Decidi

Deciding Children's Futures addresses the thorny task of how to assess parents and children who belong to struggling families where there are issues of neglect or significant harm, and when separating parents are contesting arrangements for the care of their children.

This is a practitioner's guide: it discusses how to create relationships that are capable of breaching natural parental defences to assessment; the importance of keeping an open mind, how to ask questions that fathom people's experiences, and how to develop understanding of their histories, narratives, worries, hopes and fears. Joyce Scaife's approach draws on practice knowledge, theory and research findings with a view to integrating the accounts of parents and children with safeguarding imperatives and government guidance, thereby enabling professionals to make informed decisions designed to impact positively on children's futures.

This accessible and comprehensive book will be of great interest to 'expert' witnesses, practising social workers, children's guardians, solicitors, barristers, magistrates and mental health professionals.

Joyce Scaife is a clinical psychologist with over 15 years of experience in carrying out assessments for the family court. She is former Director of Clinical Practice for the Doctor of Clinical Psychology training course at the University of Sheffield.

'This is a welcome and timely book in light of the well received Munro Review. It provides an excellent assessment guide for professionals across disciplines, working with families involved with Children's Social Care. This book is eminently readable and user friendly; it is challenging; it uses the author's significant experience to guide and suggest ways to conduct assessments of adults and children in an environment where a "watch your back culture" often predominates.

The book resonates with the voices of many parents and children and these serve as a powerful reminder of the unintentional harm that professionals can inflict upon the vulnerable. The words respect, dignity, empathy, understanding and compassion litter the pages. The reader is left in no doubt that these are essential attributes when conducting assessments that are thorough, balanced and informative; assessments that ensure the welfare and safety of children are paramount but which allow parents a voice and in many cases empower them. The book also acts as a valuable resource guide providing information on assessment tools easily accessible to all, relevant texts and research findings and signposts to a multitude of relevant organisations.

If practitioners were to use only one book to help them to carry out complex assessments this should be the one; I cannot recommend it highly enough.'

– Christine Carter, Co Founder and Co Director of Carter Brown Associates Family Expert Witness Service

Deciding Children's Futures

An expert guide to assessments
for safeguarding and promoting
children's welfare in the family court

Joyce Scaife

Routledge
Taylor & Francis Group

LONDON AND NEW YORK

First published 2013
by Routledge
27 Church Road, Hove, East Sussex BN3 2FA

Simultaneously published in the USA and Canada
by Routledge
711 Third Avenue, New York NY 10017

Routledge is an imprint of the Taylor & Francis Group, an informa business

© 2013 Joyce Scaife

British Library Cataloguing in Publication Data
A catalogue record for this book is available from the British Library

Library of Congress Cataloging in Publication Data
Scaife, Joyce, 1950–
Deciding children's futures : an expert guide to assessments for safeguarding and promoting children's welfare in family court / Joyce Scaife. – 1st ed.
    p. cm.
Includes bibliographical references and index.
ISBN 978-0-415-59635-0 (978-0-415-59634-3) 1. Child welfare. 2. Public welfare. 3. Social work with children. 4. Domestic relations courts. I. Title.
HV713.S323 2012
346.01'50269–dc23   2012013181

ISBN: 978-0-415-59635-0 (hbk)
ISBN: 978-0-415-59634-3 (pbk)
ISBN: 978-0-203-09413-6 (ebk)

Typeset in Garamond
by Cenveo Publisher Services

Printed and bound by CPI Group (UK) Ltd, Croydon, CR0 4YY

Contents

Illustrations

Figures

Tables

Preface

At a time when child welfare workers find themselves operating in a climate of increasingly prescriptive legislation, procedural guidelines and managerial visions, the ability to think is in danger of being lost. Yet, informed, reflective thought is the only way for those in the thick of practice to keep their bearings and to remain present and available to both children and their parents.

(Howe *et al.*, 1999: 4)

Aims of the book

In 2011 the Munro report highlighted that, 'professionals are, in particular, constrained from keeping a focus on the child by the demands and rigidity created by inspection and regulation' (Munro, 2011: 9). She continued, 'Knowing *what* data to collect is useful, but it is equally useful to know *how* to collect it; how to get through the front door and create a relationship where the parent is willing to tell the social worker anything about the child and family; how to ask challenging questions about very sensitive matters; and having the expertise to sense that the child or parent is being evasive. Above all, it is important to be able to work directly with children and young people to understand their experiences, worries, hopes and dreams' (Munro, 2011: 36). This book is about how the aspirations of David Howe and Eileen Munro might be accomplished in the thorny domain of safeguarding children's welfare.

I aim to describe an approach to assessment which draws on practice knowledge and places at the centre the relationship between me, the practitioner, and the families I am tasked to assess. If I were to be the subject of such a process myself, I would want to feel fairly and compassionately treated. I would not want the approach to be based on a narrow rational-technical vision of assessment in which workers seemed to remain emotionally distant from me because they had become exhausted by the role and needed to make their work more manageable (Munro, 2002). I would not want the power differential between the roles of assessor and assessed to block the issue of our shared humanity. I would want my assessors to keep in mind the primary role of helper. When the welfare of a child is at stake, the practitioner's task too readily may become redefined as a quest for evidence, particularly in the harshly critical environment of social work fostered by the popular press following another apparent failure to prevent the death of a child.

Purposes of assessment

Assessment has multiple possible purposes and purpose constrains form. This means that as a practitioner I need to keep clearly in mind why I am doing this and adjust my approach accordingly. The initial assessment (I am using the term 'initial' generically but in the UK it is also used to denote enquiries carried out as a Child in Need referral under section 17 of the Children Act, 1989) is for my (the assessor's) benefit. Its purpose is for my learning, enabling me to gain perspectives on the current practice, knowledge, skills, attitudes and values of the care-givers I have been asked to assess and to explore the developmental status, behaviour, wishes and feelings of the children. In educational settings this is known as 'diagnostic' assessment (Scaife and Wellington, 2010). Diagnostic assessment operates through an attitude of open-minded curiosity and 'attunedness' on the part of the assessor to the issues and concerns of family members. This can be a difficult process because the questions I ask can too often seem very intrusive, with the character of interrogations designed to find out how the parents' practice is wanting. David Boud (2001) argues that the usual conventions of assessment demand that people display their best work. Parents are unlikely to want to reveal their deficiencies to me with the attendant risk of losing the right to care for their children. I might reasonably expect them to try and hide what they see as negative indicators.

In addition to its diagnostic qualities, the initial assessment also has the purpose of informing a decision about the immediate safety of the children and whether they can be left in the care of the parent whilst interventions, if needed, take place. This gives it some of the characteristics of summative assessment: a judgement of fitness to occupy the parental role. 'High stakes testing' – when the results of summative assessment have important consequences – has been shown to have a number of negative effects. These include lowering the self-esteem of people who are doing badly, and increasing anxiety (Harlen, 2003). I need to be mindful of this negative impact and try to conduct my initial assessment in ways that focus constructively on strengths from which improved parental practice can build.

There is also an argument for the initial assessment to serve the purpose of a very thorough screening to ensure that significant issues (such as a child's heretofore undiagnosed genetic condition) are not overlooked.

In a paper published in 1995, Martin Seligman pointed out that psychotherapy in the field is self-correcting – if one approach is ineffective, another is usually tried. People in psychotherapy usually report multiple problems and the aim is for 'improvement in general functioning as well as amelioration of a disorder and relief of specific, presenting symptoms' (Seligman, 1995: 3). These factors also characterise the families that I see in my court work: multiple problems, the need for flexible approaches to intervention, and the aim of improving general functioning as well as solving specific problems. It seems to me that such commonalities suggest the benefits of seeing assessment as an ongoing process in which initial ideas are continually revised as new information enters the arena. This requires the thinking and critically reflective practitioner advocated by Eileen Munro, David Howe and his colleagues, and also by Danielle Turney *et al.* (2011), who concluded from a review of social work assessments of children in need that a clinically focused approach emphasising assessment knowledge and skills is required.

The initial assessment results in provisional hypotheses or explanations about how the presenting situation has developed. It is easy to forget that these are provisional and when the outcome of an intervention seems consistent with the proposed explanation or further data seems to support the initial formulation, the account may become consolidated into a 'truth' which is ever more difficult to dislodge, even though a different perspective would cast doubt on its credibility. These 'truths' may also derive from what have become our habitual explanations. Alex Gitterman (1991) argues:

> Like other professionals we become socialized to special philosophical, theoretical, and practice perspectives. Our favourite theories are often so overly cherished that we inevitably begin to fit people and their situations into them. These conceptual security blankets can become worn and frayed. We always have to deal with ambiguity and yet act with confidence.
>
> (Gitterman, 1991: 15)

Acting with confidence may not seem to fit neatly with an attitude of open-mindedness. Legal and organisational factors can impact inadvertently and not always constructively on the decision-making process. In my experience, courts tend to prefer certainty. The mandate for courts to prioritise the child's welfare as the 'paramount consideration' (Children Act 1989 s1[1]) may foster an approach that plays down the needs of the parent, overlooking the inextricable interweaving of both. In order to provide sensitively responsive care to a child, parents need first to look after themselves. Legislation that intends to make removal of a child from the care of the birth parents an exceptional event emphasises that a formal order should only be made where 'no order' is not an option. In a 'watch your back' culture, this can lead professionals strongly to make a case for the removal of a child by 'proving' the parents' incapabilities, thereby focussing on weaknesses to the exclusion of strengths. This is despite attempts to shift emphasis solely from those parts of the Children Act (1989) that deal with the need to detect and rescue children at risk of harm and towards those sections offering family support (Sargent, 1999).

As the assessment process continues beyond the initial stage (in the UK this might be by progression through a strategy meeting, a core assessment, a section 47 investigation and beyond), another purpose that benefits the assessor is that of finding out whether my intervention strategies are bringing about desired learning and changes. This is a further example of diagnostic assessment which may lead me to revise my strategies and methods. My habitual ways of working may not suit this parent and I need to monitor the impact of my interventions and make adjustments that acknowledge the individuality and specific needs of this particular family.

When the purpose of assessment is to foster the family's learning and development, it is typically known as 'formative' assessment, also known as 'assessment *for* learning' (AfL). There is extensive research evidence documenting the benefits of formative assessment in improving learning and fostering change, particularly when it is executed at a time and in a manner that people can respond to by making improvements (Black and Wiliam, 1998; Harlen, 2009). Formative assessment involves asking questions, providing feedback and occasionally 'telling' people things that aid learning.

Formative assessment is underpinned by a belief in the possibility of improvement. Because self-esteem is involved, there is a need for care in providing formative feedback – not only because feelings can be hurt and hackles raised, but also because pre-existing levels of self-esteem are thought to condition how people will receive the feedback (Young, 2000). I find that parents in care proceedings often experience low self-esteem, making it difficult for them to show openness to learning, to accept the views of the practitioner, and to change their practices on the basis of professional advice. I want this book to reflect my view that assessments have a formative purpose and have a significant role to play also as interventions with the potential to impact positively on families in addition to helping the professional system in its decision making.

However objective or scientific we try to be, ultimately we have only our own experiences to go on. We cannot step outside our individual experiential worlds to know and feel first-hand what it is like to be in the shoes of another. Different individuals who observe 'the same' event will give different accounts of their experience. We are always dealing with multiple 'realities'. Sally Holland (2004: 3) argues that this 'liberates practitioners from the view that they must discover the "truth" during an assessment and come to *the* correct solution.' Instead she exhorts us to listen hard to each participant's account and value it as such. This requires us to give our undivided attention to everyone's narrative and make a subsequent critical evaluation in light of the full range of information available. This is sometimes termed an 'ecological transactional perspective', which 'requires a dynamic, not a static understanding and assessment of children and their families' (Brandon *et al.*, 2009: 10).

In this book I have drawn on accounts given by people who have been subject to assessments in which children's welfare has been in question. They are composite accounts based on 'real' narratives but with details and identifiers altered in order to ensure confidentiality. They are intended to be a reminder of the difficulties faced by families in court proceedings.

There is a temptation to locate 'the problem' within an 'other', whether this be a problem family, problem child, a poor practitioner who fails in the task of protecting children, or a broken society that denies growth opportunities to families and fails to take collective responsibility for the well-being of its people. This book is not about identifying bad people who are bringing up their children badly. A disposition of enquiry is likely to be more fruitful than a perspective which seeks to allocate blame. What we do know is that mass disorders are not eradicated through interventions that target individuals (Albee, 1983). If we are truly to improve the lot of children throughout our communities we need to look not only at families in trouble but also at the social conditions such as poverty, poor education and absence of social support that make the task of parenting so difficult. Although this book is about the assessment of individual children and families, this is not to underestimate the impact of context and community.

A great deal of luck and accident determines which families come to the attention of the authorities; parents often point out that the care they have provided to their child is better than that being provided by their neighbour. A detached house affords the privacy that keeps prying eyes and ears away from my own attempts at parenting. The resources I have at my disposal support me in meeting my children's needs. I am fortunate. I need to be mindful that with a few different twists and turns in my life I could be the other party in the assessor-assessed coupling.

The subsequent chapters focus on assessments that may be carried out by a social worker, expert witness, psychologist, psychiatrist, health care worker, employee of a voluntary agency or any professional involved in the assessment of families where there are issues of safeguarding. I hope that it will act as a useful reference for advocates, barristers and judges. It is not intended to be profession-specific and I have generally signposted materials that are not restricted in use to particular disciplines. My aim is to encourage the development of practitioner confidence to carry out the assessment process in a state of open-minded compassionate concern. I did not find space, as I had hoped, to write in detail about legal frameworks, the history of child protection and the meaning of childhood, the specific demands of assessments in private law proceedings, preventive interventions that do not involve the courts, the special needs of trauma sufferers and asylum seekers, the important role of fathers, approaches to children with learning difficulties, report writing, giving evidence and much more. Some of the appendices are intended to compensate for the absence of these topics in the main text and do not necessarily link directly with topics addressed in individual chapters. Appendix 5 describes the process of application for a care order, something with which social workers will be familiar, but which is meant to act as a reference for workers from other disciplines. What I do hope that I have achieved is a text that translates imperatives and government guidance into a practical approach focused on the question of '*how?*'

Acknowledgements

This book has been a long time growing, ever since I first began to carry out assessments for the family court and struggled to find the kind of text that would help me to adapt my usual ways of working to the specific demands of public and private law settings. During that time I have benefitted from the advice and ideas of many colleagues for which I am enormously grateful. As with my previous writing, it could not have been completed without the unerring emotional, intellectual and practical support of Jon Scaife, whose ideas he allows me to steal unashamedly. Neither could I have managed without the technical support of the two Jon's in my life so thank you both for being available at a moment's notice to fix my computer when it seems to have had a mind of its own, and to Hannah for her unwavering positive attitude to whatever I do.

For constructive and timely feedback on my writing I would like particularly to thank Mike Pomerantz for his ready availability, unerring enthusiasm and encouragement. I would especially like to thank Chris Carter who took time from her busy schedule to read in depth an earlier version. I am sure that as a result a better book has emerged. I also want to thank Graham Turpin who provided very helpful and positive comments on the original proposal as well as the completed manuscript, and Amie Stead who has shared her extensive knowledge and experience in many informative conversations as the manuscript took shape. My thanks are also due to Lisa Oliver from Carter Brown who willingly shared her knowledge of suitable resource material, and Matthew Richardson for his regular succinct summaries of articles from the *Family Law* journal.

I am very grateful to people, some of whom I have never met, who have responded to my email requests for help and shared their ideas. These include David Spiegelhalter for his advice on displaying data to illustrate risk assessment; Gearoidin Farrell and Anne Hales of the Irish National Educational Psychology Service, who directed me to very helpful material concerning approaches to breaking bad news; Edward Melhuish for his paper on the evaluation and value of Sure Start programmes; Chris Pamplin (UK Register of Expert Witnesses) for his advice regarding record keeping and access to Factsheet 58 'Retention of Documents'; Gemma Gray for a copy of her presentation to a British Psychological Society training event on assessments of parents with learning difficulties; Nigel Beail for a copy of his presentation made at the same event; Martin Hughes for helping me to understand how Q-sorts might be adapted to the assessment of parenting; and Liza Monaghan, whose supervision has proved invaluable in helping me to untangle my confusing thoughts and feelings both in regard to my assessments and my writing. My thanks are due to Paul Livock, a multi-talented colleague who very kindly drew the cartoon on page 130 and gave me permission to use it again for free.

Acknowledgement is also due for permissions as follows: Dr Sarah Beglin for figure 9.1 Diagrammatic Formulation, which was published online at www.bps.org.uk/downloadfile.cfm?file_uuid=26D76984-1143-DFD0-7E8B-80F0BD2968EF&ext=ppt in 2007; Isaac Prilleltensky for figures 7.1 Cake of Well-being and 7.2 Mountain of Risk, which he presented together with Ora Prilleltensky on a speaking tour in five Australian cities (Melbourne, Canberra, Sydney, Brisbane and Perth) in November 2006; Richard Stevens for figure 5.1 the Needs Jigsaw and Sue McGaw for figure 4.1 Example of Worksheet from Parent Assessment Manual; an epigraph from Howe, D., Brandon, M., Hinings, D. and Schofield, G. (1999), *Attachment theory, child maltreatment and family support* (London: Palgrave), reproduced with permission of Palgrave Macmillan; Georges Borchardt, Inc. and Penguin UK for an epigraph from *Discipline and Punish* by Michel Foucault published by Pantheon in 1978 and Penguin in 1995.

Last but far from least, I have much appreciated the ongoing support of Joanne Forshaw, Jane Harris and Kirsten Buchanan from Routledge who have good humouredly steered the book through all of the stages that turn an initial idea and draft script into a book that I can hold satisfyingly in my hand.

1 Introduction

> The judges of normality are present everywhere. We are in the society of the teacher-judge, the doctor-judge, the educator-judge, the 'social-worker'-judge; it is on them that the universal reign of the normative is based; and each individual, wherever he may find himself, subjects to it his body, his gestures, his behaviour, his aptitudes, his achievements.
>
> (Foucault, 1977: 304)

Being assessed

I retain a strong memory of being assessed as a new secondary school pupil. My father was a tailor and my mother a seamstress of enviable skill who carried out sewing alterations from home. Growing up in such an environment meant that I had used a needle and thread from infancy and was as familiar with driving our treadle sewing machine as I was with riding my bike. The girls at my school took mandatory needlework (the boys, woodwork, which I would much have preferred) and our first project was to make an underslip. I was incensed when my own effort was graded 'C' and such was the impact that I can still feel myself both fuming and laughing about it fifty years later. In the second half of the year we made an embroidered stuffed ball for which I received an 'A' grade with the comment 'has improved'. I knew that I had not improved − I should have had an 'A' from the start − and tucked away the knowledge that my own and someone else's assessment of me (or of my performance) could be at serious odds. I was an expert on 'me' whereas the teacher was assessing my performance over a very brief period with only limited knowledge of my sewing history and prior experience.

The people I assess in family proceedings are experts on themselves too. My task is to learn as much about them as I can in a relatively short period of time, using multiple sources of information through a fair process in order to reach a perspective that can inform further professional action. In a nutshell, this is all I need to do. It is a research process; investigating, finding out, making meaning from our experiences, juggling the data to work out what fits and what is inconsistent, and reaching an understanding, a formulation, a set of hypotheses or ideas that lead to action. Included in the data are my own beliefs, values and tendencies to see things in particular ways. In order to be fair, my vision needs to include I-sight, an awareness of what I bring to my assessment that is based on my life experiences to date. At least my needlework teacher was able to make a different judgement on the second occasion that she assessed my work. She was not trapped by her initial vision into a perspective that saw me as a 'C student' fixed and forever.

It is my belief that at the centre of the assessment process are the worker's personal qualities. Although technique may assist, what is crucial is that I mind about and respect the people I assess, that I am prepared to acknowledge my misunderstandings and change my mind, that I remember what it is like to be on the receiving end when being judged, that I use my feelings as information and not as an excuse to distance myself, and that I genuinely want to learn about this family and the challenges that they are struggling with in raising their children.

Here are the voices of two people who have been the subjects of assessment processes in family court proceedings. The first was perceived by the professionals involved as aggressive and threatening – a view that I have often encountered, particularly of fathers, in care proceedings and also in disputes concerning residence and contact.

> I'm forthright. I say what I mean. I've got quite a loud voice. If I've got something to say I say it. I've got to let them know. They may take it as threatening but it isn't. It's because I'm well built and tall. All this is stress related. I raise my voice when I'm talking. I'm finding it hard to concentrate; my attention span is dreadful. Before these proceedings, I could concentrate for England. What's happened and why it's happened has had an effect. I get terrible headaches and pressure above my eyes. Normally I wouldn't be like this. What's happened has made me ill and agitated. It's a feeling of complete bewilderment. When I get anxious I can have trouble with my breathing and it makes me feel hot and unwell. I get this terrible feeling in the pit of my stomach. In years gone by I was always confident. I could attend interviews. Now what was natural at one point is alien, it's very worrying, disconcerting. I don't know how I feel and I'm finding this utterly harrowing.

The mother in the following excerpt was eventually diagnosed with a neurological condition. As a result of her disability she had difficulties in meeting the physical care needs of her children. Here she describes the trauma and confusion of the children being removed.

> I'm sitting here on my own, Gracie and Toby were in bed, and a knock came on the door. The social workers came in and they said, 'Have you got someone who can look after the children tonight, we're going to have to remove them,' so I had to get them up and take them to a friend of mine who lives in the flat underneath. They stayed the night with

Tracy and the next morning I went down with their clothes because of it being a school day and took them to school. They said, 'We believe the children here are at risk.' From then it's a complete blur because it upsets me so much. I went to court and they told me on the day they were going to take the children into local authority care. 'Won't I have time to get them some things and say goodbye to them?' I had to tell the children and they cried and I cried. They gave me a lift home and that was it. It was horrible. I had lost the two dearest things in the world and I just sat and thought and thought and I didn't know where all this was going.

Phyllida Parsloe (1999: 12) states that, 'an assessment is a major intrusion into anyone's privacy and it could well be argued that it should require the same kind of informed consent as is necessary in medical interventions. Anyone being assessed is likely to be in a vulnerable position and this vulnerability may be increased if they belong to one of the oppressed groups in society.' I find that I need constantly to remind myself of the assessed person's perspective, an act which is not always easy to sustain, especially under extreme workload pressure and when it appears that this person may have severely harmed a child. These experiences are emotionally charged not only for the assessed person but also for me. How am I to maintain an open-minded, empathic and caring stance when faced with, and sometimes overwhelmed by, the extent of people's distress, reflected in anger and frustration towards me as a representative of what they perceive to be the oppressive or ineffective system?

Feelings associated with assessment

It helps to remind myself that their reaction towards me is not personal. Reactance theory (Beutler *et al.*, 2002) asserts that freedom of choice and action is generally valued and so we tend to react negatively to perceived, implied or actual threats to our 'free behaviours' as a normal response to stress and perceived threat. Not surprisingly, since practising professionals are agents of social control, our involvement can readily be perceived as a threat to clients' rights to self-determination. When under investigation we rarely attribute our difficult circumstances to our own actions, but rather are prone to develop a view of ourselves as victims of circumstance or other people's malevolence (Kirmayer, 1990). Reactance is seen as being both a state and a trait which can be played out consciously or unconsciously. It is enacted in resentful compliance, passive resistance or angry direct refusal to cooperate.

How else can a worker relate in ways that reduce the likelihood of reactance? Beutler *et al.* (2002) advise that it helps to reduce the level of directiveness. Telling people what to do when they are in a state of reactance will almost inevitably generate resistance which arises out of the client's perception that the worker's intervention is illegitimate (Strong and Matross, 1973). Discussing the other person's understandable anger or fear and how it is affecting the relationship may also be helpful (Beutler and Harwood, 2000), particularly if the worker accepts responsibility for generating these feelings. Carl Rogers (Rogers *et al.*, 1967) described how, over time, he came increasingly to focus on the source of his feelings towards clients. He would ask himself, 'Why do I feel this way?' His feelings might have included a desire to be rude, finding himself hurried, embarrassed, avoidant, or feeling 'on the spot'. I see this self-questioning as reflecting an orientation in which workers take responsibility for their own feelings, rather than attributing them to the client's behaviour:

> We tend to express the *outer* edges of our feelings. That leaves *us* protected and makes the other person unsafe. We say, "This and this (which *you* did) hurt me." We do not say, "This and this weakness of mine *made me* be hurt when you did this and this." To find this inward edge of my feelings, I need only ask myself, "Why?" Then, instead of "You bore me," or "This makes me mad," I find the "why" *in me* which makes it so. That is always more personal and positive, and much safer to express. Instead of "You bore me," I find, "I want to hear more personally from you," or, "You tell me what happened, but I want to hear also what it all meant to you."
>
> (Rogers *et al.*, 1967: 390)

It is worth asking a question (to self and other) about how the people who are the subject of the assessment might take greater control over the assessment process. It is important for them to feel free to express their negative feelings and to assert their perspective about what is taking place. This requires practitioners to respond in a non-defensive manner and to accept responsibility for their contribution to the process (Safran *et al.*, 2002). This may include being explicit about *me* being appointed to assess *you* and we are therefore 'in it together'.

Following the introduction of the guidelines laid down by the Department of Health (2000a) in the Framework for Assessing Children in Need and their Families, Brian Corby and his colleagues (2002) explored what parents thought of the way assessments were carried out, with a view to identifying how professionals could build on and improve their practice. They interviewed 34 sets of parents and carers (10 who were involved in initial assessments and 24 who were involved in core assessments) and gathered additional information from case files, initial and core assessment records and questionnaires. Their sample included in particular disabled children, older children presenting behavioural difficulties within their families and children seen as in need of safeguarding.

> The most significant finding in relation to both initial and core assessments was that the key to their success with parents is the achievement of some form of congruence of views between the assessors and those being assessed. Achieving such congruence is not easy, particularly in situations where there are major disagreements and disputes about the care of

children between parents and professionals, which was the case with several of the core assessments in particular .... Successful intervention also depends on reaching agreement about the nature of the problem. This requires honesty about the causes for concern. If service users do not share the views of the assessors that there is a problem, then the assessment and any subsequent intervention may be viewed negatively. The direct questions in the relevant sections of the framework for assessment provided a helpful platform for this in many cases.

(Corby *et al.*, 2002)

For parents who were themselves brought up in the care system and perceive it to have failed them, resentment of the assessment process can make their experience seem even more highly charged. The assessor may occupy the dual role of care system representative and ostensibly 'neutral' professional. Workers may find themselves facing the wrath of vulnerable, agitated and sometimes highly unstable parents who are responding to reminders of their adverse history rather than the qualities of the individual practitioner (Dale *et al.*, 2005).

Here is a young mother's description of her experiences with her birth family and in the care system. Her mother was also brought up in care and her own son was taken from her at the age of five years. She explains how difficult it is for her to respond to what she perceives as being told what to do:

When I was upset as a child my mum never really did anything although I think she tried her best. She couldn't really be bothered. She'd just do her own thing. I used to think she was trying to teach me to be independent and to look after myself and one day I realised she didn't know how to. When she went out I used to look after my brothers and I could cook a meal and clean the house but they were a pain in the neck. I always felt on my own and the odd one out somehow, then mum dropped the bombshell that Steve wasn't my dad. My mum used to try to get us to do things but when she realised she wasn't going to succeed she would give up. I never listened to her and I always did the opposite of what I was told. I was a pain in the arse basically, the worst daughter you could ever imagine. I was smoking at nine and stealing cigarettes from my mum. One day I stood at the top of the stairs, spitting at her and calling her a 'slag'.

I don't remember much about school. I went to five different primary schools and six secondaries. I ended up at a school for naughty kids. I put myself into care when I was 14 because my mum couldn't stand living with me. We had a gigantic argument in the middle of the night. The police came and I went to a foster home the next day. It would have been all right but I started to steal from them so I was moved to live with a couple who had another girl called Ellie. I didn't want to live with them. They were too old. They were boring and they favoured Ellie over me and they always showed it. I said I'd rather be in a home so I went to Greenstiles. I loved it there but I kept getting arrested for criminal damage and assault. I started getting in with the wrong people at school and I started drinking and taking cannabis. I always argue to this day because I can't stand being told what to do. I've grown up to think I'll do what I want, when I want, how I want. It's the best policy.

This woman struggled to have relationships with anyone in authority, including her representative solicitor. She chose violent partners and could not accept those who showed her care and affection because it was such an alien experience in which she was unable to trust.

Confidence and trust

There was a time, and there still are such interludes, when I was consumed by doubt about my skills as a professional helper. Being infected by doubt is an unpleasant experience, but I would not like to think that I had become so consumed by hubris as to believe that I have reached a position of all-knowing professional wisdom. The work that we do entails uncertainty and I have come to view this as a desirable, if still uncomfortable, state. It helps me to know that others have similar self-doubts. The work we do and the people with whom we do it can not only generate self-doubt but paralysing fear, particularly when we are confronted by someone's profound distress and rage.

This is an account by Gerald Jampolsky (2011) who had been called to a patient on a locked psychiatric ward at 2 a.m. one Sunday morning:

> I looked through the small window in the door, and saw a man six feet four inches tall weighing 280 pounds. He was running around the room nude, carrying this large piece of wood with nails sticking out, and talking gibberish. I really didn't know what to do. There were two male nurses, both of whom seemed scarcely five feet tall, who said, 'We will be right behind you, Doc.' I didn't find that reassuring.
>
> As I continued to look through the window, I began to recognize how scared the patient was, and then it began to trickle into my consciousness how scared I was. All of a sudden it occurred to me that he and I had a common bond that might allow for unity – namely, that we were both scared.
>
> Not knowing what else to do, I yelled through the thick door, 'My name is Dr Jampolsky and I want to come in and help you, but I'm scared. I'm scared that I might get hurt, and I'm scared you might get hurt, and I can't help wondering if you aren't scared too.' With this, he stopped his gibberish, turned around and said, 'You're goddam right I'm scared.'
>
> I continued yelling to him, telling him how scared I was, and he was yelling back how scared he was .... As we talked our fear disappeared and our voices calmed down.
>
> (Jampolsky, 2011: 128)

I am not arguing that it is invariably appropriate to disclose feelings of fear, rather for the important step of recognising the feeling in order to moderate its impact on how we act. Bob Johnson, also a psychiatrist, described his fear when he was accosted on the way to his office by Eddie, a heavily-built prisoner on a maximum security hospital wing who bristled up to him with the accusation, 'Why did you tell me to fuck off yesterday?' (Johnson, 1996: 188). Johnson argued that one response to his fear, 'a hidden agenda in me which said this man is scum, he needs taking down a peg or two,' could have led him to use disciplinary action which would have been entirely counterproductive. He says, 'Fears are toxic to learning, and hidden fears are most toxic of all … fear acts like a lethal mist, wiping out all traces of what was supposed to have been learnt yesterday, and heavily impeding progress today' (Johnson, 1996: 191).

I was struck in these examples by the power of the emotions that can be generated when we meet with people in the course of our work whom we perceive as hostile or frighteningly unpredictable. If this generates anger or fear in us, we risk responding by exercising our authority in retribution, by protective withdrawal from the relationship, or other defensive reactions that crush our empathy and creativity.

In my experience, the pressure of the safeguarding process on professionals can inadvertently generate a stance from which strengths and positives tend to be overlooked or minimised. Pamela Davies (2011) highlighted the invidious position of workers at the 'front end' of the investigative process. They (we) walk a tightrope characterised by crisis, limited resources, negative public views and are designated to do a job involving the generation of strong and frightening emotions both in clients and in the workers themselves. The responsibilities of the task are daunting and it can be dangerous; threats to workers by enraged clients are not rare.

Nevertheless, Johnson argues that we need to generate trust, to learn to trust others and most importantly to trust ourselves, which is accomplished through developing feelings of confidence. I can identify with this idea and have learned to remind myself, when faced with a situation that frightens me, that if I know how to do just one thing adequately then I can have sufficient confidence to get me through. I may be interviewing a person with a history of violent offences. I need to take sensible precautions such as making others aware of my whereabouts, and I have also learned to trust my capability to recognise if my questions are acting as a wind-up, and to defuse the situation, although this has very rarely been necessary. It is quite hard to hit someone who is sitting quietly and inoffensively on a sofa. People who are subject to court proceedings are quite understandably and frequently fearful, irritable and frustrated. If I listen, try to understand and show them respect, I am unlikely to provoke a direct attack. My fears will reduce if I face them, but have a bad habit of magnifying if I avoid them. A very good friend of mine years ago was a junior manager of a Berni Inn. He told me that as he stood at the door closing up for the night he was confronted by a group of young 'thugs' who threatened, 'Let us in or you'll be shitting yourself.' His retort,

'Mate, I already have,' was greeted with laughter and they went on their way. He acknowledged his own fear and was prepared openly to admit it.

Research findings provide evidence that workers' anxiety adversely affects performance. When feeling anxious, practitioners are more likely to ignore the respondent's expressed feelings including those towards the practitioner, and inaccurately recall material from the session (Hayes and Gelso, 1991). Anxiety, fear and worry alert us to the need to keep ourselves safe, hopefully in ways that still allow us to listen, accept and try our best to understand the people we are assessing.

Relationship, alliance and the temptation to 'rescue'

Looking back on myself as a young practitioner, I think that I had a tendency to assume that if something was wrong with the child, the parents must have had a hand in the cause. I wanted all parents to be unremittingly child-centred and follow Penelope Leach's advice to, 'look at the baby's feelings from his, rather than your, point of view' (Leach, 1977: 199). I had an urge to rescue the child from their less-than-perfect parents and sometimes experienced unfounded confidence that I might have been able to do better. I have learned to shift my focus in recognition that parenting is a demanding role in which most people are doing their best. Although a child may need rescuing from an environment that is proving harmful to development, I need to make an alliance with the parents if they are to trust me with what has been happening and if I am to make a positive impact on the adverse circumstances. Making an alliance with the parents does not prevent me from protecting the child, even when this requires removal to a substitute care-giver.

At different stages of my career I have taken different approaches to my work, and what seems to matter is that I have some belief in the efficacy and effectiveness of the theory or models to which I subscribe, that I am able to convince my clients of this, that I really want them to improve their quality of life and that I mind about them. Richard Bentall, who has written extensively about working with people with severe and enduring mental health difficulties, says that it takes a particular kind of person to do this work; someone who, 'can sit with people for long periods and can both be simultaneously empathic and organised' (Bentall, 2010: 150). This is not to say that theory and technique do not matter, rather that they have a place but it is not centre stage. At the centre lie practitioners' interpersonal skills and their genuine desire to help coupled with the client's willingness (even reluctant willingness) to take part in the enterprise. This alliance has consistently been shown in psychotherapy outcome research to be the main contributory factor to positive change (Blow and Sprenkle, 2001; Duncan *et al.*, 2009; Lambert, 2007; Lambert and Ogles, 2004). In a thorough review of outcome research Mick Cooper concluded that, 'the evidence suggests that the key predictor of outcomes remains the extent to which the client is willing and able to make use of whatever the therapist provides'(Cooper, 2008: 157) and, 'positive outcomes are associated with a collaborative, caring, empathic, skilled way of relating' (Cooper, 2008: 156).

> From a client perspective, the most important aspects of therapy typically are the "nontechnological" factors: having a time and place to talk; having someone care, listen and understand; having someone provide encouragement and reassurance; and having someone offer an external perspective and advice.
>
> (Bohart and Tallman, 1999: 51)

When assessing parents in family proceedings we are not their therapists, they may not even need or wish to change, but I believe that assessments have a significant role to play also as interventions that have the *potential* positively to impact on the people whom we are assessing, in addition to helping the professional system in its decision making. This function is encapsulated in the UK Department of Health Framework for the Assessment of Children in Need and their Families: 'The process of assessment should be therapeutic in itself' (Department of Health, 2000a: 15). If the assessment results in the removal of children from their birth families, this is with the intention of providing better life chances for them. From the parents' perspective the removal of their children will almost certainly be experienced as negative. The outcome, though, does not preclude the assessment process from featuring therapeutic characteristics which may bear fruit in the longer term.

We can't always do very much about the client's desire and commitment to change. Some have such consolidated experiences of lacking agency and feeling unable to affect outcomes that the proceedings take an almost inevitable lemming-like journey that serves to confirm them in their helplessness. But I have met parents who have failed in their bid to take care of their children through multiple sets of proceedings and who have finally reached a position in which they have made significant strides, sufficient to convince the authorities that this time they can meet the needs of their child.

> Before, I didn't used to talk. I ring Lucy (social worker) up quite a few times now and make contact with the workers. I've got to change my life. I can't keep doing what I did. It doesn't get me anywhere. Getting all worked up didn't get me nowhere. I talk to Annie. I didn't used to do that before. I used to keep myself to myself, quiet. I feel more confident to talk. I'm starting to talk to the contact workers at Churchgate. I've been isolated. I sat back one day and thought I had to change or I'm just going to be left on my own. Even Lucy said, 'If ever you want to talk phone me up.' My sister was with me at the review, and I thought I've got to keep things positive so I stayed to the end of the meeting. I could have got emotional but I stayed calm. I used to get all teary-eyed in review meetings. Some of the things they say make me

feel stressed and angry but I've learned to calm myself down and go for a walk. I used to get hysterical. Sometimes I look at myself. I think I could improve myself and I want to lose a bit of weight. I've changed in my getting angry in front of the children. We were just playing and laughing and I want them to be happy instead of me getting emotional and hysterical. I've still got my factory job and I get on well with my bosses. I have a laugh and a joke with them. I'm contented doing the job, I like doing it. I like to go shopping and I've been going for walks. I've walked it to contact. It takes about half an hour, it's exercise.

What helps the alliance to develop, and what might impede it? Graybeal and Konrad (2008: 186) argue that the practitioner's attitude is central. Positive outcomes are related to a practitioner's belief in the care-giver's capability to change, skill in conveying confidence and optimism and the capacity for empathic listening. Strengths-based assessment involves learning about and paying respect to care-givers' and children's perspectives, believing what they say unless and until there is irrefutable contrary evidence, exploring their aspirations, goals and dreams, understanding their unique concerns and life histories, using language that they can understand, avoiding blame, labelling, and being wary of engaging in cause-and-effect thinking (Saleebey, 2006). This is not to propose that staff subject their critical professional judgement to a 'rule of optimism' (Dingwall *et al.*, 1983) and leave children in situations of high risk.

I think it almost inevitable that in the context of stressful court proceedings, relationships between professionals and clients will from time to time be strained. These strains can lead to impasses or ruptures which have long been described in the counselling and psychotherapy literature and also in supervisory relationships. Ruptures can often be tracked to issues of transference (the unconscious redirection of feelings developed in one relationship into another). Both assessor and assessed bring prior experiences of relationships involving authority, and I would find it surprising if this did not bear on the assessment process. Isca Salzberger-Wittenberg (1983: 12) stated, 'Any new relationship tends to arouse hope and dread, and these exist side by side in our minds. The less we know about the new person the freer we are to invest him with extremes of good and bad qualities.' She argues that helpers such as teachers, counsellors and doctors are often imbued with immense power for good and evil.

Research evidence suggests that workers are not always skilful in recognising such tensions (Lambert *et al.*, 2005). In a series of studies, clients completed questionnaire measures, including information about their experience of the therapeutic relationship, prior to each session (Harmon *et al.*, 2007). This information was given to the therapist before the client's next appointment. Client outcomes were enhanced, particularly for those who had been predicted to deteriorate. Therapists reported using the data in different ways but some discussed the results with the client,

using them as a prompt to discuss the relationship, to explore process issues, and to review the client's expectations and goals.

(Scaife, 2009: 57)

I see no reason why workers carrying out assessments in the context of
child protection could not obtain regular feedback from parents about their
experiences of being assessed, and use the information to negotiate future
sessions. It might constitute an additional way in which the people being
assessed could experience themselves as being 'heard' and 'seen'.

Confidentiality

In relationships between professionals and the general public, it is usually
reasonable to expect confidentiality of information shared, as between a doctor
and patient, or between social workers, counsellors or lawyers and their
clients. It is generally accepted that all information is provided in confidence,
whether or not it is directly relevant to the medical, social care or personal
matter that is the main reason for the relationship. Where this cannot be
assured, it is helpful to give an explanation at the outset so that people know
what may be shared, with whom, and for what purpose. However, in English
law, if there are concerns that a child is, or may be, at risk of significant harm,
the overriding consideration is to safeguard the child. When there is reasonable cause to believe that there are safeguarding concerns, consent is not
required from families to obtain information from professionals who know
them, but in order to foster trust and mutuality, it is wise to inform parents
of this process and to seek their agreement, providing it does not compromise
the welfare of the child. Legislation requires that the information shared is
necessary for the purpose, is shared only with those people who need to know,
is accurate and up-to-date, is shared in a timely fashion, and is shared securely
(HM Government, 2008). It is advised to keep a record of the reasoning
behind the decision to share information, particularly when parental consent
has been withheld. Once care proceedings have been instigated, it is clear that
a child may be at risk of harm and most professionals will share their knowledge of the family providing they are assured that the person requesting the
information is bona fide. A record of all such conversations is essential. Whilst
a child's medical records may be obtained without parental consent, consent
is needed for parents' medical records to be disclosed. In my experience, the
vast majority of parents do consent to disclosure, if only for fear that refusal
may give a negative impression.

Not infrequently when carrying out assessments in family proceedings,
parents ask to discuss an issue 'off the record' and it is important to stop them
immediately in order to remind them that 'off the record' does not exist in
this setting. Many go on to talk about the matter even after this reminder, but
it does serve to reinforce the directness that features in relationships of
trust. Shemmings and Shemmings (1995) use the word 'mutuality' to refer to

practitioners treating the adults they are assessing in a manner that they would wish to be treated themselves. Clarity about the impossibility of confidentiality at least offers parents a degree of control in terms of what they decide to share. Expert witnesses however, do not share information with other parties except in their report which is served on the court and distributed through the lead solicitor. The report becomes the property of the court.

A focus on strengths

Approaches to assessment are predicated upon (often implicit) underlying philosophies. These vary by culture and across time. Are we trying to prevent harm, in particular the highly publicised child deaths that have occurred at the hands of parents and relatives, perhaps beginning in the UK with that of Maria Coldwell in 1973? Nigel Parton (1996) argued that these deaths have resulted in moral panic and preoccupation with culpability, blame and retribution. Or are we interested in child welfare and how to allocate scarce resources to families in need? These two aims are closely related but can result in a different emphasis in approaches to assessment. If we focus on the former, we may tend to explain harm to children as arising from stable dispositional characteristics of parents which leads us to categorise them as perpetrators and non-perpetrators with fixed causes located inside the person.

Alternatively (or additionally) we may approach the issue of welfare by focusing on context so that we see harm as arising from people's situations and circumstances, which are dynamic and lie on a continuum rather than being categorical. These different perspectives will influence what we do when carrying out our assessment role and tasks.

> The difference between the European and British systems is well illustrated by the common characterisation of the first child protection visit in which the British child protection worker comments: 'I am here to investigate a report of suspected abuse against your child.' The European child protection worker comments on the other hand: 'I am here to see if I can help you with any problems you might have with your child.'
>
> (Trotter *et al.*, 2001: 9)

A strengths-based approach contrasts with assessments that spotlight parental deficits. An audit of the impact of the Assessment Framework by Cleaver *et al.* (2004) suggested that in the UK, assessments of children in need led by the local authority have tended to focus primarily on issues of abuse and neglect rather than a holistic assessment of children's developmental needs. In my view, this does not derive from the orientation of individual workers, but reflects the context: a culture of 'watch your back' and risk aversion. If the organisation is risk averse, workers are required to convince the court that parents are doing a poor job. A deficit focus is built into the safeguarding process.

The language we use reflects cultural imperatives and can constrain what we see. In the UK we focus on 'safeguarding', in Canada on 'family preservation and support'. Whilst I believe that the term, 'risk assessment' can serve a useful purpose, it may nonetheless encourage a perspective that focuses on threats rather than possibilities. The context of care proceedings can itself work against a strengths-based approach:

> many assessments are disproportionately deficit focused – collating dossiers of parental inadequacy, disturbance, and apparent reluctance or refusal to cooperate with agencies ... It can be very difficult for local authority social workers to be seen to be undertaking fair assessments when at the same time they are accumulating evidence for court proceedings about parental failings, and perhaps also 'concurrently planning' the compulsory adoption of the infant in question.
>
> (Dale *et al.*, 2005: 164)

> The risk is that an emphasis on pathology, symptoms and failings may divert practitioners from the curiosity, compassion, and connection that are necessary for building effective and productive therapeutic alliances.
>
> (Graybeal and Konrad, 2008: 187)

Dale *et al.* (2005) argue against the separation of assessment and intervention which they see as two aspects of a single process. Assessment is not a one-off event but rather an ongoing process which informs action throughout the whole period of clients' involvement with services. The tendency to see assessment as a single event has been reinforced by the prevalence of statutory guidance, targets and local rules, bureaucracy which has reduced workers' capacity to stay child-centred, and to work directly with children, young people and families (Munro, 2011). In the same report Munro argues for a change from a 'compliance' to a learning culture which would serve to encourage a focus on and development of family strengths.

Art or science, analytical or intuitive judgements, quantitative or qualitative methods?

In the literature on risk assessment, child custody evaluations (as assessments regarding residence and contact following parental separation are known and described in the USA), effective child protection and safeguarding, there are extensive discussions regarding the value of science-art, actuarial-intuitive and quantitative-qualitative approaches to assessment. These are often presented as dichotomies: 'either or' choices.

I do not think we need to choose between these dichotomies but rather adjust our approach at different stages of the assessment process. We may use our intuition providing we subject it to critical checks and balances. Having a 'feel' for something may result from important learning that has taken place through 'osmosis' unconsciously in what Guy Claxton (1998) has called 'the undermind'. He argues that the non-conscious mind extracts patterns from the rich perceptual data arising out of extensive first-hand experience. He cites much evidence to show that this kind of learning accounts for our skilled performance on many tasks. Conscious thinking can interfere in a negative way, but in a second stage we can attempt to bring our knowledge to consciousness, challenging ourselves to identify and name the experiences that have generated what we intuit. This step is essential to ensure that we do not allow ourselves unreasonably to be dominated by our biases and prejudices.

For the purpose of testing my impressions of a family, I have found the concept of 'triangulation' particularly useful. It is discussed in more detail in Chapter 10. This involves cross-checking by obtaining data from multiple sources (data triangulation), from multiple investigators (investigator triangulation) and/or using multiple methods (method triangulation). In the case of assessments of children and families, methods can include semi-structured interviews, self-report questionnaires, direct behavioural observations, reviews of relevant records, psychological tests and 'collateral' interviews with others who are involved with the family (Gould and Martindale, 2009). Primary data can be of particular importance and I like to ask for photographs, recordings, school reports, and medical assessments that provide contemporaneous data through which it is possible to challenge recent judgements based on hindsight. Such data allows the testing of claims that a child is making more rapid developmental progress in one context than in another. Catalogued and dated photographs showing the child's environment can provide evidence about the cleanliness and tidiness of the home and the presence or absence of appropriate playthings.

It is also my belief that in order to give our assessments credibility they need to pay some homage to research findings and to relevant theories. In the domain of assessments of children and families, relevant evidenced theories include attachment theory and learning theories. Where we find deficiencies in parenting skills we might account for these in childhood experiences of chaotic care-giving and/or distorted learning about ways of being through exposure to domestic violence or brutal interpersonal relationships. There is evidence for the development of poor mental health outcomes for children exposed to high levels of 'expressed emotion' or verbal hostility (McCarty *et al.*, 2004) in their families of origin.

Research evidence is not necessarily grounded in theory but may derive from studies which seek and examine factors that discriminate between groups. Such groups may include parents known to have caused physical injury, known to have neglected their children, or known to have provided adequate levels of care. In practice it is very difficult to identify factors unique to each group. Such research focuses on the identification of factors which are more prevalent in one group than the other: factors which correlate with particular outcomes. There are many studies which have compared the characteristics of the families of children who have been harmed with those who have not. The results produce 'risk' factors such as poverty, alcohol and drug misuse, rigid expectations of child behaviour, high levels of parental distress and social isolation. These studies have led to the development of structured forms of assessment such as questionnaire measures on which parents may show profiles similar to those who are known to have harmed a child. There are complex questions of interpretation relating to such measures in terms of identifying 'true positives' amongst the many 'false positives'; these are explored in more depth in Chapter 8.

Actuarial approaches are a-theoretical, insofar as they are not based on explanations about what might cause a parent to harm a child. They were originally developed in the field of economics when companies needed to make predictions about matters such as future insurance claims in order to derive policy costs for consumers that ensured the company was able to pay out and meanwhile make a profit. They involve the derivation of mathematical formulae and tables that predict likely future outcomes based on what has happened to date. In the field of child protection and safeguarding they include the Violence Risk Appraisal Guide (VRAG) and the Sex Offender Risk Appraisal Guide (SORAG) which have been used since the late 1990s to predict recidivism, influencing decisions about the level of dangerousness that offenders pose to society and whether they should be detained or set free (Nieto and Jung, 2006).

The use of these actuarial tools results in predictions (from zero to 100 per cent) based on the measured relationship between the outcome (in this case violent recidivism) and several variables (e.g. age, marital status and criminal record). Variables are selected based on the extent of their correlation with the known outcome in a large number of previous cases, and weights for each variable are computed. Formulae and tables are used to predict outcome for new cases.

In Chapter 3, I express my reservations about aspects of testing, and in Chapter 8 about the use of actuarial tools when attempting to predict rare events. But in my assessments, in addition to interviews, I usually ask parents to complete some questionnaires about specific matters such as their relationships with romantic partners, symptoms of depression and anxiety, or experiences in the parental role. There is an enormous array of such measures available, many of which are free to download from the internet; others which may be purchased from a variety of sources. Some provide 'norms' which indicate to what extent this person's result conforms to or differs from the average of the general population. The number of restrictions on professional use varies but of the ones that I cite, the majority are available for use by all practitioners in health and social care settings. In this book I want to signpost interested parties to their sources whilst emphasising that the results of questionnaire measures are only adjuncts to understanding. They may contribute to the process of triangulation and sometimes stimulate conversations with care-givers which lead to improved insight into parental perspectives. On the advice of colleagues I have placed some of them in appendices for fear that they appear to take centre stage. Their value in the context of assessment in family proceedings is limited by the imperative to do well which may prevail over accurate self-disclosure.

To my mind, the research process in which we are trying to make the best decisions about children's futures does not require particular methods defined as 'scientific', 'intuitive', 'quantitative' or 'qualitative'. It is about selecting methods that are suited to purpose. Hammond *et al.* (1987) describe this approach as a 'third way' which allows both intuition and systematic research findings to influence the professional judgements that drive decision making. Hammond *et al.* describe a 'cognitive continuum' of judgement. Intuition may be all that is available when under pressure to make an immediate judgement. Next along the continuum is peer-aided judgement, including the use of supervision, system or protocol-aided judgement. Next there is the option to engage with a quasi-experiment (try things out) and finally, recourse to actuarial judgement. This is not to suggest that all stages on the continuum may be relevant or followed in a specific order.

Fairness

Fairness can be of particular salience when cultural differences pertain. What adjustments am I to make when assessing family members with ethnicity, gender, social class, age, faith or sexuality that differs from my own? At times I have found it difficult to keep pace with rapidly changing social and political mores and their attendant preferred vocabularies: do I talk about 'handicap', 'impairment' or 'disability'? Awareness of difference can begin with an internal sense of discomfort evoked by apparently small but significant differences between myself and others, such as the newspaper that I choose to read, the products that give me a distinctive smell, and the kind of food I have on my plate. More embarrassing can be an acute sense of having got things 'wrong'.

The 'myth of sameness' (Smith, 1981: 141–85) refers to the assumption that the skills of the helper are generic and applicable to all individuals irrespective of their backgrounds and personal qualities. But minority and dominant groups do not occupy a level playing field. When applied to minorities, methods devised by the dominant group can be questionable and of dubious value, as in the misapplication of Western-derived intelligence tests (Poortinga, 1995). Training in non-discriminatory practice, unless embedded in all aspects of a course, can lead to a mistaken impression that all is well because the topic has been 'covered'. It is my intention to revisit the issue of diversity throughout this text, rather than allocate it a single section, reflecting my view that a significant degree of continuous effort and imagination is required in order to address issues of difference and fair assessment. Lumping members of a minority group together (e.g. 'Asians') can make for misleading conclusions about needs and appropriate responses, although it can be helpful to have some knowledge of cultural traditions, so long as assumptions are not made about specific individuals. For example, the Chinese practice of subordination to authority may impact on the assessor-assessed relationship (Tsui, Ho and Lam, 2005). Miscommunication is easy when the participants are used to contrasting forms of talking.

Sexuality is one example of a salient feature in which individuals' preferences are diverse, but unlike more visible differences such as ethnicity and gender, it can be revealed, partially revealed (for example, we both know this about me, but the rule is that it doesn't get mentioned) or can be kept effectively and totally hidden (Hitchings, 1999). I will need to question the relevance of enquiries about sexuality to the assessment and to consider the double or triple jeopardy experienced by clients where sexuality, religious affiliation and ethnicity may interact. Eleftheriadou (1994: 80) advises, 'aim to achieve a delicate balance; to include the cultural background of the client, but not to make it the prime issue unless the client has already indicated that it is an area of importance.'

Overall process of assessment

Posing apt questions

Assessment is a research process in which questions are posed and answers are sought from a range of different kinds of data. The data-set is organised through a process of pattern seeking. Where are there consistencies and inconsistencies? How can the inconsistencies be further investigated? How can the data-set be explained? What predictions does it allow us to make and how accurate are they? Fundamentally, these questions are about whether this family's immediate and wider social context can provide care for the children that will produce capable adult citizens. In disputes of residence and contact (UK) or custody and visitation (USA) the task is to determine what arrangements for care will produce the best outcomes for children.

The first stage is the preparation of questions that the assessment is designed to address. What are we trying to find out? As a researcher, I regard this as the most important stage in the process because the design of the study follows from these initial questions, and whilst the process is likely to change and develop as the study unfolds, I can return time and again to my initial queries and see if I am still on track. The questions will need to be adapted to fit the particular circumstances. But when children's needs are in focus and their welfare is at stake, many of the questions will focus on the care-givers' general functioning and parenting skills. There are many frameworks available that can guide the process, one of the most widely used in the UK being the Framework for the Assessment of Children in Need and their Families (Department of Health, 2000). This focuses on three central questions: What are the child's developmental needs? How well are the parents able to meet these needs? What supporting resources are available in the wider family and community? In my role as an 'expert' the questions that I am asked usually fall within the following list, some being similar to those described in the practice direction for expert witnesses in proceedings relating to children (Ministry of Justice, 2008).

- What are the features of the involved people in terms of personal characteristics and their emotional/psychological/developmental profile?
- How do these characteristics or other factors, such as their physical and mental health, learning difficulties or their own history of being parented impact upon the adult's skills as a parent?
- What strengths and weaknesses/areas of needed development does this person bring to the role and tasks of parenting?
- What is the quality of attachment of the children to the parent and of the bond that the parent has with each of the children?
- To what extent does the parent understand and meet the needs of the children across all areas of development?
- What special needs does this child have over and above those of every child?
- Is the adult able to provide appropriate protection for the children?
- How safe are the children whilst in the care of this person?
- What is the person's understanding and acceptance of any concerns about her or his parenting?
- What sources of support does the person have from family, friends and local community?
- If there are any particular needs or difficulties, what input would be helpful in order to effect change?
- What services are available to provide the necessary input?
- How willing and able is the care-giver to work with professionals to achieve change?
- How motivated and committed is the care-giver to bringing about change?
- What is the potential for change, the likely prognosis and timescale?
- If the children are unable to return to the care of the birth parent/s, what kind of alternative placement would best suit their needs?
- What should be the contact arrangements for the children with members of their birth family and each other? Consider the advantages, disadvantages and implications for each of the children.
- What is the capacity of each parent to manage contact in the best interests of the child?

Whilst frameworks, structures and checklists may usefully guide the practitioner in collecting information, there is a danger that these act to constrain the enquiry and become the straightjackets of a bureaucratic culture, closing down thinking and suppressing creativity. This is described by Phyllida Parsloe (1999: 11) who states, 'Much effort in social service agencies is expended on ensuring that procedures are followed so that, in the event of trouble, the agency can show that it acted appropriately and followed the rules, whether these were provided by legislation, by central government or by local agreements. The problem is that professional judgement may be hampered by a rigid application of procedural rules.' Once the questions have been posed and relevant information collected, the task of the practitioner is to analyse and synthesise the data in order to create hypotheses or provisional explanations and understanding which lead on to decision making and ongoing review in which the cycle repeats.

Stages of judgement and decision making

Judgement is about the ways in which people 'integrate multiple probabilistic, potentially conflicting cues to arrive at an *understanding* of the situation' (Goldstein and Hogarth, 1997: 4). Decision making requires people to, '*choose* what to do next, especially in the face of uncertain consequences and conflicting goals' (Goldstein and Hogarth, 1997: 4).

> A helpful aspect to the process is to think of professional judgement as a sequence. In the early stages of a case, a worker makes holding judgements with the intention of ensuring safety for the child and gaining stability in which to make further enquiries. These holding judgements are further characterised by, as far as is possible, not compromising future plans. The next stage of judgement making concerns the issues in the case. It involves a careful analysis of the case to understand the mechanisms that are creating needs in the child, for example not just 'mother is drinking', but 'mother drinks because of the pain of her childhood memories and these combined factors mean that she is not able to *develop* an emotional relationship with her child.' Having analysed the issues, the next judgement stage is to make strategic judgements, i.e. what is to be done and how. The final type of judgement is an evaluative judgement, in which the worker and manager, together with the service user, can assess the effectiveness of interventions and establish the reasons for any undesirable outcome.
>
> (Hollows and Nelson, n.d.: 8)

The overall investigative process is cyclical, repeating the loop that involves posing questions, collecting relevant information, analysing and synthesising the cues and data in a reflective process, reaching tentative explanations and judgements which lead to decisions and actions. The analytical process involves deciding what weight to give particular pieces of information. The final stage of review; finding out how the interventions are impacting on the family's circumstances, leads on to another lap of the cycle. The above quotes already show that authors use different vocabulary to describe what I experience as the same thing. What Goldstein and Hogarth (1997) call 'decision making', Hollows and Nelson (n.d.) call 'strategic judgements'.

What can go wrong and how to avoid it

One of the well-documented dangers in carrying out assessments is the influence of bias, which may take many forms. It can derive from over-emphasis of particular information at the expense of other or missing data. This is an extract from a report concerning a mother who, on IQ testing, achieved a result that suggested she had learning difficulties:

> Ms Bleasdale is currently functioning in the severe to moderate learning disabled range of intelligence. Her thinking is concrete and she is unable to understand abstract concepts, reflect on her experiences or show evidence of understanding the court process. Although she appears to be quite articulate in interview, she does not fully understand what she says. She presents as someone significantly more able than she actually is. She is likely to have great difficulty in recognising her daughter's needs, particularly if she had to deal with novel or non-routine situations. She has little idea about the impact of her behaviour on Natasha and her cognitive limitations will make her management of Natasha's behaviour very inconsistent. It is highly unlikely that she could parent a child on her own without ongoing intensive support. She is likely to have great difficulty were she to move out of her current home in which she has managed within very restricted routines in which her behaviour has been 'over-learned'.

Although standing alone this paragraph may seem reasonable, there is conflicting information from other sources that warrants deeper consideration. At this time Natasha was being cared for by her father who had been awarded residence. As a result of his mental health difficulties he would disappear out of Natasha's life on an unpredictable basis, leaving her with Ms Bleasdale without notice. Ms Bleasdale would pick up the reins, ensure that Natasha received good physical care, take her to school on time and be observed to provide warm and affectionate care although Natasha could 'wind her round her little finger'. Ms Bleasdale had been educated in mainstream schools, single-handedly ran her own home, had no outstanding debts, had passed her driving test and managed all of the written correspondence sent to her by the authorities. In this case, her score on a one-off IQ test was not set against other information that gave a different picture. Ms Bleasdale's account of the assessment was that the interviewer had spoken in an accent that she struggled to understand. She did not have the confidence to raise this in the session, fearing to alienate the assessor and doubting her own experience of the process. There lies danger in over-reliance on one piece of information, however well-regarded might be the method by which it was obtained.

Known as 'fundamental attribution error', people have a propensity to ascribe causality to a person rather than the person's context, the latter tending to be perceived as background (Lassiter *et al.*, 2002). This has been reported even when the person making the judgement is aware of situational constraints, and it is more common in individualistic cultures (Miller, 1984). The phenomenon links, for me, with our apparent obsession in the West with finding someone to blame whenever anything goes wrong. One of the difficulties with such an orientation is that it can close down options for constructive intervention.

My personal thinking habits can lead to unfair and unjust assessments which close down possibilities for understanding the people whom I have been tasked to assess. In order to limit the influence of my prejudices and bias I need a good understanding of me and an orientation in which I continuously reflect on what I bring to the process. Methods for facilitating such learning are described in Scaife (2010) and usually benefit from the involvement of another person such as a supervisor. I also need to be alert to the impact upon me of cultural imperatives which influence how I construct my ways of being, including how I do my job. They are at work constantly through the media and reinforced in daily interactions. I may thoughtlessly engage in stereotyping on an automatic basis. Our jobs expose us to compassion stress – we are upset by repeatedly hearing clients' stories of hardship and suffering. This readily leads to staff burnout, vicarious traumatisation and compassion fatigue (Bennett *et al.*, 2005; Figley, 1995, 2002; Myers and Wee, 2005; Rothschild and Rand, 2006). We have a duty to care not only for our clients but also for ourselves and through reflective practice with colleagues, to ensure that we do not become inured to our clients' pain and anguish.

Skills

Peter Dale *et al.* (2005) argue that there are key skills, irrespective of discipline, that are needed for conducting assessments in family proceedings:

- research knowledge (awareness of relevant research and methodological limitations in applying research findings in individual cases);
- skills in engagement with family members (who are likely to be anxious, defensive, angry, etc.);
- skills in history taking (being able to create a constructive environment to obtain relevant information from family members in a systematic way);
- observational skills (especially regarding parent-child interactions);
- interviewing skills (listening, communicating, understanding, giving feedback, exploring responses to feedback, probing, etc.);

- skills in regulating the emotional intensity of interviews (given that family members invariably have strong feelings about their situation);
- thinking and analytic skills (synthesising complex information and developing and exploring hypotheses from a neutral perspective);
- monitoring counter-transferential responses to a family, and other potential sources of assessment bias;
- knowledge and skills in assessing potential for change in view of identified personal and family problems;
- writing skills (assessment reports need to be cogent, authoritative, clear and balanced documents).

(Dale *et al.*, 2005: 156)

At the beginning of this chapter I argued that our task as assessors is to learn as much about families as we can in a relatively short period of time, using multiple sources of information through a fair process in order to reach a perspective that can inform professional decision making. I have argued the case for constructive assessment which involves keeping an open mind, active and critical listening, asking the kinds of questions that encourage openness rather than defensiveness, and recognition of strengths which may be developed. Whilst I agree with Peter Dale and his colleagues about the skills that are needed for carrying out this task, I also believe that at the centre are the worker's personal qualities; an orientation of minding about and respecting our clients, believing in them, treating them as we would like to be treated ourselves, trying to be aware of our biases, remembering what it feels like to be assessed, owning our own feelings, and being authentic in our way of relating to these parents who, for the most part and despite their difficulties, genuinely want to do well for their children.

2   Interviewing

In this chapter I want to argue that what emerges from interviews is highly dependent on the nature of the relationship that can be built between the participants and how they experience its tasks and purposes. I want to persuade you that in the initial stages, assessment is more about the interviewer than the interviewee. It is about what preconceptions the interviewer brings, and about what learning the interviewer can achieve through the interviewing process. The families we see may have goals that differ from those of the involved professionals:

> At first it was not very good – I kept losing my temper – which is bound to happen when they are threatening to take your son off you .... As its gone along, things have got better ... we've got more friendly – we talk to each other – instead of shouting and bawling at each other (laughs) .... She actually stayed quite calm – she tried to calm me down. I just couldn't hold my temper back – I had to let it out. She either just sat there and let me say what I had to say – or she'd sit there and talk to me and tell me to calm down. (Ms Durgan)
>
> (Dale, 2004: 150)

> ... he nigh on interrogated me. It was the questions he asked, and I wasn't in a fit state to talk to anyone. He was very much accusing.
>
> (Thoburn et al., 1995: 55)

> All along, social services seemed to be testing and pushing us. They wanted to see how far we would go. They were just waiting for us to snap. Waiting for us to make any little mistake. I don't think they really thought we were human then.
>
> (Lindley, 1994: 32)

In my interviews I want to hear the respondents' first-hand account of their experiences, learn about and gain understanding of their lives and how things got to be as they are now. I want to know about their hopes and aspirations. The importance of listening, empathy and respect for the individual has been described as an important traditional social work skill by Corby *et al.* (2002).

Like most people, I have had a number of experiences of interviewing and being interviewed, in my case many more of the former than the latter. My experience as interviewee derives largely from job applications. I have some recall of such interviews going back many years, particularly those at which I was unsuccessful, or in which I came away feeling small or stupid. In the 'hot seat' I often experienced anxiety, sometimes at a level that enhanced my performance, but on occasions that interfered with my ability to think. The trouble is that being the subject of an assessment interview can feel exposing, can evoke uncertainties and feelings of powerlessness. And these were only job interviews. How much more potentially threatening would be an interview that could result in the loss of my children. I try to keep my own experience of anxiety in mind when I meet with and interview people who are contesting the right to care for their children.

I see the task of the assessment interviewer, at least in the first instance, as giving the interviewee the floor, using an approach that has parallels with qualitative research methods. Stan Lester (1999) describes a method aimed at gathering 'deep' information, the purpose of which is to understand events as they are perceived by the individual respondent. This involves cutting through taken-for-granted assumptions and habitual ways of perceiving. The approach emphasises the personal knowledge and subjective experience of the interviewee, an exploration of which can be a powerful process for gaining insights into people's motivations and actions.

The perspective and aims of this approach are encapsulated by McCracken (1988: 17). 'Qualitative research does not survey the terrain, it mines it.' He draws attention to the difficulty for the interviewer of bringing an open mind to the process. He says, 'Those who work in their own culture do not have this critical distance from what they study. They carry with them a large number of assumptions that can create a treacherous sense of familiarity .... With these assumptions in place, an invisible hand directs inquiry and forecloses the range and the kind of things the investigator can observe and understand' (McCracken, 1988: 22). McCracken invites the investigator to try and 'manufacture distance' in order to create a critical awareness of matters with which we have a deep and blinding familiarity (Marcus and Fischer, 1986: 137–64).

What is more, even with an open mind, interviewers cannot help by their actions but convey to the interviewee a sense of what it is they may be seeking, and this may take place out of conscious awareness. If the practitioner says, 'Tell me more about that,' a sense of direction is being conveyed. If the worker only nods and smiles, giving encouragement to continue, that is also directive. If interviewers turn their body away from the other person or frown, they are conveying that this is not the sort of thing they want to hear (Haley, 1987). Rom Harré (1998) argues that the interviewer is embedded in the social scene of the interview, and cannot therefore be independent of the respondent's replies.

Despite the challenges of interviewing, I regard this as the central plank of enquiry when undertaking family assessments. A person-centred and respectful approach is regarded as being particularly appropriate for the study of sensitive personal experiences (Lee, 1993). The interviewer encourages, clarifies, and probes, explores exceptions, contradictions, ambiguities, and ambivalence in order to gain as deep an understanding as possible of the interviewee's experience. It is about me trying to enter into the client's 'reality' whilst trying to suspend my own.

Issues in interviewing

Roles and responsibilities of interviewer

Interviews are verbal exchanges which have much in common with but differ from social conversations. They involve a more formal structure than a social conversation, a clearly defined distinction between roles, and a different set of norms regulating the process of interaction. Adults usually have some shared understanding of these structural factors, whilst children may not yet have been socialised into the interview norms of turn-taking and clarity about who is asking the questions and who is answering. Interviews that take place with a view to safeguarding children are generally with troubled people or people in trouble. This behoves sensitivity to the respondents' emotions, allowing space for them to experience and express feelings which may include sadness, anger and fear, whilst ensuring that at the close of the interview they are not left in a heightened emotional state that would disable their functioning after we have parted.

It is the interviewer who provides structure and organisation for the conversation, whilst following the leads provided by the interviewee. I aim to make it possible for my fellow participants to tell me about themselves as openly as possible in the circumstances. They need to feel that I can empathise with their situation and that I will give them a fair and attentive hearing. When listening to people expressing very different ideas from my own, I find it helpful to bear in mind that, whatever they say, it makes some kind of sense to them. Although I have a structure in mind, and written questions to address, much of the interview cannot be determined in advance and benefits from an improvised sequential response as the dialogue unfolds.

Conveying a desire to understand

Given the opportunity, I find that people generally love to tell stories about themselves. If I can minimise the impact of the context, in which the other person feels assessed and I feel like the assessor or judge, and am able to create conditions in which respondents feel comfortable, the chances are they will begin to relax and tell me about themselves. This needs supporting conditions, often the person's own home, and a relatively uninterrupted extensive

period of time. If I feel under pressure of time or an imperative to get particular answers to specific questions, such conditions are unlikely to prevail. If I
am there with an authentic attitude of curiosity and genuine desire to understand just how the person's life turned out this way, my manner will convey
attentive and curious listening and encouragement to elaborate.

An incidental advantage of long interviews undertaken in respondents' homes
is the information that it provides about their ways of life. I have witnessed debt
collectors call, young people congregate to share illicit substances, partners from
whom respondents allege that they have separated stagger sleepily downstairs,
friends and family phone insistently, neighbours bring their children while they
go to the shops, dogs barking incessantly in the next room.

Interviewer assumptions and bias

It is inevitable that interviewers will bring assumptions and personal biases
to their interviews, based on their own predispositions, family and professional history, beliefs and values. Mary Main (n.d.) cautions against a tendency
for interviewers to probe significantly more positive than negative events and
vice versa. Professionals have been found to use their interviewing techniques
to 'shape' assessments, seeking or finding data that fitted a favourite theoretical model (Sheldon, 1995). This is called 'confirmation bias'; an inclina-
tion to seek and notice information that fits with a pre-conceived account
(Sutherland, 2007: 99). Strohmer *et al.* (1990) showed that when counsellors
were asked to consider a specific clinical hypothesis, they found more
confirmatory than disconfirmatory evidence in a narrative report, despite the
presence of a greater number of examples of the latter.

Whilst confirmation bias is regarded as a process that may occur out of
awareness, some authors argue for the presence, in custody or residence disputes,
of intentional distortion, selective reporting or skewed interpretation of the
data in a process of 'confirmatory distortion' (Martindale, 2005: 33). This
suggests that interviews benefit from being conducted with a view to seeking
evidence that counteracts any predisposition to see family members and their
functioning in a particular light. Being aware of the picture I have formed of
the interviewee before we have even met can help to ensure that I monitor any
tendency to notice data that fits and shut out that which conflicts. Open-
minded interviewing can be particularly challenging against a background of
highly distasteful allegations. I cannot 'unknow' such information and I have
found myself harbouring feelings of anger towards clients I have known even
for a very long time when it appears that they have behaved in ways that I
have found repugnant. At such times I like to try and think of them as the
'child become adult'. What happened to them during their childhood that
could generate such actions in the adult? This helps particularly when parents'
own children present as severely neglected or ill-treated.

In addition to the influences of my personal history and tendency towards
confirmation bias, I have been socialised into my professional culture. In my

employing organisation there will also be habitual ways of doing things that reflect both explicit and implicit policies, practices and values. A typology of cultural dynamics is described in Hawkins and Shohet (2006: 196). These include 'hunt the personal pathology', 'strive for bureaucratic efficiency', 'watch your back', 'driven by crisis' and 'the addictive organization'. You may recognise these from your own experience and they can operate simultaneously. In my experience these imperatives tend to get pushed down the line and I can find myself treating my clients in similar ways to those I am experiencing in my work culture. If, for example, I am constantly watching my back at work, I may risk emphasising negatives and avoidance of risk rather than bringing to the client my optimism for change.

Steps in interpretation of an interview

Whenever an interview is conducted for the purposes of an assessment, there are a number of steps of interpretation. This begins with what the respondent reports, followed by what the interviewer interprets as the meaning of what was said, how this is translated from the conversation to the written word and finally, there is an interpretation placed upon the text by the reader. There is a risk of the interviewee's meaning being 'lost in translation'. The nuances, context, emphasis, etc. are all lost once the spoken word is converted to text. In each step, new and potentially different meanings are made by the interviewer and the report reader. And in each step the reader, or interpreter, inevitably brings to bear her or his cognitive schemata, the mental models and meaning-making structures that have developed over a lifetime. What we make of what we hear or read may say more about us than about the interviewee.

> Having received the incoming signal we process it; this involves making sense of the message received. The processing consists of recalling stored information, relating other information relevant to the message, thinking about the message, evaluating the message, and translating it so that the message is coherent within the receiver's frame of reference. As receivers we select certain items from the incoming message, ignore others, and rearrange what we hear into interpretable patterns. We then formulate a message in response.
>
> (Kadushin and Kadushin, 1997: 27)

It is as well to remember that as Alfred North Whitehead (1978: 264) said, 'Spoken language is merely a series of squeaks.'

The interviewer/interviewee divide

I find it helpful to remind myself that the relationship between me and the interviewee does not start off on neutral territory. I have a title; social worker, psychologist, psychiatrist, teacher, health visitor, and there are popular conceptions of the meaning of these. Clients will say that they have an appointment to see 'the shrink'; social workers are people who take your children away. People are likely to be anxious about meeting with me because of my assessment role. Sometimes they are very frightened. They want to do well and this includes children as well as adults. Even very young children have learned that there are 'right' answers and these are what they want to give (Holt, 1969). If I am to learn as much as possible about the interviewee I need to try to build a trusting relationship in a very short space of time, and this requires me to create an atmosphere in which the respondent does not feel 'done to':

> Participants feel a personal involvement with the researcher in the collaborative development of each unique interview as opposed to being someone who is 'done to' according to criteria and a process that they had no part in devising. The significance of this distinction should not be underestimated in personally sensitive areas of research, especially with people who have histories of abuse, exploitation, manipulation and neglect.
>
> (Dale and Allen, 1998: 802)

Although there is a role divide between us, it is as well to remember that whilst today it is your turn to be interviewed, tomorrow it may be mine. A shift in my circumstances may put me in the 'hot seat'. I was starkly reminded of this fact when my daughter was little. She came home from school one day, telling me that the teacher had inquired into the cause of the red mark on her neck.

The respondent's preoccupations

I have had children greet me by saying, 'My mummy's poorly,' and 'I'm not allowed in the playground because I just hit James,' before I introduced myself or asked a single question. This tells me that they have preoccupations that may have nothing to do with my purposes in interviewing them. There are times when I am talking to someone else and I realise later that I have heard almost nothing because of the primacy of my internal dialogue with myself. This tells me that respondents may need to get things off their chests before they are able to attend to the questions that I am asking, and if I do not allow this, how will I get them to hear me?

Method of recording

In my interviews for the family court I usually rely on my written notes rather than a voice recording. I could give many reasons for this decision but it is primarily one of practicality. Transcription is a lengthy process. Nevertheless, there are many advantages to voice recording and when I do choose this option I appreciate the opportunity to review what was said, which usually improves accuracy and helps my understanding. I have written at length about the issues involved in recording interviews and the approaches that I have found least intrusive in Scaife (2009).

Purpose of interviews

In my professional context, the well-being of others is the focus and purpose of my work. My task is to encourage respondents to talk about themselves, their experiences and, in the case of parents, their parenting as this relates to the questions being posed. It is not for me, the interviewer, to speak about or impress upon the other person my own views and experiences. 'The best probes are when the interviewer says little, gives quick, short prompts where the function is to get the participant going again. If you sound like you are saying a mouth full or a full paragraph you are off target' (Crowell and Treboux, n.d.).

Interviews involve interpersonal interaction for a specific purpose. The purpose may be mutually agreed by the participants, as in job selection for example. But in interviews which aim to help determine children's best interests, interviewees may be participating under duress without commonly agreed goals. Interviews have a significant role to play in the negotiation of goals and also as interventions that have the potential to impact on clients, in addition to helping the professional system in its decision making. If these purposes are to be accomplished, interviews will need to enable people to identify their strengths and development needs through a holistic approach, differentiated according to the child's or family's unique circumstances.

> Social workers need to identify services users' competencies and to affirm their experiences so that self-confidence can grow. This requires asking for their stories; listening and taking them seriously helps to build confidence and a sense of being valued.
>
> (Milner and O'Byrne, 2002: 37)

> Interview listening requires a different approach from social listening. Interviewers need to feel comfortable and unthreatened by anything the interviewee says in order to devote all their energy to listening freely. Although interviewers recognize that what is being said may be contrary to their own values and attitudes, workers are not called on to defend their values and attitudes in the interview.
>
> (Kadushin and Kadushin, 1997: 54)

> The accepting worker seeks to explain the individual's behaviour rather than to determine the worth of such behaviour .... Striving to understand what explains, motivates, or supports the behaviour that needs changing does not imply approval of the behaviour.
>
> (Kadushin and Kadushin, 1997: 104)

The role of checklists and formal structures for interviewing

A judge instructed the local authority to carry out a parenting assessment. The local authority barrister replied that the social worker had underway a Core Assessment. The judge responded, 'In my experience over 80 per cent of Core Assessments are not worth the paper they're written on. I don't want a social worker to go with a checklist. I want them to start with a blank piece of paper.' For me, this encapsulates one of the central dilemmas in interviewing. The Department of Health Framework and associated guidance emerged out of what were regarded as previous failures to secure the well-being of children. Assessments were to become 'comprehensive' – and how else might this be accomplished other than through the use of a standard set of headings in order to avert idiosyncratic interviewing practices, thereby ensuring that a common set of relevant topics was explored. A social work colleague tells me that in her department the initial response to a family identified as having children in need or at risk of harm is to complete the Core Assessment form and ensure that all the boxes are ticked, after which the true assessment begins. I fear that this approach has the potential negatively to impact on interviewees before 'true' assessment has begun.

The Assessment Framework comprises a detailed set of questions. The Core Assessment Record for children aged 5–9 years has 36 pages, many of which require a tick of a yes/no box with one line available for qualitative comments. Sally Holland (2004) argues that its authors never anticipated that interviewers would use these questions exactly as set, but that they should aim to complete the form by the end of the assessment. In her study, she found that there were three types of approach used by social workers in response to the Assessment Framework.

> With the Core Assessment [form] I don't actually use it with the clients, or the family. Usually I expect them first time just to tell me anything they want to tell me, and the questions I ask I think of then, and then go back on a second visit really to try and fill in the gaps. (Interview with Gaynor, City Social Services).
>
> To be frank, you know you need to get x, y and z information so you know you do it instinctively, do you know what I mean? It is not necessarily by following the format to the nth degree because if you have done it for quite a while you are doing it quite naturally. It is surprising how much information you can actually pick up in a very short period of time if you are experienced. (Interview with Lillian, City Social Services).
>
> It is very clear because you are actually taking the assessment forms with you and saying that they need to complete these and I need to work with it. And they get to see the information that you are writing about, which I think is really good and it does involve people a lot more. (Interview with Caitlin, City Social Services).
>
> (Holland, 2004: 117)

Grant McCracken (1988) attempts to balance focus with breadth in his 'long interview' method. He advocates an initial review of existing information and the construction of a focussed questionnaire based on this knowledge. The subsequent intensive interview is a sharply focused and relatively rapid process that seeks to diminish the indeterminacy and redundancy that can attend less structured interviews whilst giving interviewers a penetrating glimpse into the minds and lives of their respondents. He advocates a process in which the kind and amount of data is controlled, 'without also artificially constraining or forcing their character' (McCracken, 1988: 12). Although there is a clear structure, the interviewer is expected to make free with prompts about issues that arise spontaneously as the interview unfolds.

> Extemporaneous strategies of investigation are often the only road to understanding. The interviewer must be able to take full advantage of the contingency of the interview and pursue any opportunity that may present itself. In sum, the questionnaire that is used to order data and free the interviewer must not be allowed to destroy the elements of freedom and variability within the interview.
>
> (McCracken, 1988: 25)

I employ a similar method for the purpose of conducting interviews in court proceedings by creating a short set of overarching questions arising out of a reading of the background information, conversation with a key professional, and/or derived from a letter of instruction. I follow this with a few relevant questionnaires which serve to broaden the field of data that will contribute to the development of an understanding.

Reflecting purpose in the start of the interview

With a view to clarifying the purpose, I usually begin assessment interviews, after a greeting, introductions and some small talk about the weather or my journey, by reading to respondents the list of questions that the interview is designed to try and address. In addition to the list outlined in the previous chapter, other general questions address issues about domestic violence, drug or alcohol misuse and the parent's understanding of its impact on the children, and quality of parenting. Specific questions may relate to any impairments or disabilities experienced by family members.

For children in private law proceedings where residence and contact are being contested, questions may also centre on a parent's capability to negotiate with the other, to support contact with the non-resident parent and to prioritise the child's needs over the contest between the parents.

Assessments of children usually focus on questions about the child's needs and developmental status, any of these that cause concern including potential explanations for presenting problems, the nature of the child's attachment to the care-givers, bonds between children, placement needs and appropriate interventions.

There are a number of reasons why I read a list of questions to interviewees at the outset, although I will usually return to them later in the interview. This is firstly to allow respondents the opportunity to weigh me up without the pressure of having to speak themselves. If they wish, they can wait until I have read through the whole list before having to speak at all. It gives a message that the assessment is prescribed and we are working together to try and provide answers to a third party. I am seeking their answers to the questions and sometimes, particularly when I am at a loss to understand what lies behind some of the questions that I have been asked to address, I invite the respondent to help me understand the source of or motivation for such questions. Such questions might take the form, 'Is Ms Hayward attention seeking?' or, 'To what extent does Mr Elliot understand the impact of his behaviour on Ms Hayward?' I feel as if I am interviewing in the dark and so I can ask, 'How have you acted that might have led someone to think that you may be attention seeking?' 'What kind of behaviour do you think might be seen as impacting on your partner?' When I do not fully understand the question myself, I cannot bring preconceptions to the exploration of the issues and I find this enlightening, especially because it tends to generate a shared sense of exploration in which I am at sea and the respondent is my guide.

This way of beginning the interview conveys my responsibility to provide some structure; to draw the session back to the questions if the content has strayed too far and is failing to shed light on them. More often though, I will follow rather than lead the respondent, trying to draw some relevant meaning from the choice of topics introduced by the interviewee. If I interrupt, it is usually to test how the person responds to such interruptions and I will try different approaches to the exploration to see what works best.

Sometimes interviewees begin to answer the questions when I am part way through the list and if this is their preference, I may follow. This may mean that the interview does not follow a logical order but this is not my major concern. I am interested in whatever the person chooses to tell me in the knowledge that I can organise the content into a different sequence at a later date, providing that I am respectful to what I take to be the person's meaning.

Making no demands for answers at the beginning can help to settle anxiety, both my own and the respondent's. Sometimes anxiety is manifest by the need to talk and respondents will tell me the whole of their life story in a few sentences that could bring the interview to a close within minutes. I have to keep in mind that there is no hurry, that we can go over the same ground more than once and that how we begin is providing me with information about this person in the context of this kind of meeting. If they feel pressure to give their account of events in order to deal with their anxiety or to impress upon me their view, then it costs me nothing to wait my turn and give them my undivided attention. I rarely if ever meet a parent to whom their relationships with their children are other than vitally important. With so much at stake it would be surprising, and perhaps even concerning, to find a relaxed interviewee. Anxiety may be manifest as pressure of speech, hesitation for fear of giving the 'wrong' answer, distraction – moving the topic from the heart of the matter to the periphery, difficulty in attending to or understanding what I am asking, or heightened affect which may present as jumpiness or a raised vocal pitch. If I am also anxious we may not get off to a good start and so I need strategies to help me to relax, whatever I meet at the door.

Confrontational and/or negative interactional style

I prefer to take it as read that the respondents are feeling anxious, under pressure and likely to respond defensively to perceived criticism. In other words, I think they are likely to be having similar feelings to me when I feel judged. In my view it is the interviewer's responsibility to frame the initial interview in a way that reduces these feelings. If not, the interview can turn into a contest, such as this:

> I asked Ms Howson why her first daughter had been taken into the care of the local authority. She minimised the difficulties and could not give me any specific reasons but said that she had been young and inexperienced. She turned her attention away from me as if she was using a tactic to avoid answering my questions. I pressed her by asking whether she understood the concerns of the local authority about her parenting. She said, 'I was always there for Kellie but I made mistakes because of my inexperience and I want another chance. I've grown up since then.' I asked how she thought that her mental health difficulties impacted on her parenting. She denied experiencing any mental health difficulties, saying that she had had 'baby blues' just like many other first-time mothers but that she had quickly recovered and this was not relevant to her current situation. I introduced some of the other specific historical concerns. Ms Howson raised her voice and said that these were not relevant because, 'I'm telling you now that I'm much older and wiser.'

The contest follows a process in which the interviewer challenges the interviewee to accept and acknowledge historical criticisms of her parenting while the interviewee attempts to defend herself through distraction and denial. Christopher Cordess (2003: 173) states, 'There is no point in aggressive confrontation which is likely to increase defensive denial … a psychotherapeutic approach … which seeks to understand the subjective experience of the 'failing' parent, can be effective in establishing an initial therapeutic alliance.' Research that has explored parents' experience of being assessed in child protection investigations suggests that they often feel unfairly treated and on the receiving end of a negative interactional style adopted by practitioners. This can lead to anxiety-derived behaviours that are interpreted as confirmatory evidence of their inability to provide adequate care for their children.

> The emotional responses of parents (such as expressions of frustration, irritation and sarcasm) to perceived negative styles of intervention may

be seen as 'evidence' that the family is totally uncooperative and even inherently dangerous. Families describe a professional mentality that can appear almost paranoid: a fear that parents are so psychopathologically devious that they will 'fake good' in disingenuous dealings with professionals and at the first manipulated opportunity are likely to pounce in cold blood and murder their baby. While some parents undoubtedly do have murderous feelings towards their offspring, acting on this is extraordinarily rare.

(Dale *et al.*, 2005: 96)

I would hold that what seem to be defensive responses provide useful information about the interviewee's anxieties and uncertainties. When we are feeling confident we may have less need to defend ourselves than in areas where we lack confidence, although even then we may experience indignation about others' opinions that differ from our self-assessment. I think that this kind of response by an interviewee is communicating that the interviewer needs to change the approach because it is generating defensiveness. The approach is likely to prevent engagement and risks creating a process in which interviewees have no opportunity either to show their strengths or to own their weaknesses.

Why not begin the above interview by asking a more general question about Ms Howson's experience of giving birth to and looking after her first child? What she had enjoyed, what she had found difficult, what was the baby's temperament, who had supported her, what she had learned? This interview seems to have begun with an assumption of incompetent parenting, probably based on a reading of the previous file. Perhaps the most helpful attitude that an interviewer can bring to the assessment is an open mind, a desire to understand the other's perspective and a will to think about how things might be made better. In a different interview the mother described above had another opportunity to talk about the reasons why her first daughter had been removed from her care. She said:

It's very terrifying when they take a baby from their mother. I was naive and had family problems. I've learned. People do change and move on. There were times that Kellie wanted to go to the park and I used to say that I wasn't feeling well. She never used to get hugs and kisses but I did make sure she was clean and I bought her good quality clothes. I really did go wrong. At that time I was with bad influence and bad company.

Would this mother be regarded as taking responsibility for her past failures? Is this a question we are trying to address? Can she have a clean sheet? Are we learning more about the interviewing style, about the anxiety and defensiveness of the mother, or more about the acceptance by the mother of past failures?

The observed quality of care of her baby by a mother such as this may well be regarded as non-problematic, and it is doubtful whether the child would have been removed without the mother's previous history. This is not a lone example. The Coastal Cities study (Holland, 2004) found that the most important factor in whether a child was rehabilitated to the care of a parent was their perceived cooperation with the local authority, not the quality of care that the child was receiving. Holland (2004: 87) observes, 'it is seen that direct parenting behaviours are observed in detail but that this is rarely a deciding factor in assessment conclusions.' Sally Holland cautions against unduly heavy reliance on interview data alone since this is a function of the worker–parent relationship and may discriminate against parents with limited verbal fluency or who lack confidence to express their views.

In the 1970s and 1980s, confrontational interviewing was an approach of choice for substance-misusing clients, based on the idea that direct confrontation was needed in order to break down defences (Miller and Rollnick, 1991). Later research suggested that the strong denial and resistance of such clients may have developed *in response* to confrontational approaches to interviewing (Miller and Rollnick, 2002). One of the other difficulties with interviews that employ forcefulness is that they may reveal more about the contribution of the interviewer to the relationship than they do about the interviewee.

> Mr Jones does not always listen unless one is quite assertive with him. He has a tendency to express himself verbally at great length, and expects by this that others will eventually conform to his point of view. When I attempted to interrupt and return him to the task in hand he was exceptionally resistant and continued with his own discourse despite my questions about other topics. He appeared to be acting out the scenes that he was describing and to be preoccupied by his own issues. He repeatedly turned to his own topics at times when it was irrelevant to do so.

What might this passage reveal concerning the beliefs of the interviewer about the role and task? These are my suggestions:

- Interviewees should listen to interviewers.
- Interviewees should not be preoccupied by their own topics.
- Some of the preoccupations of interviewees are irrelevant.
- Interviewee responses should not be lengthy.
- Lengthy responses might indicate an attempt to change the listener's viewpoint to that of the interviewee.

Without more information about Mr Jones' behaviour in other circumstances, the danger is that this passage tells us at least as much about the interviewer as about the interviewee. Maybe Mr Jones did not feel heard or adequately understood. Maybe the interviewer did not speak in an accent that

Mr Jones was able readily to follow and he had difficulty in understanding the questions. Almost certainly Mr Jones was frightened.

First questions

I usually begin initial interviews by exploring one of three general areas – of parental history ('Were you born locally?'), of parental relationship ('How did you and your partner meet?'/'How did you two meet?'), or history of involvement with the local authority. This has features in common with the beginning of an unstructured interview described by Dale (2004) in a qualitative research study. Interviews began with an open-ended 'grand tour' type question (Spradley, 1989), along the lines of 'Perhaps you could begin by telling me how the child protection services first became involved with your family?' Grand tour questions are open-ended questions that allow the interviewee to set the direction of the interview. The interviewer then follows the leads that the interviewee provides. The interviewer can always return to pre-planned interview questions after the leads have been followed. The interviewer's interventions are to encourage, clarify, probe and explore exceptions, contradictions and ambiguity, as well as drawing out similarities and differences of view. For these purposes 'open' questions are generally more productive than 'closed' questions, which require only a yes/no or other very brief response. 'Do you get on well with your partner?' is closed. 'What is your relationship with your partner like?' is open.

The continuing interview

Differences of style; clinical/questionnaire format

The interviewing style that I propose differs from those which follow a questionnaire format and also from a clinical interview; it has a different purpose. The former tends to produce brief responses, often encouraging people to give yes/no answers to closed questions. In my experience, the kind of interview that provides the most useful information follows a style advocated by Mary Main (n.d.) in her advice regarding the Adult Attachment Interview. She argues that interviewees need time to reflect and that the interviewer should not hasten to new questions or interrupt as people try to formulate their thoughts. Where answers require reflection, encouragement to continue can be given by active gentle affirmations of interest. If the end of an initial response is met by interjections such as 'UhHUH' or 'OhKAY' this can signal that it is time to move onto the next question and may have the effect of shutting up the respondent. She argues that the participant should be given a full conversational turn in order to have time to give due thought to the question asked. A listening attitude can be conveyed by allowing reasonable silences, by the use of soft encouraging sounds and by body orientation towards the interviewee. For the purposes of accurate reporting I find it helpful to write down as much as possible of what the interviewee has to say and this has the added benefit of encouraging me to leave gaps in the conversation whilst I catch up with what is being said.

Overly informal style

Mary Main also draws attention to difficulties arising from an overly informal style. This occurs when interviewers join in the conversation by offering their own opinions and experiences or by moving away from the central questions to peripheral matters. It can be tempting to share experiences with a view to fostering the development of rapport, but such sharing risks turning the interview away from the purpose of finding out about the interviewee. Main counsels against interviewer contributions such as 'I remember feeling rejected when my mother took my sister on holiday without me.'

Avoid giving the interviewer's interpretation or view

Empathic statements such as, 'That sounds very difficult', or, 'That must have been hard,' can be encouraging but may be even more effective when posed as questions beginning with the word, 'How?' It is usually unhelpful to guess about the nature of the feelings generated by an experience lest this pressures the respondent to agree, shutting down the possibility for the expression of other feelings that may have been more central in the interviewee's experience. Main advocates the use of empathic statements only when interviewees have already described the emotions that accompanied their experience. If you can encourage interviewees to identify their own feelings you are not putting words into their mouths.

Leading vs non-leading questions

Leading questions or prompts invite interviewees to agree with you or to respond with the interviewer's interpretation of the reported experience. I have found that leading questions can have a place in interviews if there appear to be gaps in the respondent's recall or they have missed out an area completely, but only after they have had an opportunity to respond to non-leading questions on the same topic. Crowell and Treboux (n.d.) offer the following example:

> I think I wasted a lot of my years.
>
> *Do you think that was because there was a lack of communication between you and your parents?* (leading)
>
> *Why do you think you wasted a lot of years?* (non-leading)
>
> 'Why' questions can be very difficult to answer and another non-leading enquiry might be, '*How did you come to that conclusion?*'

Kinds of prompts

People vary in the degree of recall that they have of their own childhood but this can be prompted by asking for early memories, how the family celebrated birthdays and other special days in the calendar, any important teachers that they recall or activities that they enjoyed. I ask about to whom they would go when hurt or upset and how that person would have responded. I ask about routines and boundaries and how their care-givers would react when they misbehaved. The answers can be connected with the present by asking about what approaches to child care they reproduce in their own parenting and what they have resolved to do differently. I ask to whom they felt most strongly attached and about other adults outside the immediate family such as grandparents, aunts and uncles, teachers and parent's friends or friends' parents who may have provided a different or compensatory experience of care-giving. I ask about relationships with siblings and explore care-giving that may have been provided or given.

Using opportunities to seek additional evidence

As respondents describe their life history I find it useful to ask for information that later might constitute evidence. I ask if they have any photographs of themselves as a child. This often provokes further memories. When discussing school attainments, some parents like to show evidence of achievements in the way of certificates or school reports. Photographs of their children can also be very revealing and provide counter-evidence to assertions that children were 'severely neglected' if they show smiling relaxed faces of children in clean and tidy homes with age-appropriate toys in the background.

Not making assumptions about apparently negative experiences

Talking about the parental history is often relatively non-threatening and can help to disarm the interviewee so that when more challenging topics are raised they are less likely to invoke a defensive response. Adults who had difficult experiences in childhood tend to offer a rehearsed a story of their childhood and its negative consequences. After hearing such accounts, I like to ask questions which turn the matter around by exploring the positive impacts of the experiences, such as developing coping strategies that have given them strength. Parents often say that the experience of having been harmed by a care-giver has made them more determined to protect their own children. This is the kind of account that an adult might give about being sexually abused as a child. Despite the huge negative impact on her life, it is possible to invite the interviewee better to understand the impact and the survival skills that have resulted:

> I was abused from about the age of five, as far back as I can remember.
> He used to make me lie down in the bathroom or in the office where

he worked. He must have been about forty, a grown man. He'd touch me down below and made me masturbate him. My mum, I can remember her being dragged to my school because they said I had over-sexualised behaviour. I thought it was a game – mummies and daddies. I was showing boys my bits at school. It got to one time in his office, and he laid on top of me and I could smell him, his aftershave, and I can remember it hurt but I can't remember how. I can't remember how it stopped. I wasn't shy of showing my bits off and I used to get called weird. I can remember mum asking me why I did it. I never told. I thought what he was doing was normal. It wasn't until much later and I thought I must have done something wrong. When I was in St Mark's hospital I used to think about it a lot. How did it happen or why did it happen or what could I have done to stop it but I couldn't come up with the answers. Dr Shaffer said it shouldn't have happened and it wasn't my fault but I never quite believed her.

Following this account with questions that enquire into, acknowledge and affirm the consequences of such abuse, in terms of feelings of powerlessness, betrayal of trust, stigmatisation and self-destructive behaviours can lead on to discussions about the ways in which the person has overcome or managed these challenges:

If I had stayed on that track then he would have won. Everybody that's victimised me, they would have won and I can't let that happen. The things that's happened to me, a lot of people wouldn't have got through. All I can do is change it and be a very strong person so that I can look after my little boy. I am very angry about how people can make you feel dirty and like a slag. I didn't used to think I could live on my own. I was scared to death. Now actually I've found I *like* being on my own and pleasing myself. I'm beginning to find out who I am and what I like. I like going to the gym and doing my friend's hair. I've found out what I'm capable of doing and I'm not thick and stupid. I come across as really bouncy and bubbly. That's what my workers and friends tell me. And if they can like me, I can like myself.

Exploring compensatory experiences of being parented

Genuine curiosity about the individual's survival skills encourages a constructive perspective. It is all too easy to assume that a difficult childhood or an emotionally distant parent disables people from becoming successful parents themselves. I would counsel against such a deterministic approach. Many compensatory experiences are out there:

There were never no cuddles from my mam. She's not for girls. My brother got everything he wanted. He was spoiled because he was a boy. My nana and grandpa lived round the corner. I used to see them every day and they called me their 'special one'. Nana would give me lots of cuddles and I used to have my tea at their house after school. My grandpa used to drive an ice-cream van and he'd take me everywhere with him. He was my world. They both were. I was closer to my granddad and close to my nana as well. I called them mum and dad and I used to stay at their house until my grandpa got ill. They used to make sure that I got up, brushed my teeth, went to school, came home, had tea, bath and bed. On Friday nights I was allowed to stay up later. Grandma would go to Bingo on one evening and granddad looked after me. He would sit me on his knee and read stories. I felt loved by my grandparents. If I misbehaved they sent me to my bedroom and I had to stay there until I realised what I had done wrong then I was allowed downstairs. I still think of him every day and that's a photo of me and him over there. I've never had anyone care for me like him. I wish he was still alive because I think my life would be different. I was upset and gutted when he died.

What needs to emerge is detail, not only generalisations. It is the detail that provides insight into the respondent's subjective experience. Interpretation of the Adult Attachment Interview (AAI) involves making judgements about the coherence of the respondent's narrative and this judgement is relevant to assessments of care-giving capabilities arising from more general interviews.

Peter Fonagy and Mary Target (1997) analysed responses to the AAI by seeking evidence for the respondents' ability to reflect on their own inner experience, and their capability to show reflection concerning the experience of other people. Thus, it is not the parents' experiences *per se* that predict their capability to bond with their children or their children's attachment style, but rather adults' capability to make sense of their experiences; to create a coherent narrative through a process of reflection.

Characteristics of respondents

Interviewees who talk at length

Mary Main (n.d.) draws attention to the issue of interviewees who may present particular challenges to interviewers by speaking on irrelevant topics or at excessive length. She regards these difficulties as particularly informative (not problematic), since they suggest tendencies that violate typical conversational turn-taking. She states, 'Knowing that she or he must artfully permit the participant to fully reveal his or her speech tendencies, the skillful [sic] interviewer allows the speaker diversions from the topic, as well as lengthy turns' (Main, n.d.). Here is an example given by Mary Main of an interviewee who diverts from the topic with a lengthy turn and then continues in the same vein following a prompt by the interviewer that aims (unsuccessfully) to return the speaker to the past.

> *You used the word 'difficult' in describing your relationship with your mother in childhood. Any incidents or memories that would tell me why you chose that word to describe your relationship in childhood?*

> My mother was a very difficult person ... I was bullied by her when I was, up to when I was 12, but I'm not bullied by her anymore. (Mm-hmm mm-hmm) And, those are things that happened over years y'know ... (Mm-hmm) and um, I just, the few times that we've seen her, um, each time it's gotten much easier and much easier, I told her I guess about 2 weeks ago 3 weeks ago, excuse me, she was angry that, I had her to dinner and she was angry that I served creamed onions, because she is sometimes allergic to onions, like, she gets these big rashes and she makes a big deal about it, and I said, it's up to you to remember your allergies, it isn't up to me, and ... (3 sec) and she's a very resentful person and these are the – little, little incidents that grow in her mind and they become more and more important and she calls up about them, and she screams about them...

> *And would you say that she was difficult in that same way in your childhood, too?*

> Definitely, and ... I said, Lookit, y'know nobody tells me what to serve to my family. It's a family matter, and you're over here as my guest, and I want you here, I really do...

Main suggests that it is appropriate for the interviewer to make one or two polite attempts to steer the conversation back in the direction of the original topic, lest the interviewee take it that the interviewer has condoned the change of subject. It is also possible that the interviewer is yet to become aware of a link in the respondent's mind between the apparent digression and the interviewer's question.

Interviewees who give very brief answers

A parallel difficulty in interviewing is with participants who veer towards exceptional succinctness. This is an example:

> *Did you ever feel rejected as a young child? Even if now you might not think you really were being rejected – well you might, but the point is I wonder whether as a child you ever felt rejected?*
>
> Yeah.

How old were you?

Ahm, ahm, twelve, twelve years old.

And, what happened that made you feel rejected?

Ahm, I wrote a couple of letters back, a couple of letters to uh, to my parents that I didn't want to stay there at the school, and uh

You mean you wrote to them from the school?

From the school at Place 7 (yeah), and I can't even remember uh, I got like one letter back for, for, for Christmas vacation and that was, and I can't, I'm amazed, and I asked them, I said, "How come I have to stay here?" They never gave me a response.

So they didn't answer your letters?

Right.

How did you feel about that? What did you do?

Ahm, un – I just, I didn't feel wanted, or loved.

You, you felt unwanted and unloved.

Yeah.

Why do you think your parents did that – do you think they realized how it was making you feel?

(Main, n.d.: 5)

Succinctness may be a habit, sometimes because people are unfamiliar with receiving undivided attention, possibly because they rarely discuss such personal matters. Short answers may be conveying a message that this person does not wish to discuss the topic or regards the questions as intrusive, in which case an enquiry such as, 'How are you finding my questions?' may clarify. A number of other interpretations are possible. From the interviewer's perspective it is important to leave sufficient space between questions for the interviewee to fill, and to ensure that the questions remain, as far as possible, open-ended.

Sometimes, in the middle of an interview I find myself beginning to feel uncomfortable, usually because I am concerned about whether I am fulfilling the intended purposes. This can involve a child who gets up and wanders around the room, an adult who takes offence at a question, or who acts in a manner that undermines my sense of professionalism with what I experience as 'narcissistic challenges'. Phil Mollon (1989) gives examples of how clients' behaviour towards novice workers in particular can generate feelings of inadequacy. This can be through direct enquiries into the worker's personal circumstances – 'Do you have children?' with the implication that to be childless disqualifies the worker from competence, or more subtle enquiries about whether this approach is going to be of help. I have to remind myself to regard what I am experiencing as information that will help me to understand respondents and their circumstances, and so whatever happens and whatever I feel, it will assist me in my effort to understand the client's world.

At such times, my regular supervision can often help me better to understand my discomfort and manage it in my interviews.

Bearing in mind that we are more similar than different and our lives could have followed a similar path

Some clients have met with life experiences that would predict difficulties as they are growing up. They have been neglected or abused, have not experienced being loved for themselves, have been frightened and insecure, have lived in poverty, or been subject to discrimination. Some are leading highly successful lives that fall apart like a house of cards due to a series of events creating a downward spiral. Mr Darley was brought up by his mother and grandparents in a close-knit working class community. He was very successful in his education and his social life revolved around football. He went to the local college of further education and obtained practical qualifications, eventually leading to a responsible job in a local firm. He was always in work, happily married with children, and his job regularly took him abroad. He began to spend his evenings away from home in his hotel bar and, whilst it did not obviously hinder his performance in the workplace, he became increasingly dependent on alcohol, especially when promotion increased his stress levels. In this situation he became vulnerable to further stressors and when he and his wife lost a child in a fatal accident at age three, he began a downward spiral which eventually saw him in prison with a conviction for an offence which was later quashed. Although the offence was wiped from his record, in the meantime he had lost his job, had separated from his wife and other children, and was confused by the turn his life had taken. This is how he described what happened on his release from gaol:

> I had a crisis of confidence when I came out. There was a year out of work. I don't have a prison record but a huge blank in my life and it was difficult to get past that on my CV, let alone in my life anyway. That summer the weather was good. There was nothing to do, and the people I was bumping into were freeloaders and I started drinking with them. I didn't realise it at the time but I must have been suffering from depression. I felt sorry for myself because I'd had all this taken from me. I hadn't seen my children for a year. I had to sell the car and it meant two bus journeys to see them. What I used to do to try and get out of this pattern, I got a travel pass and I used to ride trains all day. In the end I went to the doctor and that's when I was diagnosed with depression and I was given a weird concoction. Seroxat made me feel really low. I went on to something else but I was still drinking, drinking from getting up. I'd get up and have to have a livener and then a few beers. I'd get a bus to the station, have a drink on the train, sit at the station and have a drink. I drank whatever was cheap. I wanted to work but I'd got into the mindset that I was incapable. And there's the loneliness, and you just don't seem to have a purpose and you're buggered up.

Then I got accused of shoplifting. By god I felt low. I'd never felt like that before in my life. I felt absolutely gutted. That really did hit me hard. I just thought, 'When is all this going to end?'

Stories like this remind me that at times my own life could have taken a trajectory that would have landed me in circumstances not too dissimilar from those of the people I am asked to assess. I think it is important for me to keep this in mind lest I begin to feel too distant from them, as if we are a different species. I need to maintain my sense of compassion and a will to encourage and support rather than condemn. I need to understand the intensity of the murderous as well as overwhelmingly loving feelings that it is possible to experience towards children so that my interviews remain open to whatever my respondent is trying to convey. This is a characteristic of the social work interviews described by Kadushin and Kadushin (1997):

> ... the social work interview is apt to be diffuse, not standardized, interviewee controlled, with no set agenda, focused on affective material, and concerned with the interpersonal interaction of participants. As a consequence social work interviewers have a difficult assignment. They generally cannot determine in advance much of what they have to do in the interview; they must respond to the situation as it develops.
>
> (Kadushin and Kadushin, 1997: 14)

> We can only know the interviewee's subjective perception and interpretation of that reality and then only to the extent that the interviewee is willing to share the details with us. The only approach the interviewer can take is to accept what the person says as the interviewee's *subjective reality*.
>
> (Kadushin and Kadushin, 1997: 20)

In this chapter I have highlighted how the purpose of interviews prescribes the roles and tasks of the participants. I regard it as the central method for obtaining relevant information for the benefit of the interviewer's developing knowledge of a family, and argue that such interviews are best conducted from a position of open-ended enquiry that is constrained by a set of research questions rather than a questionnaire or proforma. If I am able to contain my anxiety as an interviewer, I can accept all that takes place as information that helps me to develop my understandings. It is crucial for me to try to keep in mind my own prejudices, habits and biases in interpreting what I see and hear.

3 Assessment of personality, profile and relationship context

> If clients are motivated to share personal information and have access to the information being requested, they are usually excellent testifiers to the presence or absence of their own mental health problems … [on the other hand] men and women being evaluated in family custody cases tend to present themselves in a highly virtuous and unrealistic manner.
>
> (Butcher and Beutler, 2003: 174, 179)

In this and the following two chapters I want to focus on assessments of individual adults in terms of their general functioning, how this might affect their role as care-givers, their potential for change in areas that would benefit from development if they are to provide satisfactory care for the well-being of their children, the nature of their relationships with romantic partners, and the kind of support or intervention that might assist if they are in difficulty. Butcher and Beutler draw attention to the idea that people usually have excellent insight into their difficulties but when they are involved in assessment with high stake outcomes, they are motivated to hide their weaknesses from the prying eyes of professionals. David Mohr and Larry Beutler suggest that, 'under the best of circumstances, the requirement of revealing oneself to a stranger is difficult. It is made even more difficult by the frequent fear that the clinician has special powers and can see things that even the patient does not know' (Mohr and Beutler, 2003: 117).

I will refer again to these issues throughout this chapter, for the meaning of the assessment to the person before me will almost certainly impact upon the impressions that I receive. Adults are not naïve about the purposes of assessments in family proceedings, which means that I do not begin my relationship with them on a neutral footing.

Because I see the assessment process as akin to a research study, the topics comprising the list of questions in Chapter 1 can act as a starting point. In this chapter I will focus on personal characteristics and behaviours, in Chapter 4 on special issues in the assessment of adults and in Chapter 5 on adults in the role of care-giver.

Personality traits and psychological profile

Although I am a psychologist by training, I confess that I do not have a great deal of confidence in the assessment of individuals by formal measures designed to assess something called 'personality', particularly when the individuals have an investment in presenting themselves in the best light. I was maybe put off personality tests as an undergraduate by what seemed to be fairly crude measures aligning humanity along dimensions such as 'extraversion' or 'neuroticism' or lumping them into discrete categories. These measures were designed by researchers such as Hans Eysenck (Eysenck Personality Inventory) and Raymond Cattell (the 16PF) with the aim of developing greater understanding of the psychology of human life through the use of 'objective' measures, although they have been applied for much more diverse purposes than originally intended. At the time, psychology was a relative newcomer to the family of sciences and strove to prove its credentials amongst its more well-established fellow disciplines. These measures elaborated on the existing armoury of projective tests, such as the Rorschach inkblots and the Thematic Apperception Test, which had evolved out of psychodynamic accounts of personality formation based on the ideas of Sigmund Freud and his followers. I experienced a degree of mystery around the interpretation of these projective tests and developed a degree of scepticism which remains with me today.

Nevertheless, the concept of personality is appealing, in that it relates to the idea of a 'self' with a degree of stability and consistency.

> Most people have some level of most personality traits .... *Personality* designations describe the relative strengths of different traits when compared to other people as well as to other traits. The pattern of behavioral traits – the relative strengths and weaknesses of the traits – forms a social profile that is used by others to describe, and distinguish among, people.
> (Beutler *et al.*, 2003: 2)

Devising measures of human complexity poses a challenge. In the nineteenth century, attempts to create instruments that could measure longitude were thwarted by the complexity of the system in question. In that case, it turned out to be possible eventually to produce a reliable instrument by taking into account multiple factors including time, but human systems are infinitely more complex and there is no such 'x' factor in personality tests which are intended to provide reliable indicators of people's future behaviour. They need to have predictive validity if they are to be of use in the family court.

Test credibility

Formal psychological tests gain their credibility from evidence of their reliability, validity and generalisability. Reliability is a measure of the test's consistency. Without reliability a test cannot be valid. It would be like using a heart rate monitor that gave erratic (unreliable) results because it was affected by fluctuations in the ambient temperature. To be reliable, personality assessment measures should give very similar results for an individual whatever the circumstances in which they are administered. Validity is about whether the test measures what it purports to measure. This is typically determined by examining the extent to which the results obtained by individuals on this measure equate to their results on different measures of the same characteristic. Because the concept of personality is abstract, there is no direct measure against which the test can be validated. Larry Beutler and colleagues usefully point out that if we can already measure a construct such as personality, why develop a new test in the first place?

A test's usefulness is also determined by its capability to predict a person's performance in relation to a criterion, such as whether they have been, or are likely to be, violent to others. The construct 'violent' would need an operational definition (such as conviction of a violent offence) in order to establish whether the test was successful in measuring this construct. A comparison may be made of the results on the test obtained from different populations or groups of people. If this person's pattern of scores for physical aggression is similar to the pattern obtained from people who have been convicted of violent offences, but different from those who have no history of such offences, then this would constitute evidence of validity. Psychologists are a long way from devising tests which are wholly valid or reliable and humans are notoriously inconsistent in their behaviours across contexts, even when behaviour is unaffected by the impact of mind-altering substances such as drugs and alcohol. Even after extensive testing, uncertainty remains. Personality tests may be seen as rough indicators, the results of which, taken in conjunction with other information, may help us better to understand the people we are assessing.

There is available a range of tests designed to assess stable characteristics of adult functioning. One of the most widely used is the MMPI-2, devised to aid understanding of individuals presenting with mental health difficulties. Others include the Personality Assessment Inventory (PAI), a self-administered questionnaire comprising 344 items that gives scores on 22 scales. The Millon Clinical Multiaxial Inventory-III (MCMI III) was designed to link with the Diagnostic and Statistical Manual (DSM-IV) for a clinical sample of people with mental health or emotional difficulties with a view to distinguishing enduring personality characteristics from acute clinical disorders. It was intended for use only with people who had already been identified with mental health difficulties. The Millon Index of Personality Styles (MIPS) addresses motivation, thinking skills and behaviour. The California Psychological Inventory (CPI) has 434 items to which a 'true' or 'false' response is given. Unlike many of the other measures, it focuses on positive attributes such as self-acceptance, tolerance, amicability and empathy. One of the principles underlying its development was that the concepts measured should be familiar to most people. These are known as 'folk concepts'.

Although they are not classified as personality tests, there have also been attempts to devise measures of what has been termed 'emotional intelligence'. These include the Goleman ECI 360 test and the Bar-On Emotional Quotient Inventory (EQi). They share the problem of any test designed to measure 'ability' – that this can only be inferred from current performance.

Typically, measures of personality employ validity scales intended to detect responses biased towards presenting a favourable or negative image. They have been standardised by obtaining results from a large sample of a 'normal' population distribution of people, and their validity and reliability have been established in a number of ways. Such measures can provide reliable information about populations of people and I think that they can also make a useful contribution to the overall set of information that helps in developing an understanding of individual people. But I would urge caution in placing too much reliance on any such questionnaire measures, because in family proceedings they are being completed by people for whom outcomes have enormously high stakes. The tests were not devised for use in such contexts (Otto and Edens, 2003; Reder *et al.*, 2003a).

By way of illustration, I began to use a specific questionnaire measure a few years ago. It is called the Child Abuse Potential Inventory (CAPI), created by Joel Milner specifically to try to identify those adults who pose a risk of physical injury to their children. The measure is well constructed and researched with impressive data concerning reliability and validity. In addition to questions designed to identify child abuse potential, it has three subscales intended to determine whether the respondent is 'faking good', 'faking bad' or is responding randomly to the various items on the questionnaire. An examination of the results of the last 40 occasions on which I have administered the questionnaire shows that three respondents presented with profiles similar to people known to have physically abused a child, one presented with a profile that was dissimilar to people known to have physically abused a child, 33 results had to be discarded because the respondent selected answers suggesting an attempt to 'fake good', one was categorised as 'faking bad' and two results were invalid because the respondent appeared to be responding randomly. I cite this not to suggest that there is a problem with the test, but to illustrate how the context influences people's responses to questionnaire measures, particularly in 'high stakes' testing when 'wrong' answers can have profoundly serious negative consequences (Harlen, 2003). If you give me a questionnaire in a high stakes test, I will be apprehensive about your motivation, and I think this is likely to be the case for other people, not just me.

When I ask people to fill in self-report questionnaires as part of my assessments in family proceedings, they sometimes show reluctance to respond, cross out particular questions, make notes alongside their answers, exercise much caution in reaching a decision about how to answer individual questions, and make comments suggesting that I may be trying to catch them out. This is apart from errors of understanding when people struggle with questions containing double negatives, or when they accidentally tick a box giving an answer that is inconsistent with most of their other responses. It would have to be a pretty good measure that was able to inveigle me into revealing what I consider to be my negative qualities and if that's the case for me, then my guess is that it may be for other respondents too. This has been confirmed in research findings (Budd and Holdsworth, 1996; Carr *et al.*, 2005). Since parents risk the catastrophic outcome of losing their children it is not surprising to find that they attempt to present themselves in the best possible light.

There have been attempts to design instruments to assess the tendency of respondents to give what they regard, consciously or unconsciously, as socially desirable responses (e.g. Marlowe–Crowne Social Desirability Scale, MCSDS). The Paulhus Deception Scale (PDS) is designed to be completed concurrently with other self-report questionnaires to give an indication of the validity of the results obtained. The PDS aims to assess socially desirable responding both as a response set (a temporary tendency caused by situational demands such as court proceedings, entitled 'impression management') and typical response style (a trait-like tendency apparent whenever the person self-reports entitled 'self-deceptive enhancement'). Whilst the measure was initially standardised on a college student group, Richard Lanyon and Adam Carle (2007) found it to be applicable to forensic populations, although for this group a single concept of favourable self-presentation was suggested by the degree of overlap between scores on the two subscales.

Another issue that I have with the concept of 'personality' is that it is essentialist. It allows no room for variation according to time, space and context. Would my parents describe my personality in a similar way to my partner, my children, colleagues, friends? How do I present myself to different people under different circumstances? I am capable of being strategic in my relationships. I am not going to be happy to show my faults and the worst of me to you if you can wield a significant influence over the rest of my life. I can probably manage myself well enough to try to hide these if you ask me to fill in a questionnaire meant to define my personality. I will also try to show myself in a good light in interviews, but if I warm to you or forget myself I may be drawn to tell you about my difficulties and problems.

Against the construct of 'personality' I am happier with the idea of a 'profile' – an outline or sketch that describes me, my experiences and the impact that they have had on the way that I see things; the ways in which I think, feel and act over a range of time, place and contexts. Such information can be obtained from interviews, whilst it benefits from being complemented by, or triangulated with, information from other sources such as previous reports from other professionals who know or have previously known the care-giver, other family members, history on files, information from medical and police records, and first hand evidence which may be provided by the respondent – photographs, school records, letters or emails. All of these have been given to me by parents when asked if they are able to support their account with such 'hard' evidence. The following example combines data from a number of sources to create a psychological profile:

Ms Robertson's description of her childhood suggested that she experienced secure attachment to her mother and maternal grandparents. She gave a coherent and detailed account of the ways in which her mother would respond when she was upset and how she continued to keep her in mind as a young teenager after she and her father separated. Although her father was not physically affectionate, he called every day on his way home from work to see Ms Robertson and would always know if she skipped school. Ms Robertson and her partner have been together for 12 years and the results of the Experiences in Close Relationships-Revised (ECR-R) gave her a score in the 'secure' quadrant, suggesting that she has been able to take her secure attachment experience into adult romantic relationships.

Ms Robertson also has substantial experience in young adulthood of living in a close-knit community, where there was a sense of collective responsibility for the care of the children. Given this pattern of secure attachment, Ms Robertson's confidence was significantly undermined by a brief episode of infidelity by her partner which occurred at the same time that her father was dying. In response she was for a time housebound and managed her shaken confidence by keeping her partner close at all times. This event may have re-evoked for her the feelings of loss or insecurity that she experienced when her mother died at a fairly critical time in her life, particularly as this meant that her younger sisters became looked after by the local authority for a brief period. Ms Robertson appears to be beginning to regain her confidence, and her son told me in interview that his mother now goes out regularly in the local community. Her lack of confidence appears to be related to face-to-face interactions with people, particularly those in positions of authority, rather than being characteristic of agoraphobia.

Ms Robertson obtained an IQ score which would suggest that her intellectual functioning is in the low average range. When I asked her to complete a sub-test concerning her verbal skills, Ms Robertson struggled to respond. She later told me that she had found the experience embarrassing as she had not attempted any such exercises since she stopped attending school aged 15 years. She uses the Internet and has created a website for her son. Her emails are reported by her son's teacher to display a good vocabulary, with limited skills in punctuation and spelling. She has successfully negotiated her way through the benefits system on behalf of her sister. Taken together this suggests that she is intellectually capable. I am of the view that Ms Robertson lacks confidence in her intellectual functioning, probably as a result of her curtailed schooling. Her actual functioning warrants a greater level of self-confidence.

Data from my interview and from questionnaire measures suggests that Ms Robertson is not suffering from anxiety, depression or feelings of worthlessness, and her self-esteem is moderate. She has a strong desire to be treated respectfully and will contest the views of people in authority. If she is not approached in the manner that she considers appropriate, her strategy for dealing with this has been to ignore communications or fail to attend appointments. Another strategy has been to argue her case either in person or by email, sometimes with a degree of forcefulness that has been found aggressive by the involved professionals. Neither strategy has helped to progress her case.

Ms Robertson has a strong moral sense. She regarded her father as a hypocrite for attempting to ensure that she attended church whilst failing to attend himself. She refuses to claim benefits fraudulently, a practice in which she is encouraged by some neighbours. She values family and relationships above all else and devoted herself to caring for her father in his terminal illness. She shows her son that he is loved through physical affection and openly telling him how much she cares. This has been observed by staff at the school her son attends and by her health visitor. She shows strong loyalty towards her partner and Karl, defending them when they are under attack from outside the family.

Karl reported to me that his mother sometimes loses her temper and can be quite frightening at times. Ms Robertson said that this is now restricted to shouting and thumping the table. She said that she used to do this when she was suffering from stress in an attempt to distract herself from ruminating on her problems. The social worker reported that she thumped the table when she threatened to remove the children. The results of the State-Trait Anger Expression Inventory (STAXI-II) suggest that she does have a somewhat angry temperament but that her anger is not used to control others. In interview her son showed some fear of his mother's anger but not of her. I am aware of no evidence to suggest that she is physically violent towards any members of her family.

In addition to the losses of extended family, Ms Robertson's unemployment has meant that the family has struggled to live on their income. Her partner is wheelchair-bound and Ms Robertson has always been the breadwinner. They do not forward plan or budget their finances, having been used to receiving her wages regularly, and spending the money without undue care. Ms Robertson described her father as hating to lose face. Ms Robertson herself is a proud person and regards herself as capable of providing for her family both materially and emotionally. She finds it very difficult when this is called into question and has experienced a great deal of shame about being unable to provide for them during her period of unemployment.

When creating such profiles, I find it usually constructive to generate a benevolent explanation for current difficulties. Parents are more likely to be able to respond positively if the profile is presented in a manner which validates their first-hand experience and does not blame them for their predicament. Richard Lewak and Sean Hogan (2003) argue for an ongoing dialogue which is responsive to resistance and in which the practitioner is not drawn into an argument about what is 'true' but rather asks further questions focused on the individual's response to the assessment. Resistance or denial can thus be used to further understand this person's experiential world, rather than being seen as defiance. These authors suggest asking clients to let them know when feedback 'hits the mark' and when it seems to be inaccurate. Here is an example of feedback to a client who seemed to have responded to test material in a defensive manner:

> You approached the testing in a somewhat cautious way, perhaps fearing being judged or criticized, or perhaps fearful that the test results were going to be used against you. You tended to put your best foot forward, going out of your way to let me know that you are a person of high moral fiber and above reproach. You have managed to convey your need to be seen that way, but unfortunately, I have not been able to get to know you as thoroughly as I would like to.
>
> (Lewak and Hogan, 2003: 372)

My starting point for creating a profile is to invite respondents to tell me about themselves in an interview based around the questions that I am trying to address, supplementing this data with information from transparent questionnaires and rating scales designed to explore specific areas of functioning and from other 'hard' evidence that is available.

Characteristics and issues that impact on parenting skills

Information from interviews will have provided a base from which further to explore specific topics and this is an area in which data from other sources can be a useful adjunct. Many questionnaires have face validity – their meaning is transparent with no lie scales or questions which might be perceived as trying to catch someone out. Amongst these are measures of depression, anxiety, anger expression, drug and alcohol use. Some are restricted to use by members of particular professions, some are costly, but many are available to download free from the internet and can be used as a screening rather than diagnostic measure so that practitioners ensure that they remain within their established area of expertise. Whilst information regarding reliability and validity of each questionnaire is available from their sources, they have not generally been standardised for use with the population of parents who are subject to assessments in family proceedings, and the results therefore need to be interpreted with great care. In my experience, they can provide useful qualitative information and may give an indication of this person's status in relation to the population at large. Where it is useful to make such a comparison, understanding of the limitations of the measures is important. Because there are so many questionnaires available that are relevant to the assessment of adults, I have located my selection in Appendix 2 for fear of giving them too much weight in the text. For each of the sub-headings below, information is given in Appendix 2 about the questionnaire measures available and where they can be accessed.

Biochemical tests of drug and alcohol use, through hair strand analysis, blood and urine testing, breathalyser or liver function testing can provide convincing evidence to validate or undermine self-report, although caution still needs to be exercised in relation to their interpretation.

Medical records are meant to document confidential transactions between doctor and patient. In my experience they are often requested in family proceedings and this can have the sometimes unfortunate effect of making them available to a range of people including solicitors, administrative staff, social workers, experts and possibly to other care-givers involved in the proceedings. The justification is that of ensuring children's welfare. I think that the balance is difficult to strike. Some solicitors are assiduous in disclosing the records only to those who have a justified need to review them and in excluding themselves.

Medical records can be an enormously useful source of information about mental and physical health, contemporaneous historical data from this adult's childhood, the frequency of visits to the GP and accident and emergency departments, injuries, commencement of sexual activity and whatever else the patient has thought to disclose to a trusted professional. In my experience they also record inaccuracies and sometimes unjustified value judgements. Whilst they are invaluable in shedding light on a person's history, they also need to be treated with circumspection and subjected to critical review in the same manner as any other data that is being used to determine children's futures.

Also obtainable are individuals' police records. These document not only offences committed and disposals, but also reports to the police that do not involve further action after investigation. In my experience, the police are assiduous in removing third party data from these records and they provide much detail which can be of assistance in understanding what has transpired between individuals.

The impact of parents' own attachment histories on their functioning is discussed in Chapter 7 and assessment of parenting in Chapter 5. What aspects of an adult's psychological profile are relevant to assessments in children's

proceedings? It seems clear to me that some personal qualities are more relevant than others to a person's parenting role. It may not matter if they are
introvert or extravert, creative or unimaginative, a leader or follower. But how
they manage their anger is likely to be a key factor in determining a child's
safety and well-being.

Aspects of profiles relevant to family proceedings

Self-esteem and experience of shame

Paul Gilbert (2010) argues that we can all suffer from a sense of shame and
that:

> No one goes through life without being criticised, doing things you later
> regret or having attributes that you'd rather not have. It's part of the
> human condition. A sense of shame can arise when we think that others
> might be looking down on us in some way, that they see us as inadequate,
> inferior and bad, or simply not up to much or not worth bothering with.
> We can also have a sense of internal shame when we feel these things
> about *ourselves.* Commonly our own sense of shame is accompanied by
> self-criticism and self-attacking. In fact, shame-based self-criticism and
> self-attacking are among the most pervasive problems in Western societ-
> ies and seriously undermine our contentment and well-being. They're
> the opposite of self-compassion. Rather than feeling support, kindness
> and enthusiasm for ourselves when things go wrong, we feel anger, disap-
> pointment, frustration or even contempt for ourselves.
>
> (Gilbert, 2010: 351)

Self-esteem is about how I see myself in terms of my overall sense of my value,
and may also be derived in relation to specific skills. I might think of myself
as a generally worthwhile and valuable person. Such a perspective may be
aided if I am skilled in specific domains such as sport, craftwork, writing or
parenting. Skill in particular domains can have an impact on a general sense
of well-being. An eight-year-old described the feeling to me like this: 'When
we play, when I'm sporty, my legs fill up. I'm like a car. It's like I'm getting
more petrol in my legs. It feels good.' At the opposite end of the spectrum,
shame involves strong negative feelings of worthlessness and self-criticism
that I experience towards myself and which I may have learned in response to
others' criticisms of me when I was growing up, wounded by what they said
to me about me. It may be more subtle and result from my failure to meet
the, maybe implicit, expectations and standards desired of me. Shame is the
feeling of being hopelessly less valuable than other human beings; a waste of
time. It is the feeling that there is something wrong with me and is not so
much about what I have done, but about who I am. If I constantly put myself
down I am likely to experience depressed mood and fail in tasks that I set
myself through lack of self-belief.

It is easy to imagine how a sense of uselessness can be all-pervasive and generate feelings of hopelessness when confronted with apparent failings as a parent and a person. Court proceedings are likely further to reinforce this perspective. Particularly when this lesson has been learned in childhood, the experience can foster the development of adult relationships in which this self-belief is reconfirmed and can result in a tendency to occupy a victim role. Shame can make me anticipate attack and my response may be one of anger or rage as a way of defending myself. Even mild criticism may send me off into a torrent of self-justification. When shame dominates, people tend to feel threatened when their actions are called into question, and this is not conducive to accepting responsibility for what has transpired and making positive changes. Paul Gilbert (2010: 238) usefully makes a distinction between the experiences of shame and guilt. Whereas shame generates a desire to hide or defend, guilt encourages the desire to make reparation, to put things right. Guilt is typically associated with particular actions that I have committed, rather than a reflection of my overarching sense of self. Feelings of guilt are associated with remorse and regret, a desire to make amends because I can empathise with the experience of others in the scenario about which I feel guilt. To this extent, guilt can result in positive changes to how I behave, whereas shame encourages me to oppress and depress myself.

People's experience of shame and self-esteem often emerge in interview and there are structured questionnaires which can supplement this data. These are summarised in Appendix 2.

Degree of self-confidence – insecurity

Whereas self-esteem is about the sense that 'I am essentially ok', self-confidence is about a feeling of capability to undertake tasks and perform actions successfully enough. The 'enough' is important because this may not mean performing at a high level compared with others, but at a level that is satisfactory in terms of my own aspirations. I believe that I am a fairly average parent, yet confident enough that I am not damaging my children irreparably through my efforts. And if you have a different opinion, I may be prepared to listen and maybe change my behaviour, and it is my confidence that allows me to be open to such criticism and advice. I know that I can do some things involved in parenting adequately. I have appropriately modest expectations of myself and so I can show you my performance and will not buckle beneath your assessment of it. What I think of my performance comes first, and after that your opinion may matter, or I may decide to reject your view.

What does matter is whether I can tolerate doing badly by my own standards and the impact that this has on me. Do I become utterly discouraged, avoid situations that make such demands on me and distance myself from my children, or do I use the experience to work at improving? Failure to reach my own standards can spur me on, whilst in some situations I may just focus my efforts elsewhere. However, if as a parent the authorities believe that I am not doing well enough, and I am faced with the possible removal of my children from my care, then I am going to have to face my failures and try to improve my performance in order to meet others' standards. I will need to practise and face up to my inadequacies without losing heart. I may need to learn to set myself higher or different standards. Sometimes these will seem unattainable, as if I have to produce 'perfect' parenting to satisfy demands. If, beneath the surface, I struggle with feelings of insecurity about my parenting I may present a false front of greater confidence than I feel in order to try to preserve some self-respect. This was described to me by a contact supervisor: 'Mum struggles to accept responsibility for any difficulties with the children and isn't prepared to accept any fault in herself. She either sees herself as a perfect parent or her demeanour masks a lack of confidence and insecurity.'

This dimension is important because what presents as resistance and refusal to change may reflect such a lack of confidence. Approaching it with criticism is unlikely to produce change; encouragement and highlighting skills which may be developed and built upon is a more constructive approach. The benefit of challenging strengths rather than weaknesses is the context of a positive frame which better supports learning and development.

Warm – distant in relationships with others – sociability

Interpersonal warmth has been defined as, 'the pleasant, contented, intimate feeling that occurs during positive interaction with others' (Andersen and Guerrero, 1998: 304). The interpersonal characteristics of warmth and sociability are likely to be associated with the development of a strong social support network, the presence of which has long been proposed as a positive indicator for developmental outcomes for children (Dunst *et al.*, 1988). Carol Coohey's (1996) study suggested that the label 'social isolation' was not sufficient accurately to describe the mothers in her study who were struggling to care for their children, since all of her participants had more than 100 contacts with members of their network in the month prior to her study. She concluded that an important factor was the *quality* of their social relationships. Emotionally close and nurturing relationships appeared positively to affect a carer's sense of well-being and in turn, how the carer approached looking after the children. Norman Polansky and his colleagues (1981) proposed a link between low levels of emotional support, loneliness, and child neglect (Polansky, 1985; Polansky *et al.*, 1985). They argued that limited access to emotionally close relationships produced an intense sense of loneliness, which was thought to result in apathy, and the failure to provide comfort and necessities to children (Polansky *et al.*, 1981). They identified something of a 'chicken and egg' situation in which neglectful carers were perceived by members of their communities to be deviant and unlikely to reciprocate any support that was offered. This contributed further to their isolation.

The attachment literature would suggest that secure attachment acts as a base from which to form warm, trusting and intimate relationships in adulthood. But in addition to this environmental influence, there is evidence that the tendency towards warmth and sociability is also a characteristic of temperament (Plomin and Dunn, 1986: 73) which impacts on the level of social support that a parent can engage when struggling with the demands of child care. It has been argued that models of social support need to be able to account for both these personal and environmental influences (Pierce *et al.*, 1997). Feelings of shyness can seriously limit a person's social contacts, and hence restrict access to the emotionally close relationships that affect well-being. Parents who struggle with shyness or a lack of sociability can nevertheless be engaged in services through which they may learn to overcome their reticence and form enduring friendships through which they learn more about their own value:

> At first I thought that the whole world was against me but now I'm taking courses at the 'Together Women' project. It's helping me to feel more self confident. At the beginning I was shy and quiet and I absolutely hated the 'ice-breaker' exercises. I just used to clam up and I felt really embarrassed but now I'm buzzing off the IT course. I don't look in the mirror any more and see myself as ugly and fat. Now I'm not scared to open my mouth and loads has come out that I never used to talk about. People on the course seem to *like* me and my brother says he hardly recognises me, I look so much better. If other people can like me then I think I can like myself. I never used to praise myself in the past but now I pat myself on the back and congratulate myself on what I've managed to do in a day. Sometimes I go to sleep thinking about all the things that I'm going to do tomorrow. I can't remember when I last felt so happy. It's fantastic.

Calm – angry

For anger to have persisted in the human condition, it can be supposed that it conveys a survival advantage, or at least does not carry a non-viable disadvantage. The energy that comes from anger can motivate people to challenge perceived injustices. Anger can provide respite from feelings of vulnerability. At its most extreme, however, anger can lead individuals to become a danger to themselves or others. Frequent angry feelings are a threat to health and can contribute to a chaotic lifestyle when they are expressed to others either in physical assaults or verbal outbursts, threats or intimidation. Relationships in which the parties experience ongoing high levels of anger arousal are also likely to be turbulent and unstable. Being subject to another's anger, particularly when the other is a key person such as a care-giver, and when it results in violence, abuse or neglect, 'is likely to have a profound effect on a child's view of themselves as a person, their emotional lives and their attachments, and on their future lives' (HM Government, 2006: 36).

Although aggression and violence may be activated by angry feelings they are not the same thing. While anger can increase the probability or intensity of aggression, it is neither a necessary nor a sufficient condition (Novaco, 2000). It is the failure to regulate angry feelings that can lead to its expression in acts of verbal or physical violence. Anger suppression can also have negative impacts in the form of developing resentment and a build-up of tension arising out of the inhibition of people's feelings about the way in which they are being treated. As Raymond Novaco puts it:

> There is now widespread recognition that this turbulent emotion, when experienced recurrently, has health impairment consequences ... the aggression-producing, harm-doing capacity of anger is unmistakable, and so is its potential to adversely affect prudent thought, core relationships, work performance, and physical well-being. The problem conditions, however, are not derivative of anger per se, but instead result from anger dysregulation.
>
> (Novaco, 2007: 3)

There is evidence that anger-related problems are often associated with the experience of multiple and chronic life stressors (Cavell and Malcolm, 2007: xxix). People with histories of recurrent abuse or trauma, and those who have experienced abandonment and rejection are often psychologically fragile. There is a tendency for this vulnerability to be hidden beneath a 'hard' exterior, particularly when the individual is feeling under threat. Piercings, studs, boots, tattoos, hairstyles and posture can make surface statements belying someone's internal state. Novaco describes this as 'character armor', the wearing of which can be generated, 'by the foreboding punitive actions of powerful social systems' (Novaco, 2007: 6) although there may be other reasons why people would choose to make such statements. Anger can serve the function of repelling threat and boost a flagging sense of self-worth.

Novaco argues for the usefulness of functional analysis in evaluating anger; of working out how anger is useful to each of us in our context. He suggests that anger can energise, and it can focus attention on environmental features that have threat significance. Angry feelings support us in the expression of negative sentiment, help us to suppress fear and defend our self-worth by externalising blame. If something has gone wrong, it is not because we have erred but the result of someone else's action. Anger may help us to feel in control of a situation and signals information to others about our emotional state. Novaco takes the view that it is important to work out how anger functions for each individual. For those trapped in toxic environments with little apparent freedom to instigate change, anger may become a chronic and habitual automatic default response, no longer activated by particular environmental stressors. This mechanism is implicated in the involvement of anger in post-traumatic stress (Novaco and Chemtob, 2002).

Perceived malevolence is a common cognition that induces anger. I have experienced this even in relation to inanimate objects such as my laptop computer which on occasion will seemingly deliberately defy my attempts to exercise control. When another person's behaviour is interpreted as intentionally harmful, anger and aggression are commonly activated. If you take away my children I am quite likely to experience justified anger which externalises blame. It is too threatening to my self-worth to turn the lens on me. People who are disposed towards frequent and intense feelings of anger are highly vigilant in threat sensing and quick to respond (Novaco, 2007: 24). This cuts down the thinking time for alternative constructions or meaning-making prior to responding. High levels of arousal can override inhibitory systems. Anger displays tend to evoke angry responses from others in an escalating cycle.

Novaco argues for interventions that disconnect feelings of anger from a person's threat detection system, normalising and legitimising the experience of anger and moderating any worries about being a 'bad' person for feeling this way. Self-worth is affirmed through the building of trust, a quality regarded as pivotal in bringing about change (Novaco, 2007: 36). Because anger can serve positive functions, Novaco suggests the aim of moderating anger intensity and building improved regulation of angry feelings rather than the unrealistic and unhealthy goal of anger suppression.

Paradoxically, the process of assessing anger may be experienced as threatening in itself. Disclosing angry feelings may represent a loss of power. What's more, one of the difficulties about assessing anger can be the difference between the perception of the intensity of anger by the person experiencing it and a recipient. I am reminded of the importance of social and cultural factors in the perception of anger each time I visit Crete, where passionate street shouting contests do not seem to presage violence as they might in the UK. Professionals involved in proceedings not infrequently say that they feel threatened by one or more of the people they are assessing. I try to remember that being assessed is frightening in itself and highly likely to arouse the human threat-response system. There are available two widely-used questionnaires that may aid in the exploration of anger and response to provocation which are described in Appendix 2.

Vulnerability – resilience in the face of stress and challenge

'People who are resilient display a greater capacity to quickly regain equilibrium physiologically, psychologically, and in social relations following stressful events' (Reich *et al.*, 2010: 4). Resilience also involves the capacity to continue forward in the face of adversity (Bonanno, 2004). It has been categorised as an individual trait, a process, and an outcome. People are regarded as differing in their inner strength, flexibility and 'reserve capacity' (Gallo *et al.*, 2005), so that although environmental forces impact on the development of resilience, individual responses to similar stressors vary. Individuals with high levels of resilience appear able to continue on a satisfying life course whatever disasters befall them. At the other end of the spectrum, vulnerable individuals are more readily thrown off track by adverse life experiences.

I regard this as an important dimension because it is too easy to assume that care-givers who have themselves experienced adverse life histories will automatically neglect or abuse their own children. Glasser *et al.* (2001) found little evidence in their retrospective study of parents to support what they described as the widespread belief in the cycle of child sexual abuse. In their study of 843 people who attended a service for 'sexual deviants and offenders', 227 (27 per cent) were found to have abused a child, and 616 (73 per cent) had not. For those men who had not abused a child, one in nine reported themselves victims of child sexual abuse; for those who reported that they had abused a child, one in three reported having been victims. Of the 41 women attending the forensic psychotherapy service who had been victims of sexual abuse, only one (about 2 per cent) was categorised as a perpetrator. The authors concluded that the data supported the notion of a victim-to-victim-iser cycle in a *minority* of men and not among women. Intergenerational cycles of physical abuse have also been proposed but appear to have been overstated (Kaufman and Zigler, 1993; Tomison, 1996; Zuravin *et al.*, 1996). Prospective studies of abused children have concluded that the best estimate for the rate of intergenerational transmission of abuse is approximately 30 per cent (Kaufman and Zigler, 1993). In both domains, the majority of adults with adverse life histories do not go on to harm their own children. In my experience, each person's abusive experience is individual and no single mechanism could account for the diverse ways in which people make sense of and respond to such adversities. Many people are able to integrate and make meaning of the abuse in ways that do not leave them vulnerable, and others benefit from compensatory experiences that give them a basis from which to take their lives forward in positive and constructive directions. This is all too difficult to keep in mind when, in my work, I am faced with an unremitting series of families who are struggling in a multitude of different ways, many of whom suffered abuse in their own childhoods and experienced periods in the care system. Self-report questionnaires that can assist in the assessment of resilience are listed in Appendix 2.

Open – closed to learning/motivation to change

In my view, openness to learning is one of the most crucial determinants of outcome for those families who come to the attention of child protection services and is an appropriate element of a personal profile. Whilst engagement in learning can be hindered by a lack of confidence and poor self-esteem, I have also encountered the phenomenon of 'presenteeism' (Proctor and Ditton, 1989: 3) in which physical presence masks a lack of engagement with the task in progress – I am there in body but not in mind or spirit. This may be a deliberate choice when a carer stubbornly resists alternative views of what constitutes adequate child care but recognises the need to be seen as compliant, and can also arise when dysfunction is so entrenched that the prospect of change is just beyond comprehension. There are parents who are unable to recognise that their actions are a reflection of who they are. Their core beliefs include themes such as, 'I am a warm and caring person,' 'Everyone loves me because I am so good.' Sometimes indulged in childhood, their construction of themselves is as a fine citizen who could not have treated others in the way that the evidence suggests. It is too frightening to face the negative emotions associated with acknowledgement of abusive behaviour towards others and a web of self-deception is constructed in defence. Actions that have been harmful to others are minimised, blame is attributed to external circumstances and people, and there is a failure to look inside and acknowledge the need to change. This contrasts with core beliefs that can derive from rejection, neglect and abuse, 'I am an evil person,' 'No-one could love me.' Both kinds of beliefs need to be challenged if significant change is to result. Quick fixes are unsuited to the radical restructuring of patterns of belief, thought and behaviour that have developed over a lifetime.

William Miller and Stephen Rollnick (2002) identify three critical components of motivation: readiness, willingness and ability. Willingness arises from the experience of a sufficient discrepancy between desires for the future and what is happening in the present. Ability is about belief in the capability to accomplish a specific change and may be described as self-efficacy. Readiness is about priorities. All of these are subject to the 'yes but' dilemma, which the authors label as the phenomenon of ambivalence. Tony Morrison (2010) argues that individuals cannot be said to be 'motivated' or 'unmotivated'. Instead, people are often beset by conflicting intentions. He gives the example of carers' desire to protect their children from a partner who constitutes a threat to their welfare conflicting with the need to avoid feelings of loneliness.

Openness to learning is revealed through interviews and observation of carer responses to suggestions and advice. The manner in which advice is given can be critical in determining the response of the recipient. Most of us do not respond well to being told that we are doing things badly; a focus on our strengths, encouragement and modelling of more effective behaviour are approaches that are more likely to activate openness to learning.

Assessing motivation to change

There are times for all of us when we struggle to manage what life throws at us. Most of the families who come to the attention of the authorities are wrestling with economic and social disadvantage. In a review of care proceedings under section 31 of the Children Act 1989 concerning allegations of ill-treatment of children by carers (Brophy, 2006) it was reported that in the mid-1990s the majority of parents in proceedings were struggling economically with over 80 per cent being dependent on income support at that point. Further evidence of vulnerability was indicated by the 40 per cent who were likely to have mental health problems and 20–30 per cent with drug or alcohol problems. Many such families led chaotic lifestyles (about 36 per cent) and almost half of the mothers had been subject to domestic violence (45–50 per cent). In Julia Brophy's most recent study, 61 per cent of parents were unable to control their children. Half of all parents were also likely to experience housing problems (Brophy *et al.*, 2003). Most applications for care orders (over 70 per cent) included allegations that the parents had failed to cooperate with involved professionals (Brophy *et al.*, 2003).

The review indicated that black children were over-represented in the sample (6 per cent compared with 2 per cent in the 1991 census); children of dual or multiple heritage were substantially over-represented (8 per cent compared with 1 per cent in census data); children with South Asian heritage were under-represented (2 per cent compared with 5 per cent in census data). Julia Brophy suggested caution in making interpretations of these figures (Brophy *et al.*, 1999).

Social and economic disadvantage makes life hard. What would be an easy task for me with my economic advantages and tertiary education can be daunting or even impossible if you have no credit for your phone, no confidence to speak to the person at the other end of the line, no energy as a result of your long-standing depression and the demanding task of caring for a number of small children. Where will carers facing these daily challenges find the energy and commitment to acknowledge their difficulties and invest in change? Failure to cooperate fully with the local authority is a significant factor at the point of statutory intervention. Refusal to cooperate was cited as a reason to commence court proceedings in 62–73 per cent of cases (Bates and Brophy, 1996; Brophy *et al.*, 2003).

A model of motivation and readiness to change was proposed by Prochaska and DiClemente (1982), Prochaska *et al.* (1992) and is described extensively in Morrison (2010). It is known as the 'Trans-theoretical Model' of change and comprises six stages, two of which represent barriers to change: Pre-contemplation (not changing and not intending to start to change) and Relapse, with four stages of intentional change termed Contemplation (not changing, but intending to change), Preparation (making some changes, but not fully, though intending to change fully), Action (has achieved all changes regularly for less than six months), and Maintenance (has maintained all changes for longer than six months). A phase of 'lapse' is also sometimes included. Progression through these stages is not smooth, but by its very nature the process of change is one of movement backwards and forwards; two steps forward, one step back. This reflects the experience of ambivalence as the immediate rewards of previous habits do battle with the longer term benefits of altered patterns. I have displayed the characteristics of the different stages in Table 3.1 (adapted from UCLA Center for Human Nutrition, n.d.), which includes suggested approaches to intervention for practitioners who are working to encourage and support people in making changes. Processes of change involve cognitive and behavioural adjustments. The former include developing increased awareness of the benefits and means of change, experiencing emotional arousal to negative consequences of continuing the current pattern, social or environmental re-evaluation and self-reappraisal. Behavioural adjustments involve stimulus control

Table 3.1 Transtheoretical Model of Change

Stage of Change	Characteristics	Intervention
Pre-contemplation	Not currently considering change or intending to take action in the foreseeable future 'Ignorance is bliss' May be uninformed regarding consequences of behaviour or have become demoralised about capability to change	• Acknowledge lack of readiness • Clarify that any decision to change is theirs • Encourage re-evaluation of current behaviour • Encourage self-exploration, not action • Explain and personalize the risk of continuing the present course of action
Contemplation	Ambivalent about change; acute awareness of pros and cons 'Sitting on the fence' Intending to change in the next six months but profound ambivalence may lead to stuckness	• Acknowledge lack of readiness • Clarify that any decision to change is theirs • Encourage evaluation of pros and cons of behaviour change • Describe and promote different positive outcome expectations of change
Preparation	Some significant action taken in past year and is beginning to try to change 'Testing the waters' Planning to act within one month and has a plan	• Identify and assist in problem solving regarding obstacles • Help to identify sources of social support and avoid temptation • Encourage perception that person has underlying skills necessary for behaviour change • Encourage small initial steps • Recruit to action-oriented change programmes

(Continued)

Table 3.1 (Continued)

Stage of Change	Characteristics	Intervention
Action	Engaging in altered behaviour for 3–6 months Vigilance against relapse is critical in this stage	• Focus on restructuring environmental cues and social support • Bolster self-efficacy for dealing with obstacles • Combat and normalise feelings of loss whilst focussing on long-term benefits
Maintenance	Continued commitment to sustaining new behaviour and experiencing reduced temptation to relapse Post-six months to five years	• Plan arrangements for follow-up support • Reinforce self-reward and satisfaction • Discuss coping with temptation, relapse and relapse prevention
Relapse	Resumption of old behaviours: 'Fall from grace'	• Evaluate trigger for relapse • Reassess motivation and barriers • Plan stronger coping strategies

(e.g. removing temptation), engaging in supportive relationships, substituting other behaviours, self-reward and making firm commitments (Velicer *et al.*, 1998).

Perhaps the most significant phase of change is that of Contemplation in which the recognition of the need to change results in a determined decision to take action. This phase is regarded as particularly complex and it has been broken down into the 'seven steps of contemplation' reported by Tony Morrison (2010). These stages comprise, 'a professional says I have a problem,' 'I accept that I have some responsibility for the problem,' 'I have some discomfort about the problem,' 'I believe that things must change,' 'I can see that I am part of the solution,' 'I can make a choice to be involved in bringing about a solution,' 'I can see some practical things that I can do.' The latter coincides with entry into the stage of Preparation.

Significant and lasting change is difficult to accomplish and people often lapse during the course of recovery. Lapses typically occur when under stress or facing a crisis. They are not considered to constitute a relapse unless there is full resumption of former patterns of behaving.

In my view, an understanding of parents' motivation to change can often only be determined by providing them with opportunities to change. This involves making a cross-sectional assessment of current functioning, agreeing targets for change with parents', engaging the parents in appropriate intervention and assessing the extent of change accomplished in an agreed timescale (Hartnett, 2007). The targets need to be realistic and meaningful both to the family and the professional. Effective interventions typically address multiple domains of family functioning, are provided in the family home and are tailored to individual families. A meta-analysis of 23 studies of parent-training concluded that such programmes are able to promote positive changes in attitudes, behaviour and parental emotional adjustment (Lundahl *et al.*, 2006).

It has been suggested to me that contact supervisors are sometimes an underutilised resource for encouraging effective change in parenting skills (Kim Burnby, personal communication, 2011). She argues that contact supervisors should be given the opportunity to support parents in behavioural change in order to ensure that the contact is as pleasurable as possible. Such support could be given at home rather than at some of the unsuitable venues arising from attempts to increase room occupancy in order to limit costs. Contact supervisors often have a great deal of first-hand parenting experience, could undertake further training, and may be perceived by parents as less threatening than members of formal professions.

Some care-givers begin to engage through surface compliance, such as agreeing to attend a parenting programme, alcohol detoxification, or domestic violence course, because this has been a condition of keeping their children. The initial engagement may be tokenistic but the resultant positive impacts may have a reinforcing effect leading to increased commitment and engagement. Research conducted by Humphreys *et al.* (2011) concluded that in the complex field of domestic violence intervention, organisations and workers are as important in the change process as the parents and children with whom they work. The process of change is not always smooth and can take a long time. Jan Horwath (2007) acutely observed that organisational performance indicators often demand rapid change and services are geared up for quick results. Following the trans-theoretical model of change, it is difficult to have confidence in the maintenance of change until the new pattern of behaviour has been established for about 12 months and this may be regarded as lying outside the child's time-frame, unless intervention is scheduled early in the assessment process.

Miller and Rollnick (2002) describe a therapeutic approach, termed 'motivational interviewing', designed to aid people in moving forward in the motivational cycle of change. This involves exploring ambivalence and building a sense of optimism and self-efficacy.

Prochaska and DiClemente have published a questionnaire, the University of Rhode Island Change Assessment (URICA), designed to assist in determining the location of a client's motivation with regard to the stages of change. The long version of the form can be downloaded from: http://casaa. unm.edu/inst/University%20of%20Rhode%20Island%20Change%20Asses sment%20%28URICA%29.pdf. From the URICA a measure of Readiness can be calculated using the method published at: http://www.umbc.edu/psyc/habits/URICA.html.

Inspired by Q methodology (which employs Q-sorts), card sorts have been used (Martin Hughes, personal communication, July 2011) to assess readiness to change in relation to parenting skills. A Q-sort involves ranking a set of items along an agree-disagree continuum, often 40–80 statements printed on small cards. The use of ranking, rather than two discrete categories of 'agree' and 'disagree', aims to reflect the notion that people think about ideas in relation to other ideas, rather than in isolation. The sample of items for a Q-set is intended to represent a wide range of statements that people might say or think about the issue under consideration. When used with single individuals, he or she is asked to rank the same set of statements under different conditions, thereby creating a comparison (similar to using a repertory grid in Personal Construct Psychology, a constructivist theory of cognition and understanding developed by George Kelly, 1955). The ranking is often a comparison between the items that describe people as they see themselves now, and a vision of their ideal selves. The process is described in more detail by Ruth Cross (2005).

Martin Hughes (School of Education, University of Sheffield) devised a Q-set with items representative of each of the stages of change such as, 'It's the professionals – they "gang up" on me,' 'I am thinking about the idea of changing my approach to parenting,' 'It's hard work, but I feel like I'm getting somewhere' and 'I have managed to stick with the changes that I have made in my parenting.' The mother in this example was asked to complete the Q-sort according to how the statements characterised her parenting at the present time and in relation to her past performance. In addition to giving an indication of the mother's readiness to change, the interpretation of the completed card sort provided a focus for discussion of parenting skills.

Assessment of social support

Parents do not bring up their children in a social vacuum. 'An understanding of a child must be located within the context of the child's family (parents or caregivers and the wider family) and of the community and culture in which he or she is growing up' (Department of Health, 2000a: 11). This has led to the proposal for an ecological approach to assessment of families in children's proceedings (Jack, 2001). Such an approach examines the child in context including the immediate and wider family, the carers' friendship network, support available in the local neighbourhood and professional sources of support. Social networks can offer very positive sources of support whilst also having the potential to increase stress if parents feel that they are subject to criticism by people who figure in them (Dunst *et al.*, 1997).

There are a number of theoretical perspectives that attempt to account for the influence of social support on health and functioning. These include the notion that social support reduces the negative effects of stressful life events

(Cutrona and Russell, 1987, 1990), that the belief that we have positive social relationships promotes a sense of positive self-esteem irrespective of the presence of stress (Lakey and Drew, 1997; Mankowski and Wyer Jr, 1997), and that relationships *per se* provide companionship, intimacy and help in maintaining low levels of conflict and high levels of social cohesion. The latter view reflects the perspective of evolutionary psychology, that such companionship fulfils a basic biological need for humans to connect with others of their species. Distinctions have been made between social networks in terms of size and constitution, social integration into these networks, and the extent to which people comprising the networks are perceived by their members as supportive. The most valued functions of social support have been described as practical help, emotional support and the provision of information and advice (Sarason *et al.*, 1990). *Perceived* support appears to be a crucial factor and, 'paradoxically, a strong sense of support seems to give people the confidence to cope without needing to marshal their network's resources' (Gottleib and Bergen, 2010: 512). The finding that perceived support was more important to health and well-being than enacted support gave rise to the idea that individual personal characteristics were important determinants of social support processes (Pierce *et al.*, 1997). These authors state:

> the support individuals perceive to be available to them partly reflects their skills in eliciting support as well as building and sustaining relationships. It is ironic that many individuals who need social support lack the skills to have developed close relationships that could be a source of support or the skills to elicit it.
>
> (Pierce *et al.*, 1997: 8)

Carers with a reliable source of support provided by a partner or close friend are at lower risk of depression than those in a relationship characterised by conflict or unreliability (Brown *et al.*, 1986). According to Pat Crittenden, the families in which children are both abused and neglected are typically characterised by unstable and conflictual relationships between the main carer and partner/s, and a restricted social network (Crittenden, 1988). Domestic violence accounts for a significant portion of parental stress (Lacharité *et al.*, 1996) and, 'the primary problem of neglectful parents concerns their inability to establish and maintain close relationships' (Lacharité *et al.*, 1996: 30).

What information provides evidence of social support and of carers' skills in forming intimate long-term relationships? The impact of early attachment experiences is relevant and described in Chapter 7. Interview data will give a perspective on the degree of support that is perceived by carers to be available to them. I have found respondents to have no difficulty in telling me their perception of their sources of support. Not infrequently they refer to enduring relationships that they experienced outside the immediate family as they were growing up; how such special people helped them to feel valued just for themselves and provided sources of recognition and achievement outside the home (Jenkins and Smith, 1990). Some of these childhood relationships endure into adulthood and when they do not, such as when a dearly loved grandparent dies, the impact can be very substantial. In addition to such interview data, various questionnaires listed in Appendix 2 may also be useful.

Assessment of parenting partnerships

It has been suggested that the best predictors of multi-type child maltreatment are poor family cohesion (family members feeling disconnected from one another), low family adaptability (rigid roles and inflexibility in relationships and communication) and the poor quality of the adults' relationship with each other (Higgins and McCabe, 2000). With these precursors it is quite likely that parental relationships in such families will be short-lived or conflicted, with the propensity for domestic violence. Pat Crittenden (1988) reported that for families who have simultaneously abused and neglected their children, the relationships between the mother and her, often sequential, partners were characterised by instability and domestic violence. The poor quality of the mother's relationship with her partner and the presence of domestic violence were also found to explain the high level of maternal stress in a study by Lacharité *et al.* (1996). These authors concluded that the mother's perception of her partner's behaviour, 'significantly influences her capacity to enjoy her relationship with her child, her state of personal well-being as a parent and, to a lesser degree, her capacity to manage her child's behaviour in terms of setting limits and gaining her child's cooperation' (Lacharité *et al.*, 1996: 31). This suggests that the quality of a couple's relationship has wider ramifications for the care of the children.

Although detailed information on the living arrangement of parents in care proceedings is fairly limited, one study (Brophy *et al.*, 2003) found that, whether married or not, most parents (85 per cent) were not living together at the point of the application (and this figure remained high across most ethnic groups). In research reported by Masson *et al.* (2004) only just over a quarter of the child's parents were living together at the time an Emergency Protection Order was made. In the remaining families, the parents were either separated, the father was deceased or his identity was unknown. In the Coastal Cities study, Sally Holland (2004) reported that, 'many couples underwent numerous separations and reunifications, without being able to provide rational explanations for these (Holland, 2004: 99). The couples struggled to negotiate the roles and responsibilities of their everyday lives and were unable to discuss matters and plan ahead. Decisions to live together had often been taken without long acquaintance, much discussion or forethought.

The assessment of how couples relate and what effects this might have on the care of the children will be impacted by cultural norms. Interdependence and clear prescription of roles characterise some cultures, with female partners joining their husbands' families in a role directed wholly to care of the home and the children. Diana English and Peter Pecora (1994) referred to the importance of family strengths and kinship relationships in the aetiology of child maltreatment, with some cultures giving greater emphasis than others to the centrality of family boundaries and relationships with the extended family. In a diverse and pluralist society I view it as important to make an effort not to impose my own values about couple relationships and to focus my assessment only on aspects of partner relations that impact on care-giving. This also means recognising that whilst all children have a male and female parent, care-giving may be provided by single sex couples, by a parent and grandparent and other combinations of adults whose relationships are subject to the vicissitudes of any other care-giving partnerships.

Through the enactment of their bond with each other, care-givers provide a model of how relationships work to their children and these patterns may be reflected in the child's future relationships with partners. The factors that I regard as particularly relevant to assessments in the family court are the extent to which the care-givers are able to collaborate, to show each other respect, and the capability to disagree and negotiate disagreements without recourse to verbal or physical violence. Stability and commitment are other material factors: the duration of the relationship, the partners' long-term plans and intentions, and the frequency with which they separate and reunite.

In assessing parenting partnerships I have found it helpful to draw on material from interviews conducted individually and together, observations of the partnership in action during contact with the children, reports of professionals who know them and previous records, including any police call-outs related to domestic violence. A number of questionnaire measures (Appendix 2) can be a useful adjunct.

Domestic violence

A significant factor that impacts the care of the children is the extent to which spouses or partners are safe with or harmful to each other. Domestic violence is known to impact negatively on the emotional development of children, and there is a possibility that they will also be directly injured when the violence is physical. According to published studies, in 30–60 percent of families characterised by domestic violence, child maltreatment also occurs; children in such families may witness parental violence, may be victims of physical abuse themselves, and may suffer neglect from parents who are focused on their partners or unresponsive to their children due to their own fears (Goldman *et al.*, 2003).

Domestic violence has been defined in a spectrum of different ways, has been theorised from a number of contrasting perspectives, and the relation-ship between domestic violence and gender continues to be a controversial and highly contested issue in the academic literature. The Children and

Family Court Advisory and Support Service (CAFCASS) in the UK defines domestic violence as:

> Any behaviour which is characterised by the misuse of power and control by one person over another within a family context and/or with whom s/he has been in an intimate relationship. This behaviour can be overt as in threatened attempted assault or actual assault or harassment. It can also be subtle, such as the imposition of social isolation on a partner and/or her/his children. It can thus take the form of emotional, financial, physical, psychological or sexual abuse or any combination of these.
>
> (CAFCASS, 2007: 6)

There is conflicting evidence about the extent to which men and women are victims and perpetrators of domestic violence. It has been suggested that men are less likely to report domestic violence because of the associated stigma, that violence against men by women is more likely to be in self-defence, and that women more often present with injuries or are killed because men have, on average, greater upper body strength. In studies by Straus and Gelles (1995), physical violence was typically mutual (both partners brawling), it was just as likely that women would strike the first blow, and the results were the same when women-only surveys were conducted. A 2001 survey carried out in the UK showed that 4 percent of women and 2 percent of men had been victims of domestic violence in the previous year. Of the most heavily abused group, 89 percent were women (Walby and Allen, 2004). Women are at much greater risk than men of being murdered by an intimate partner. In 2010 in England and Wales, 21 men and about 100 women were killed by their partners or former partners (BBC, 2011). The frequency of such incidents has led to a decision by the British government to make mandatory automatic multi-agency case reviews for every death resulting from domestic abuse. This may help in giving recognition to the serious and enduring impact of domestic violence in families, whether men or women are the protagonists (Archer, 2002).

Research into domestic violence is challenged by the associated stigma and shame which affect willingness to report; by non-standard definitions of abuse; and because such patterns of interaction can seem 'normal' when well established and are therefore not reported. It has been argued that it is the impact and function of domestic violence rather than the frequency of individual acts that is crucial, on the basis that its purpose is to control and intimidate rather than to hurt or injure (Jacobson and Gottman, 1998). But Janice Haaken argues that, 'it is not ethical to take the position that men are violent simply because they consciously choose to assert power and control over their partners' (Haakens, 2011: 515). Not every hurtful word, angry outburst or ugly interchange constitutes abuse, and valid assessments focus on the motivation of the parties, the history of the relationship and the impact of the behaviour.

In helping couples and individuals to understand the concept of domestic violence and reflect on the extent to which this characterises their relationships, I have found the Duluth framework useful (Domestic Abuse Intervention Programs, 2008). The framework is somewhat controversial because it is based on the presumption that perpetrators are male and that their aim is to exercise power and control. I have found a non-gendered modified version to be accessible to families and of value in prompting a discussion about the behaviours that constitute domestic violence, and to what extent each partner experiences these behaviours in their relationship (see Figure 3.1). It also allows for discussion of violence between same sex couples.

Appendix 2 lists a number of risk assessment instruments for intimate partner violence. A study which examined the validity of such questionnaires (Hanson *et al.*, 2007) reported that the victims' assessment of risk had similar levels of predictive accuracy to structured approaches to risk assessment. General

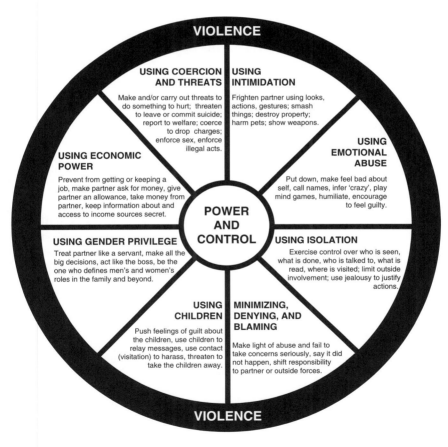

Figure 3.1 Adaptation of Duluth wheel of power and control.

risk assessment tools for violent behaviour performed as well as the specialised measures. The authors proposed that consideration be given to the combination of the partners' judgement of risk with other risk-relevant information.

It is not uncommon in the families I meet in care proceedings who have been embroiled in domestic violence that a condition for consideration of a return of the children is for a couple to maintain a state of separation. This is inordinately difficult for some people and may take several attempts, during which it is determined that the children cannot wait. Assessments not atypically include reports from privately hired surveillance companies as well as reported sightings in the community. There is to my mind a paradox in that children do best when separated parents are able to sustain a cooperative and negotiated relationship. For couples who have formerly engaged in domestic violence, complete separation and an absence of communication are usually prescribed. If couples are seen shopping together this is taken as evidence of cohabitation. Careful and critical scrutiny of the data is required in such examples because when couples do continue their partnership against the proscription, they often engage in secrecy and deceit.

I have found that information provided by children is often the most compelling in making an assessment of the degree of domestic violence, especially when they are able to provide a detailed account of their first-hand experiences. This child described the extent to which the parental hostilities worried him:

> Julie and dad were starting to argue yesterday, shouting at each other and stuff in their room. I was in the computer room. I just worry what's happening 'cause Julie used to hit dad sometimes. I've seen her throw a hairbrush at him before. It just makes me worry 'cause he might be getting hurt or something. He's had some scratches on his arm from the hairbrush. He just tries to walk away 'cause he doesn't want to hit her. The arguing stopped for ages but now it just started again yesterday. Julie went to her friend's house and slept last night. They normally argued 'cause of Lizzie. I don't know why. And now they're starting again. I've been fairly worried all day. I didn't see Julie this morning. I'm worried what's going to happen. They might start arguing and if it's at night I can't get to sleep. It keeps me awake when they argue and I can hear them. They might split up but that seems a good thing. They'd stop arguing wouldn't they?

Parental reports of specific incidents can also reveal the kind of detail that gives authenticity to the account:

> We were going to a works dinner and he bought me this really really lovely dress. It was black crushed velvet with a really floaty feather boa. We sat at the table and had a nice meal and wine was flowing. I wasn't drinking too much. Graham was. I just wanted water. He was dancing

and said, 'Come and dance,' and he turned his back on me to talk to his colleague so I walked off. He came back to the table: 'Don't you ever embarrass me like that again.' People were looking and his friend's wife gave me a glass of wine. 'Will he be okay?' 'No, he's getting drunk.' He went slumped in his chair so I was dancing with Melanie, and we were having a laugh and a chat and when I got to the table, 'What have you been talking to her for? My work is nothing to do with you. Keep your ugly nose out of it.' We got on the coach and he started being so abusive. He was saying, 'Wait until I get you home you f'ing lesbian, you dancing with her. Bitch, ugly cow.' He really really laid into me and Jenny tapped me on the shoulder and put her head nearer and said, 'Are you all right?' We got off the coach and he went, 'I'm going to kill you. Best you hide from me.' My friend was babysitting for me and we got in the house and, 'Right you can f off.' He gave her some money and she went home and he went for it big style. He chased me up the stairs and ripped the back off my dress. He ripped my underwear from me, hitting and kicking me and threw me downstairs. He started biting me and pulling my hair. He dragged me downstairs and back up and I didn't lash out once. I was just numb to it and couldn't feel any emotion. I went and got into bed. He took the quilt off me and pushed me out of bed and I went to the spare room. In the morning I ached. I phoned Jenny up and said, 'Can I come round?' and went to her house and she phoned the police and the police came to her house and made a note of all the injuries. They cautioned him but again I wouldn't press charges.

Police logs often provide useful evidence. If couples are to remain apart, then research studies have suggested that in order to achieve lasting independence from a partner who has been abusive, the provision of legal assistance can be helpful (Farmer and Tiefenthaler, 2003). The research by these authors concluded that a decline in the incidence of domestic violence in the 1990s was accounted for by the aging of the population, improvements in the economic status of women, and the provision of legal assistance. Legal assistance can facilitate essential safety planning, allay fears of a loss of residence or custody, and provide advice about relevant government benefits.

Irrespective of the presence or absence of domestic violence, I have found that the extent to which the partnership is based on cooperation, negotiation, stability and safety is reflected in the following observations and interview data:

- Talks calmly and pleasantly to partner in joint interviews.
- Talks warmly *about* partner.
- Can de-centre, understand and empathise with partner's experience of the relationship.
- Expresses satisfaction/dissatisfaction with the relationship.
- Has been/is able to negotiate how to bring up the child.

- Talks about value of stability in interview.
- Has made active choice of partnership and thought of impacts on children of choices and actions in relation to partnerships.
- Understands impact of own experiences in childhood on approach to relationships with partners.
- Shows commitment to the integrity of the family as a basis for bringing up children.

In this chapter I have explored issues and approaches to assessing the adults who hold the key to the welfare of children. As an assessor, if I can understand their histories, motivations, struggles, strengths and weaknesses and the challenging contexts in which they are trying to raise children, this is a good starting point from which to encourage the changes that will enable them to provide quality care for their children, even when this is against the odds. The seeds of change are small beginnings. It helps if I am not a detached professional scrutinising and finding wanting their parenting practices, but rather someone who learns about their hopes and fears and shares their desire for the welfare of their children. Even though it is particularly difficult for practitioners tasked with making judgements that may lead to removal of a child to create the kind of working relationship with parents that involves trust and cooperation, I think that their children would want us to try.

4   Special issues in the assessment of adults

In order for children to feel safe and secure it seems to me that they need to experience a reasonable degree of stability which may be provided in a number of ways, not all of which are necessary, but the presence of at least some of which are desirable. This may be stability of carer, of the carer's mood state, of housing and neighbourhood, of nursery or school and of routines for daily living. These factors are most often disrupted when a parent is struggling with mental health issues, drug or alcohol misuse, financial or housing problems, domestic violence and/or transitional relationships. People with significant learning difficulties may also find parenting to be a challenge beyond them unless they have extensive and ongoing support from friends, family and professionals.

Mental health difficulties

Not all parents with mental health issues will experience significant difficulties in caring for their children but it has been estimated that in 50–90 per cent of families on the caseload of social workers in child care settings, the parents have mental health problems, alcohol or substance misuse issues (Office of the Deputy Prime Minister, ODPM, 2004).

The most common mental health presentations that arise both in the general population and amongst parents in proceedings are those of anxiety and depression, phobias, obsessive-compulsive and panic disorders. In the UK an estimated one in six people is experiencing a common mental health problem at any one time (Department of Health, 2000b). Excessive anxiety can serve to prevent people from being able to undertake tasks involved in daily living and may be a general state, specific to certain contexts (typically known as a phobia) or a transitional state arising out of particular life experiences. Depression is a very debilitating condition involving disturbances of mood, appetite and sleep. It contributes to increased irritability and exhaustion. The associated emotions are those of anger and sadness. When sadness dominates, self-harm may result, and when anger dominates, uncontrolled outbursts may be a consequence, although anger can have a useful energising effect. Anxiety and depression are frequently experienced together.

There are many readily-available questionnaire measures that can screen for such conditions which may be used by a range of professionals. Social workers may be understandably reluctant to use them for fear of being accused of straying from their domain of professional expertise, and may regard this process as more appropriately conducted by a health professional. Assessments resulting in diagnoses of mental health conditions are appropriately conducted by psychiatrists but the screening measures described in Appendix 2 can be used to gain a perspective on the involvement of mental health difficulties in the client's profile, and to determine whether referral to an expert is indicated. I have found parents typically to be open about their difficulties with anxiety and depression and these short scales have a face validity with which they are able to identify. Screening for more unusual or severe presentations is appropriately referred to specialists.

Although diagnoses of anxiety and depression are widely accepted within Western culture, concepts of health and illness are by no means universal. For example, Ahmed (2000) summarised these concepts within an Islamic framework:

> Traditional Islamic teaching considers disease states of two kinds: spiritual and physical. Spiritual ill health is the more serious since the Prophet taught; 'Allah does not look to your bodies nor your forms, but rather He looks to your hearts'.
>
> Islamic teaching obliges Muslims to seek cures for both spiritual and physical disease. The former are usually sought from those trained in understanding inner realities, i.e. teachers of religion, while the latter are sought from those trained in the physical sciences – many in the Muslim world are trained in both of these disciplines. Cure, however, comes solely from Allah and these individuals and institutions are simply Allah's instruments for effecting cure.
>
> Ahmed (2000: 38)

Ahmed argued that within Islam, illnesses are seen as 'tests' from Allah. According to tradition, sickness and tribulation bring an opportunity to earn reward through patience and steadfastness and are a cause for the cleansing of one's sins. This means that British Muslims may be caught between contrasting and sometimes conflicting world-views regarding personal interpretations of health and disease. These different perspectives may lead to inner turmoil. In Ahmed's view, the 'aches and pains' and 'heartache' so common among Muslims may represent an attempt to articulate this turmoil in a form that clinicians can understand. I have found that if I enquire, people are usually willing to try to explain to me their faith beliefs and how these impact on their health beliefs and approaches to family life. Some parents have offered me literature and drawn my attention to television programmes, for example broadcasts by imams about parenting, in order to further my understanding. Websites may also be a source of information about the concerns of parents within specific cultures and the advice that they may be receiving from their community leaders (http://www.askimam.org/fatwa/fatwaList.php?fid=7). This sometimes helps to clarify dilemmas faced by parents confronted with different advice from their community and the State.

Some parents have received a diagnosis indicative of severe and enduring mental health difficulties. It would be easy to 'write them off' as self-evidently incapable of providing the quality of care needed by their children, but I would caution against automatic assumptions, firstly that the diagnosis has been warranted, and secondly that such conditions are life sentences. This parent had experienced severe psychotic symptoms over a number of years, which in retrospect appeared to have been drug induced:

> I was first given a diagnosis of schizophrenia when I was 17. I used to hear voices and hallucinate. The voices were sometimes squeaky and sometimes shouted at me and they always told me to smash things up or run in front of cars or buses or swallow razor blades or hang myself. I used to cut myself really deeply and it was like a release. It was like undoing a zip to let out the voices. I've got scars all the way up my arms and on my back and legs. I got sectioned loads of times and they gave me Risperidone and Olanzapine and I took them along with my street drugs. When I was in hospital my dealer would bring my drugs in and I stopped taking the prescribed ones. I used to hide them under my tongue and then spit them out in the sink. I was done for supplying heroin a couple of years ago and it was the best thing that's ever happened to me. It helped me to get clean. My drugs counsellor was great and I went on a methadone programme and I decided to stop taking my prescription stuff. Now I'm really healthy. I go to the gym every day with a mate. I've moved away from the town where all the people I knew were druggies and I'm the happiest I've ever been.

Some mental health diagnoses, such as the class of personality disorders, are associated with instability and unpredictability of mood and behaviour. I have known people with such a label to experience a degree of fluctuation in functioning that made the risks to their children palpable, whilst I have also found myself puzzling over how the label came to be allocated to this particular parent. It has been argued that the personality traits defining the disorders are present in some people who are regarded as living apparently successful lives. 'Many senior managers have Narcissistic Personality Disorder' (Furnham and Taylor, 2011: 70). At one time such disorders were seen as unresponsive to any kind of treatment but more recently approaches including dialectical behaviour therapy (Linehan, 2007), cognitive therapy (Binks *et al.*, 2006) and approaches based on mentalization (Fonagy and Bateman, 2006) have been shown to be promising.

Fabricated and induced illness

For some parents involved in children's proceedings who are experiencing severe mental health problems, these difficulties may be shown in florid symptoms, but they may also be masked beneath apparently stable functioning. This can be the case in the controversial condition now known as Fabricated and Induced Illness in a Child (FII) (formerly known as Munchausen Syndrome by Proxy (MSbP), which involves a carer harming a child through the seeking of unnecessary medical attention. At its most severe, this may involve causing illness through the administration of poisonous substances, attempted suffocation, or contaminating samples taken for investigation. I give it space here because it is rare and poorly understood but can prove fatal to children. I have encountered only two possible cases in my entire career, and lack of familiarity makes this a particularly difficult condition to detect for most professionals. The causes are debated and the motives of the carer are uncertain although it has generally been suggested that the adult benefits vicariously from the attention paid by medical professionals and/or from a sense of power and influence. Courts are reluctant to accept that the behaviour constitutes a syndrome, whilst it is clear that some care-givers do deliberately harm children in a manner which results in unnecessary medical attention and can be fatal. Julia Macur QC (2005) cautions advisers and advocates to resist the use of generic terms such as 'Factitious Illness by Proxy' at the fact-finding stage of proceedings and advises insistence on a careful evaluation of the base material to assist the court and to promote the welfare of the child.

In my experience, professionals often find it very difficult to accept that a parent may have intentionally harmed a child, particularly because a picture is presented of a very caring mother (it is largely mothers who have been found to harm their children in this way) who is close to her child, who is sociable on the ward when the child is admitted to hospital, and who forms close relationships with nurses, junior medical staff and other parents. A thorough exposition of FII can be found in a book by Christopher Bools (2007). Guidance is also provided by the UK Department for Children, Schools and Families (2008b). Presenting medical conditions and symptoms have included apnoea, fits, allergies, asthma, developmental disorder, bleeding, diabetes, vomiting, poisoning, diarrhoea, skin rash, failure to thrive through withholding food, smothering and skin rash.

The literature about FII suggests that perpetrators are extremely difficult to identify and treat. They are described as being skilled at evoking sympathy and doubt, at deception, and at becoming, chameleon-like, whatever is called for in the situation (Lasher and Sheridan, 2004: 279). Carers who have developed such habits are archetypally closed to learning. The payoffs for their learned behaviours prevent the kind of self-examination that is necessary if change is to occur. This is not to say that change is impossible but rather that the first step is a motivational one, and ultimately the motivation needs to come from within rather than be externally driven. This is militated against by the involvement of the courts. For professionals involved with carers suspected of FII, I would advise an attitude involving scrupulously critical examination of evidence and clarity about role. The literature currently tends to emphasise the dangerousness of perpetrators to their children (Lasher and Sheridan, 2004) whilst also addressing ways to approach the therapeutic needs of the carer (Parnell and Day, 1998). If you are the assessor, it is crucial to keep this role to the fore and resist being drawn into the web of deception spun by the perpetrator. This does not preclude empathy for the care-giver, whilst keeping an open mind that enables scrutiny and integration of all the evidence becomes of utmost importance.

Drug or alcohol misuse

Marc Schuckit tells us that, 'two out of three men and women in the United States are drinkers at some point in their lives' (Schuckit, 2000: 8) and that the, 'pattern of substance use in most parts of the world is prodigious, even without considering the intake of illegal substances' (Schuckit, 2000: 8). In a 1997 survey conducted in the USA, 35.6 per cent of people admitted to having used an illegal substance (Substance Abuse and Mental Health Services Administration, Office of Applied Studies, 1998) and this was across all socioeconomic groups and ethnicities. A survey of 3000 university students in the UK revealed that 65 per cent admitted to having used an illicit drug (Webb *et al.*, 1996).

Can such wide-spread phenomena be considered deviant? I imagine that most people would agree that the use of psychoactive substances in itself is insufficient to disqualify parents from providing adequate care for their children. What is important is the extent to which the pattern of use is 'maladaptive' or 'harmful', leading to significant levels of impairment or distress. Substance use becomes problematic when the priority given to it interferes with the fulfilment of major role obligations, when the use impairs functioning and judgement in contexts likely to be hazardous such as driving or operating machinery, and when persistent or recurrent social or interpersonal problems result.

High risk groups for the development of problems with substance use are young people who have been diagnosed with conduct disorders (Myers *et al.*, 1998) and health care workers, who are regarded as being more likely to have access than the general population (Schuckit, 2000). Drug and alcohol misuse are also regarded as, 'tending to thrive in areas of multiple deprivation, with high unemployment and low-quality housing, and where the surrounding infrastructure of local services is fractured and poorly resourced' (Rassool, 2009: 49). Whilst drugs are used for multiple purposes including experimentation and recreation, substance misuse refers to the use of a psychoactive substance in a way for which it was not intended and which causes physical, social and/or psychological harm (Rassool, 2009). The term 'addictive disorder' tends to be used when the problems caused have escalated to a state of dependency. The World Health Organization uses the terms 'hazardous' to refer to use of a drug that increases the risk of harm or dysfunction, 'dysfunctional use' when it is leading to impaired psychological or social functioning such as loss of employment or marital problems, and 'harmful use' when drug use is causing damage to health through tissue damage or psychiatric disorders (World Health Organization, 2010b).

For parents in children's proceedings, my experience is that problematic substance use has often begun in people's teen years and has developed into a way of escaping strong negative emotions. This can lead to the development of a lifestyle in which the drug takes centre stage. It dictates relationships, demands funding, involves deception and supports avoidance of difficult issues or life histories. It serves to protect the user from thinking about painful and difficult experiences and may lead to physiological and/or psychological dependence. Chaos tends to result because judgement is impaired and priorities are distorted. Here is an account from a mother who was trying to change her life pattern after over 20 years of drug and alcohol misuse.

> I lived with my mum and dad until I was nine. My dad used to beat up my mum and lock her out. One day my dad threw a knife at her that ended up in the back of my head and it scared me to death. My mum used to try and hide it but I remember that me and my sister used to let her in after my dad had locked her out all night. She used to have black eyes and one day I went in the kitchen and my dad had my mum over the table with his hands round her neck. My mum was never affectionate with us. She was always having different men and that drove my dad wild.

> I had an uncle who used to pay special attention to me and was always wanting me to sit on his knee and he'd tickle me. He had a shop and he used to take me into the back room and started to touch me down below. At the time I didn't know what he was doing but he was making these jiggling movements and I remember he had a horrible smell about him. Then he made me masturbate him and one time he pinned me down on the settee and told me we were playing a game of 'mummies and daddies'. He used to bribe me with sweets and presents. I'd have this awful sticky stuff on my tummy and I used to get in the bath and scrub myself so hard that my skin bled. I felt dirty and ashamed. I don't know how it came to stop but I just hated having anything to do with him and I was angry all the time about no-one noticing or asking me what was the matter.

> When I was ten I stole some money from my mum's purse and went to the shop with my friends to buy some food for a picnic. The owner phoned my mum because I had so much money and she shouted at me

and hit me with a belt across the top of my legs. I just skeltered out of control from then. I was running away all the time. My life just became chaotic. I was expelled from school at thirteen. I was sexually precocious and I went with anyone. My life's been like a roundabout that I got on when I was just a kid. I feel robbed of a childhood. When I was fourteen I got locked up in a secure unit for a bit. The staff were all right and at least I did learn to read, but the other kids were just like me. When I got out I became a working girl and I was sort of looked after by Clive. I thought I was special to him but he just hooked me on cocaine and I couldn't escape. After that I've had different men that just come with the drugs. I don't want to be on drugs, I want a normal life.

Last year I got introduced to a sex workers' outreach service by another woman on the street. I was crying and telling this volunteer how I didn't know where to find the strength to come off the drugs and she referred me to the drugs service. When you take drugs you hate yourself, you detest yourself. I don't feel ashamed anymore. The staff are fantastic and I've started caring about myself for the first time. What I do now is I steer clear of anyone who's on drugs. I can ring any of the workers during the day, Sarah Louise or Annie, weekends or night. I used to be scared of being on my own. They've got me a benefits advisor and Debbie from Hope House is like family. Sarah Louise is like the mother I never had. I used to have no self-esteem, no self-worth. Sarah Louise has taken me to the gym and now I take more care of myself. I've been on courses to help me develop myself and they've drummed it in to me that I can be all right. Simple things like cookery classes and helping me get furniture. All I have to do is keep it clean. That's another thing I've never done in the past. The house was in a state. I thought I was cleaning it. At the beginning when I came off drugs they helped me. I was so anguished about my children, and furious with myself. I felt loss and lost. I kept feeling sorry for myself and I've had to learn not to do that because it gets me into trouble. 'Poor me' is an unhelpful thought. At the beginning the workers believed in me and now I believe in myself. They would have done things for me but now I do it for myself. Before, I wouldn't have anything to do with workers. I always thought they just wanted to take my children. I wouldn't turn up for appointments and I'd be out if I thought someone was going to visit me. I thought they looked down on me. Every time they took one of the children it sent me back over the edge.

Sometimes I still get feelings that I can't take it any more but not massive volcanoes of feeling that I can't control. I get tempted to use and I've had a couple of lapses. I wouldn't call them relapses because it's just been one spliff and then I get back on track. Sometimes I feel happy and it's such a wonder. I can't think of the last time I knew what that was like.

There are a number of questionnaire measures which enquire into drug and alcohol use but perhaps the most reliable data is that from hair strand testing. Since hair takes time to grow, use in the immediate term cannot be determined in this way, but for this purpose, substance use can be adjudged on the basis of breath, urine and blood tests. Breathalysers are sometimes administered at each appointment by alcohol counselling services. Hair strand testing of drug use is considered to be very reliable, that of alcohol testing less so because the results can be affected by bleaching and frequent washing of the hair. False positives can be obtained because simply being in a pub is enough for traces of alcohol to find their way into the hair. Caution has been urged in a judgement in the UK by Mr Justice Moylan; London Borough of Richmond upon Thames v B & W & B & CB [2010] EWCA 2903 (Fam), which was reported in Lamb (2010). The judgement warns against the use of hair strand analysis to test for lower levels of alcohol use and states:

> Research has shown that there is a relationship between alcohol consumption and the concentration of these markers in hair. There are many factors which will affect the level of the concentration of the markers, as a result of which there is no direct correlation between alcohol consumption and the level of concentration of the markers. However, research has shown that there is sufficient of a relationship to justify using these markers to identify those who abuse alcohol. The definition used is that provided by the World Health Organisation of an average of 60 grams of ethanol per day over the course of several months .... Balancing the strengths and weaknesses of the tests for both EtG and FAEEs in hair has led to it being generally acknowledged that, currently, they should only be used to ascertain whether the results are consistent with excessive consumption.
>
> (Lamb, 2010: no page numbers)

The advantage of hair drug testing over urine or serum drug tests is said to be that these tests can provide evidence of the pattern of use over a time period of several months. Hair analysis not only determines the use of the drug, but it can also provide an accurate historical record of its consumption. This helps in differentiating between one-off and regular use. Because human hair grows at about one centimetre per month (there is some variation between cultures), a three-centimetre sample can provide a history of drug use over a three-month period. When professionals consider that drug and alcohol misuse may be an issue, chemical analysis is likely to provide the most convincing evidence. Self-report measures may also assist in exploration of the issue and are listed in Appendix 2.

It sometimes appears obvious that drug or alcohol use is creating chaos in a family but it is also important to remember that some medical conditions can masquerade as intoxication, producing behaviours such as staggering and slurring of speech when no substance has been consumed. It is easy to draw false conclusions without the back-up of chemical analysis. Similarly, people who use to excess can become skilful at concealment and deception as their increasing use gradually takes them over.

> When the domestic violence started that's when I started being a secret drinker where I'd be hiding vodka in Evian water bottles. People have described it as a sort of escapism and it went on for quite a while. The relationship was fading and I knew it was going and I'd got quite a lot of pressure at work, targets. I used to stop off at the local shop and get a bottle of vodka and Evian water and I'd drink half the water and top it up with vodka and leave the half vodka in the car and take the Evian water into the house and put it in the fridge. When he'd go to work I'd drink it and it was a relief. I'd finish the bottle of Evian water and then I could do with another one and I'd bring the vodka from the car and when that was gone I'd go outside and put the vodka bottle into the wheelie bin, then the situation is normal. On the way home from work, this was when it started to get daily. Each time I thought to myself, 'If I leave half a bottle in the car I won't have to buy any tomorrow,' but just knowing it was there was the temptation.

As their life stories unfold in interview, I find that people often show how easy it can be in a state of unhappiness to seek solace from a mind-altering substance and it is only later that its destructive effects take over.

Physical impairment

To my surprise, when I was researching this book, I found that under the heading 'disability' are often lumped together physical and intellectual disability, mental health issues and even domestic violence. I wondered what this said about the meaning of disability in my culture. Just under 11 per cent of families in the USA have one or more disabled parents (Olkin, 1999: 125), this being a broad term including a heterogeneous group of parents who may have very little in common. Jenny Morris and Michele Wates (2006) tell us that in the UK there is no one source of information that can enlighten us about parents with impairments but the Labour Force Survey uses the definition of disabled person contained in the Disability Discrimination Act 1995: that is, anyone with a long-term health problem or disability which has a substantial and long-term adverse effect on the ability to carry out normal day-to-day activities. Using this definition, about 12 per cent (1.7 million) of Britain's 14.1 million parents are disabled and 1.1 million households with dependent children have at least one disabled parent (Stickland and Olsen, 2005: 137–8). This definition of disability includes parents with physical disabilities, intellectual disabilities, support needs arising from mental health difficulties, parents with HIV/Aids and drug and alcohol dependency.

This ubiquitous over-generalisation across different impairments fails to consider the differences in functional levels that pertain even within one category of disability (Kirshbaum and Olkin, 2002). A parent's impairment can be congenital or adventitious, stable, progressive or varying. 'The specific circumstances, degree and characteristics of a parent's disability can affect not only the parent's routine functioning and life experiences, but can also impact aspects of the parenting role as well as the child's experience' (Preston, 2010: no page numbers). Children tend to be seen as victims of parents' disabilities, with, 'implicit and explicit criticism of disabled parents, their values, their choices and even their right to have children at all' (Olsen, 1996: 42).

Freda Olkin is herself a wheelchair-user and a parent. She contrasts the medical, moral and minority models of disability. From the perspective of the moral model, which has the longest history, disability is viewed as a defect caused by a moral lapse or sin; a test of faith. The medical model sees disability as residing within the individual, being a pathological defect in or failure of a bodily system. Olkin (1999) argues convincingly for a minority (social) model which proposes that the problem of disability lies within the environment that leads to discrimination and prejudice. The minority model takes the problem out of the realm of the individual and places it in the world of culture, politics and society. This view places, for example, the responsibility for everyone to have physical access, firmly in the built environment. It leads to the provision of induction loops, enabled buildings and public transport, and the availability of assistive devices as a matter of course, reflecting the notion of inclusion whereby people with disabilities are able to participate in all activities, sites and interactions within society. Reflecting the minority or 'social' model, it is advised that the term 'disabled parent' is preferred to 'parent with a disability' since the latter assumes that the disability lies with the individual. Whilst a parent may have an impairment, the disablement arising from it lies within society (Olsen and Clarke, 2003).

Freda Olkin provides helpful information about what it is like to be a physically disabled parent, and the misconceptions that can easily be held by professionals:

- For a parent with a disability, everything takes longer, whether this is changing a nappy or cooking a family dinner. This is not necessarily disadvantageous as it may provide opportunities for extended interaction.
- Children may need to be taught very specific limits such as always remaining within voice range of a parent with limited physical movement or a visual impairment.
- There is a crucial role for assistive devices.
- Schools and other organisations involved with the children can helpfully recognise that parents will have had to devise a style of parenting that takes into account their disability.
- Disability restricts parental energy so children's social activities may be delineated by the parent's level of fatigue and mobility.

- Children of parents with a disability may imitate the disability but this does not imply that they have difficulties with issues such as body image.
- Children of parents with disabilities may become members of a disability community which provides different but not inferior opportunities.
- Children may show sensitivity about a parent with a disability but any issues arising should not automatically be assumed to result specifically from the disability.
- Although a child may assist a disabled parent to complete tasks, this does not reverse the care-giving roles and it is inappropriate to think of this as 'parentification' of the child.
- The essential functions of parenting – its joys and challenges, remain relatively unaffected by the presence of physical or sensory disabilities.

(Olkin, 1999: 129–132)

A briefing by the UK Social Care Institute for Excellence (2005) does focus exclusively on the group of parents who experience physical and sensory impairments. It describes how they experience negative attitudes from other people towards their parenting, especially assumptions that they either cannot be a parent or are not able to look after their children properly. They can therefore feel that they have to work harder than other parents in order to be accepted as competent (Grue and Laerum, 2002). The report highlights how disabled parents can experience the double problem of lower incomes and higher living costs, which in turn leads to social exclusion. Interventions from social services were found seldom to focus on the whole family or on how to support and help the parents in the discharge of their parental duties in their social setting (Goodinge, 2000). 'There were services to meet their personal needs and services for their children but there was a lack of flexibility, to bring these all together to support them in undertaking their parenting role' (Goodinge, 2000: 1).

One of the difficulties for people with physical and sensory impairments is the day-to-day experience, like other minority groups, of prejudice and stereotyping. Freda Olkin describes how disability can frame a person's world view:

One day I came back to my car with my infant son and a cart full of groceries. I took my son up into my arms, and as I was opening the trunk a woman stopped and said, "May I help you?" I gratefully accepted. To my amazement, instead of helping me load the groceries she forcefully took my son out of my arms. Both he and I freaked, and I took my crying son back. The woman turned to walk away, saying, "I know, I know, you people like to do it all yourselves." This emotionally powerful incident

might have remained an isolated one, but within the next few years I read
about Tiffany Callo (which, whether accurate or not, I remember as the
case of a mother with a disability losing custody of her baby in large part
because of her disability) and then read a newspaper account of a
Michigan case of two parents with disabilities who used personal attend-
ants (they lost custody of their son because they were unable to care for
him without assistance.) I read in a scholarly journal that "disabled
women are at risk for a range of undesirable outcomes, including ... loss
of child custody" (Kallianes and Rubenfeld, 1997: 203). Thus four events
helped shape my view – one personal experience and three I read about
that had a personal meaning for me – that I, as a mother with a disability,
could lose my child more easily than a mother without a disability.

(Olkin, 1999: 83)

Olkin argues that such experiences repeatedly shape the perspective of a
person with an impairment. She says that, 'being a person with a stigmatized
condition hones skills in detecting nuances of nonverbal responses in others'
(Olkin, 1999: 85). 'Having a disability means always being noticed, standing
out, being different, *everywhere you go*. People will respond to your different-
ness' (Olkin, 1999: 80). Insightfully she also states:

I am not like everyone else. I am the exception. Things don't apply to
me. This is a form of narcissism I sense in myself and others with disabilities. We are so used to pushing and shoving our way in, being our
own advocates, being on the outskirts, being the exception, being different, we start to think we are the exception in ways and situations other
than those related to the disability. Clinicians must understand this
process and not mislabel it as a personality disorder.

In my practice I have encountered parents with physical impairments who
have been disadvantaged in contested residence and contact disputes and who
have been given the label of 'personality disorder'. Here is an account by a
mother with a life-long condition, of the many ways in which this can impact
on and shape a way of being:

When I first started school I couldn't walk so I got carried around everywhere and had a frame. It was really overwhelming and scary. The other
kids didn't want to sit with me.

All members of the family were totally opposed to my first pregnancy.
'You must have a termination, you've got a disability.' His mother said
the child would be on the 'at-risk register' because I wouldn't cope.
I'd end up crying. They said I'd never be able to hold the baby or bath
her. It erodes your self-esteem. I was a nervous wreck the whole time.
I couldn't share anything with them. I couldn't go baby shopping.

They didn't want to know about the scan. When I went to the hospital I felt completely defeated and humiliated. They took over and made all the decisions because they didn't believe in my body's ability to give birth. It should have been a spiritual experience. I felt like a piece of meat.

I'm angry these days about people's attitude. The anger helps. They look at my legs and just make these judgements about my person. Some people as I was growing up would talk to you in this really slow way and I used to talk back and take the piss out of these able-bodied people. Most people say, 'How did that happen?' which I'm sick of telling people. The, 'Oh, gosh, how do you cope?' After we split up and I was trying to get residence of Jamie-Lee, it's because of my disability that I got ordered to have a parenting assessment and John didn't. When the health visitor came she took one look at me and said, 'Oh dear,' about my disability and the fact that there were steps outside. She thought I couldn't manage the pushchair. When you get bullied and battered your whole life it makes you feisty. You have to be like that, otherwise they trample on you.

One fundamental lesson that I have learned over the years about diversity is that to achieve fairness, everyone cannot be treated the same. People with impairments and those without do not start off on a level playing field. Apparently equal opportunities are often inequitable. If my assessment is to be fair I have to take this into account and listen with care to the stories of people whose perspective on life has been shaped by their disability experience, whilst ensuring that I do not automatically assume that their impairment is implicated in any issues that arise. This requires a deliberate and continuous effort of imagination rather than reliance upon a culturally determined set of unquestioned assumptions. Here is an account by Isabella Devani, a wheelchair user who describes how she and her son have adapted to their circumstances:

At 16 months old, my son is an unstoppable, toddling force. Running, scrambling, exploring and investigating, his day begins at seven in the morning and ends 12 hours later – if I'm lucky! As a permanent wheelchair user, I'm often confronted with the question "How *do* you manage?" Whether spoken in admiration or disbelief, it remains an irritating affront to my disability consciousness. Having become a wheelchair user only four years ago, I still find myself in defensive mode when it comes to other people highlighting my disabilities ....

Bonding with my son has taken place through song, rhyme and use of mirrors rather than through floor play. To sit my son on my lap in front of a full length mirror allows ample opportunity for sharing eye contact and facial expression. A few choruses of an adapted classic *The wheels on mummy go round and round* still result in hilarity for us all. We have also learned baby signing over the last six months, giving my son a chance to express himself more fully and giving me the added time to physically meet his signed requests. The closeness of our relationship has been a vital element to making our experience work.

So how *do* I manage? Managing for me has been a combination of basic equipment, practical support and continuous innovation. Being a mummy who doesn't walk has been much easier than I had anticipated. No longer held back by my own preconceptions has paved the way for wider avenues of experience and the discovery of useful techniques for meeting essential developmental goals. Far from struggling to carry out the basics, my fears have been diminished as I grow in confidence in my own abilities and my child's own instinctual path.

(Devani, 2007: 3–4)

My assessment also needs to take account of the different kinds of support that may benefit people with physical impairments. This may mean cutting across service boundaries and 'normal' rules for the provision of aid. In a study by Olsen and Clarke (2003), the level of support available to parents in their own right was sometimes so poor that the question of support with parenting was not even on the agenda. Here are two accounts of such difficulties in accessing support involving children:

The OT [occupational therapist] asked me if I needed any help but I've been told that I can't have it. They've said they would help with personal care .... They would cook for me but not for them [the children].

Well, they had agreed to take me shopping and everything was fine, but then they phoned me back and said they could not take children as passengers on insurance grounds. This meant that I simply couldn't use it. I mean, it's as if they assume that disabled people just don't have children. In the end, I argued with them and they got back to me, saying "Yes, you can bring your children, but only because you're a single parent", which I thought was a strange thing to say.

(Olsen and Clarke, 2003: 41)

Learning difficulties

The World Health Organization (2010a) defines intellectual disability as 'a significantly reduced ability to understand new or complex information and to learn and apply new skills (impaired intelligence). This results in a reduced ability to cope independently (impaired social functioning), and begins before adulthood, with a lasting effect on development.' The terms 'learning difficulty', 'mental retardation', 'mental handicap', 'developmental disability' and 'cognitive disability' have all been used to denote this generalised difficulty with learning. For the purposes of this book I will use interchangeably the terms 'learning difficulties' (excluding specific learning difficulties such as dyslexia) 'learning disability', and 'intellectual impairment'. First and foremost, parents with learning difficulties are more similar than different from other parents who become involved in family proceedings, although they are highly likely to experience poverty and deprivation. Tim and Wendy Booth (1993) argue that:

> ... parents with learning difficulties who come to the attention of child protection services share many characteristics with parents in the general population who experience similar caretaking problems. Foremost among these characteristics are inadequate incomes, unemployment, poor vocational skills, a disadvantaged childhood, isolation from their extended family, an insufficiency of social supports, stressed marital relationships, large families, and a lack of ordinary living experiences (Mickelson, 1949; Rosenberg and McTate, 1982). In short, the factors that make it hard for parents with learning difficulties to cope are mostly the same as those that make it hard for people who do not have learning difficulties to be good parents (Gath, 1988).
>
> (Booth and Booth, 1993: 463)

Research carried out by Philip Swain and Nadine Cameron (2003) in Australia gave support to the anecdotal experience of parents with a learning disability that, like their counterparts with physical and sensory impairments, their capacity to care was likely to be more harshly judged than that of non-disabled parents. Parents with generalised learning difficulties are evaluated against more stringent standards than their non-disabled peers and these criteria may never be made explicit (Levesque, 1996; Painz, 1993). The removal of children from parents with learning difficulties has been reported as a common occurrence (McGaw and Newman, 2005; Ray *et al.*, 1994; Tarleton *et al.*, 2006) and disproportionate compared with those parents who do not have a learning difficulty (Booth *et al.*, 2005; McConnell and Llewellyn, 2000). David McConnell and Gwynnyth Llewellyn argue that intellectual disability *per se* is a poor predictor of parenting competence and that any deficits are largely remediable. It has been argued that there is evidence of systemic bias against parents with intellectual impairments. These parents may be falsely presumed incompetent, incapable of learning and of overcoming perceived parenting difficulties (McConnell *et al.*, 2011). In Canada, David McConnell and his colleagues (2008: 722) found that, 'investigations involving parents with cognitive impairments were substantially more likely to result in (a) the substantiation of maltreatment (61% vs. 46% of all other cases); (b) the case remaining open for ongoing protective services after the initial investigation (55% vs. 25%); and, to remain open even when maltreatment was not substantiated (30% vs. 12%).'

Tim Booth (2000) argued that the central features of professional practice and service organisation undermine parents with learning difficulties and heighten their vulnerability. The presumption of incompetence and the belief that intellectual disability automatically disqualifies people with learning difficulties from parenthood encourages a focus on deficits. Some of the support that is offered has the impact of de-skilling parents and reinforcing feelings of inadequacy. They are less likely to have received appropriate and adequate support for parenting prior to the commencement of care proceedings. They face the difficulty that staff working in children's agencies lack training and expertise in working with parents with learning difficulties and, 'agencies with the most expertise in developmental disabilities are the least likely to be involved with families' (Mandeville, 1990 cited in Booth, 2000: 180). There is a lack of co-ordination among services which results in many families 'falling through the service net' (Whitman and Accardo, 1990).

As a result of the lack of fit with organisational boundaries, particularly at a time of tight budgets, funding for the needs of parents with intellectual impairments may become disowned by all. Children's services are not funded to provide intensive services which may be needed over the long term. Parents with intellectual impairments can be disadvantaged by their difficulties in understanding rules of evidence and procedure. It has been suggested that legal services are poorly equipped to support such parents in responding to the legal process and in working out how best to present their case (Keyzer *et al.*, 1997 cited in Booth, 2000).

Robert Hayman (1990) surveyed cases reported in the USA since 1965 and concluded that, 'the fact of mental retardation, once established, often has the effect of shifting the various burdens of proof from the state to the parent' (Hayman, 1990: 1237). '[O]nce a court is satisfied that it is in fact dealing with a mentally retarded parent, it often insists that the parent bear the burden of proving her fitness or potential for fitness, thereby presumptively equating mental retardation with inadequate parenting skills' (Hayman, 1990: 1239).

In consequence, many such parents are reluctant to approach supportive services with their problems for fear of inviting professional scrutiny that carries negative assumptions about their coping skills, and which risks the loss of their children to the care system (McGaw *et al.*, 2010). As a result, parents with learning difficulties frequently receive professional intervention only during crises when their parenting difficulties become more evident (McGaw, 1996).

Sue McGaw *et al.*'s (2010) study of over 100 parents with learning difficulties concluded that their children were at greater risk of harm if parental learning difficulties were compounded by additional factors. These included parent childhood trauma, co-morbidity of disability (such as mental health difficulties), and caring for children with special needs. Another significant risk factor arose for parents with partners whose histories involved criminal activity and/or anti-social behaviour (including sexual offences, domestic violence, or substance misuse). This would constitute a risk factor in any family but it has been suggested that women with learning difficulties are 4–10 times more likely to experience sexual violence, physical violence, and homicide by their spouses, dates, or sexual partners than women without disabilities (Sobsey, 2000). Risk factors identified by Feldman *et al.* (2002) include limited social support, maternal stress and child behaviour problems. It is also the case that children of care-givers with learning difficulties are often aware of the discrimination to which their parents are subject, and which they may experience through association:

> The worst bit was her coat, she always wore the same coat. It was a long, fur coat and she wore it summer and winter. All my mates laughed at her and she laughed with them. I hated that she would laugh at her own weaknesses. I think she had learned that this was better than being shouted at. The teachers would come to the gate and show her off. They didn't know how to talk to her really. But at home it was different, no one teased us there – we had great times. She would make things she had seen on the TV during the day and I would help her. She wasn't very good at cutting out and she would get me to do that. The other bit I hated was the neighbours. They didn't like us and they called mum names.
>
> (Morgan and Goff, 2004: 18)

When dealing with a discriminated-against group it behoves professionals to take an active approach that counters prevailing cultural assumptions and stereotypes. Parents with learning difficulties are a heterogeneous group of individuals. 'Some will not present any significant needs, some will present with relatively simple or transient needs, and still others will present with a complex of inter-related problems which will endure throughout the child's development' (McGaw and Sturmey, 1994: 37). The assessment needs to take account of parents' individuality and be respectful of the particular difficulties that they experience without being patronising. This mother gave an account of the many professionals with whom she had relationships, and the approaches that she found valuable.

> I get MENCAP. They come and help. They clean the house and do a bit of washing and tidy up. They help me a lot. They come every day and I'm happy with that. They ring me up and see if I'm all right. They read letters to me that I don't understand and explain and that. I don't want more MENCAP help; I like to be independent and show them I can do it off my own bat. It's important to be independent to prove to the social worker that I can do it but she keeps pushing me and pushing me saying Tom's clothes are too small. I've got him a new pushchair upstairs because he can't walk with his splint on; he cries. He'll walk so far and then his leg gives in. The social worker doesn't like him being in a pushchair. If she tells me to get rid of it I'll tell her I won't have Tom in one of those special prams 'cause I won't have people take it out on him. I'm more for Tom because of his disability problems.

The health visitor comes now and again. She's helpful. The advocate, she's on the social worker's side. She won't listen to what I say. She's supposed to write down what I say and what I want. The community nurse, I see her at the doctor's. I went to the hospital and I don't get on fine with them because they want to adjust my medication: in and out of hospital. I said I'd rather go to the doctor's and see the nurse there. I can't be in hospital and look after Tom. The nursery nurse and pre-school teacher were unhelpful, telling me how to potty train Tom; teach him to read and write and do his name and I said, 'Look, I'm doing what I can.' The social worker pulls him down and says he's slow at learning but no way. He bosses you around playing the teacher. He stands with his hands on his hips. He said, 'You've got to eat your dinner mummy or no pudding.'

I used to find respite care useful but Tom's getting fed up of going, now he's just about living there. He's starting to play up in the foster home. They don't do him a proper meal, they take him out to McDonald's. At home he had five meals a day; when he come home from school, dinner, tea, supper. If I've got any money I buy an Indian. He gets everything. I'm the only one with nothing. The social worker's saying there's no food in the house. She's making things up as she goes along, making sure that I don't have Tom back. I won't listen to them. It makes me feel hopeless and stressful. It makes my heart beat faster but not with MENCAP. They ask should they do anything. They're very caring with me being a bit slow to understand.

Difficulties experienced by parents with learning difficulties and their children

Although they are a diverse group, some outcomes for children are on average poorer for children of parents with learning difficulties. The average performance of children of parents with learning difficulties on tests of reading, spelling and maths has been found to be lower than those of a comparison group matched for characteristics such as low income, ethnicity and number of children. Behaviour problems are more frequent amongst children of parents with learning difficulties (Feldman and Walton-Allen, 1997; Keltner *et al.*, 1999). Morgan and Goff (2004) describe a number of factors which may impact on children's development when their parents have a learning difficulty. These characteristics need to be taken into account in devising suitable interventions. This is in the context that no clear relationship has been demonstrated between parenting competence and intelligence (Haavik and Menninger, 1981; Schilling *et al.*, 1982) and the ability of a parent to provide good-enough child care is not predictable on the basis of intelligence alone (Booth and Booth, 1993; Rosenberg and McTate, 1982).

Difficulty in generalising from the specific and concrete

Significant challenges for people with intellectual impairments are posed by the difficulties that they can experience in transferring learning from one context to another and in the maintenance of learning over time (Dowdney and Skuse, 1993). 'That is, much of the learning of people with a learning disability is specific both to context and time' (Young *et al.*, 1997: 59). These authors suggest that carers with a learning disability may need physical demonstrations of skills and reminders on a regular basis because they do not automatically adjust their parenting approaches as a child develops. There is a greater reliance on concrete experiences from which the parent may be unable to extrapolate to the abstract. Morgan and Goff (2004) cite an example of a parent who was following a teaching programme.

> Her task was to go to the library, choose a book with her son, and then go through the pictures with him. The plan was twofold; to help with attachment, as the activity was to take place on the mother's lap, thereby providing an opportunity for intimate contact and to help with development by looking at books. The parents reported back to the worker after three weeks that the activity was not working. It became apparent that the book had not been changed and the child had become bored with the same pictures. Nobody had explained to the parents that the book needed to be changed.
>
> (Morgan and Goff, 2004: 13)

In a focus group for parents with learning difficulties, the majority acknowledged that they were unable to read materials, but many indicated that, 'they could learn if information was presented to them more slowly and if they were allowed to try things out' (Tymchuk, 1999: 70).

Tendency to over-generalise

Parenting requires constant adjustment over time as the child grows and develops. This improvisation can be more difficult for parents with intellectual impairments. There may be a tendency for skills suited to the parenting of younger children to perseverate. Whitman *et al.* (1989) gave an example of a mother with a learning disability who took her sick child to casualty and was told to give the child only clear liquids. No time limit was specified and she was not told when to change back to solids. Three weeks later the infant was admitted to hospital for failure to thrive.

Lack of stimulation

Research findings suggest that children's speech and language development is particularly susceptible to delay when care-givers have learning difficulties

(Accardo and Whitman, 1990; McGaw and Sturmey, 1994). Because creativity and imagination are core features of play, Morgan and Goff (2004) suggest that the skills of parents with learning difficulties may limit them in creating stimulating play situations. They may benefit from demonstrations of alternative ways of using toys and encouragement to engage in 'messy' play. Some parents, and in my experience not only those with learning difficulties, feel embarrassed and shy about engaging in play in the presence of professionals. It can be very freeing if professionals confidently model playing and singing games alongside the child and care-giver, showing that there is no need to feel shy or embarrassed (Morgan and Goff, 2004: 84).

Difficulty in incorporating child care routines

Some basic aspects of care may need to be demonstrated to parents with learning difficulties, and these may benefit from being repeated on several occasions to ensure that they have been understood and incorporated into family routines. These may include how to dress an infant appropriately for the weather, or how to manage a baby or child whilst doing the shopping. All of these issues pose problems for any parent, but the organisational demands may be more taxing for a parent with learning disability (Young *et al.*, 1997: 66).

Responsiveness to child's needs

Sue McGaw and Peter Sturmey (1994) wrote that mothers with a learning disability, 'are less likely to show affection, reinforce, support, stimulate and bond with their child in contrast to mothers who do not have learning difficulties' (McGaw and Sturmey 1994: 47). Margaret Flynn (1989) highlighted concerns about parents' skills in providing appropriate stimulation, showing awareness of children's needs and in providing appropriate and consistent discipline.

Whilst parents with learning difficulties are able to learn parenting skills, using them responsively to the child's needs is likely to present a challenge. In order to know not only *how* to change a child's nappy but also *when* to do so requires reasoning which may be beyond the carer's capability. Carers have to work out what to do when a baby cries rather than make the same causal attribution on each occasion. They need to be able to attend to more than one thing at a time, keeping their eye on their child at the same time as attending to telephone calls and avoiding attending to the person who shouts the loudest. There may be a tendency for parents to assume that their own needs and the child's are identical.

Despite this level of agreement among authors on potential skill deficits, other factors are also seen as playing a part when children's development lags behind their peers. McGaw and Sturmey (1994) identified that, 'factors such as poverty and the child's IQ may also significantly affect the parent-child relationship' (McGaw and Sturmey, 1994: 47), and Ann Gath argued that the number, ages and spacing of children can be critical (Gath, 1995: 198). Tim and Wendy Booth concluded that, 'many of the problems experienced by parents with learning disabilities derive more from poverty, poor housing, harassment, victimization and lack of support, than from their own deficits in parental competence' (Booth and Booth, 1993: 475).

In assessments of parents with learning difficulties, many of the static risk factors are identical to those that are relevant in any family, including poor childhood experiences, institutional care, a history of abuse and neglect, lack of family support or larger family size (Nigel Beail, personal communication, 7 March 2011). A limited internal model of parenting may derive from poor memory. An IQ score below 55–60 would signify difficulties with comprehension and reasoning, or being able to hold in mind the needs of more than one person at a time. Dynamic risk factors include lack of parenting knowledge and skills, lack of coordinated interactional style with the child, absence of environmental support, presence of psychological difficulties or mental disorder or the absence of a child-centred focus (Nigel Beail, personal communication, 7 March 2011). Inadequate models on which to build parenting skills, low self-esteem, and limited knowledge of supportive resources were noted by Whitman *et al.* (1989).

Parents with a learning difficulty whose children are removed from their care may struggle to understand the issues of concern and as a result of low self-esteem may respond defensively. Being observed during contact with their children may be particularly difficult.

> At contact it's like a prison. They're in the room writing on their note pads. I've not seen none of the contact notes. They just sit and watch at contact. They don't explain what they've wrote down. I don't even hear from my solicitor; a fortnight. I don't think he's helping, myself. The first day in court he came out with a sneer on his face and when I phone he's never there and he doesn't ring me back. When I'm in court he goes over to her, the social worker. He said it's to explain how it goes from my point of view. I just want her (social worker) to stay away from my door. I want an injunction against her. I'm taking it out on the kids 'cause they're asking me when they can come home. It's just destroying me and I just feel like I don't want to go and see them because it upsets the kids and it upsets me when I have to leave them there.

The challenges faced by parents with learning difficulties have generally been addressed through parent education and training programmes which have universally concluded that parents benefit, are able to develop their parenting skills and can learn to take care of their children successfully (Llewellyn *et al.*, 2003, 2010; Wade *et al.*, 2008). These approaches were pioneered by Alexander Tymchuk and Maurice Feldman (1991) in the USA. They used applied behavioural approaches which emphasised the opportunity to learn skills *in situ* (Booth and Booth, 1993), the breaking down of skills into small steps (McGaw, 2011), the use of illustrated materials, demonstration and the provision of opportunities for practice with positive reinforcement, and matched to the parents' level of understanding (McGaw and Newman, 2005). These authors were able to show that parents were able to learn child care, home safety, child health and parent–child interaction skills (Llewellyn and McConnell, 2005). Long term intervention was often desirable (McGaw, 2012).

Appropriate assistance is responsive to particular learning and support needs which may involve intermittent support over the longer term. A positive attitude on the part of the professionals is one of the most powerful determinants of outcome. The approach is most helpful when it promotes parental competence, strengthens supportive relationships, reduces parental stress levels and addresses educational needs (Aunos *et al.*, 2010; Llewellyn and McConnell, 2002).

The results of studies by Llewellyn (1995) suggest that the techniques and direct intervention offered to people with learning disabilities are of less importance than the quality of the relationship formed between the professional and family and the subsequent psycho-social support offered. The literature suggests a strong association between supportive social networks and the positive psychological well-being of parents with learning disabilities (Cotson *et al.*, 2001; Kroese *et al.*, 2002; McGaw *et al.*, 2002). Some parents with learning disabilities report a preference for support groups because they are helped to gain confidence, improve their self-esteem and assertiveness, and enhance feelings of control (Booth and Booth, 2003). Such groups can provide the social support that is often missing from the lives of parents with learning difficulties.

Parenting assessments, when learning disability is a factor, benefit from an approach that takes into account the difficulties that parents may have in expressing their skills in interview. A recent version of the Parent Assessment Manual (PAMS 3.0), originally published by Sue McGaw *et al.* (1998) is available from Pill Creek Publishing at http://www.pamsweb.co.uk/publications.html. The first section comprises forms for professionals and care-givers that give structure to the initial stages of screening and planning. Section 2 contains in-depth assessment tools including a skills index, worksheets, a frequency observation form and a summary sheet (see Figure 4.1). This section includes cartoons designed to assess knowledge of parenting skills. Observation of skills is regarded as a more reliable indicator than performance on formal tests of knowledge. Section 3 focuses on risk and generates a visual profile of carers' personal and child care skills. It facilitates planning for present and future needs. The materials can be used to assess verbal communication, literacy, understanding of time, budgeting skills, capability to travel and use transport independently, cooking, hygiene and emergency knowledge and skills.

Practitioners may need to adjust their communication style by using straightforward language, avoiding abstract concepts and keeping to one

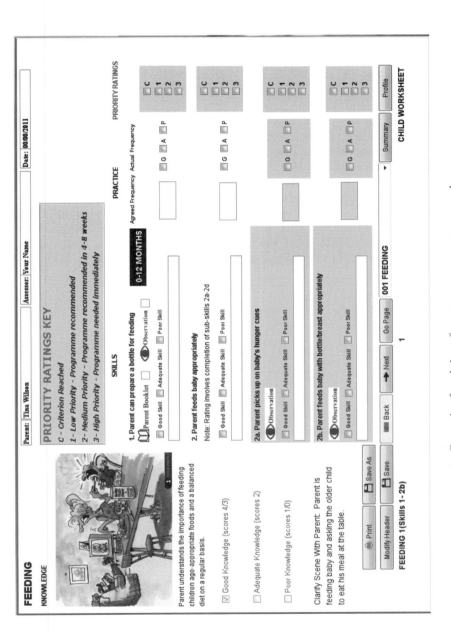

Figure 4.1 Example of worksheet from parent assessment manual.

point at a time (Booth and Booth, 1994). Supporting texts with pictorial information can help to clarify any information provided. For the purpose of explaining the court process to parents with a learning disability, illustrated texts have been written by David Hawkins and Sarah Jane Lynch. They can be downloaded free from: www.changepeople.co.uk. 'For many care-givers the assessment will indicate the need for significant levels of intervention and support' (Cotson *et al.*, 2001: 298) over a lengthy period of time during which reassessment will show to what extent the carer is able to adapt as children grow and develop.

The Division of Clinical Psychology Faculty of Learning Disabilities of the British Psychological Society has produced excellent guidance regarding issues in the assessment of parents with learning disabilities which is widely applicable (Baum *et al.*, 2011). It can be obtained from: http://www.bpsshop. org.uk/Good-Practice-Guidance-for-Clinical-Psychologists-when-Assessing-Parents-with-Learning-Disabilities-P1322.aspx.

For the most part, the assessment of adults with a learning difficulty benefits from an approach that has much in common with the assessment of any care-givers, the focus of which is the following chapter. This may be supplemented by functional assessments, examples of which are listed in Appendix 2.

5   Assessment of parenting

Precautions

Cultural assumptions

When I was a child at primary school, which I like to think is not all that long ago, it was not uncommon for my fellow students to be sent to the head to be caned. At age seven I remember one of my teachers, for mild misdemeanours, used to make us stand on our desks whilst she slapped our legs with a ruler. It was not so much the slapping as the humiliation in front of our classmates that upset us. No one batted an eyelid then about what now would be regarded as unacceptable treatment of young children at school.

In a UK study (Nobes *et al.*, 1999), over 90 per cent of parents said that they had smacked, slapped or hit their child at some time, and a greater proportion of mothers than fathers smacked weekly or more often (25.1 per cent). In a retrospective study reported in New Zealand by Jane Millichamp *et al.* (2006), 80 per cent of participants reported that they had been exposed to physical punishment in childhood. This would have taken place in the 1970s and 1980s. In conjunction with findings reported from the USA the authors argue that rates of physical punishment have not altered greatly over the past few decades. There continue to be different opinions about whether it is permissible to smack children and the impact upon them of physical punishments which in some countries are outlawed and in others are not. The high frequency of such behaviour towards children suggests the need to look beyond the physical punishment itself to explain negative and damaging outcomes for children. 'A consistent finding with physically abused children is that it is the emotional quality of the parenting, rather than the actual physical abuse, that is so psychologically damaging' (Fitzpatrick *et al.*, 1995: 56). There is also evidence that the category of abuse and the degree of physical severity does not predict the future well-being or safety of a child, rather it is the degree of disturbance in parenting (Donald and Jureidini, 2004).

I cite this example to make the point that views about what constitutes appropriate behaviour towards children by adult care-givers is culturally determined and time-dependent. Even at the most severe end of the spectrum of unacceptable parenting the concept of 'child abuse' is evolving and influenced by social attitudes to children, theories of child development, professional practice, political initiatives and changes in legislation (Reder *et al.*, 2003b: 4). It follows that ideas about what constitutes satisfactory parenting will similarly be impacted by changing cultural mores and the personal views and experiences of the assessor. Attempts to create standardised checklists or proformas for assessing parenting have been dogged by these social changes, typically rendering them inappropriate to a subsequent generation (Holland, 2004: 96). There is also a debate about whether standards are set higher or lower for those parents who find themselves in the family court (Hill *et al.*, 1992; Reder *et al.*, 1993) with different authors taking contrasting perspectives on this issue.

Some authors have made a strong case that attempting to define 'good' or 'good enough' parenting in precise terms is a complex endeavour, the results of which are open to ambiguity (Taylor *et al.*, 2000). These authors argue that poverty and socioeconomic status are major determinants of what has been described as poor parenting and that it is convenient for politicians to suggest that poor parenting results from deliberate choice and matters of personal responsibility. They state, 'Parenting is a proximal variable in the causal pathway to adverse outcomes in childhood and adolescence, of which material disadvantage and economic hardship are distal variables. Behavioural problems and temper tantrums among young children have been shown to increase as a result of parenting changes associated with economic hardship' (Taylor *et al.*, 2000: 115). They argue that parenting can only be understood in its social and economic context, particularly the impact of increasing income inequality which results in a large group of socially excluded families. Children in such families experience acute and chronic material deprivation in a context in which advertising leads them to desire and expect availability of expensive toys, designer clothing and gadgets.

A study of health visitor judgements regarding what constituted poor parenting (Taylor *et al.*, 2009) reported that these practitioners relied on only a narrow range of the available factors in reaching a decision. Significant predictors were parental boundary setting, health behaviours and the type of housing that the family occupied. 'For example, if a mother lived in privately rented accommodation, the child had dental caries and they cuddled their child to sleep on the sofa until they dropped off to sleep, the health visitor was more likely to form a judgement of poor mothering and parenting' (Taylor *et al.*, 2009: 1186).

The influence of cultural assumptions was highlighted by Azar and Cote (2002), who suggested that it is easy to assume that parenting strategies of single parents living in a high-crime neighbourhood should be similar to those of a middle-class mother in a suburban environment. Embedded cultural assumptions may lead to judgements that generalise socialisation goals (self-reliance as opposed to inter-dependence), whereas in many cultures the extended family network is responsible for socialisation and care of the child. Assessors risk constructing all families in the image of the Western, middle class nuclear family, a form which is not universal (Kağıtçıbaşı, 2006).

Successful parenting of one child does not necessarily mean that a carer is able to meet the needs of another. There is a question of goodness of fit (Azar *et al.*, 1998). Sometimes it appears that one child is picked out and becomes the scapegoat for all of the family's ills. It may well be possible that a parent can successfully parent one child, but the nature or demands of another child are beyond that parent's capacity.

Ensuring the assessment process is fair, just, and perceived as such by all parties

A study by Joe Smeeton and Kathy Boxall (2011) concluded that parents' voices are rarely heard in contested care proceedings when parents do not agree voluntarily to relinquish their children to the care of others. Although reports to the court are intended to present all evidence, however favourable or unfavourable it may be to birth parents, where the local authority has determined that children's future needs would best be met through long-term care, there is a tendency to emphasise parenting failures and shortcomings in order to establish that the threshold criteria have been reached. Once the children are removed, contact between them and their birth parents becomes supervised. Parents feel the pressure of such scrutiny and are often unaware of the criteria by which their parenting skills are being assessed:

> I was on like, walking on eggshells ... because I was scared of making one slight mistake where they could jump on me in court and say he's done that wrong .... So I was having to think everything through before I even said something, just so they couldn't use it against me, and it like, it put a lot of stress on me and pressure ... and no matter what I did, it was wrong.
>
> (Smeeton and Boxall, 2011: 6)

> It was supervised, which wasn't very comfortable for me, because I didn't know what to say to my children, I didn't know how to act with them or anything ... I didn't have a clue what they were looking for. All I knew, that it was supervised for the hour, both hours a week and I didn't know why.
>
> (Smeeton and Boxall, 2011: 6)

The experience of the three parents in their study was that once proceedings began, they felt that professionals were purposely betraying them and providing written evidence that was obscure and intended to confuse. These parents had little confidence in the legal system and felt poorly represented by their advocates in court. Birth parents often perceived a 'cosy' relationship between the various advocates and judges who appeared collectively to conspire against them. Although involvement of the local authority had initially focused on support for the family, as soon as concerns escalated, the focus shifted away from the parents to centre exclusively on the child.

The authors make a number of recommendations regarding the process of conducting parenting assessments, which I have summarised below:

- Provide clear information in accessible formats for birth parents about the roles and responsibilities of the different parties involved.
- Provide open and honest information about the processes involved and possible outcomes.
- Work with parents from a perspective which acknowledges that they have strengths and does not just emphasize their 'deficits' or failures.
- Ensure that assessment reports do not automatically read as a catalogue of failures and are written in as balanced a way as possible.
- Try to ensure that parents feel welcomed in the contact situation and also have a clear sense of the criteria on which they are being assessed and judged.
- Make every effort to ensure that the overall process is perceived by all parties as fair, impartial and just.

Empathy for parents' perspectives in the context of the child's needs being paramount

When the child's needs are paramount and evidence is being sought to show that the threshold criteria for significant harm or risk of significant harm have been met, it is easy to lose sight of the experience of the birth parent. I have found that the vast majority of parents are trying to meet the needs of their children whilst labouring under constraints bestowed by the poor parenting that they themselves received, lack of social and practical support, and inadequate personal or material resources. Parenting is a challenge under the best of circumstances. I remind myself that many of the children who are removed from the care of a parent will do their best to locate them at a future time out of curiosity, a need to know about their origins, when seeking to understand who they are and in the hope of receiving the love and affection that they feel is a right to expect from a birth parent. Despite the aim of permanence, many children will eventually reinstate some manner of contact with members of their birth family (Child Welfare Information Gateway, n.d.). Professional sensitivity to the experience of the parents and the way that their difficulties are recorded in notes and reports will in the longer term be of benefit for the child as an adult, trying to make sense of the experience of enforced separation.

Sensitivity to the experience of parents was found to be lacking in a study of social work students by Susan Gair (2010). Students were presented with a range of vignettes or narratives, intended to help them develop empathy through a process of reflection. Of four different narratives, that of a birth mother who had given up her child to adoption received the second lowest score in terms of its capacity to evoke empathy. Many of the students' comments appeared to convey 'conditional empathy' or what Gair refers to as 'dispassionate empathy'.

> I couldn't understand the passage – I found it too confusing to give any feeling …. I can understand the person is going through something quite profound.

> It's hard to determine the exact focus of Christine's need for help, so as a client I would ask her for more information.

> The situation is personal – the subjective nature of the scenario abandoned my interest to judge the feelings involved.

> (Gair, 2010: 45)

Students' explanation for their difficulties with empathy was that they lacked similar experiences in their own lives. They, 'could not link the experience to their own values or background, framed their comments with moral inference and demonstrated a remoteness or lack of willingness to emotionally engage' (Gair, 2010: 45). If workers lack empathy or compassion for groups of people who have experienced marginalisation and who may have been demonised in the popular press, then they may (inadvertently) contribute further to the social exclusion process, rather than maintaining a stance that works against further discrimination (Astell, 2004).

The part played by parenting assessments in outcomes for children

As a final precautionary note, I would have expected assessments of parenting to play a significant role in decisions concerning children's placements but this may not be so. Surprisingly, Sally Holland (2004) found that the assessment of practical parenting skills seemed to have had little effect on assessment outcome decisions. She states:

> Positive assessments of parenting skills were associated with all types of assessment recommendation. For example, some parents who were assessed as having good parenting skills had recommendations that they be reunited with their children, whilst others faced recommendations that they should not be reunited. Even fairly negative assessments of parenting skills led, occasionally, to decisions to rehabilitate children. It therefore might be suggested that, whilst parenting skills featured strongly in all of the assessment reports, this area was not seen as representing the decisive core of the assessment.

> (Holland, 2004: 98)

What matters in parenting?

In the late 1990s, Susan Golombok found herself being inundated by requests from the media about what really matters in parenting. The context was that there had been a rapid increase in the diversity of family structures in which children were being brought up. Traditional structures were being expanded to include gay and lesbian couples, divorced and single-parent families, step-families and children born through surrogacy. This led her to investigate the research base concerning the impact of family structure as against family process on parenting outcomes. Assumptions were being made that non-traditional structures were in some way inferior to the traditional nuclear family and would have negative impacts on children. Her aim in writing *Parenting: what really counts?* (Golombok, 2000) was to address the question, 'What aspects of family life really matter for children's healthy psychological development?' Her survey of the literature concluded that what matters is a secure attachment developed out of sensitively responsive reactions by carers to their infants, the ability to administer discipline whilst remaining warm and affectionate, the absence of significant levels of conflict between care-givers, support provided by the social context, and adequate basic care. A further factor is the impact of the temperaments of the children themselves.

A study conducted by Genelle Sawyer and colleagues (2002) reported an association between heightened potential for physical abuse and the follow-ing: parents' failure to complete secondary education, receiving little emotional support and practical help in the role of parent, deriving little satisfaction from parenting, having difficulty in accepting their child's expression of independence, and lacking confidence in effecting the parental role. For parents with profiles similar to those who were known to have physically harmed their child, dissatisfaction with the parental role was the most influential characteristic.

The literature on parenting assessments repeatedly refers to the difficulty in defining what constitutes 'good enough' parenting, a construct arising out of the writing of Donald Winnicott, by which he meant the care that was provided intuitively by mothers to their babies.

> You all know the kind of person who goes about saying, 'I simply *adore* babies'. But you wonder, do they love them? A mother's love is a pretty crude affair. There's possessiveness in it, appetite, even a 'drat the kid' element; there's generosity in it, and power, as well as humility. But sen-timentality is outside it altogether, and is repugnant to mothers.
>
> (Winnicott, 1964: 17)

I like Donald Winnicott's version of a mother's love because it equates with my first-hand experience and because it does not sound too unrealistic in terms of its demands. It sounds like a hard kind of love that allows me to feel anger towards my child and to take control and wield my power when I deem it necessary. It does not sound entirely unconditional and it allows that I have needs myself that may have to take precedence at times if I am to be able also to provide for my child.

A definition of good enough parenting provided by Masud Hoghughi and Nigel Speight is helpful in drawing attention to the changes in what is expected over time and cultural context:

> We can define good enough parenting as a process that adequately meets the child's needs, according to prevailing cultural standards which can change from generation to generation. Of course all children need physical care, nutrition, and protection. Over and above these basics, the child's emotional needs can be regarded under the following three headings: (1) love, care, and commitment; (2) consistent limit setting; (3) the facilitation of development.
>
> (Hoghughi and Speight, 1998: 294)

It follows from a 'loose' definition of good enough parenting that it may be accomplished in a diversity of ways. The results of longitudinal research that have followed the developmental outcomes for representative samples of children suggest that, 'some children arrive in the same place by following the same route, some follow different routes to reach the same destination, some set out along the same route but branch off to arrive in different places, and others follow pathways that never meet' (Golombok, 2000: 103). She concludes that what matters is the quality of family life and this cannot be determined by matters such as family structure.

> "Everybody has different parenting styles, as I say to the families, we don't have a tick chart that says "Yes, yes, yes, that's it – you're a brilliant parent". Everybody develops their own style of parenting and there is not a wrong or right way." (Family support worker)
>
> (Kellett and Apps, 2009: 3)

Acknowledgement that there is no single parenting route to positive outcomes for children encourages open-mindedness to different cultural practices. Research findings suggest that high levels of parental control are associated with the perception of hostility and rejection by white Americans and Puerto Ricans but with warmth and love by Korean adolescents (Rohner and Pettengill, 1985). This difference is attributed to cultural imperatives whereby Korean adults and their offspring honour an ideology which emphasises the, 'cardinal importance of the family, obedience to its authority, and deference to its elders' (Rohner and Pettengill, 1985: 524). Similar findings have been reported from Japan (Trommsdorf, 1985).

> The clearer rules for social behavior exhibited in some ethnic groups may be perceived by children as greater involvement and concern, and may

provide a sense of security, rather than be a source of risk. Moreover, some cultural groups that are viewed as engaging in harsher punishment and less overt positive affection (e.g., Chinese Americans) still have more positive child outcomes (academic achievement; Uba, 1994).

(Azar and Cote, 2002: 197)

The literature on the assessment of care-giving discusses parenting 'competence' and 'capabilities'. I find a problem with the term 'capabilities' since it requires a judgement of the carer's ultimate performance and this can only be inferred from current practice. We never really know what standard might be achieved through ongoing development. 'Competence' might also vary according to context; competent under what conditions? I prefer to consider care-giving under the headings of knowledge (that which can be stated or 'knowing that'), skills (that can be observed), values, and the attitudes which reflect underlying values. Consideration of values allows attention to cultural norms which will vary between and within different ethnic and social groups. Goals of parenting may be valued more or less highly than others (e.g. developing a child's autonomy as opposed to deference to others). I also include understanding, such as being able to make a critical choice from a range of possible actions which equates to flexibility and adaptability in meeting a child's changing needs. The use of these headings acknowledges that as a carer I may have these qualities in sufficient measure to meet my child's needs, even if they are not apparent in my current performance.

Sources of evidence

Information that sheds light on parenting skills comes from a number of different sources. Particularly in the care of younger children, observation of parent–child interaction is likely to provide useful information although interaction conducted under the constraints of observation may not always provide an accurate picture of how the parent behaves at home.

I have found that parents frequently have a great deal of difficulty in responding to unanticipated questions about the needs of the child, often responding with, 'He needs me to be there for him.' Even attempts to deconstruct what this means in practice seem to terminate in dead ends. Although parents may be unable to answer such questions, their knowledge is implicit and may be inferred from their interactions with the child. It is also possible to infer a lack of judgement and sensitivity from the actions that have been taken by a parent. If carers tell you that they have often shared a child's bed in order to avoid their partner's drunken violent attacks, this suggests that self-preservation has come before the child's needs for protection.

Nevertheless, the parent's and child's needs are bound together and at times, in order to ensure long term well-being, the parent may have apparently put their own needs first, such as prioritising going to work over remaining at home when a child is ill. In this example, the child's needs are prioritised in an indirect way.

Parents are often able to respond to questions about specific scenarios in ways that reveal sensitivity to a child. A father described to me how one of his children, who had been abandoned by her mother, would sleep fretfully and come to the top of the stairs, asking if he was going out. He described how he responded, 'Why no, darling, daddy's not going out, he's wearing his slippers,' thus providing not only verbal reassurance but evidence by which the child could judge the veracity of his statement. Scenarios put to parents can investigate their awareness of the need to be flexible as the child grows and her or his needs change. So, in addition to questions such as, 'What would you do if ...?', 'What are your thoughts when ...?' it is also possible to preface enquiries with, 'When he's six ... '

A major source of evidence about the parenting comes from the child's behaviour. There is a great deal of normal individual variation and temperamental difference which may account for problematic behaviour. But if the child's behaviour is relatively extreme, for example, excluded from mainstream school at the age of five, then this suggests that the child has not been subject to warm administration of boundaries or provided with appropriate guidance. If the child is very shy and withdrawn this may be an indicator of parenting difficulties. Then there is what the child tells you. Sometimes the child will not speak to you but a person who knows the child well will be able to provide a profile.

In summary, sources of evidence come from:

- Child behaviour
- Parent behaviour both currently and in the past
- Parent interview
- Data from child interviews including use of play materials
- Reports from other professionals and family members
- Questionnaires
- Data from other professional sources, e.g. police records, medical records

Useful data often emerges from other professionals who have known the child and parent for some time. Teachers, nursery staff and health visitors can provide useful insights because, as members of universal services, the parent is less likely to have regarded them as agents of social control.

A framework for the assessment of care-giving

The Child Welfare Information Gateway *et al.* (2010) identifies as important in parenting, the protective factors of Nurturing and Attachment (emotional warmth, guidance and boundaries), Knowledge of Parenting and Youth Development (understanding child development and able to put this into practice, stimulation), Parental Resilience (able to handle everyday stressors and able to accept and recognise their own challenges such as inappropriate parenting in their own childhood), Social Connections (from trusted and caring family and friends who provide emotional support, encouragement and assistance), and Concrete Support (to provide basic care).

These protective factors are regarded as critical for all parents and caregivers, regardless of the child's age, sex, ethnicity, economic status, special needs, or whether he or she is raised by a single, married, or divorced parent or other caregivers. All of these factors work together to reinforce each other; for example, parents are more likely to be resilient in times of stress when they have social connections and a strong bond with their child. Protective factors can provide a helpful conceptual framework for guiding any practitioner's work with children and their families.

In the UK, the Framework for the Assessment of Children in Need and their Families suggests that carers need to provide: Basic Care, Safety, Emotional Warmth, Stimulation, Guidance and Boundaries, and Stability. If I couple these with knowledge, skills, values, attitudes and understanding, flexibility and adaptability then I have a framework within which to research the match between this care-giver and a loose standard of 'good enough' (see Table 5.1).

Basic care

This refers to the practical issues of provision of food, drink, warmth, shelter, clean and appropriate clothing, personal and dental hygiene and engagement in securing universal services where necessary (doctor, dentist, optician), as outlined in the UK Common Assessment Framework (CAF) (Children's Workforce Development Council, 2009). Some authors (Horwath, 2007) also include under this heading evidence that care-givers are able to manage their finances in order to improve home conditions, prioritise spending and budget effectively to meet the needs of the child. For the purposes of considering the environment in which the child is being cared for the Home Conditions Assessment may be used (Cox and Bentovim, 2000; Davie *et al.*, 1984). Evidence of the extent to which the parent is meeting the child's basic care needs is most usually apparent in the physical appearance of the home and of the child, both of which are reflections of the carer's skills. But knowledge and understanding is also important. The carer needs to be able to recognise the signs when infants need a nappy change, when they are still hungry or satiated, the age-appropriateness of the help that they give to a child who is learning to feed her or himself, and sensitivity to symptoms of illness.

Even in the domain of basic care, standards and 'fashions' change. An example as I write is the recommended age at which infants should be introduced to solid food. Whilst it was common in the 1960s and 1970s to introduce infants to solids before the age of four months, the widespread advice since 2002 has been that the introduction of solid food should be deferred

Table 5.1 Data for Assessment of Care-giving (Based on Department of Health Framework for the Assessment of Children in Need and Their Families)

DH Framework	Skills	Knowledge and Understanding	Values and Attitudes	Flexibility and Adaptability
Basic Care	• Appearance of the child • Physical appearance of the home • Shows 'how to' make a bottle, change a nappy etc. • Child's account of who does what in running the household • How child has presented to foster carer in placement – degree of familiarity with routines • Evidence of planning and management of resources	• Can describe 'how to', e.g. make up a bottle • Can describe how to respond age-appropriately for child's developmental level, e.g. self-help/ feeding • Knows *when* to use skills, e.g. understands child's communication of hunger or pain	• In interview shows values regarding cleanliness, appropriate tidiness of home, even if not meeting own standards • Shows and describes value of health care and of organisation of home to support basic care needs	• Adapts expectations of child according to developing capability to contribute to own basic care • 'Reads' child if ill and makes judgement about appropriate action • Describes giving more choice and autonomy as child grows older
Safety	• Home observation of use of age-appropriate safety measures • Provides appropriate supervision of child in home and community • Protects from potentially dangerous others • Management of parental stress without recourse to substance misuse • Children's accounts of dangerous behaviour, domestic violence • Police records of convictions or call-outs	• Parent interview concerning knowledge of issues of safety • Pictorial stimuli and cartoons or scenarios may be useful to present potentially unsafe situations • Shows age-appropriate expectations regarding need to protect • Shows knowledge of changing issues of safety according to age of child	• In interview shows awareness of role of supervision in protection • Understands need to protect child from dangers in and out of home • Attitude towards substance misuse, mental health difficulties and domestic violence • Values preparation of older children for threats from environment and ensures child is educated regarding safe sex, drugs, etc.	• Evidence of ability to de-centre and show awareness of safety from child's perspective, e.g. emotional impact of domestic violence • Evidence that parent is able to adapt issues of safety according to the needs of the individual child, irrespective of age

(Continued)

Table 5.1 (Continued)

DH Framework	Skills	Knowledge and Understanding	Values and Attitudes	Flexibility and Adaptability
Stimulation	• Observation of parent-child interaction. Parent shows child-centred play • Interest shown in child/attention/listening • Reciprocal play and eye contact • Support for schooling and homework • Child's description of daily/weekend activities • Child's developmental status although a range of factors may account for any delays	• Parental knowledge of activities the child enjoys • Description of bedtime and morning routines • Describes activities built around child's interests and needs	• Beliefs about value of interaction and play with child • Beliefs about value of school work and child's learning	• Choice of appropriate play materials • 'Reads' child's interest or lack of engagement and adapts play • Builds from child-initiated activities
Emotional Warmth	• Observation of greetings, partings and warmth of interaction during contact • Body language and eye contact positive towards child • Shows sensitivity to child's feelings • Talks warmly to child • Observations of teachers, nursery staff regarding warmth, hostility shown to child	• Describes child's personality in detail • Shows empathy for child's perspective on events	• Describes child warmly in interview • Talks warmly *about* child in front of child and about role as a parent • Expresses satisfaction/dissatisfaction with the role of parent • The meaning of the child to the parent – motivation for conception, association of child with other important emotional events	• Sensitive to child's responses to shows of affection • Shows flexible expectations and allowances for child's behaviour

Guidance and Boundaries	• Child 'runs rings' round parent • Parent gives explanations for prohibitions • Parent focuses on building positive/reinforcing negative behaviours • Parent gives choices • Parent follows through on imperatives • Parents shouts/restrains/shows aggression towards child • Child describes parental approach	• Parent describes underlying approach to discipline and boundaries • Parent able to describe how approach is influenced by own experience of being parented • Able to give examples of managing child's behaviour constructively	• Carer recognises the role of parent's modelling of behaviour for child, e.g. respect, persuasion, compromise • Clear about when boundaries are flexible and when they may need to be rigid • Attitude to child's behaviour, e.g. sees child as being deliberately defiant, or presents as a conflict of interest between child and parent • Evidence of a clear set of family rules	• Parent shows flexible responses to individual presentation of child • Adapts boundaries to age, characteristics of child and individual circumstances
Stability	• Evidence of ongoing membership of a stable community and/or extended family • Frequency of house moves • Number of changes of school • Number of changes of care-giver/changes of partner • Stability of own mental health • Management of own emotions in presence of child	• Shows understanding of impact of instability on child • Able to describe how child's feelings are affected by changes and by unpredictable behaviour • Shows awareness of impact of own negative emotions and behaviours on child	• Talks about value of stability in interview • Impact of own experiences in childhood on approach to parenting • Recognises impact of own life choices on child's experience • Shows commitment to the integrity of the family and to child rearing	• Preparedness to subjugate own preferences and needs to sustaining child's relationships with extended family and neighbourhood

until the infant reaches six months of age (Department of Health, 2010; World Health Organization, 2011). The World Health Organization advice, whilst still extant in 2011, was first published in 2002. An article by Mary Fewtrell and colleagues published in the *British Medical Journal* in January 2011 caused something of a furore by suggesting that the evidence in support of this advice is ambiguous. The authors concluded that, 'Exclusive breast feeding for six months is readily defendable in resource poor countries with high morbidity and mortality from infections' (Fewtrell *et al.*, 2011: 210) but in developed countries may confer a *higher* risk of iron deficiency anaemia, food allergies and coeliac disease than the introduction of solid foods from the age of about four months. In the UK 2005 Infant Feeding Survey, less than 1 per cent of parents were following the recommendation to exclusively breast feed for six months although the trend was to delay the introduction of solids from an average of 15 weeks in 2000 to 19 weeks in 2005 (Bolling *et al.*, 2007). I have known failure to follow health visiting advice regarding the introduction of solid foods to be cited as one of the factors showing that the threshold criteria for 'significant harm' have been met.

Inevitably, the practitioner will exercise judgement in reaching conclusions regarding the parents' skills and knowledge in providing basic care. I have found that consultation with other professionals who visit the home is a useful check and balance when looking into matters of basic care, especially discussion with those who make unscheduled visits.

It is also helpful to talk to children about who takes responsibility in the home for making meals, washing up, vacuuming, shopping, making sure that they are clean and have brushed their teeth, washing clothes and mending things that are broken. These are relatively innocuous questions that children are usually happy to answer, showing pride in their independence and often describing in detail aspects of the care of the home.

> The house weren't clean. The cans were all over the place. When we were chucking sweet wrappers on the floor. There were toys all over the floor as well. It was just like messy and the toilet wouldn't work you know, the chain where you pull it. My dad was trying to .... It wouldn't flush and had loads of pooh in it so my dad had to get this glove on and get this stick and do that down the toilet. He kept doing it for hours and hours and had this mask over his face.

Where children have been removed from the care of their birth family, substitute care-givers are usually an excellent source of information about how they presented when first placed; whether they were used to routines, whether they knew how to wash themselves and clean their teeth, how independent they expected to be, what kinds of food they were used to, the appropriateness of their self-help skills and the stories that they have told about the care previously given. Whilst this information is usually enlightening, there are times when it seems that a child's skills initially dip on placement away from the birth family. This is presented as a rapid increase in facility following placement; learning to ride a bike in an afternoon, language explosions and rapid development of self-help skills. Such acceleration may represent a recovery of previously learned skills that have been disrupted by the emotional upheaval of separation from the birth family and I prefer to treat the meaning of them with caution.

Ensuring safety

In addition to ensuring that the child is protected from basic hazards in the home and garden such as open fires, trailing wires, ponds and hotplates, this dimension includes parental behaviour such as alcohol and drug use and domestic violence, protection from unsafe adults and other children, and safeguarding of the child from danger in the neighbourhood. One of the most obviously dangerous times is as a child begins to toddle and it becomes necessary to 'baby-proof' the environment with stair gates and guards to sources of heat, power and chemical products. Active toddlers typically need a carer's full attention, which is easily distracted in the presence of other adults, children and compelling conversations on mobile phones. Misuse of alcohol and drugs may leave a child inadequately supervised as the parent's judgement becomes impaired. Here are three different examples of situations that constitute potential danger to a child:

> They all knew I was smoking dope when they decided that I could look after Hannah. That's why it's so hard for me to give it up. I've had no incentive to give it up. This stuff doesn't cause me problems; it gets rid of so much heartache. I don't want to have all the feelings floating round in my head; that's what frightens me most; going back to the depression and suicide. I've even sat all night looking at a bottle of pills a couple of months ago. I thought what the hell am I thinking of? I am hepatitis B positive. People seem to have got the idea that I'm hepatitis C positive as well but it's not true and you can check it out with the staff at the GU clinic. I've talked to them about how to keep Hannah safe and they told me to lock up my lady shaver and tooth brush and make sure that there's no contact with body fluids. I know all about the dangers and I'm meticulous in keeping things out of her reach.

> As I was leaving the property Shelley (4) and Ben (6) came out of the house and grabbed onto the back of my car. I drove off slowly and turned the car round and they kept standing in the middle of the road until a truck came down. Last time I visited, after I left, Shelley came out with Milly in her pushchair and was walking up the footpath to cross the road. She wasn't tall enough to see over the top. When I raised this with their mum on my next visit she denied that the children had been out of the house on either occasion.

On my second visit the couple were reluctant to show me the kitchen. They said that it was clean and there were adequate supplies of food, but the dogs would have urinated on the floor because they had not been out that morning. The dogs barked and whined throughout the time I was there. When I visited for the third time the house was very cold and the couple told me that they had run out of coal on the previous evening and would be purchasing more later that day.

Although these examples show convincing evidence of risk to children, I have found it essential to explore the issues in as much depth as possible to see if the carers recognise the hazards, have the motivation to address them and the resources to effect change. Sometimes the best evidence comes from children. It is the level of detail of their accounts that can give a convincing portrayal of life at home.

Dad used to get Jenny (7) and me (8) to do the jobs round the house; washing the pots and doing the vacuuming. I had to clean the bathroom and the toilet because I was the oldest. I put bleach on the bath and sink and left it for a few minutes then I wiped them and rinsed them out while my dad used to sit at his computer. I had to be very careful with the bleach. You know the ones you press hard on the lid to get it open and squirt it round the toilet rim and then it all comes out. It was one of those child-proof ones and then when you put the lid on you twist it so it goes on properly. I spilt it on my hands once. Then when I went to tell my dad he told me to put it under some cold water fast or it'll start to burn. But you know me, I don't like to do what I'm told. I left it and it started burning so I did what my dad told me to.

My mum gets some white powder and puts it on some foil on a teaspoon and then she sets fire to it with her lighter and she breathes in the smoke with, like, a straw, and then she's right calm. When she can't get any she has a real bad head and I have to keep the others in the bedroom so we don't get on her nerves. Billie's only eight months so he doesn't understand and sometimes I have to put my hand over his mouth to stop him crying and making a noise because she can't stand a noise. Then when she has some she's right nice to us and she makes us breakfast and gets us clean clothes ready for school.

One night Kelly, Amie and me were being naughty, 'cause we ran across the road when my dad went to the shop. We ran across the road to get some sweets at night time and there were a car coming and it nearly ran us over. Daddy came back and we were downstairs eating sweets.

Issues of safety inevitably change as a child grows older and parents will need to be able to adapt to allow for growing independence, showing understanding of these developing needs. The establishment of trust and openness in the relationship between parent and child will have been critical if parents are to be alive to the activities of their teenagers. Where is the line between freedom and independence, continuing supervision and oversight when a child has access to the internet, social networking sites and emails, the task being made more challenging by the child's probable greater facility with the relevant technology? At what age and degree of maturity might a child be allowed to play out unsupervised, within what distance from home and during what hours of the day? The answers to these questions are likely to vary according to the nature of the surrounding neighbourhood and the extent of involvement of the community in the care of all of its children. Can older children adequately supervise their younger siblings? Growing children need to learn to be street-wise, to be educated about safe sex and to understand the impact of substance misuse. In my experience parents are often ill-prepared and anxious about discussing such subjects with their children, often relying on the school to introduce and educate on these issues. Opposite-sex parents often say how uncomfortable they would feel talking about menstruation, contraception, erections and wet dreams with their sons and daughters, even when they have been disadvantaged through ignorance themselves.

Stimulation

Probably the most interesting source of stimulation for a child is another being. Even newborns show a preference for a care-giver's face (Pascalis *et al.*, 1995). Toys are not essential to stimulating play as there is plenty of interest in the natural environment and in imaginative conversations between the carer and child. Interest shown in the child, attentive listening and conversational turn-taking are indicators of a care-giver's skills in providing stimulation to the growing child. Selection of age-appropriate toys and activities can show insight and understanding of the child's stage of development. Evidence is also provided by the care-giver's support to the child's socialisation with other children and adults, and the encouragement of regular school, playgroup or nursery attendance.

In addition to data obtained from first-hand observation, one of the ways of accessing information about levels of stimulation is to enquire about the kinds of activities that the child enjoys. Descriptions of bed-time routines are often enlightening, revealing whether children take the major responsibility for putting themselves to bed or benefit from some conversation, a story and a routine that involves repetition and reciprocity.

If a child is set homework, parents can encourage a positive attitude towards learning by ensuring that it is completed and supporting the child's learning. Attendance at parents' evenings and other school events shows the child that the parent values active participation in the opportunities for learning and socialisation that schools provide.

Praise, warmth and encouragement are discussed by some authors under the heading of Stimulation but I prefer to consider these within the category of Emotional Warmth.

Emotional warmth

This dimension of the Framework for the Assessment of Children in Need and their Families is likely to reflect the nature of the bond between the care-giver and child. In my view, along with the maintenance of boundaries and routines, showing a child warmth, affection and positive regard is the most important aspect of parenting. Children who have been shown love and affection by care-givers who are reasonably sensitive to their needs and who strive to understand the meaning of the child's behaviour are likely to grow up with a sense of self-worth and of their own value which will see them through the ups and downs of their ongoing experience. There is a great deal of evidence to suggest that even children who have experienced corporal punishment ('the use of physical force with the intention of causing a child to experience pain but not injury for the purposes of correction or control of the child's behavior' (Straus, 1994: 4)) and/or physical abuse do not show evidence of negative outcomes providing that they simultaneously experience high levels of emotional support and do not feel rejected (Gershoff, 2002; McLoyd and Smith, 2002; Rohner *et al.*, 1996). It is the meaning of the punishment made by the child in the context of the parent–child relationship that matters.

In a study by Joanne Kellett and Joanna Apps (2009), practitioners made judgements of warmth and engagement between the parent and child through observation of the parent-child relationship, noting how carers talked to the child, shows of demonstrable affection and how parents talked *about* their children. Professionals appeared to make a judgement of the balance of positive and negative messages given to the child. Concerns were elevated if the parent's communication to and about the child was largely negative:

> [Parents] would say very negative things. They would say, 'He's a night-mare, he's naughty, he's horrible, he's mad' in front of the child, they would use extremely negative words. They would have their faces looking extremely negative and angry. They would stop or say things to the child in a very negative way. 'Stop that. Don't do that. I didn't say that to you', that kind of tone they would have with the child, which is continually negative. So all that they're saying to you or to the child is negative. You don't have to look for any other markers. That's [a] very cruel fact.

> (Paediatrician 1, area 1)
> (Kellett and Apps, 2009: 14)

An example I can think of is a parent who [often] greeted or left a child without showing any kind of affection, just [saying], 'Go on, in you go' or picking up time, 'Come on you', or instantly swearing and shouting at them, even if the child has got a picture in their hand or something to show them, it's ignored and they're pulled along ... I think you do pick [that] up.

(Teacher 9, area 2)
(Kellett and Apps, 2009: 15)

In Kellett and Apps' research, practitioners looked for verbal and physical expressions of care and affection, positive body language, mutual eye contact, and whether children were offered encouragement, support and praise. A key theme to emerge in defining 'good enough' care was that parents appeared to try their best within their means to give priority to their children's needs by being available, spending time with them, paying them attention and providing consistent care. Suggested areas of focus for observations of parent-child interaction by Daniel Hynan (2003) included signs of emotional attachment, communication skills, reasonableness of parental expectations for children, the appropriateness of toys and other materials brought to the session and how children are addressed.

In assessing the dimensions of knowledge and understanding, skills, values, and flexibility in relation to emotional warmth, it is appropriate to focus on what carers show in their behaviour, their knowledge of this child, their attitudes about the desirability of showing positive behaviours towards the child and their capability to be flexible in the way that they show their affection. Lack of parental empathy is associated with poorer outcomes for children (Kilpatrick, 2005; Kilpatrick and Hine, 2005). Parental empathy for the child can be explored by asking care-givers to describe their child's individual personality or character and by asking them to de-centre and describe some events from their child's perspective. I sometimes do this by asking the parent to tell me how they think their child would reply if I were to ask them a specific question about their home life. This can involve what the child would have been thinking and feeling.

A parent's description of a child can vary from, 'he's just like me', or 'she's funny' to a level of detail that shows the extent of parents' knowledge of the child's personality and their attempts to understand and accommodate the individual foibles of the child.

Jamie-Lee prefers to play with the younger children and she can seem a bit immature compared with other children of her age. It might be because she was quite slow to talk and a bit awkward about talking to other children. She's just beginning to enjoy pretend games and really loves dressing up as a fairy and a nurse. She's begun to suck her thumb or finger and she likes to play peek-a-boo if I wrap her in a blanket.

At bedtime she wraps her Thomas blanket round her and likes to have a lullaby. She knows if I change anything. She has a very loving side to her nature. She came with me to visit my friend in a young disabled unit. She asked if she could feed her. She was very loving and calm and was fantastic with her. If I hurt myself she wants to kiss it better.

Jamie-Lee likes books and she's learning new words really quickly. She likes me to sing nursery rhymes and songs, she's learning her colours and she can count up to ten. As a character she's really stubborn and strong willed to the extent that she's prepared to deprive herself of something just to stick to her guns. On the way back from nursery she was holding two teddies, one in each hand. I asked her to give me one because she had to hold my hand to cross the road. She didn't want to let go and when I insisted she said that now she didn't want either. One day I went to help her to move her bike because she'd got it stuck in some paving stones. She was determined to do it herself and wouldn't listen to explanations. Her mood changed and she started slamming things around and when I came in she put the bike back where it had been even though it meant she couldn't ride it. A bit later she came in and was a bit weepy. She sobs when she doesn't get her own way. One day she really cried for a simple thing so I hugged her until she stopped then I tried to get her to explain what was wrong.

Not all carers have this level of verbal facility and may need prompts and encouragement to describe specific examples that illustrate the child's temperament and behaviour.

Guidance and boundaries

In Kellett and Apps' study, guidance and boundaries were seen as central by practitioners in all professional groups. Guidance involved care-givers taking responsibility for their child, being in control and setting clear limits and boundaries.

> You can actually see a child that's absolutely running rings round the parent, to the point where you almost feel that that child could be putting themselves into danger .... So a child who habitually, for example, leaves the school and you see them just run straight ahead and across a road and they're not called back to hold a hand or something or they arrive at least three, four minutes before the parent and the parent just says very offhand, 'Oh he always runs away from me and across that road'.
>
> (Teacher 9, area 2)
> (Kellett and Apps, 2009: 30)

This is one domain in which parents often show understanding which is not necessarily reflected in action. One reason frequently given is that their contact with their child is limited and they do not want to be refusing the child's requests or imposing sanctions during the short period of time that they have together – an understandable attitude. This is also an area in which intervention is often provided through parenting classes, and with which many parents engage.

One purpose of implementing boundaries for children's behaviour is to help them to learn to regulate their own emotions and behaviour in order to fit into their community by building self-discipline. Parents can accomplish this through demonstrating and modelling appropriate behaviour, through discussion and explanation and through implementing consequences when a boundary is violated. Children's accounts sometimes show evidence of a lack of structure and organisation to the child's day:

> Sometimes we used to stay up late and sometimes a little bit late. Annie's gone first sometimes and I gone second and me and the baby and my mum gone to bed together sometimes. We was all in my mum's room and Jordan slept in his own bedroom sometimes. There were two beds and we broke my mum's bed by jumping on it and my mum had to get another bed. She's getting another bed now. Sometimes we rolled out of bed and fell on the floor and it bangs doesn't it?

Observation of parent–child interaction will provide information about whether the parent models politeness, consideration and cooperation. Do parents encourage considerate behaviour or inadvertently encourage temper tantrums, whining, shouting or rudeness by following it with something that the child finds rewarding? Do parents give explanations and focus on what the child can do rather than what the child cannot do? Penelope Leach (1979: 435) gives the example: 'You can't leave your tricycle there,' compared with, 'Put your tricycle over by the wall so that nobody trips over it.' The former statement presents a challenge which is inclined to generate resistance. Is the parent clear in explaining to the child what is required? 'Behave yourself,' does not give the child information about what behaviour the parent wants or the reasons why.

In some circumstances clear 'dos' and 'don'ts' are needed. These are the rules that keep a child safe and need to be implemented with as much consistency as possible so that the child recognises that the activity is forbidden. This is because any violation may result in harm. They include imperatives such as never crossing the road without an adult, never poking anything into an electrical socket, and never going with a stranger. Can the carer describe the rules that they operate for the child's behaviour and how they ensure that the child complies? Is this consistent with observations of the child and parent together in contact? How many rules does the parent have and how often do they give the child an instruction? Are they thinking about obedience and disobedience or are they thinking in terms of a conflict of interest between themselves and the child (he wants to carry on playing, I want him to go to bed now) and how to induce cooperation through compromise and discussion.

Values come into play in this domain in the form of beliefs about the most appropriate ways to bring up children. These are sometimes reflected in 'sayings' that are widespread in a culture at a particular time such as, 'Spare the rod and spoil the child.' Parents are influenced in their beliefs about parenting by their own socialization and past experiences as well as the cultural context and dominant discourse about child rearing. Since 1960, Diana Baumrind of the University of California at Berkeley (cited in Azar and Cote, 2002) has interviewed and observed parents' child rearing styles and methods of exerting discipline. She proposed a typology of styles of parenting linking emotional warmth with the provision of guidance and boundaries. She originally described 'authoritative', 'authoritarian' and 'permissive' parenting styles, later adding a further category of 'neglectful' parenting characterised by care-givers who provide little warmth, exercise little control, are pre-occupied with their own issues and show disinterest in the child. Teachers can often provide information that informs the assessment of this kind of parenting:

> There are people that we never see ... the ones that don't turn up to parents' evenings, children are constantly late, lots of unauthorised days or unauthorised absence. Parents who send their children to school on their own, even some of the young ones ... and then parents who really don't engage when things go wrong and we want to offer help. I guess all of those are risky.
>
> (Teacher 1, area 1)
> (Kellett and Apps, 2009: 30)

Authoritative parenting involves a high degree of control over children, coupled with warm displays of affection. In contrast, although an authoritarian style additionally involves exercising a high level of control this is coupled with less warmth and greater emotional detachment. Permissive parenting involves a lack of control and few demands made, coupled with expressions of warmth and affection. Baumrind (1978) argued that children who have been subject to authoritative parenting have the 'best' outcomes, showing competence in their positive relationships with peers, cooperation with adults and engagement in purposeful activities.

Stability

A central aspect of stability is an enduring functional relationship between child and care-giver/s. Stability is also conferred by the maintenance of ongoing affectional relationships between the primary care-giver and a wider family and friendship network. Protecting the child from too many moves of home and school helps to create a sense of continuity and stability although this may not be possible in travelling cultures and the armed forces where security is provided through continuity of care rather than continuity of environment. Recognition and understanding of the child's need for day-to-day predictability can be shown in interview and demonstrated in action.

Threats to stability in wider society include poverty, extreme inequality, rapid population growth, environmental degradation and poor governance (Verstegen *et al.*, 2005). These features are believed to make societies more vulnerable to violence, conflict and breakdown. I am struck by the parallels with factors that can increase the likelihood of family breakdown. As family size increases and resources, both emotional and practical, become stretched, so stress increases on parental capability to maintain the home, manage and respond to everyone's needs. Parents' forward-thinking and planning for children's future well-being can be shown through their insight into the way their growing family has been planned and their thoughtful management of resources.

Instability is associated with drug and alcohol misuse and compromised mental health. 'Many adults have times when they suffer from anxiety or depression, have unstable relationships with partners or drink alcohol to excess and increasing numbers have used drugs, both licit and illicit, but this does not mean that they are poor parents. It is the extremity or combination of these stressors, particularly the association with violence, which may place children at risk of significant harm' (Cleaver, 2002: 263). All of these difficulties tend to have social consequences for families. Living standards are impacted as jobs may be lost and family income reduced. Financial resources may be diverted from the provision of food, utilities and clothing towards funding of the dependent substance. Social isolation may result as the quality of contact with friends and family deteriorates, and partner violence may erupt with the attendant negative impacts upon the children. When parents have difficulty in organising their day-to-day lives, school attendance may become sporadic, children may lack appropriate supervision, health checks are missed and physical needs may be neglected. When children present at school with poor personal hygiene and a dishevelled appearance this is likely to impact negatively on their peer relationships, jeopardising friendships and engendering a sense of shame.

Here is an account by a parent given in response to questions designed to explore some of these factors, and in particular to assess his knowledge of skills in parenting that would meet the child's emotional needs. He is describing a three-year-old, not his own child, for whom he wishes to provide a home because he looks after her older brother and, on account of their history, believes that the bond between the siblings means that a joint placement is crucial for their future well-being.

She has got one or two problems. She has a lot of tantrums. She won't listen to me when I talk to her. She blanks me. She has this thing about not wanting to hold my hand crossing the road. She's still tugging away from me. I've explained about the traffic and cars. She won't put her coat on when it's cold. I don't understand the reason. There are a lot of ways she'd have to change. I think it'd take time. I think she'd probably get used to how me and Ben's living; time to blend in. Perhaps she's had a lot of her own way at Penny's (current foster carer). I don't really know how she's treated there. I don't really like Melonie's tantrums. It goes through my mind, thinking am I doing the right thing. I couldn't cope with that for the rest of my life. I said that week (a week in April when Melonie was scheduled to stay with him whilst her carer was on holiday) will be a testing point for me and I will tell the truth. She's a lovely little girl and I can cope with her and I do cope with her. Little ways I never had to cope with Ben, especially that ignoring me. It's probably what she's experienced living with her mum. If she's been bawling and shouting; been blanking her. Melonie wouldn't have understood her mum's depression and upset. She might have thought her mum didn't care. Penny has done well with her. I can't see Penny letting her get away with it. When she's trying it on with me she could be doing it because she's got a bit of freedom.

There was a time when she didn't like Terry picking her up. I had some right do's with her, having tantrums in the yard not wanting to go, proper throwing herself around. I had to carry her from the bedroom. Penny managed to carry her to the car. She were nearly upside down. And you could hear her proper screaming and that happened three times, a proper tantrum. She weren't having none of it. She wouldn't listen to you, throwing herself on the floor and shoving on her knees. I'm being honest, if that happened every day it would be a proper nightmare. I'd just try and calm her down and talk to her. I should imagine she'd have to have a good reason to paddy like that. I think there was a lot of fear in her. She might have been frightened. I think it's because she didn't want to leave Ben because they'd just got settled. Either that or she doesn't like men, but I've not seen her around other men so I don't know. Because there was a problem at school some months back. They'd got nobody to pick Melonie up so they sent a support worker; a man she'd never seen before and she was hysterical. I were a bit annoyed about that actually because social services know Melonie's background so why send a man who she's never met before?

In my view this father showed the following strengths:

- the capability to de-centre and understand how a child might be feeling from a child-centred perspective

- recognition of the need to be truthful with the children
- an ability to see challenging behaviour as the result of underlying emotions such as fear
- the ability to interpret children's behaviour in a number of different ways
- preparedness strongly to defend a child against criticism, negativity or thoughtlessness
- showing no resentment towards the children having good relationships with other adults in addition to himself
- acceptance of Melonie's need to grieve the loss of her foster carer and the need to allow her time to adjust
- recognition of his own limitations
- awareness of age-appropriate responses to children
- recognition of the need to allow relationships to grow rather than forcing them
- a preference for compassionate explanations of Melonie's mother's difficulties in his explanations to the children

I have found it more useful to collect such information through an open-ended interview and not only through the completion of a standard checklist or questionnaire. The data can always be transferred later to a questionnaire measure if necessary or desirable. My experience suggests that the undivided attention of the practitioner helps parents to feel that they are being seen as respected individuals with valuable views and opinions of their own. This is in the spirit of the Framework for the Assessment of Children in Need and their Families (Department of Health, 2000a: 15):

> Undertaking an assessment with a family can begin a process of understanding and change by key family members. A practitioner may, during the process of gathering information, be instrumental in bringing about change by the questions asked, by listening to members of the family, by validating the family's difficulties or concerns, and by providing information and advice. The process of assessment should be therapeutic in itself. This does not preclude taking timely action either to provide immediate services or to take steps to protect a child who is suffering or is likely to suffer significant harm. Action and services should be provided according to the needs of the child and family, in parallel with assessment where necessary, and not await completion of the assessment.

Whilst I have proposed a structure for thinking about parenting based on the Framework for the Assessment of Children in Need and Their Families, other options are available. These include that proposed by Peter Reder and Clare Lucey (1995) which addresses the parent's relationship to the role of parenting, the parent's relationship with the child, family influences, interaction with the external world and the potential for change.

Formal assessment measures of parenting

A number of more formal measures of parenting have been developed in research settings, some of which are described below. Whilst they can be used with caution to provide additional perspectives on aspects of parenting, the choice of measure is not critical.

Home Observation and Measurement of the Environment (HOME)

The HOME Inventory (Home Observation and Measurement of the Environment) (Caldwell and Bradley, 2001; Cox, 2008; Totsika and Sylva, 2004) comprises subscales and items that have been shown to be associated with the developmental tasks of childhood. There are different versions for different ages of children (birth to three, 3–6, 6–10, and a fourth edition for young people aged 10–15 years). The subscales include 'learning materials', 'language stimulation', 'academic stimulation', 'physical environment', 'parental responsivity', 'variety', 'acceptance' and 'modelling'. A judgement is made regarding the presence or absence of behavioural markers such as, 'Parent holds child close for 10–15 minutes per day,' 'Parent converses with child at least twice during visit,' Child is encouraged to learn colours,' 'Child is encouraged to learn patterned speech,' 'Some delay in food gratification is expected,' and 'TV is used judiciously.' It has been argued that there is no single conclusion that can be reached about the way that the HOME Inventory is appropriately used in different cultures and contexts because, 'the instrument reflects a western theoretical background and has been normed on middle class samples, thus relating more to a western-type middle class family setting' (Totsika and Sylva, 2004: 28).

The measure usefully provides specific time limits as a framework for the conversation between care-giver and assessor by focusing on the facts of a very specific day of the week (yesterday). This may encourage the use of evidence and factual information. However, there is no standardised procedure for administration and the binary yes/no scale makes for easier scoring but does not capture more subtle distinctions. If the parent reports that the child has been physically chastised on one occasion during the previous week this is scored as a 'yes', the same score that would be obtained if the child was being physically punished several times every week. Vasiliki Totsika and Kathy Sylva (2004: 33) conclude that, 'HOME might be considered a broad but valid brush for painting the child's caring environment.'

Marschak Interaction Method (MIM)

The Marschak Interaction Method (MIM) (Lindaman *et al.*, 2000) is a structured approach to observing and assessing the nature of the relationship between two people. It employs the categories 'Structure', 'Engagement', 'Nurture' and 'Challenge'. The dimension 'structure' concerns the skills of the parent in setting limits and providing a structured environment involving the implementation of guidance and boundaries. 'Engagement' captures the parent's interest in the child and attunedness to the child's feelings and behaviours. 'Nurture' addresses the adult's provision of comfort, soothing and care to the child whilst 'challenge' reflects the parent's efforts to help the child accomplish tasks at a developmentally appropriate level. The parent and child are given nine cards that direct specific interactions relating to the four assessed areas. Their task is to complete the activities outlined on the cards. The method aims to elicit behaviour which allows an assessment of the strengths and weaknesses of the relationship between child and adult. There are a number of variants of the assessment method suited to different age groups from pre-natal to adolescent. Dependent upon age of the child, the parent–child dyad is presented with tasks such as puzzles, block building, pat-a-cake, peek-a-boo, doll-play, naming objects and nursery rhymes.

The MIM is a clinical measure which has not been standardised on a normative population sample. Assessments are qualitative whilst being undertaken within a defined structure, and the authors argue that extensive clinical experience is essential to its administration. Generally a MIM session takes about 30–45 minutes and is recorded with a view to follow-up discussion with the parents (Brooke, 2004). The MIM materials can be obtained from the Theraplay Institute at: http://www.theraplay.org/18401.html.

Needs Jigsaw

The Needs Jigsaw (see Figure 5.1) was developed by Kathy Stevens of Wakefield Social Services as a means of supporting practitioners' discussions with parents about their children's needs and developmental status. The pieces represent different domains of a child's needs which are added to the jigsaw when participants raise a relevant topic in interview. Missing pieces may represent gaps in knowledge with which the parent may need support. There is second version for adolescents and young people. They can be obtained from the Educational Resource Centre, Crigglestone, West Yorkshire WF4 3LB or: http://www.familyworkresources.co.uk/resources.htm.

Play-based Assessment

A range of play-based approaches to assessment of interaction between carer and young child is described by Lori Roggman and colleagues (2000). They focus on the carer's involvement in pretend play which is regarded as significant in the child's development of symbolic representation. The adult's involvement has been found to facilitate higher levels and longer periods of such play. A focus on games can show the skills of the parent in playing together with their children in ways that involve turn-taking, reciprocity and matching the degree of complexity to the child's age and developmental

Figure 5.1 Needs jigsaw.

level. Such games include banging a drum together, the adult stacking blocks and the child knocking them over, and rolling a ball back and forth.

The infant's visual attention to the mother's activity and mutual gaze are further indicators of the quality of the relationship that is developing. Both may look at the same object or one may watch the other play. Parents may use attention-directing strategies and toy sharing or exchange, whereby the adult helps the child to manipulate objects. Interaction may be characterised by varying degrees of affective expression with smiling, social referencing, physical contact and proximity seeking.

Such observations have been carried out in free play situations and may also be structured. The adult's behaviour may be restricted by the instructions given, or by controlling the infant through the use of a high chair or fixed seat. It has been argued that the quality of information is enhanced by unobtrusive observation (e.g. use of a one-way screen) and by allowing time for acclimatisation to the unusual circumstance of the observation.

Working Model of the Child Interview (WMCI)

The WMCI (Zeanah *et al.*, 1993, Zeanah and Benoit, 1995) is a one-hour semi-structured interview which aims systematically to assess the parent's subjective experience of the child. The interview focuses on the child's character, challenging behaviour, parental expectations and the relationship with the child. The approach involves eliciting the carer's account of the parent-child relationship from pregnancy to the present. Coding of either a recording or transcript of the interview is carried out, resulting in classification of the carer's working model as 'balanced', 'disengaged', or 'distorted'. The interview focuses on the parent's relationship with one child and has similarities to the Adult Attachment Interview. It has been shown to have reasonable reliability and validity (Benoit *et al.*, 1997), although scoring is not regarded as necessary when the interview is used for clinical purposes. The interview can be downloaded from: http://www.oaimh.org/newsFiles/Working_Model_of_the_Child_Interview.pdf and from: http://cooscurry-courts.org/ZTTWorkshop/Site/doc/Conference%20Materials/new_materials/WMCI%20bio%20parent.pdf.

In addition to these observational, interactional and interview methods, there are many helpful questionnaires that have been devised with a view to assessing quality of parenting. These are listed and described in Appendix 3.

Prioritising data in assessments of care-giving

Which, if any, types and sources of data have primacy when making an assessment of parenting? Data that gives an indication of the parent's capacity to provide empathic, child-focused parenting has been argued as the tipping point by Terry Donald and Jon Jureidini (2004). These authors believe that behavioural observations made of interactions between carer and child are of limited value. Their first priority in judging parenting is to assess the adequacy of the emotional relationship between parent and child. First, the parent must recognise and accept responsibility for the harm caused, so assessment ideally follows rather than precedes the establishment of significant harm. The assessment explores the extent to which parents not only accept the harm and their role in perpetrating the harm, but are able to 'de-centre' and show empathy for the child's experience. Parents need to demonstrate that they are able to avoid dangerous impulsiveness and take responsibility for their own behaviour. The authors cite the following example:

> A young infant was admitted with a fracture dislocation of one elbow and several metaphyseal fractures. No explanation was proffered to account for the injuries, which were judged to be inflicted. A 'standard parenting assessment', which surveyed the three domains (parental factors, child factors and environmental factors), failed to identify the presence of any major adverse factors in any of the domains. The parents were well educated, had good supports and the child had no handicaps. When the injuries were reviewed with the parents, the child's father was clearly distressed, seeking reassurance that the pain resulting from the fractures

would not affect the baby long term. However, the mother seemed not to share his reaction, only expressing concern as to what disease the baby must have to cause such fractures. Further careful exploration failed to identify any capacity for the mother to feel what it must have been like for the baby. Thus, while the 'standard assessment' did not identify any grounds for concern, we concluded from the mother's lack of empathy for the baby that her ongoing care of her infant, in the context of the unexplained inflicted injuries, would continue to expose the baby to high risk of further harm.

(Donald and Jureidini, 2004: 15)

Whilst I agree with Donald and Jureidini that parental empathy for the child is crucial, I believe that it is also incumbent on professionals involved in such testing and distressing processes involving the potential permanent separation of a child from the parents, to show empathy themselves in the manner in which investigations are conducted. There are many reasons why a parent in the scenario above may *appear* to lack empathy. In the following extract Pamela Davies, a principal lecturer in criminology, describes her own experience as a parent 'victim' of the child protection system:

On the evening of his first birthday in April 2005 our son Frederick rolled off the sofa in our living room. The sofa is low and the floor is carpeted. Afterwards he seemed fine. His father was in the room nearby and I was watching from the hall. However, 2 days later, it was obvious that Frederick had sustained a head injury. A visit to hospital resulted in a child protection investigation .... During the initial examinations made on Frederick, I explained what I knew of the swelling to nurses, doctors and consultants. As I did so, it became clear to me that this was appearing unsatisfactory. My perception of their disquiet seems to have suggested that I had caused the injury and was attempting to conceal this ....

I was telling all I knew. A crime and/or abuse had not taken place and none of this was enough to preserve our family .... It seemed that a strong basis from which to challenge the absence of an obvious explanation for a serious unexplained injury was another paediatrician. This centring and ranking of the experts left me feeling even more powerless in the process of which I was a key part. My 'evidence' was of a lower status than that of professionals and there were rankings of professional evidence too. I had no ability to stop the system being put into gear, I was powerless to stop it going into overdrive and felt powerless in preventing it from crashing .... It seemed to me that in the social service system, 'parents are treated as guilty until proven innocent' (Jardine, 2006). Our outcome felt even less satisfactory and more victimizing. We were never proven or deemed innocent.

(Davies, 2011: 201–6)

Data from all of the sources described above can be integrated to answer some of the questions posed at the outset of the investigation:

- What strengths and weaknesses/areas of needed development does this person bring to the role and tasks of parenting?
- To what extent does the adult understand and meet the emotional and physical needs of the children?
- Is the person able to provide appropriate protection for the children?
- What is the person's understanding and acceptance of any concerns about her or his parenting?

Interventions and sources of support

Although Article 8 of the Human Rights Act does not require that domestic authorities make *endless* attempts at maintaining children in their birth family it does require that they take all steps that can reasonably be demanded to facilitate the maintenance of the family or reunification of children and their parents (English, 2011). In order to establish whether care-givers can meet the standards needed for a child to remain safely in their care, it follows that they must be given an opportunity to improve.

Effecting meaningful change is a complex and challenging task whether this be for individuals or families. In making the changes that are demanded in order to gain approval to look after my children, I may be motivated extrinsically or intrinsically. Learning and change that is motivated by recognition of the need for change, interest in changing, a willingness to take responsibility for my weak areas, and a desire to accomplish particular goals are positive indicators for success. If I am told to change or if I participate in prescribed interventions under duress in order to 'get the authorities off my back' I am externally motivated and, at least initially, may only be concerned to 'pass' the assessment in order to satisfy external demands. Whether such change will be sustained after the intervention comes to an end is in question. It follows that whatever the specific intervention prescribed, the relationship between intervener and parent-participant is crucial to outcome. Too often I think that the relationship is experienced by care-givers in children's proceedings as shown in Figure 5.2.

Whatever the intervention, if they are to become intrinsically motivated, carers need to believe that the professional helper is on their side. And in my view, being on the side of the child usually also means being on the side of the carer. A variety of relationship models put the worker and client alongside each other. In an educational context, the term 'critical friend' has been used to denote a relationship of trust which allows for constructive challenge:

> A critical friend, as the name suggests, is a trusted person who asks provocative questions, provides data to be examined through another lens, and offers critique of a person's work as a friend. A critical friend takes

Figure 5.2 Dragon cartoon.

the time to fully understand the context of the work presented and the outcomes that the person or group is working toward. The friend is an advocate for the success of that work .... Many people equate *critique* with *judgement,* and when someone offers criticism, they brace themselves for negative comments .... Critical friendships, therefore, must begin through building trust.

(Costa and Kallick, 1993: 50)

The process of critical friendship involves people in selecting and describing a practice about which they would like feedback and identifying the desired outcomes for the interaction between them. This puts the learner firmly in control. The critical friend asks questions in order to develop understanding of the issues and context, gives feedback which involves more than cursory praise and provides a perspective that helps to illuminate the issues. Further open-ended questions encourage the learner to see the issue from multiple perspectives. What I take from the notion of a critical friend for the purposes of assessment in family proceedings is the usefulness of a questioning approach and the centrality of trust. Telling things to people who don't want to meet with you anyway is highly unlikely to bring about change. As a game show contestant (http://www.youtube.com/watch?v=LsOm3Yt7nR0) said, 'I'm listening to what you're saying but I only hear what I want to.' Far more effective is the judicious use of questions, recognising that people have to change their own minds. Establishing trust is particularly challenging because families in court proceedings usually have not invited the worker to become involved.

Ideas about effective working relationships can also be drawn from the coaching and mentoring literature. Coaching and mentoring processes are described as follows by David Megginson and David Clutterbuck (2005):

> Coaching relates primarily to performance improvement (often over the short term) in a specific skills area. The goals, or at least the intermediate or sub-goals, are typically set with or at the suggestion of the coach. While the learner has primary ownership of the goal, the coach has primary ownership of the process. In most cases, coaching involves direct extrinsic feedback (i.e. the coach reports to the coachee what s/he has observed.)
>
> Mentoring relates primarily to the identification and nurturing of potential for the whole person. It can be a long-term relationship, where the goals may change but are always set by the learner. The learner owns both the goals and the process. Feedback comes from within the mentee – the mentor helps them to develop insight and understanding through intrinsic observation (i.e. becoming more aware of their own experiences).
>
> (Megginson and Clutterbuck, 2005: 4)

I am not arguing for interventions by coaches, mentors or critical friends with families who are struggling, but rather that a mind-set in the worker which draws on some of these ideas can support the development of constructive relationships out of which learning and development may emerge. The features common to these approaches are the encouragement of self-kindness, self-compassion and self-celebration, with the assistance of someone who genuinely minds about me and wants to see my life improve.

I think it behoves me as a professional to maintain an orientation of kindness and compassion to the people I have been tasked to assess, even when I abhor the actions of a care-giver who has harmed or even killed a child. Such an attitude does not mean that the needs of the child have to move from centre stage or that children will be left in dangerous or damaging circumstances. Maintaining an empathic stance towards parents can pose a serious challenge and I am assisted in the task by bringing to mind this adult as a child. What hurt this adult as a child that has led to such repugnant acts? In my assessment I want to know. And if I am to intervene in a useful way, I want to keep this understanding in mind as I work out how to build a relationship from which he or she may derive benefit. Within this common frame of a functional trusting and empathic relationship what kinds of interventions might assist adults who are struggling to provide for their children?

Universal services can be accessed by all families, including those with children in proceedings, or as a preventive intervention, and there may be less stigma attached to engaging with such facilities (e.g. Sure Start Children's Centres) than to specifically targeted interventions. It has also been argued that such, 'general services in the community need to be available in order to reinforce direct interventions' (Bentovim, 2009: 277). There are many websites which provide information about support services for carers and families. These may be national or local, broad-based or particular to parents of children with specific difficulties, aimed at particular groups of parents such as those from black and ethnic minority backgrounds, and provided by statutory or voluntary organisations. UK-wide services include: http://www. equip.nhs.uk/HealthTopics/parents_family.aspx; http://www.togetherfdc.org/ for parents of children with a disability; https://www.education.gov.uk/publi-cations/standard/publicationDetail/Page1/DCSF-RR166, which describes the family-nurse partnership (FNP) programme of support to vulnerable young mothers; http://www.frg.org.uk/, which is a charity set up to advise carers whose children are involved with or need children's social care services. They promote policies and practices, including family group conferences, designed to enable children to be parented safely in their birth families.

- The NSPCC provides a range of local services and can be contacted via their website: http://www.nspcc.org.uk/default.html
- Services for parents with a learning disability are provided by MENCAP, which can be accessed at: http://www.mencap.org.uk/
- At the time of writing, Barnardo's at http://www.barnardos.org.uk/ runs 415 projects across the UK.
- A number of services and centres are provided by the Children's Society (http://www.childrenssociety.org.uk/).
- Save the Children runs projects designed to support children, young people and their families to run six-month change projects on a range of issues that impact children in poverty (http://www.savethechildren.org.uk/en/in-my-back-yard.htm).
- The National Children's Bureau (NCB) (http://www.ncb.org.uk/support_services/home.aspx) hosts many single-issue or single client groups, networks, forums, councils and partnership programmes.
- Action for Children (http://www.actionforchildren.org.uk/) supports local authorities to provide, at the earliest opportunity, a range of

flexible services to children, young people and their families and family support (http://www.actionforchildren.org.uk/content/437/Family-support).

Practical support can be offered to assist carers with establishing and maintaining daily routines, organisation of cleaning, cooking and shopping, applications for benefit entitlements, budgeting, basic literacy and practical baby and child care. Such tasks may be provided by home care assistants or family support workers employed by the local authority. Emotional support is often an adjunct to the practical support offered. Throughout the UK there is a network of women's centres that offer a range of services including one-to-one sessions, support groups, educational groups and advice on hazardous drug and alcohol use. Some centres offer counselling and psychotherapy and others are oriented towards particular communities such as Asian women. A range of programmes is available to assist care-givers to gain in confidence, become more assertive, understand and prevent victimisation, bullying and domestic violence. These are often provided by specialist women's services such as Women's Aid (http://www.womensaid.org.uk/). A number of local authorities provide such services under the term 'Freedom Project'. There are services to aid people in reducing and managing drug and/or alcohol intake and specialist services for adults with learning disabilities. Often a range of criteria need to be met in order to access such services.

More specialist therapeutic services addressing mental health difficulties can be accessed in the first place through GP practices, although they are also provided by the private and voluntary sectors. Many are listed at: http://www.counselling-directory.org.uk/, and they include services which charge on a capability-to-pay basis such as SHARE, based in Sheffield (http://www.sharepsychotherapy.org/index.php) and the Sherwood Therapy Centre which is based in Mansfield, Nottinghamshire (http://www.counselling-directory.org.uk/counsellor_20811.html). Similar services in other UK locations may be found at: http://www.counselling-directory.org.uk/counsellor_21485.html. Since 2008 'Improving Access to Psychological Therapy' (IAPT) has been rolled out across the UK. It provides low and high intensity services according to client need and is available via general practitioners for people experiencing symptoms of anxiety and depression. Information can be accessed at: http://www.iapt.nhs.uk/. IAPT services for children and young people are also beginning to be available through GP practices. Information can be accessed at: http://www.iapt.nhs.uk/children-and-young-peoples-iapt/meeting-under-18s-specific-needs/.

A variety of intervention programmes concentrate on the promotion of positive interactions between carers and children and on helping parents to learn more about how to support and manage their children emotionally and behaviourally. These may be provided generically by local services for looked-after children, and by Child and Adolescent Mental Health Services (CAMHS). More specialist interventions include:

- Theraplay (Booth and Jernberg, 2010). Agencies in the UK with Theraplay trained staff can be found through: http://www.theraplay. org/8454.html/
- Dyadic Developmental Psychotherapy (DDP) (Becker-Weidman and Hughes, 2008; Hughes, 2009) was originated by Dan Hughes and information regarding certified therapists can be found at: http://www. dyadicdevelopmentalpsychotherapy.org/certifiedtherapists.html
- Relationship Play (Binney *et al.*, 1994) is aimed at enhancing attachments of young children to carers through the medium of play.
- Video Interaction Guidance (VIG) (Kennedy *et al.*, 2011) aims to build positive relationships and promote interactive attunement between adults and children through filming and feedback sessions.

Evidence for the effectiveness of group parenting programmes has been reviewed by Gibbs *et al.* (2003). Evidence-based programmes oriented towards building understanding of children's development and enhancing skills in parenting include:

- Families and Schools Together (FAST) (Crozier *et al.*, 2010) (http://familiesandschools.org/)
- Mellow Parenting (http://www.mellowparenting.org/) (Puckering *et al.*, 1994)
- Strengthening Families (SFP10-14) (Spoth *et al.*, 2001, 2008) (http:// www.mystrongfamily.org/)
- Triple P Positive Parenting (http://www8.triplep.net/) (de Graaf *et al.*, 2008)
- Webster-Stratton (Webster-Stratton, 1990; Webster-Stratton *et al.*, 2004) (http://www.incredibleyears.com/)
- There is also a significant outcome literature for Parent Effectiveness Training (PET) (http://www.gordontraining.com/parentingclass.html) based on the ideas of Carl Rogers (Cedar and Levant, 1990; Wood and Davidson, 2002)
- Sue Jenner has described an approach termed 'the Parent-Child Game' which can also be used as a parenting assessment tool (Jenner, 1997)

I am conscious that I may be giving the impression that there is a wealth and richness of resources available to families in court proceedings. Realistically, there are significant limitations and inadequate resources to support struggling families, even though the cost of removing children to substitute care is substantial. This problem is reflected in analyses of serious case reviews which highlight, '… overwhelming workload, high staff turnover and vacancy rates alongside very high numbers of unallocated cases over a period of several years' (Brandon *et al.*, 2009: 43). Political and social philosophies, policies and economic climates impact the allocation of resources. Whilst there is no point in recommending an intervention that is not available, there is also a risk that failing to describe what would assist may serve to sustain the resource status quo.

I want to end this chapter by encouraging a focus on strengths. Change is more readily accomplished by challenging strengths rather than prompting defensiveness through attention to weaknesses (Egan, 2002). Peter Choate (2009), drawing on the work of Trivette and Dunst (1990) describes the qualities of 'strong' families as:

> ... commitment to the well being of family members; appreciation for what each member does; commitment to spend time together; a sense of purpose in the family allowing them to keep going in good and bad times; congruence amongst family members on values and commitment to family goals; the ability to communicate effectively and to see the positives; a clear set of family rules, values, and beliefs that are tied to expectations about acceptable and desirable behaviors; a variety of coping strategies; the ability to effectively engage problem solving; positive crisis management; flexibility, adaptability, and a balanced use of internal and external resources for coping and adapting to life events.
>
> (Choate, 2009: no page number)

In our assessments let us seek to uncover such strengths, acknowledge the challenges of the job of being a good parent and, whilst giving primacy to the well-being of the child, use our imaginations metaphorically to 'walk a mile in their shoes' (Eckermann *et al.*, 2006).

6 Assessment of children and young people

Introduction

Children of all ages frequently surprise me with what they are able to communicate about their experiences. Their concerns can be conveyed in a spectrum of behaviours as well as through direct verbal expression. In my experience they generally have very strong feelings about their relationships with parents and other care-givers, which, given the opportunity, they are usually willing to share with an adult who will listen respectfully. Sometimes their preoccupations are revealed by what they say first. Pre-schoolers are typically uninhibited about what they are prepared to disclose to strangers. On one occasion, before I had a chance to introduce myself or explain the reason for my visit to the nursery, a child who had just turned four opened the conversation with, 'My mummy's poorly.' And on another, a child of five greeted me in the reception area with, 'I'm not allowed in the playground because I just hit James.' 'Oh,' I said, 'How does that feel?' 'Sad and angry,' he replied.

Removing children from the care of their birth family has a major impact, even when the quality of care that they were previously receiving has been found wanting. This is often all they have ever known, and the familiar has many benefits despite the harm that results when their parents are struggling or in trouble. The following statements are from children of a range of different ages, all eloquently expressing how 'home' is difficult to reproduce in substitute care and how confused they often are about the reasons for being looked-after:

> All I want is just to go home. Right from the beginning just go home to our mum. I can be myself. If I'm with my foster parents; you have to put on .... It just doesn't feel right, acting, acting rather than being. We can be ourselves but it doesn't like, feel like being yourself, like slouching down on the sofa and turning the channels to see what's on. I can do that more at my mum's house. I want to go back home that's definite. There's no other answer.
>
> (13-year-old boy)

At home I could be more myself. Here I feel cheeky. I don't like asking for things. With my family I would just do what I want and say what I want. I don't like asking for most things. If we're shopping I'd like to ask for some money, not a lot, to go to the shop and spend. It feels cheeky. I don't know why. When I was with my family I liked going out with my friends to the shops, talking; normal things that friends do. Have a laugh and mess about. My friends dance but I don't. I don't think I'm good at dancing but I do if I'm messing about. I'm a bit frightened to ask for something here. If someone was annoying me I'd be frightened to say that what they was doing was annoying me. Barbara said she'd buy me a nose stud but she forgot. I didn't like to ask. If it was one of my friends' mums I would ask them. I think Barbara will think I'm dead cheeky. If Barbara's watching something on telly I don't like to ask to change the channel. I don't go up to my bedroom to watch telly because they always shout me and say, 'What are you doing?' I don't think they trust me. If I go into the kitchen she (foster carer's daughter) goes in. If she's left her bag in here she'd move it and give it to her mum. I don't even like to go to the toilet to do a number two here because someone might be listening. I don't mind with my family.

(10-year-old girl)

I asked Sameera (aged 8) the reason why she had come into care. She said, 'Because we didn't used to go to school. Well, we did used to. Sometimes we felt ill but my mum always looked after us all the time and I think she was well enough. She used to cook, clean, make sure we was in bed. What other reason we came in is mum used to drink. We didn't never see her [drinking]. I want to go home to mum because she's stopped it all now and she can definitely look after me. Half of the time we went to school and we used to have headaches and that and I still get headaches at night through thinking of my mum. When I'm lying down I keep thinking about my mum and I want to go home even during the day. I think like I want to go home and I want to be with my brother and have the times we used to do going out, shopping and spend time together.

In the next example a ten-year-old explains how she experienced being taken from her family:

Sylvia dropped us off here with another worker. We were on a day out and we came back in. As soon as we opened the door they said, 'You have to go into foster care,' and it was really sad. There was nothing we could do about it. I was scared because I didn't know what it was. I thought it was a house where people beat you up. We had to pack our bags and put them in the boot of the car. Mum helped pack. They said, 'You have to go into care.' We dropped off my brother first. It was a really long way away and then we had to get dropped off here. I was really nervous because I didn't know where I was going. I didn't know Mark was going to be in the same place. I don't even know why I'm here really; they didn't tell us why. My mum used to drink and then she stopped. On Sunday at contact she looked normal. I don't know why she's in a mental ward though. She was just normal to me. She just looked like she had a sore throat. When she hadn't had a drink she could run the house and look after the baby. When she had had a drink she could still do everything normal but she'd go to sleep at about 10 o'clock until three. I'd change Tilly's nappy if my mum was doing something. If Tilly went upstairs I'd follow her because she gets nail varnish and paints everywhere. She ends up with the bathroom flooded or something.

In this final example, the 11-year-old describes what he has noticed about changes that his parents had made following local authority intervention. The parents had finally acknowledged their drug misuse and engaged in treatment:

We've got better with money 'cos I used to worry about it and they've told me not to worry. I get to take money to school for break. We have more food in the house. I think it's 'cos my dad's going out to work and mum's not spending so much on herself no more. The arguing's miles better. My mum makes things for us and for Amber like a fairy castle and masks; fairy princess masks. She loves princess masks. All of us made the masks, mum and Amber and me. I don't get into trouble with the kids in the close. I don't see them no more. I just hang out with kids my own age from school. My mum and dad stopped me playing with them. Now we've got regular bedtimes. Bedtime for me it's 9.30 and for Amber it's nine. Bath time's about seven o'clock. It's been like that for about a month. I like it. I like these changes. The changes started in about the middle of the six week holiday. Mum and dad, they're miles happier than they used to be because they're always smiling and not getting angry any more.

Legislation and the voice of the child

The United Nations Convention on the Rights of the Child (UNCRC) was adopted into international law in 1989 and ratified in the UK in 1991. The Children Act 1989 aimed to enshrine consistency with the UNCRC approach. Although the Convention has not been incorporated into English law its provisions have influenced subsequent legislation (Freeman, 2007) including the Children Act 2004, Every Child Matters (HM Government, 2004) and policy for 0–19 year olds set out in the Government's 2007 Children's Plan (HM Government, 2007). Article 12 of the UNCRC states:

> States Parties shall assure to the child who is capable of forming his or her own views the right to express those views freely in all matters affecting the child, the views of the child being given due weight in accordance with the age and maturity of the child.
>
> For this purpose, the child shall in particular be provided the opportunity to be heard in any judicial and administrative proceedings affecting the child, either directly, or through a representative or an appropriate body, in a manner consistent with the procedural rules of national law.

The Convention makes clear that it is the right of children to have a voice, to be heard and have their views taken into account. This does not mean that they have rights and responsibilities for making decisions. Courts may well reach conclusions that depart from the wishes of children when welfare issues dictate contrary determinations.

In proceedings under Parts 2 and 4 of the Children Act 1989, the court must have regard to the ascertainable wishes and feelings of the child, considered in light of their age and understanding (section 1[3][a]). This also applies to decisions relating to the adoption of a child. The Children and Family Court Advisory and Support Service (CAFCASS) was established by the Criminal Justice and Court Services Act (2000) with aims that include provision for children to be represented in order to safeguard their interests. Local authorities are obliged under the Children Act 1989 to take children's wishes and feelings into account in most actions that will concern them. This is also underlined in statutory guidance, such as the 'Framework for the Assessment of Children in Need' and the 'Working Together to Safeguard Children' guidance.

There is no age and stage limit to their right to have their ascertainable views and feelings heard. Schofield and Thoburn (1996) suggest that even pre-school children are able to contribute a perspective. They argue that children should not be ruled out of decision making but that they need help to maximise their level of understanding by being provided with information about options and time to discuss them.

> Betrayal of trust and hurt within the family, the absence of secure emotional relationships, will severely prejudice a child's capacity to make sense of their experiences. This is not an argument for not listening to children or reframing and qualifying what they say but it is an argument for professionals to devote more time and develop greater skills in helping children think through their situation, to give them a better understanding of the options and to enable children to sort out their feelings for themselves.
>
> (Schofield and Thoburn, 1996: 14)

Children and young people present particular challenges to the process of assessment. This may in part account for the finding of analyses of serious case reviews that children's voices are often missing (Brandon *et al.*, 2009). Young children are unlikely to 'obey' the social rules of the interview (I ask the questions and you answer them). Inferences often have to be made from children's behaviour and it is easy to make 'folk psychology' causal links that take no account of well-established research findings. It is important that inadvertent pressure is not put on children through the use of inappropriately direct questions. Open, non-leading and non-direct questions are particularly helpful as they prevent us from leading a child to say what they think the adult wants to hear. An approach which circles around the perimeter of an issue can allow children to express their wishes and feelings without being burdened with the responsibility for what need to be adult decisions. Greg Mantle *et al.* (2007) make the point that the assessment of a child's experience and views is not merely a straightforward 'collecting of information' but a, 'professional, highly charged, investigative and interpretative endeavour' (Mantle *et al.*, 2007: 786).

> In their efforts to discover and relay the authentic wishes and feelings of children, CAFCASS reporters are required both to employ a wide mix of skills and to shoulder a heavy responsibility. They interview young, older and teen-aged children who are often distressed, and parents/carers who are in dispute with each other. Their powers of interpretation are frequently put to the test and the difficulties they face in making sense of the information they receive, in a limited time, can readily be appreciated. To illustrate the point, consider some of the interpretations that could be made about a child's expressed dislike for one of their parents or carers: (i) the dislike is authentic and justified; (ii) the child has been manipulated by the other adult or by a sibling; (iii) the child has an insecure attachment to the disliked parent; or (iv) the child feels rejected by the non-resident parent.
>
> (Mantle *et al.*, 2007: 801)

Making sense of behavioural indicators

We all communicate not only through what we say, but also through our demeanour, non-verbal actions and our behaviour. When we know each other well we can often 'read' these signals with relative ease. Children also communicate through their behaviour. Sometimes this is the only way that they can let us know about what is happening to them and how they are feeling. As adults we try to make meaning of the child's actions in order to decide how best to respond. With children we are often engaging in guesswork, creating hypotheses about the meaning of the behaviour which can then be tested out through our responses to them. When making such interpretations I find it helpful to remind myself that for any behaviour there are multiple possible meanings and to do justice to the child I need to hold my reading tentatively. It is one piece of the investigative jigsaw which can be turned this way and that in order to determine the best fit.

Virtually all children show behaviours at times that could be considered 'disturbed'. These may include difficulties around sleeping, eating, wetting, soiling, biting, disobedience, temper tantrums, stealing and lying. The presence of such behaviours by no means indicates that the child has experienced adversity. Searching for explicit indicators of particular experiences is fruitless (Jones, 2003). Whether such an inference can reasonably be made depends on the circumstances surrounding the behaviour, the age of the child, whether the behaviour is primary or secondary (the child has gained age-appropriate control but lost it) and the developmental status of the child. Children who experience delays in their cognitive development or are slow to develop language skills may be unable to express themselves effectively by more direct means.

I have often encountered the term 'withdrawal' to describe a child's behaviour. Social withdrawal can be a way of communicating a child's struggles. It is one way of 'hiding' from potentially threatening or challenging interpersonal exchanges. There may be a relatively straightforward explanation. Children learn from an early age that adults are often seeking a 'right' answer and to be wrong is shameful. In the following example, a child aged five years was being asked to complete the Vocabulary Scale of the Wechsler Pre-school and Primary Scale of Intelligence. The way that such tests are designed is to present items of gradually increasing difficulty. The first question to Liam was, 'Where is your nose? Show me your nose?' His response, 'That's a silly question.' I would contend that he may have chosen this response because he could not believe that this was all that was required of him. It was too 'easy'. As the questions became more difficult and went beyond his current capability he decided to change the rules. 'I know, you say a word and I'll say it back as fast as I can.' When the pressure increased further he offered, 'We'll play a game. Shut your eyes. Abracadabra, Liam disappears,' and he went to hide behind the curtain.

Even as adults we continue sometimes to prefer to be invisible in educational settings and I encounter this in training workshops where the front row is the last to fill up and volunteers are hard to find. Whilst withdrawal may be a way of coping with feelings of insecurity, it is as well to remember that this may be situation specific. I have met children who have been utterly silent in nursery, in school or when they meet me, who shout, chatter and jump about excitedly when they see their favourite grandmother. This reminds me to be careful not to generalise. Whilst the child is withdrawn and emotionally 'flat' in one context, this tells me nothing about her or his general demeanour. I need to extend the scope of my investigation in order to determine what this behaviour might mean. If different adults give different accounts this does not mean that one or the other is incorrect or trying to deceive, rather that I have to take the child's situation-specific behaviour into account in developing my explanatory story.

Some children presenting as withdrawn across contexts are showing their sadness or despair. They may have given up expecting that their specific or general needs are going to be met. They are presenting as 'depressed'. Natural childish ebullience is absent. They may be uniformly compliant, reminding us that 'good behaviour' does not necessarily reflect a well-adjusted child. Early studies of hospitalised children by John and Joyce Robertson (1971) showed that following separation from their parents children tended to progress through the three stages of protest, despair and denial/detachment. In the 'protest' stage children showed difficult, angry and challenging behaviour during and following parental visits. This behaviour was used to make an argument for restricted parental visiting. The Robertsons' research prompted a case to be made for unrestricted visiting in recognition that the stage of denial/detachment was maladaptive, even though the children were easier for staff to manage. Looked-after children typically have contact arrangements with their birth parents while investigations proceed. I have often seen a case made to reduce the frequency of contact on the grounds that the children are distressed during or following these meetings with their birth family. But the children's behaviour does not necessarily mean that they want to see less of these attachment figures, even if the attachment that they developed has been insecure. For a while, as a pre-schooler, my own son cried without fail at being left with substitute care-givers, even when he knew them well. When we were reunited he would daily protest with angry outbursts, conveying his fury that he had been abandoned yet again.

Withdrawn behaviour cannot be taken to have a specific meaning; it needs to be understood in context. Parents may have been unable to help their child to process adverse experiences or provide sufficiently sensitively responsive care. Such children may be unable to understand their fears and transform them into words and thought. Withdrawal or 'shutting down' their feelings is an option. Some children are temperamentally 'shy' or less confident than others. It has been argued (Evans, 1987: 171) that reticence or shyness is a characteristic of about 14 per cent of the elementary school population. I have encountered selectively mute children who have developed this powerful device as a way of controlling adults when other methods have failed. In nursery and school it can be a very effective way of avoiding joining in, usually receiving a sympathetic and cautious approach from staff. It may reflect a parent's difficulty in enforcing boundaries for the child's behaviour. This child, when thwarted, may try a succession of controlling behaviours in order to reproduce her or his known experience. Children are usually able to learn that different behaviours are expected of them in different settings.

Above, I have taken the example of withdrawn behaviour and explored a range of possible meanings. The same can be said of other presenting behavioural difficulties such as angry 'acting out', and hyperactive behaviour.

I have seen children who are unable to remain still because they cannot bear the thoughts and feelings that threaten to overwhelm them if they cease to be on the move. I have engaged in therapy walking around a town centre when it was the only way that a child could bear to talk about the abuses that he had experienced. But caution is needed in interpreting apparently difficult or 'disturbed' behaviour in this way without credible supporting evidence. It is tempting to read more into the many ordinary difficulties of childhood than they warrant. Enuresis (bed wetting) and encopresis (soiling) more often are down to genetic or physiological than psychological causes. If they are secondary (reversion after control had been obtained) there is a greater likelihood that they are stress related. Deliberate smearing of faeces is likely to be a clearer communication. There is no evidence that night terrors (the child shouts out or appears terrified in the night but is not awake) are related to stress whilst nightmares may be. Many children at some stage show 'picky' eating or refuse food. Stuffing food in and hoarding may be more concerning. Stealing, lying, smoking, drinking alcohol and even self-harm are not invariable indicators of disturbance. Such behaviours are often peer-induced or occur when children enter a stage of experimentation as their identities develop and they begin to individuate from their families of origin.

Here is a description of a child's behaviour by her concerned foster carer:

At first I wasn't concerned about Leanne. She seemed to settle quickly and all the professionals were worried about William because he was so withdrawn. I thought he was fine and it was really difficult to get my concerns about Leanne taken seriously. I've got diaries full of William because they only ever wanted to know about William. I was worried because Leanne just didn't show her feelings. She was never upset, she didn't like a hug or a cuddle and she just seemed too self-sufficient. That led to appointments with CAMHS and two of them talked to me but they didn't see Leanne. She's been here for 3½ years now and when William left she didn't show any feelings. I was distraught and she tapped me on the back and said, 'It's okay mam, I'm here.' She still doesn't show her feelings but she'll have massive blow-outs where she's screaming her head off and crying; it'll be over something very tiny, like she can't take off her socks. I think she holds her sadness in and then a tiny incident can set her off. I think she's really upset that she doesn't live with her mum, about the whole thing. Unsettled and upset because she doesn't know what's happening. She's been told that she will be living with someone else for three years now. When she first came to us she was upset and crying because she missed her mummy. She said, 'I want my mummy.' I worry because she gets really excited about things we do but once the activity's happened she tends to have a blank expression. She wants things, but when she gets them it's a disappointment. Once she's got it, it hasn't quite done it for her.

This child had been promised a new family three years earlier. The local authority was unsuccessful in finding a placement for both siblings and her younger brother had recently been adopted. Her excellent inexperienced foster carer made much of Leanne's difficulties to the local authority because she had been unable to make her ordinary concerns heard. This led to a diagnosis of attachment disorder, made without sight of the child or full review of the history. An alternative explanation, that this child had had a secure bond with her mother and was holding herself back from making substitute attachments when she knew that her placement was temporary, had not been considered.

There is one set of behaviours that almost invariably cause alarm bells in the minds of carers and professionals alike and they are usually described as 'sexualised'. IngBeth Larsson (2000) conducted a thorough review of studies of normal and deviant sexual behaviour in children. Sexual behaviour is referred to as 'sexualised' where it is known to have arisen as a sequel to sexual abuse. Larson's review reached the following conclusions:

- Children are naturally curious about their own bodies and those of others and can take part in sexual investigations of their own body and in games with other children. Children vary in their interest in sexuality.
- Behaviours which appear to imitate adult sexuality, e.g. attempted intercourse or imitation of sex with another child or dolls/soft toys; attempts to insert objects in the child's own anus or vagina or the anus or vagina of another child; oral-genital contact and demanding that others take part in specific sexual activities with the child, are very uncommon in observations of normal groups of children but are more common among children who have been the victims of abuse.
- Problematic sexual interaction between children seems to be characterised by force, threats, dominance, violence, aggression and compulsiveness, unlike sex play which is spontaneous, good-humoured and mutual in nature.

In some studies, up to 9 per cent of pre-school age children were reported to masturbate sometimes or often and children were reported to do this more when they were worried, had appetite problems or mood swings. Larsson's review suggests that children can use masturbation to reduce tension related to loneliness, fear, boredom or anxiety. She cautions:

> Besides the behaviour in itself, it is important to look at the child's entire situation: level of development, anxiety, shame, guilt, pain, relationships with adults and friends, the environment in which the child lives and is growing up and the total family situation, etc. What is considered to be sexualised behaviour, with an explicit sexual content, may be due to the

child having been the victim of abuse, but it is important to be aware that similar behaviour can also have other causes.

(Larsson, 2000: 7)

Interviewing children

Getting started

Approaches to interviewing children take their starting point from the idea of purpose. Ascertaining a child's wishes and feelings in relation to residence and contact with separated parents will require approaches both common to and different from talking to children alleged to have been abused. In the latter case, the interview may need to be conducted within guidelines set out to ensure that the evidence thus produced is credible in forensic settings. In the UK this means following the guidance of the Memorandum of Good Practice on video-recorded interviews for child witnesses in criminal proceedings. The Memorandum usefully suggests four stages to such interviews: establishing rapport, obtaining a free narrative account, questioning, and closing the interview.

In this chapter it is not my intention specifically to address forensic interviews. Excellent guidance can be found in works by Aldridge and Wood (1998), Kuehnle and Connell (2009), Lamb *et al.* (2008), and Westcott *et al.* (2002). Nevertheless, the guidance for such interviews has relevance for all assessment conversations with children, particularly in avoiding leading questions and encouraging free narrative.

Consent is usually needed prior to interviewing a child. This may be the consent of the parent or of the court. Whilst consent is needed only from one parent with parental responsibility, where it is shared, it is usually wise to obtain the consent of both. In the UK, parental consent may be forgone if to seek consent would place the child at risk of significant harm (Department of Health *et al.*, 1999). Jones (2003: 94) argues that, 'formal consent is not feasible or relevant to the initial responses to uncertain situations where the purpose of the practitioner's communication is to see whether there is cause for concern'. Older children's consent can be explicitly obtained. Younger children tend to 'vote with their feet'. If they do not consent they remain silent or choose to leave or disrupt the session. This phenomenon has been described by Wood *et al.* (1996). In one interview a child pulled her black leather jacket over her head then zipped it up. Another child sat with her back to the video camera and refused to answer questions. They report that strategies such as coaxing, comforting and repeating questions invariably failed, prolonging the child's discomfort and the interviewer's frustration. Confidentiality cannot be offered and this has to be stated explicitly to children who request it. Such refusal benefits from an accompanying explanation.

Practicalities

I have found it helpful to consider first of all the conditions conducive to children being able to relax with me and talk freely about their experiences. I have experimented with different environments. Over 20 per cent of participants in a study reported by Aldridge and Wood (1998) were of the view that it was unfair to expect a child to settle in a false setting in unfamiliar surroundings. I have a preference to see children at their school or nursery because they have been socialised into particular ways of behaving and talking in this environment which they tend to transfer to the interview. Sometimes it is difficult to find an uninterrupted space but in general I have found staff in schools to be very supportive to the process. If a child is reluctant to be seen alone, or I am struggling to understand the speech of a child with whom I am unfamiliar, school staff are usually happy to be present and assist me in the task. Homes and foster placements can also be suitable venues, providing a quiet room is available and other children are not present to distract. In disputes between separated parents over contact and residence, it is usually important for the venue to be seen as 'neutral' so that the child's testimony can be accepted by both parents as uninfluenced by the presence of the other, or by the child being swayed by the setting in which one parent dominates the child's life.

An argument against seeing a child in the relatively neutral environment of the school is that this may be a particularly safe place for the child. The intrusion of the interview may threaten the child's sense of security, particularly when a stranger may turn up at any time to interview them. They may feel under pressure to explain where they have been to their peers and the process benefits by consideration being given to timing so that the child does not need to go back to class at the end of the session and be faced by the curious enquiries of peers. Staff and children themselves can be very good guides to timing and location of interviews, making the session fit as naturally as possible into the usual school day. Children need to eat and drink at regular intervals. They often do not like to miss playtime or particular activities and this also benefits from consideration. Aldridge and Wood (1998) similarly emphasise the importance of fitting interviews around the child's routines.

In my experience, I am able to communicate with children more effectively when we have a joint focus. I prefer to engage with them in activities on a table top or on the floor. This also means dressing in a way that allows me to be comfortable. Sometimes children tell me the most interesting things when we are both travelling in a car and I sometimes arrange to go with a carer and the child on an outing, for a meal or on the way to a venue for contact with their parents. The naturalistic setting can help a child feel relaxed.

Before seeing a child I usually talk to the carer about how they might explain my session to the child. An over-emphasis on the purpose of the meeting and what will happen to the data can be constraining. Children have variable knowledge about the proceedings, some being fully aware and others having only vague ideas about what is happening, about why they are in care, or about the involvement of a judge and a court. I ask carers to tell the child that I will be coming to see them, and to keep this low-key and 'just in time' lest the child's anxiety escalates. I ask the carer for advice on whether to write to the child as a way of introducing myself and the purpose of the interview. In my letter I will say that I am often asked to talk to children who are not living with their birth families or both of their parents, to find out what they think and feel about it. If they are living with their birth parents I explain that I am sometimes asked to see children because there are concerns about the care that they are receiving. If I am also speaking to their parents I will let the child know this in my letter. I give them a contact number for me and the details of the appointment, suggesting that if the arrangements are unsuitable they can either contact me directly or with the help of an adult to whom I will refer by name. I end by saying that I look forward to meeting them. I use simple language whilst trying not to be condescending. I ask carers if they consider it preferable to hand the letter to the child, who then knows that the carer is aware of the contents.

It can be helpful to find out in advance about a child's special interests and to build rapport by asking questions about the topic: 'Who do you think is the best midfield player in the England team?' I only take this approach when I have some knowledge of the subject myself lest I convey a false interest. Wood *et al.* (1996: 223) advise against viewing, 'rapport building as a formality that must be observed, before getting down to the real business of talking about abuse.'

When I meet with the child I introduce myself by name and give the explanation above about my role. Beginning with statements rather than questions can convey to a child that I will take care of the structure of the interview, that they need not take responsibility, and gives them a chance to settle down with me before there is any pressure to say anything themselves. I explain that it is my job to try to understand what has happened and what they think and feel about it. If I know that the child is aware of the involvement of the court I may add that I have been asked to do this by the court. I offer them the opportunity to ask me questions at the beginning and as we go along. As in my interviews with adults, I may read to them a list of the questions that I am trying to answer. If I am making a recording of the session I explain that this is because I can then give them my full attention and make sure that I am clear about what they have said, so that I do not make mistakes in my understanding. I always make extensive notes and if children ask about this at all it is usually to comment in awe about how many pages I have written. Unlike a forensic interview I do not establish that the child understands the nature of truth, but rather go forward on the assumption that they will tell me the truth as they understand it. Like the child and family reporters in a study by Greg Mantle *et al.* (2007: 798), I also find that, 'most children are amazingly honest.' To introduce the idea of lying, would in my view arouse potential confusion when children's natural instinct is typically to say what they think, providing I am accepting rather than critical of their contributions. This was also the experience of participants in a study by Michelle Aldridge and Joanne Wood (1998), one of whom said, 'When I mention these, I think the children think I expect them not to tell the truth' (Aldridge and Wood, 1998: 12). By writing down what they say, I am showing a genuine interest in their ideas. At the end of the interview I can check that the child is happy with what he or she has told me, I can ask if there is anything that they would like to tell me that I have not asked them about and, if appropriate, ask if there is any message that they would like to convey through my report to the court.

My experience is that children will behave in all kinds of ways during an interview, from cart-wheeling up and down the room, to slapping me and tearing up my materials. I have to accept that whatever they do is providing information. It is telling me something about this child, and maybe something about my approach, and this is useful and informative. Most children understand the social requirements of the session and are polite, open and friendly. Some are more guarded. Some are quiet and shrug their shoulders in response to my questions or respond with 'I don't know'. This is information. It is telling me something about this child and I can review my own experience in light of knowledge about how the child responds to others. In order to make sense of my own experience of the child I need to talk to familiar others such as care-givers, teachers, nursery staff and/or those who transport them to and from different venues.

I like to bring a range of activities to sessions with children. Sometimes it can take an hour before the child begins to relax and talk more freely. Other sessions may only last 10 minutes because that is as long as the child is able or willing to concentrate. At other times children will talk happily for a three hour session and choose to miss their break time in order to continue. I ensure that in such cases they have refreshments as we continue. The advice given for investigative interviews conducted within the guidelines of the Memorandum of Good Practice is a time limit of an hour. However, many professionals regard this as insufficient time for disclosure to take place (Aldridge and Wood, 1998) and I much prefer to be able to take my time and go at the child's pace.

With such possible variation in the length of interviews, a prior discussion with the staff or carers is necessary in order to be assured that the venue is available for the full time period and that staff are not unduly concerned about the child's long absence. In schools there are almost invariably some interruptions and I accept these as part of the life of the school. If a child wants to leave a session, I generally allow this since a coerced child will not provide information that will contribute usefully to the assessment. I will encourage a child who is distractible to stay for a little longer in order to complete an activity. In my experience, if I am relaxed and calm the child generally is happy to remain in the session. To help me stay calm I remind myself of Norma Howes' comment that, 'Children are very forgiving of … what they perceive as stupid questions, as long as the practitioner is genuine, properly curious without being voyeuristic and engages well with them in an age-appropriate and respectful way' (Howes, 2010: 126).

I like to begin with an activity called the 'Bag of Feelings' which I learned from Alice Swann, a Belfast-based paediatrician, and to which almost all children from the age of three years upwards seem able to relate. This has been written up by Binney and Wright (1997). The interviewer draws a sack on a sheet of paper and invites the child to imagine that the sack is the inside of her or himself, containing all of the feelings that are inside them. The child is then invited to identify a feeling that is inside them, to choose a coloured pen or pencil and to show the interviewer how much space this feeling takes up. Many children will immediately choose a pen and name a feeling. For those who are unsure I ask if they would like me to give some examples of feelings and then list some such as happy, angry, sad, excited, worried, upset, cross, confused and so on. I have never experienced a child who was unable to identify or take up one of the offered feelings although some very young children may struggle and older ones may be reluctant to proceed beyond a fairly short focus on this task. It has been argued that young children have a very restricted vocabulary for emotions (Aldridge and Wood, 1998) and although I agree, this does not mean that children cannot relate to the Bag of Feelings. Even at age five and below their responses are sometimes very revealing. Lewis, who was almost five years of age told me in response to the initial question that he had the feeling 'nasty' inside him. He showed on the drawing that this took up a great deal of space inside him. I asked what made him feel nasty and he said:

> When people don't let me play with them. I like to play lots of games with Wayne and George, Ben Ten. I asks why I can't play with them and they say, 'Because you've been nasty,' and I haven't. And I feel nasty because my dad threw a glass at my mum but it missed because she ran out of the way. I helped mum but she said, 'Don't because you might cut yourself.' I don't feel nasty when they weren't fighting. It feels horrible.

The child shows the extent of the feeling by colouring in part of the sack and it may be labelled by the child or by the interviewer. Children sometimes ask for help with spelling. The interviewer then proceeds to ask a series of questions about the feeling such as how often the child experiences it, what they do when they feel it and whether anyone helps them with the feeling. They might be asked if anyone in particular is around when the feeling comes along, or whether the feeling is stronger or weaker when they are in a particular setting or at a particular time. When one feeling has been fully explored the child is asked to choose another feeling that is inside them. In my experience this method produces a very open-ended conversation. It is led by the child and unconstrained by the interviewer. It might last for five minutes or 50 minutes. Here are some examples of the kind of information that can emerge.

> I'm upset by what my mum's done to me and why she's done it. Because on my sixth birthday I spent in foster care. I spent another one in foster care 'cause I'm eight now. When she's brushing my hair she rags it. She doesn't care. There's loads of other things which I can't remember. All the time I'm upset but inside not really outside. She's just never nice to me. She's always nice to the others. When I wet the bed she slapped me and punched me and one day nearly pulled my hair up, pulled so tight. I want to know why she's been doing it. When I'm upset I don't do nowt. I cry and feel sad, not really on the outside. Sometimes you can see it in my eyes though. Some people just notice; me mostly. Nobody helps because they don't know. I go and be upset in my room. I also get to think I want to see my brother again. I feel really sad 'cos I love my brother. I've been trying to ring him but he's not answering the phone.

This 10-year-old child talked about his feelings of fear and anger:

> I feel scared when I don't see my mum and stuff. Like I'm scared I won't go back home and that the others won't either: that I'd never get to see my mum again and my little brother and sister and Katie. I love my little brother the most out of all the family and I love all my brothers and sisters. I love my mum the most. I won't be there on Katie's birthday. Mum takes us bowling and stuff and to the pictures and McDonald's then we go home and have a party with a cake and stuff and my mates and Katie's mates. We get a cake from Tesco. Mum usually does the shopping, about £100, or Lidl. Normally I always go with her. My dad looked after the others but I usually always take Nathan and push him around in the trolley. We go on the bus and come back in a taxi or granddad takes us. Every time I speak to my mum she starts crying and shouts down the phone, 'I want my babies.' I just get all scared and stuff and start crying. About twice she sounds different and all the times I've rung she sounds the same. I said to her not to have anybody in the house because the people who come round they drink as well. This woman lets her kids smoke weed and drink. I want to know why our mum got us took off her 'cos she doesn't let us smoke and that. She won't let me smoke because I've got asthma. She'll shout at me or ground me. Once in Bradingley this girl said, 'Your mum's a junkie and your dad's a druggie.' And we kept fighting and I wouldn't give up so a teacher had to come and stop us.

I find that this method both helps to establish rapport and tends to produce a free narrative that may encompass a wide range of topics. It has the advantage of providing a unique picture of young people's preoccupations and feelings, eliciting material that is not easily obtained through more formal approaches which tend to constrain the dialogue. It provides a very individual and descriptive account of a young person's experience and often yields more than a direct conversation focussing on issues introduced by the interviewer. The interviewer uses simple language which can be adjusted to suit the developmental capabilities of the child. The questions are open and non-leading.

If this approach has opened up the conversation then I may move onto a more direct interview with the child. I normally write myself a list of prompt questions designed to ensure that I do not lead and in order to keep the interview as open as possible. I juxtapose positive and negative items. The list typically comprises the following:

Questions for young people

When you were living/now you are living with your mum/dad/foster carer what did you like to do?
What were/are the best times?
What were/are the most unhappy or difficult times?
How did/do you spend your birthdays?
How did/do you spend Christmas (or other religious festivals)?
What did you used to do/do now at weekends?
Where did/do you go for holidays?
What did/do you do when you were/are upset or hurt?
Who made/makes sure that you were/are safe and didn't/don't run across the road or get lost?
What used to happen/happens when you were/are naughty?
Who used to cook/cooks the dinner?
Who cleaned/cleans the house?
Who fixed/fixes things that stopped working?
Who combed/combs your hair?
Who made/makes sure you were/are clean?
Who made/makes sure you cleaned/clean your teeth?
What happened/happens at bedtime?
How did/do your mum/dad/granddad and her/his boyfriend/girlfriend get on together?
When they fell/fall out what used to happen/happens?
How were/are they nice to each other?
What things made/make you feel good when you were/are with them/him/her?
What things made/make you feel bad when you were/are with them/him/her?
What friends did you used to have/do you have?
Where did you used to meet them?
How many places have you lived?

What was it like moving house?
What schools did you go to?
What was it like moving schools?
Which house did you like best?
Which did you like least?
Which of your brothers and sisters do you get on with best?
What do you like doing with them?
Which do you get on with least well?
What don't you like about them?
What do you miss about being away from your mum/dad/grandparents?
What are you pleased to be away from?
What's it like seeing your mum/dad/grandparents?
Is there anyone else you miss?
What do you think your mum/dad/other carer worry about?
How can you tell?
What happens when they're worried?
What kind of things make them happy?
What kind of things make them mad?
If I had a magic wand and could arrange anything/three things you wanted
about your family what would it/they be?

I tend not to ask direct questions about a child's wishes and preferences since this can place them in a loyalty trap or put pressure on them to state an opinion in which they have been coached. It may also carry the implication that they are responsible for the decisions that are going to be made. Instead, I do sometimes ask them to mind-read a sibling. 'What would your sister Lucy think about that?' or to make a judgement about what would be the best arrangement for a sibling. 'What do you think should happen next to Lucy?' During the course of the interview children often state their own opinion without being asked. Sometimes, when there is a great deal of information going back in time, I take a summary or parts of the file with me and explain that this has been provided for me. Older children are often very interested in the early history and I have at times read out entries and asked the child to comment. In my experience they rarely have any difficulty in disagreeing with what is on file, and also spontaneously elaborate on specific incidents. This can have the effect of rapport-building with children who are reluctant to talk. It can also have a therapeutic impact for children who, alone in their family, are being looked-after and do not understand why they have been picked out.

Showing interest in the child, rather than saying that you are interested, is more effective and meaningful. Children are more likely to convey information in an interview if they feel they understand its purpose, are reasonably at ease, and feel supported by the interviewer and by the context in which the interview takes place (Jones, 2003).

Structured approaches to the assessment of children

Norm-referenced tests

There is a tradition of assessing children that dates from the early twentieth century when the French government commissioned Alfred Binet to develop a method of identifying 'intellectually deficient' children for their placement in special education programmes. This led to the production of a range of formal assessments based on the bell curve, a graph of measurements made of the general population which produces a 'normal' distribution. These measures typically focus on cognitive skills and one example is the IQ test. They are 'norm-referenced' and have standardised formal procedures for administration, timing and scoring with the aim of the results being valid and reliable. They allow this child's score to be compared with that of other children of this child's age. Such tests have been criticised by Binet himself who said, 'Some ... seem to have given their moral support to such lamentable verdicts, asserting that intelligence is a fixed quantity, a quantity that cannot be increased. We must protest and react against this brutal pessimism and show that it doesn't have any foundation' (Binet, cited in Brown, 1985: 323). More recent authors, such as Stephen Jay Gould, have expressed serious doubts about the construct of intelligence itself. 'This book, then, is about the abstraction of intelligence as a single entity, its location within the brain, its quantification as one number for each individual, and the use of these numbers to rank people in a single series of worthiness, invariably to find that oppressed and disadvantaged groups – races, classes, or sexes – are innately inferior and deserve their status' (Gould, 1996: 21). I will not be describing norm-referenced tests in this chapter. Their use is restricted to particular professional groups and I believe that such scores, whilst sometimes useful, should be treated with caution.

Criterion-referenced measures

These measures compare the child's performance of specific behaviours with a criterion. This can tell us whether a child's behaviour has changed over time. Such measures are often used in nurseries and schools to map the progress of a child's development in domains such as motor skills, speech and language development, thinking skills and social development. The child's performance is mapped against an expected average performance for a child of the same age. The results give an indication as to whether this child's development is progressing as expected. If not, a variety of explanations are possible. The data can be helpful in tracking a child's progress over time. A widely used developmental checklist devised by Mary Sheridan can be accessed in the UK Department of Health's practice guidance for assessing children in need and their families (2000a: 23–28) from: http://www.dh.gov. uk/prod_consum_dh/groups/dh_digitalassets/@dh/@en/documents/

digitalasset/dh_4079383.pdf. The Early Years Foundation Stage Handbook is used by nurseries in the UK to track student progress in the pre-school years and can be downloaded from: http://webarchive.nationalarchives.gov.uk/20110809101133/wsassets.s3.amazonaws.com/ws/nso/pdf/7b6667e4e7ca29914d2d087da50710a3.pdf.

Slow progress is sometimes used to argue the case for poor levels of stimulation in the family environment but care must be taken to keep an open mind about causality. If the child's performance is reported to differ between locations then it is important to make observations in both settings. There are many possible explanations for slow progress including growth spurts and plateaus, a shy disposition that modulates performance in some settings, limited stimulation in the child's environment, and specific learning difficulties. A variety of checklists and rating scales are available on which the child's behaviours may be mapped – either following direct observation of children in their natural settings, through enquiry of care-givers or by asking young people to complete such scales themselves.

Structured methods for enquiring about emotional involvement and attachment

In this section I describe a selection of tests and questionnaires that I have used or adapted for use in assessing children in court proceedings. Like the 'Bag of Feelings' they provide a joint focus which can be more comfortable for interviewer and child than a face-to-face interview. Many such activities are available and this is a short selection of those that I have enjoyed over time. Training, in the form of short courses, is available in the UK for those methods for which it is required or desirable.

The Bené–Anthony Family Relations Test

This comprises a set of posting boxes on the front of which are drawn line figures. The child selects figures to represent family members and is presented with a series of cards on which are written positive and negative outgoing and incoming feelings such as, 'This person likes to cuddle me,' 'I sometimes wish this person was not in my family.' The child posts the cards into the box representing the person that the statements fit best. If the statements do not fit any family members they can be posted into 'Mr Nobody'. The test provides a measure of level of emotional involvement, which can be seen as related to attachment, based on total cards posted into each character, and of the direction and degree of feelings that the child experiences in relation to each of the characters. The results also give an indication of defensive strategies that the child may be adopting such as 'denial' when all or most of the negative cards are posted into 'Mr Nobody' and 'splitting' when the characters are awarded either almost entirely positive or all negative cards. Denial involves the avoidance of any negative thoughts and images, these being too difficult to contemplate. Denial acts as a self-protective mechanism. The problem with denial is that it interferes with a process of learning to accept and cope with adversity. In 'splitting', children tend to view the world in a 'black and white' or 'all or nothing' way rather than taking a more balanced view of good and bad in most people. This can result when children are struggling to manage the internal tension and anxiety they feel.

The Family Relations Test is an 'old' test dating from 1957 which I have generally found engages children from the age of three upwards. There is also an adult version. The posting of cards seems to create a distance which some-times allows strong emotional expression which would not otherwise be vocalised. Psychologists who used the test with children aged from four to 16 years reported that it facilitated the development of more complex under-standings of family dynamics and improved clarification of the experience of negativity within the family (Brand, 1996).

In My Shoes

This is a computer-assisted interview for children, providing a broad-based assessment of the child's experiences and emotions in a range of settings and with significant people. There are a number of different modules in the programme which allow children to choose a figure to represent themselves. Pictorial representations of different places where they are living or have lived can be created, in which they can place figures and family pets from a number of different sets. 'Speech bubbles' and 'thinks bubbles' can be dragged and dropped on the different figures and the child or interviewer fills them in on the computer keyboard. A number of scenes can be offered, representing school venues, leisure activities, a birthday celebration, bedrooms, bath-rooms and playgrounds. There is also a palette showing line drawings of the front and back of a child. This is used to explore places on the body that the child has experienced an injury or soreness. The results are recorded within the programme and they can be printed off if required. I have known children to hide what they have typed from me but this is not lost because it appears in the results file. The programme is flexible, allowing the interviewer to focus on different topics in addition to the standard questions asked by the on-board programme guide. In order to use these materials interviewers need to complete a training course and submit examples of their work. Studies based on the programme have been conducted by Rachel Calam *et al.* (2000) and David Glasgow and Rachel Crossley (2004). Training can be accessed through Child and Family Training, online at childandfamilytraining.org.uk, a not-for-profit organisation which is directed by Arnon Bentovim and Liza Bingley Miller.

Narrative Story Stem Approaches

Story stem approaches offer young children the opportunity to complete narratives introduced by the interviewer using a limited range of suitable props such as doll and animal figures with the possible additional use of house furniture and outdoor scenes. The interviewer begins the story and children are invited to show and tell what happens next. A list of such approaches can be found in Appendix 1.

In the MacArthur Story Stem Battery (MSSB), story scripts include a stamping elephant, a child falling off a bicycle, a child taking home from school a picture of which they are proud, a child spilling juice after reaching across a table, a conflict between being requested by a parent to play quietly juxtaposed with a friend's visit, 'three's a crowd', a burned hand when a child reaches for a hot pan, lost keys over which parents are arguing, a 'burglar in the dark', and an 'exclusion story' in which the parents tell the child that they want time alone together. The story stems may involve separation and reunion with parents, jealousy, dependency, resolution of conflict, anger and distress.

The Story Stem Assessment Profile (SSAP) comprises 13 narrative stems that have been used for clinical assessment and for research. Norms for children who have been maltreated and non-maltreated children have been produced which can be used to derive attachment construct scores for security, insecurity, disorganisation and defensive avoidance. Research based on the Manchester Child Attachment Story Task (MCAST) (Wan and Green, 2010) reported that children presenting with clinical-level behaviour disorders could be differentiated from other children by their use of themes including role reversal (the child taking on the parental role by caring for or preoccupation with the mother), maternal injury and maternal sadness. The more prominent were the themes, the more severe the children's disruptive behaviour.

These approaches build on the rich traditions of play therapy and comprise a systematic group of story beginnings enacted in play, which can open a window on the representational worlds of pre-school and primary age children. The children are not asked direct questions about their family which might create conflict and anxiety, yet the method can shed some light on the child's expectations and perceptions of family roles, attachments and relationships. More details of each of these story stem approaches can be found in Prior and Glaser (2006) including information concerning validity and reliability. I have found the approaches adaptable for the exploration of sibling relationships in addition to relationships between children and their parents. Care needs to be taken to integrate the information obtained through these methods with other data in constructing a formulation of family functioning.

My Needs, Wishes and Feelings Pack/How it Looks to Me

These materials take the form of two booklets that can be completed by the child or young person with the help of the interviewer. They were designed for use in both public and private law proceedings and allow the child's responses to be written into the booklets and appended to an assessment report. The booklets are described online (Children and Family Court Advisory and Support Service, CAFCASS, n.d.) and can also be viewed at: http://www.youtube.com/watch?v=SWIJZNCT840. They can be downloaded free from: http://www.cafcass.gov.uk/publications.aspx.

I'll Go First

This is a planning and review toolkit specifically designed for use with children with disabilities. The original 1999 version has recently been updated and is available from the Children's Society (Kirkbride and Piper, n.d.). It is also available on CD and is described at: http://sites.childrenssociety.org.uk/disabilitytoolkit/toolkit/resource.aspx?id=11. It comprises a planning and review toolkit which includes stickers and illustrated boards. The accompanying good practice guide offers comprehensive advice on how to use the pack. It covers practical aspects of organising sessions with children and different approaches to how children's views can be recorded and presented.

Draw on Your Emotions

This is a workbook (Sunderland and Engleheart, 2005) that contains a series of structured, easy-to-do picture exercises designed to help people of all ages, especially those aged 10–18, express, communicate and deal more effectively with their emotions in everyday life. The photocopiable illustrations are intended to ease the process of talking about feelings. It can be used in a social care or psychological setting to help young people to look back over events in their lives that have affected them. It focuses on self perceptions and young people's aspirations for the future. A record comprising writing and drawing is produced.

Strength Cards for Kids

This is a conversation-building set of humorously-illustrated laminated cards. They were devised with the aim of facilitating conversations that help children to identify and build on their strengths. There is also an adult version that can be used with families. They are marketed by Innovative Resources and can be viewed at: http://www.innovativeresources.org/default. asp?cmd=products&productgroup=779.

Further structured methods

In a study of CAFCASS officers, Christine Robbie (2009) found that a variety of materials and approaches were used to encourage children to talk.

Family trees or genograms were popular, as were sculpting (arranging objects in space to represent relationship patterns), scaling (asking questions to invite rank order from most to least on a numerical scale, typically 0–10 or 1–100), and asking the child for three wishes. There were other examples mentioned by only one participant in each case which included role play, role reversal, a board game, 'treasure box' and 'a desert island'. In the latter, children are invited to imagine being ship-wrecked upon an island. They are invited to draw or write the names of the other people they would wish to be present. The child's attention might then be brought to people in the family who have not been included. In the 'treasure box' task, an invitation is offered to place special or happy memories in a treasure chest, followed by another activity placing 'memories which upset me' into a balloon. A further invitation to place items in the treasure chest follows, thereby balancing activities with the potential for positive and negative emotional reactions (Humphreys *et al.*, 2011).

Questionnaires for children

There are very many questionnaires for children that aim to shed light on their social and emotional development. For example, there is a searchable inventory of instruments designed specifically to assess violent behaviour and related constructs in children and adolescents which lists more than 200 different scales and questionnaires at http://vinst.umdnj.edu/VAID/browse. asp. I have used only a very small number of those available. It is as well to consider the validity and reliability studies that have been conducted on such measures before making a selection. It is beyond the scope of this chapter to explore this issue in depth; it is well covered by George Dunbar (2005) and Cathy Lewin (2005). Below I describe a selection of measures which I have found useful, easy to administer and that have been reasonably appealing to children and young people. They can be completed either independently or with help.

Beck Youth Inventory-II second edition (Harcourt Assessment, 2005)

This comprises five self-report scales that may be used separately or in combination to assess a child's experience of symptoms of depression, anxiety, anger, disruptive behaviour, and their self-concept. It is designed for use with children and adolescents between the ages of 7 and 18 years. The inventories require children to respond to a set of statements such as 'I get nervous,' 'I have problems sleeping' and provide information based on the conscious awareness of a child about any difficulties that they are experiencing. Aside from the self-concept inventory, the questionnaires can convey a sense of negativity since they are largely focussed on symptomatology.

The B/G-Steem Primary Scale (Lucky Duck Publishing Ltd, 1988)

This is a questionnaire measure designed to aid in the identification of children with a poor self-concept. It also provides an indication of the child's Locus of Control (the extent to which people believe that internal or external factors control events that affect them). The majority of items are positive in direction and it comprises statements that require a child to answer 'yes' or 'no'. Items include, 'I am the best looking in my class,' 'I can do things without help,' and 'My teacher notices when I do good work.'

Strengths and Difficulties Questionnaires (SDQs)
(Goodman, 1997; Goodman et al., 1998)

These scales are used to screen for emotional and behavioural problems in children and adolescents, focussing on a child's emotional and behavioural strengths as well as difficulties. The questionnaires incorporate five scales: pro-social, hyperactivity, emotional problems, conduct (behavioural) problems and peer problems. There are versions to be completed by care-givers and, for older children, by the young people themselves. Scores can be computed for individual scales and for overall difficulties, indicating high, medium or low need.

Youth Self Report (YSR) (Achenbach, 1991; Achenbach and Rescorla, 2001)

These scales are devised from the Achenbach Behaviour Scales which are completed by parents and teachers. There are separate scales assessing competence, somatic complaints, anxiety and depression, social problems, thought problems, attention problems, delinquent rule-breaking behaviours, and aggressive behaviours. Scores may be obtained for overall 'internalizing' and 'externalizing' of difficult experiences. The scores relate to DSM-criteria (the Diagnostic and Statistical Manual for identifying mental health difficulties). The Youth Self Report (YSR) provides self-ratings for 20 competence and problem items paralleling those of the Child Behavior Checklist (CBCL)/ Ages 6–18. The YSR also includes open-ended responses to items covering physical problems, concerns and strengths. Young people rate themselves on a three-point scale for how true each item is now or was during the previous six months.

Questionnaires popular with colleagues of mine include the Self Image Profile for Children (SIP-C) which provides a visual display of self-image and self-esteem. There are different versions for children, adolescents and adults. The SIP-C provides a measure of self-image by contrasting ratings for 'actual self' (How I am) with 'ideal self' (How I would like to be). The discrepancy provides an estimate of the child's self-esteem (Butler and Green, 2001). The Feelings, Attitudes and Behaviors Scale for Children (FAB-C) (Beitchman, 1996) available from Multi-Health Systems and Psychological Assessments

Australia (PAA) is designed to assess a range of emotional and behavioural problems in children aged 6–13 years. It provides a profile of scores on the subscales 'conduct problems', 'self-image', 'worry', 'negative peer relations' and 'antisocial attitudes'. It incorporates a 'lie scale' and an overall 'problem index'. The Nowicki–Strickland scales (Nowicki and Strickland, 1973) are designed to assess Locus of Control. They may be obtained from Educational Testing Service, Princeton, New Jersey (www.ets.org). The Resiliency Scales for Children and Adolescents (RSCA) (Prince-Embury, 2007) give an indication of sense of mastery, sense of relatedness and emotional reactivity in children between the ages of 9 and 18 years. They include items such as, 'If I try hard it makes a difference,' 'I can make up with friends after a fight,' and 'When I get upset, I stay upset for several days.' They can be purchased from Harcourt Assessment and are available to practitioners certified by a professional organisation.

In a recent development in the UK for improving access to psychological therapies for children and young people (CYP-IAPT) routine administration of the SDQ and the Revised Child Anxiety and Depression Scale (RCADS) (Chorpita *et al.*, 2005) are envisaged. The latter is an adaptation of the Spence Children's Anxiety Scale designed to correspond more closely to selected DSM-IV anxiety disorders and includes a scale for major depression. Whilst useful for diagnostic purposes, Bruce Chorpita and colleagues state, 'Comparative analyses with traditional measures of anxiety and depression suggest that these other measures may be preferable for different conditions of use, for example in screening for trait dimensions or personality features, whereas the RCADS is keyed more closely to specific clinical symptoms' (Chorpita *et al.*, 2005: 321). It can be downloaded free along with other questionnaire measures for children from: http://www.childfirst.ucla.edu/resources.html.

Sentence Completion Tests (SCTs)

Sentence completion tests are regarded by some practitioners as projective techniques, allowing access to unconscious material, whilst others argue that respondents are fully aware of what they are revealing about themselves (Campbell, 1957). They comprise a series of sentence stems which young people are asked to complete. The responses are thought to provide some insight into attitudes, beliefs, motivation and aspects of their lives with which people are struggling. Margot Holaday *et al.* (2000) surveyed practitioners' ways of using 15 different sentence completion tests. Most respondents did not use a scoring method but the information contributed to a wider assessment. Practitioners relied on their clinical skills to interpret the content of responses according to their own theoretical orientation. In their survey, the most popular SCT for children, adolescents and adults was Rotter *et al.*'s (1992) Incomplete Sentences Blank which was designed for use with secondary school and college students. Their respondents reported using it to assess children and older adults. They tended to establish their own informal norms based on typical and unusual responses. Margot Holaday gave the example that in her experience the response 'I like ... my mom' was highly atypical for 16-year-old young men. Practitioners also reported using SCTs to obtain quotes that could lend support to their overall conclusions, to, 'find out what the client wants you to know,' and to provide information that had not emerged from other sources. 'I feel ... like crying' and, 'At bedtime ... I have trouble sleeping' could be linked to depression. 'I regret ... nothing,' could be indicative of the defence of 'denial'.

The Hart Sentence Completion Test (HSCT) (Hart, 2003) was devised specifically for use with children aged 6–18 years. A concerted effort was made to establish scoring criteria, reliability and criterion-related validity but it nevertheless lacks adequate standardisation data. It comprises 40 items designed to elucidate the child's experience of family, peers, school and self. Sample items include, 'I like ...', 'I can't ...' and 'The best thing about me ...'

In my experience, questionnaire and self-report measures can be useful in providing alternative formats through which children and young people, particularly those who are awkward in conversation, may express their ideas. Like the other ways of obtaining information described in this chapter, they can contribute to an assessment by offering additional perspectives with which to view the overall circumstances of the child. Substantive descriptions and reviews of such approaches can be found in texts by Jack Cummings (2003), Kenneth Merrell (2003) and Gerald Oster and Patricia Crone (2004). Whilst assessment methods are often focussed on deficiencies and difficulties faced by young people, I would like to end this chapter with a reminder that many children in trouble show remarkable resilience:

> Early ideas about resilience demarcated certain outstanding qualities and protective factors available to children that contributed to their ability to surmount risk and traumatic events (Masten, 2001; Werner and Smith, 1992). These factors include: a sense of humour, a sense of mission or direction, strong intelligence, insight, adaptive distancing, self efficacy, the possession of a talent or special skill, effective coping strategies and the presence of at least one mentoring relationship (Masten, 2001; Turner, 2001; Werner and Smith, 1992; Wolin and Wolin, 1993).
>
> (Graybeal and Konrad, 2008: 188)

The presence of such mentoring relationships was encouraging the development of resilience in this child who had been subject to long-term sexual abuse within her birth family:

> One particular teacher could control me in primary school, Mrs Flowers, and I was devastated when she left. She was fantastic. She liked me. She used to give up a lot of her time. Not rushed. She always used to spoil me and pay me a lot of attention. She'd buy me a book. It was somebody who actually knows what I like and what I don't like. At my secondary

school now, my teachers never put red biro on my book. They always use a green pen. I think they understand. I see red and I explode. I study so hard in lessons. Teachers say I'm clever but it doesn't show on my paper work so I think I'm stupid. I can't handle lunch breaks because I don't know how to get on with some of the other kids, so they've made me a prefect and they let me help in the library. I'm getting better. I can control myself more all the time and I'm beginning to think I might be able to do something with my life.

7   Assessing attachment

The primary focus of this chapter is on attachment theory and its implications for assessment. Attachment theory appears to me the most popular contemporary explanatory account of a child's social and emotional development, a domain that is critical to assessments that determine whether a child can safely be left in the care of the birth parents. This accounts for its prominence here, alongside encouragement to apply it critically, interwoven with alternative or complementary theoretical perspectives including social learning theory, ecological theories and the constructivist ideas of Jean Piaget and Lev Vygotsky about how children learn which I describe briefly in Chapter 10. I aim to explore the relevance of childhood attachment experiences for the quality of care that adults are able to give when they undertake the role of parent and to signpost methods by which attachment style may be assessed.

Attachment and learning theories

Attachment style is a characteristic of a child's behaviour in relation to a care-giver. The carer's responses to and feelings for the child are known as the care-giver's bond. Attachment theory developed out of John Bowlby's exploration of the long-term impact of children's separation from their primary care-givers as either war orphans or evacuees. In conjunction with John Robertson (Robertson and Bowlby, 1952) he observed that young children who were hospitalised initially protested with inconsolable crying, clung to or tried to find or follow the carer. After a few days there followed a period of despair, apathy and listlessness. If the separation continued for a longer period the child would become quietly detached and withdrawn, showing an apparent lack of interest in the lost care-giver. If reunion took place after this long separation, the child showed a mixture of anger, crying, clinging and rejection (Robertson and Robertson, 1971). As a result of this research and the Robertsons' moving film of hospitalised children, parent visiting hours to hospitalised children became liberalised. An important message for me arising from this initial research is that children will produce all manner of behaviours in response to separation from a main carer, which alone are usually inadequate as a basis for judging the quality of the parent-child relationship.

Attachment theory has a biological base. Infants are more likely to have their needs met at this fragile stage of human existence when they are physically unable to take care of themselves if they are able to elicit care from proximal adults through the production of attachment behaviours. The baby's state of anxiety is said to activate infant attachment behaviours with the purpose of increasing the closeness of the child to the adult care-giver, thereby enhancing the likelihood of the infant's physical and emotional needs being met. As an undergraduate I was fascinated by the research findings of Harry Harlow and his team (1958) who studied neonatal monkeys. They observed that the babies showed strong emotions in relation to the cloth pads which were used to cover the wire mesh floors of their cages, clinging to them and engaging in violent temper tantrums when the pads were removed and replaced for sanitary reasons. In subsequent experiments, when faced with the unenviable choice between a wire 'mother substitute' that provided milk, and a cuddly inanimate cloth alternative, infant monkeys spent much more time clinging to the soft variant than to the food source. It was a powerful lesson about the importance of apes' needs for comfort, not only physical sustenance. Attachment theory provides an account that emphasises the importance of the human infant's need to be soothed and to learn self-soothing as a means of reducing anxiety.

Attachment theory proposes that over time infants learn to 'read' care-giver behaviours and adapt their own behaviour accordingly. Sensitively responsive care provides a context to which the infant may readily adapt, whereas adults who respond unpredictably or with angry and frightening behaviours present a greater challenge. Newborns have a very limited repertoire of behaviours on which they are able to call; initially sleeping, crying, quietness, and very soon grasping, smiling, cooing and laughing. Three broad categories of infant behaviour have been described by Jay Belsky and Jude Cassidy (1994: 374):

• Signals from the child that indicate interest in social interaction. These include smiling, cooing and laughter.
• Behaviours from the child that the care-giver finds aversive and wishes to terminate. These include crying and fussing.
• Active behaviours that take the child to the carer such as crawling and following.

It is argued that these broad types of attachment behaviour continue throughout life and can be seen in socially appealing or coy behaviours, distress signals that attract attention and concern, and active approaches to others for the benefits of intimacy (Howe *et al.*, 1999). Attachment theory (Bowlby, 1969) proposes a number of phases to the development of attachment which relate to the age of the child. The phases are important for assessments in family proceedings because they limit what can be asserted about a child's attachment style according to age. For example, it is not possible to make an assessment of attachment style in an infant younger than nine months, although this is sometimes requested in instructions to expert witnesses.

The initial stage extends from birth to 8–12 weeks in which behaviours such as grasping, smiling, babbling and crying are directed at anyone in the vicinity of the child. It is thought that even in these early days infants are learning to discriminate between adults (Prior and Glaser, 2006). During the second stage, from eight weeks to about six months, as infants' sensory systems develop, they learn increasingly to discriminate between familiar and unfamiliar adults, gradually becoming selectively responsive to their primary care-giver/s.

In stage three, from six months onwards, the theory proposes that infants increasingly learn about the conditions that terminate distress and create the experience of security. John Bowlby (1969) believed that by this stage babies have learned to organise their behaviour in a manner that encourages care-givers to provide the conditions that alleviate distress. By the time that they are nine months old most infants have begun to develop preferences for famil-iar figures who have been involved in meeting their needs, seeking proximity to these central figures whenever they experience stressors such as hunger or unfamiliarity which can heighten fear. The child anticipates that the attach-ment figure will act to alleviate the stressors and return her or him to a calm state. With the development of independent movement, babies typically begin to use their carers as bases from which to explore. In phase four, usually beginning in the second or third year, the child's mental world shows evidence of a developing awareness of the care-giver as an independent person, sowing the seeds of a more complex infant-carer relationship which Bowlby termed a 'partnership' (Bowlby, 1969). As they gain greater facility with language, children become increasingly able to articulate this awareness. Even children as young as seven are sometimes able to show an almost adult-like empathy about what is happening in their families:

> The social didn't give us any money, or the bank, and we needed to ask someone else for some nappies 'cos we'd run out. My mum and me asked one of her best mates. We used to go to respite an' it was all right because it gave my mum a break and she needs a break because we make lots of noise and get on her nerves. Sometimes I have a feeling my mum and dad's going to break up. It makes me feel really really scared and terrified. Sometimes it's quite small and sometimes quite big. Sometimes she slams doors, sometimes she shouts and it scares me and when she tears her hair out it upsets me. Sometimes when we have no money my dad starts getting mad because there's nowt in the house. It makes me feel bad about eating all the food and I want mum and dad to eat as well, not give it to me, so they can live longer. They don't eat much, only a bit of chocolate and they say, 'Here you are, you can have it.' She wants to be there for me when I grow up. And she gets sad that we might have to go and she's scared she'll lose us because of

when there's no food in the house. We're saying we're hungry and we'll have to borrow money off friends and we have to ask for more and more. They can't give us more and more. It's not fair if I had more things than them.

Although showing awareness of adult issues beyond her years, this child has an empathic understanding of her carers and there may be no evidence to suggest role reversal of care-giving in the child's actions which might then indicate an attachment issue. Despite the difficulties under which families such as this labour, it cannot be assumed that they have always struggled to meet the children's physical and emotional needs. Such difficulties may be relatively short-term, arising in response to life events that may include significant losses. With sensitively responsive professional intervention, parents in such circumstances are often able to resume former levels of functioning. Their more usual practice can be undermined during periods of transition such as the birth of further children, the breakdown of partnerships, the loss of social support when a parent dies or becomes ill, or through the loss of a significant role such as being the breadwinner.

The attachment system is thought to provide a context for the development of the capacity to regulate strong feelings. When infants experience strong emotions they learn to seek the comfort of their care-givers, thereby decreasing their emotional arousal. It is also thought to aid the development of 'reflective functioning' or 'mentalization' by which humans are able learn about their own and others' intentions, desires and thoughts (Fonagy *et al.*, 2002) and develop understanding of social relationships.

Bowlby argued that young children gradually construct internal working models which enable them to make predictions (not necessarily consciously) about what will happen in response to their own behaviours and act accordingly in order to optimise the chance of having their needs met. In order to be useful, such working models need to be subject to modification in light of ongoing experience. As social and psychological systems become increasingly complex with age, significant modifications to internal working models may pose an increasingly greater challenge. Thus, the effects of early experience are thought to be carried forward even as the internal models undergo change (Goldberg, 2000). Bowlby (1969: 82) argued that, 'Clinical evidence suggests that the necessary revisions of model are not always easy to achieve. Usually they are completed but only slowly, often they are done imperfectly, and sometimes not done at all.' I find this a useful idea in contributing to an account of some parents' ongoing relationship difficulties.

Piaget's theory of learning

Bowlby's notion of internal working models fits for me with Jean Piaget's (1972) theory about how we learn. An infant may learn in early childhood that fussing and loud crying elicit adult care-giving behaviours. The internal working model (called a 'schema' or 'action scheme' by Piaget) contains this pattern. Will fussing and loud crying work in school? Probably not. Will they work in new intimate relationships? Maybe. If the established behaviour works (i.e. the outcome of the fussing and crying fits with the current schema by producing care-giving from the other), the experience is 'assimilated' into the action scheme which retains its integrity. Glasersfeld (1995: 62) summarised thus: 'assimilation is a process of treating new material as an instance of something known.' But if it does not fit, a state of 'cognitive dissonance' or 'cognitive conflict' arises. This may be resolved either by disengagement from the situation associated with the conflict (emotional withdrawal and a state of 'denial') or engagement which requires a deep review of the new experience leading to revision of the internal working model or action scheme. This process is known as accommodation. Unlike assimilation, accommodation involves radical restructuring and is typically accompanied by feelings of confusion. States of confusion can be very fertile ground for significant learning, but can also result in resistance which accounts for the persistence of ways of relating developed in early childhood. For this and other reasons, the experience of parents in their own infancy and throughout their childhood is important for understanding the internal working models that they bring to the role of care-giver. In addition to long-standing habits of response, parents also draw on their conscious memories of parenting, resolving in some instances to act in similar ways to their own parents (described by John Byng-Hall [1995] as a 'replicative script') or to take a different approach ('corrective script').

Adults who have learned and retained the action schema that fussing and loud crying is necessary to evoke care-giving may not be minded to respond at lower levels of intensity to the demands of their own children unless they have accommodated their schema in response to other compensatory experiences of care. Exploration of the life history of parents involved in family proceedings can help to illuminate the ways of relating that they bring to the parental role and needs to take account not only of their primary care-receiving experiences but also of attachments to a wider community of adults who may have shown them a different way of being looked after. Receiving support from members of the extended family and from the community of professionals outside the immediate family who cared for children as pre-schoolers and at school has been identified as a protective factor in research by DuMont *et al.* (2007). It can be especially helpful to know about any compensatory experiences, which may be very extensive, as in the case of the following mother:

> My parents had a volatile relationship and there was lots of domestic violence, especially when they'd been drinking. The police used to get called and my mum had broken bones and black eyes. They used to fight and it was horrible and I was scared. When my mum has a drink she's really loud and aggressive and it caused problems with the

neighbours. The house was a right mess. My sister's five years older than me and she used to hide me in the bedroom when things took off. My big brother's 18 years older than me. He used to live round the corner. I used to go over to his house nearly every day and have my tea there. He was really good with me. He'd talk to me. He minded about me. My brother was caring more than anybody. He had a daughter about the same age as me. I used to sleep there and he took me for days out and to get new clothes and my hair cut. He was really good with me.

I find Piaget's and Byng-Hall's ideas about learning to be congruent with attachment theory and they encourage me to seek multiple historical and current environmental and internal factors in accounting for a child or adult's presentation.

The impact of infant temperament

Individual differences in attachment style may also be impacted by infant temperament. Research by Alexander Thomas *et al.* (1968) identified nine dimensions of temperamental differences between infants that were present at birth and shown to have a degree of long-term stability. These were termed Activity Level (child's physical energy), Adaptability (how long it takes a child to adjust to new situations), Approach/Withdrawal (response to new people or places), Distractibility (tendency to be side-tracked), Intensity, Persistence (length of time on task despite distractions), Quality of Mood (general tendency towards a happy or unhappy demeanour), Rhythmicity (predictability in terms of fitting into routines) and Threshold of Response (ease with which child is disturbed by changes in the environment). Thomas and his colleagues condensed the categories to identify three groups of children: 'easy', 'difficult' and 'slow to warm up'.

Most of the parents of my acquaintance with more than one child will agree that despite being exposed to more or less similar child rearing practices, their children have differed substantially from each other in temperament, evoking different care-giving on the basis of differential reactions to parenting strategies. Some show more settled and calm responses whilst others are more prone to grizzle and fuss, cry a lot, show irregular feeding and sleeping patterns, and tend to respond with high intensity ('difficult' in the condensed category of Thomas *et al.*). Broad patterns of temperamental characteristics have been found to be modestly stable throughout childhood (Chess and Thomas, 1986).

I think that a perspective on the child's temperament is important when making assessments in family proceedings, yet it is often left out of the equation. 'Difficult' infants tend not to produce the behaviours that readily evoke tender care-giving and I find it important to recognise how intense can be the feelings (hostile or warm, love or hate) that are generated in care-givers when providing round-the-clock care.

Parental factors affecting the development of attachment and categorisations of attachment style

Having focussed on the infant's important contribution to the developing attachment system, I want to explore the impact on the infant of different kinds of responsiveness from their primary care-givers. This was the subject of an extensive series of studies by Mary Ainsworth and her colleagues who devised the Strange Situation Protocol which resulted in the classification of infants according to their behaviour in response to separation from and reunification with their main care-giver. As the researchers did not wish to assign descriptive labels, in the initial study infants were classified into three groups, A, B and C. These have subsequently been labelled as 'secure' (B), 'insecure-avoidant' (A) and insecure-ambivalent/resistant' (C). In all of these cases, infants were regarded as having developed an *organised* strategy by which they attempted to have their needs met.

Carers were rated along four dimensions of sensitivity-insensitivity, acceptance-rejection, cooperation-interference and accessibility-ignoring. Care-givers who tried to understand and respond to the infant's signals and inferred emotions were defined by Ainsworth (1973) as having high levels of sensitivity. Care-giver sensitivity is thought to enable the regulation of feelings and behaviours, whereas infants subject to less sensitively responsive care-giving are likely to find this more difficult.

The Strange Situation Protocol is a series of three-minute episodes which begin with a young child aged about 9–18 months and one of the child's main care-givers being introduced to a playroom by the researcher. The child is allowed to explore the playroom for three minutes after which time a stranger enters. For the first minute the stranger is silent then converses with the care-giver prior to approaching the child. The carer leaves the room as unobtrusively as possible. The stranger interacts with the child and after a further three minutes the carer returns, greets and re-settles the child whilst the stranger leaves. The carer leaves for a second time, saying 'bye-bye' to the child who is left alone. After three minutes the stranger returns and after a final three minutes the carer returns, greets the child and the stranger leaves unobtrusively (Prior and Glaser, 2006). The whole episode is recorded and the child's behaviour rated by trained observers. In addition to the original three categories of child behaviour, category D ('disorganised/ disoriented insecure') was later created by Mary Main and Judith Soloman (1986). Table 7.1 provides a summary of child and adult behaviour patterns associated with each category.

Although infants showing avoidant patterns appear to be relatively self-sufficient, Mary Ainsworth and her colleagues (1978) argued that they are also anxious and have rarely experienced the adult soothing that reduces their emotional arousal. The continued frustration arising out of a failure to have their attachment needs met may result in expressions of frustration and outbursts of anger. Disorganised attachment patterns are the only kind in

Table 7.1 Summary of observed child and caregiver behaviour patterns in the Strange Situation Test at the age of 9–18 months

Attachment Pattern	Child	Care-giver
Secure	Infant protests at care-giver's departure, seeks proximity and comfort on return. Quickly soothed and returns to exploratory behaviour. May accept comfort from stranger but shows clear preference for care-giver.	Provides comfort to distressed child. Responds sensitively, promptly and consistently to distress.
Avoidant	Infant shows indifference and little or no distress on care-giver's departure, little or no response to return, ignores or turns away with no effort to maintain contact if picked up. Responds in similar way to stranger and care-giver.	Little or no response if child shows distress. Discourages crying and encourages independence. May move away or avert gaze.
Ambivalent/ Resistant	Infant shows distress on separation with ambivalence, anger, or reluctance to approach and return to play on care-giver's return. Appears preoccupied with question of care-giver's availability. May seek contact but resist angrily when comfort is provided. Not easily soothed by care-giver or stranger.	Care-giver unpredictable, showing both sensitively responsive care and neglectful responses.
Disorganised	Infant seems confused and may show stereotyped behaviours on care-giver's return such as freezing or rocking. May show fearful facial expressions, odd postures. Displays contradictory, disoriented behaviours such as approaching but with back turned. Shows rapid changes of emotional expression.	May show frightened or frightening behaviour, insensitivity, intrusion, poor communication and timing. May show negativity towards infant.

which it is thought that the child has been unable to develop a coordinated strategy in response to care-giver behaviours. Their behaviour suggests that they do not know what to do in order to have their attachment needs met. Secure attachment patterns are thought to aid infants in learning that they are lovable and enable the development of age-appropriate autonomy. Such infants also learn to anticipate that others will be available, cooperative and dependable.

In a study by Mary Main and Jude Cassidy (1988), responses to parents of children at age six were found to be predictable from assessments of infant attachment by the Strange Situation test. At age six, children in the 'disorganised' group were found to show a variety of different kinds of controlling behaviour. Some, described as 'controlling-punitive', showed behaviours that appeared to humiliate or reject the carer such as saying, 'I told you to keep quiet.' A second group, termed 'controlling-care-giving', showed protective and sensitive care and concern towards the adult which appeared as a partial role-reversal, sometimes known as a 'parentified' child. The children who had been classified as showing disorganised attachment in infancy had typically developed an organised strategy at age six years, evidence that children are not necessarily harmed forever by adverse experiences in their early years:

> We now know that whatever stresses an individual may have encountered in the early years, he or she need not be for ever more at the mercy of the past. There are survivors as well as victims; children's resilience must be acknowledged every bit as much as their vulnerability; single horrific experiences, however traumatic at the time, need not lead to permanent harm but can be modified and reversed by subsequent experiences; children who miss out on particular experiences at the usual time may well make up for them subsequently; and healthy development can occur under a far wider range of circumstances than was thought possible at one time.
>
> (Schaffer, 2000: 40)

Whilst infants are thought to be biologically adapted to participate in goal-directed patterns of interaction, I believe that they are capable of developing a range of behavioural patterns in response to different adults in their lives, in a similar way that infants are able to learn to speak different languages with different individuals if they live in a bi-lingual or multi-lingual context. In later revisions of his theory, John Bowlby (1982) drew attention to the importance of the infant's learned responses to environmental cues which allowed that they were able to develop attachments to multiple care-givers. This does not necessarily mean that they do not develop preferences for specific care-givers. It has been suggested that, within families, multiple relationships have reciprocal influences upon each other (McHale, 2007). On the basis of a longitudinal study of infants and their families, four distinctive family alliance patterns were proposed by Fivaz-Depeursinge and Corboz-Warnery (1999). These were labelled 'disordered', 'collusive', 'stressed', and 'cooperative'. James McHale states, 'the perceived cohesiveness of the full family unit, as much as any single care-giver/child dyad, is what ultimately serves as the young child's central locus of security or insecurity' (McHale, 2007: 373). I find this appealing in explaining how some children when growing up develop strong attachments to siblings, grandparents and family members with whom they spend large parts of the day. In interview, parents often recall adults outside the immediate family who have had a critical influence on the development of their ideas about and actions in the parenting role. Such a view also provides a perspective on how the interactions between family members may affect a child's developing sense of security, such as in contexts characterised by domestic violence.

John Bowlby was of the view that in the first two or three years the child is flexible in responding differentially to changes of care-giver behaviour, so that the pattern of attachment could be regarded as a characteristic of each infant-adult pair. Bowlby also argued that securely attached children are more capable of modifying their working models in light of experience, whereas this is more difficult for anxiously attached children. As the child grows older the pattern is viewed (Bowlby, 1969) as increasingly based on the child's internal working model/s, becoming more stable and resistant to change.

The theory of attachment is well-established, and evidence for stable and enduring patterns has been provided by Belsky *et al.* (1996), Fraley (2002), Grossmann *et al.* (2005), van Ijzendoorn *et al.* (1999), Waters *et al.* (2000), and Weinfield *et al.* (2004). Evidence linking adverse childhood experiences, abuse and maltreatment to the development of highly insecure disorganised attachment patterns has been provided by Carlson (1998), Cicchetti and Toth (1995), and Maugham and Cicchetti (2002).

Adult attachments

The term 'attachment' applies to the child's relationship with the care-giver, and the term 'attachment figure' describes the primary carer (Prior and Glaser, 2006: 15). These authors argue that it is incorrect to refer to a parent's attachment to a child, rather that this is appropriately called a 'care-giving bond'.

Attachment theorists have been interested in the impact of early experiences of care-receiving on adult memories of and feelings about attachment; how these constructions affect the ways in which adults respond to their children's security needs, and how they influence the ways in which adults relate to others within romantic relationships. The Adult Attachment Interview (devised by George *et al.*, (1984) and described in Prior and Glaser (2006) and Main (n.d.)) is an hour-long interview designed to explore childhood experiences of loss, separation and rejection, emotional distress, injury and sickness in addition to experiences of love and acceptance. The interview can raise the interviewee's level of anxiety and stress through its focus on such matters. Coding is based not so much on the content but rather on the way that the interviewee's story unfolds in terms of its coherence, relevance to the questions asked, its clarity, the way in which the respondent collaborates with the interviewer, and the level of detail of the account. If the participant has developed insecure mental constructions of attachment, childhood memories may be vague, detail to back up general comments may be missing, information may be rich but confused and there may be contradictions in the account (Howe *et al.*, 1999). A link between the coherence of parents' accounts of the care that they received in childhood and the pattern of attachment shown in their infant's behaviour has been repeatedly demonstrated in research findings (Main *et al.*, 1985; van Ijzendoorn, 1995) even when adult representations of attachment are assessed ante-natally (Steele *et al.*, 1996).

The interview results in classification into one of four patterns of states of mind with respect to attachment which correspond to the four childhood patterns and are named 'secure-autonomous', 'dismissing' (equivalent to avoidant), 'pre-occupied-entangled' (equivalent to ambivalent) and 'unresolved-disorganised' (Howe *et al.*, 1999: 38).

Several attempts have been made to explore the idea that adult representations of attachment arising out of childhood experiences will impact not only on how they provide care to their children, but also on ways of relating to romantic partners. Cindy Hazan and Phillip Shaver (1987) suggested that adult love could be conceptualised as an attachment process. They developed a self-report measure for the purpose of classifying adult representations of attachment. They proposed a three-category classification of secure, avoidant and anxious-ambivalent. This has been developed further in a number of subsequent studies (Bartholomew and Horowitz, 1991; Feeney *et al.*, 1995; Fraley *et al.*, 2000). The latter group of authors devised 'The Experiences in Close Relationships – Revised (ECR-R)'. This is a questionnaire measure designed to assess individual differences with respect to attachment-related anxiety (i.e. the extent to which people feel insecure vs secure about the extent of their partner's availability and responsiveness) and attachment-related avoidance (i.e. the extent to which people are uncomfortable being close to others vs secure dependence on others). Responses are scored along these two dimensions, which intersect to form four quadrants with resultant classifications of 'secure', 'dismissive', 'preoccupied' and 'fearful'. The results may provide insights into adult conceptualisations of intimate relationships including orientations towards the attachment behaviours of their children. Bartholomew and Horowitz's classification is based on whether people see themselves positively or negatively, and whether others are viewed positively or negatively. This results in the following:

> *Secure:* positive view of self, positive view of others
> *Dismissive:* positive view of self, negative view of others
> *Preoccupied:* negative view of self, positive view of others
> *Fearful:* negative view of self, negative view of others

I find it more informative to think of the relative value with which people regard themselves in relation to others, rather than allocation of an individual to a category.

Attachment disorder

A diagnosis of 'attachment disorder' is a relatively recent addition to the American (The Diagnostic and Statistical Manual of Mental Disorders,

Fourth Edition, Text Revision [DSM-IV-TR], American Psychiatric Association, 2000) and British (International Statistical Classification of Diseases and Related Health Problems, Tenth Revision [ICD 10], World Health Organization, 1992) classifications of mental disorders. In the British system, two distinct disorders are identified, Reactive Attachment Disorder of Childhood (RAD) and Disinhibited Attachment Disorder of Childhood (DAD). The American system identifies Reactive Attachment Disorder of Infancy or Early Childhood (RAD) with the two sub-types of Inhibited and Disinhibited. Within these diagnostic manuals clinicians are cautioned that there continues to be extensive debate about what features might warrant such a diagnosis. Pathogenic care (including abuse and/or neglect or frequent changes of care-giver) is described as the aetiology of attachment disorders (Zeanah *et al.*, 2004). Most of the examples and evidence in the literature have been drawn from studies of children who have spent much, if not all, of their early childhoods in institutional care before being placed for adoption. As it stands, the only group of children who match current definitions are those who suffered early and severe deprivation in institutionalised care (Howe, 2003). There is no current agreement as to methods of assessment or appropriate treatments (Schofield and Beek, 2006: 39).

Maladaptive behaviours stated to be associated with the disorder have included stealing, lying, cruelty to animals and other people, avoidance of eye contact, indiscriminate affection with relative strangers and a refusal to express affection with family members, destruction of property, gorging of food, abnormal speech patterns, lack of remorse, impulsivity, inappropriate sexual behaviour, and over-activity (Kay Hall and Geher, 2003). But, Prior and Glaser (2006) caution against the demonising tone of some of these attributes and descriptions which do not accord with the core features described in the statistical manuals. These are much more circumspect and emphasise the importance of a history of *severe* neglect and developmentally inappropriate social relatedness. These authors have summarised the findings of academic studies of children who have experienced severe neglect and conclude that:

- the inhibited and disinhibited forms of attachment disorder may coexist under conditions of extreme neglect;
- the inhibited form mostly remits in children adopted out of institutions;
- the disinhibited attachment disorder can endure even after children are placed with sensitive caregivers;
- the disinhibited form can continue alongside structured attachment behaviour towards the child's permanent caregivers;
- these attachments may be of the A, B, C or D type, or may be atypical

(Prior and Glaser, 2006: 216)

Many children who come into care have experienced helplessness and fear in relationships with their primary care-givers and therefore develop a number of controlling and maladaptive strategies in an attempt to ensure their own safety and survival. However, I have also seen these strategies adopted by children who are fearful for other reasons – for example when having been removed from a primary carer with whom they have experienced security. These behaviours need to be interpreted in context; there is no clear one-to-one correspondence between a child's behavioural presentation and a specific explanation for its appearance. The vast majority of children encountered in family proceedings will *not* have developed an attachment disorder, whilst it may be helpful to explore current relational patterns, attachment style or difficulties.

Critiques of attachment theory

I regard attachment theory as a useful and important framework applicable to assessments in family proceedings, whilst I want to raise a caveat against making any assumptions that explanations for a child's behaviour in response to adult care-givers are located *exclusively* in the development of the attachment system in infancy. Attachment theory was proposed at a time when women in the West took a much more central role than today as the home-maker and primary care-giver. Although the theory is not gender- or parent-specific, the early writings tended to describe the primary care-giver as 'mother', with the implication that when the attachment system 'went wrong' it was the mother's 'fault' for failing to provide the necessary sensitively responsive care. As a mother, can I provide the sensitively responsive care-giving that would ensure the development of secure attachment? What about the impact on my children of the substitute care-giving that I organise so that I can go about my daily work? In twenty-first century contemporary society, children are likely to experience care given by a range of adults both within and outside the family, a factor which needs to be included in current conceptualisations of the attachment system.

I also have reservations about the classification of attachment into discrete categories. It would surprise me if it were possible to fit us all into one of just four such categories. My experience suggests that for most characteristics, human variation is continuous, and that behaviour is strongly impacted by the context in which it occurs. A study by Fraley and Spieker (2003) who examined data from 1,139 15-month-olds provided empirical evidence that variation in attachment patterns is continuous rather than discrete.

A meta-analysis of parental antecedents of secure attachment by de Wolff and van Ijzendoorn (1997) reported that the association between maternal sensitivity and attachment behaviours in infants was much weaker for low-income families and when care-givers were experiencing mental health difficulties. Claire Hughes (2003) suggests that the stresses and strains of financial disadvantage and psychiatric problems may overburden potentially sensitive carers, and that sensitivity itself may be a feature of the carer-infant dyad rather than a unique characteristic of the adult participant. In Main and Cassidy's (1988) study, whilst classifications based on the Strange Situation Protocol predicted attachment relationships at age six years, for some partnerships there was a marked change of classification. This finding was attributed to specific stressful events impacting at particular stages of development which were thought to have interfered with sensitively responsive care-giving during a particular period of time. The authors argued the importance of investigating change in families and the impact of change on developing attachments. When assessing individual children and families, continuity and stability of attachment style cannot be presumed.

It has been argued that the Strange Situation taps just one manifestation of a child's attachment behaviours which may be expressed differently in other settings (Rutter, 1995). Although findings arising from studies employing the Strange Situation Protocol have been replicated in many different cultures, it has been argued that their generalisability may be constrained by the meaning afforded to separation and unification in different cultures. In Japan, under normal circumstances infants are rarely separated from their care-giver. The results of a study conducted in Japan nevertheless provided evidence that the classification of care-givers using the Adult Attachment Interview was predictive of children's reunion behaviour at age six years (Behrens *et al.*, 2007).

Some infants are thought to be particularly susceptible to the stress of unpredictable or hostile relationships with care-givers in the early years by virtue of temperamental factors such as high levels of motor activity and negative emotional reactions to stimulation (Marshall and Fox, 2005). Whilst variations in infant temperament mean that concerning childhood behaviours may develop even when the child is provided with highly sensitive responsive care, specific learning difficulties, physical health problems, differential rates of development and current environmental factors may also be implicated when adults are struggling with their responses to children's emotions and behaviour. Children who are given a diagnosis of autistic spectrum disorder including Asperger's syndrome show difficulties with reciprocal social interactions. This does not necessarily mean that they are unable to develop secure and organised attachment patterns (Rutgers *et al.*, 2004). However, in Anne Rutgers and colleagues' studies of children with autism, which adopted the Strange Situation test, a lower proportion of children were categorised as securely attached than in the general population. Children with poorer intellectual attainments were more likely to be classified as insecurely attached.

In any system which has an inherent complexity (many different factors are involved) and/or where there is a significant time lag between the action of the 'input' variables (parenting behaviours) and the outcomes (attachment style); where various paths of causality or causal loops may be involved, then a measurable or a clear and direct simple connection between input and outcome is unlikely to be established (Jon Scaife, 2004, personal communication). Plasticity is now regarded as a key property of the human brain (Flanagan, 1992). Each individual has a unique dynamic fine structure of neuronal connections: 'the plastic brain is capable of reorganising itself adaptively in response to the particular novelties encountered in the organism's environment' (Dennett, 1991). This adaptive flexibility is particularly strong in children. It is not therefore surprising that the results of studies of children brought up in conditions of severe neglect, such as those raised in institutional environments where care-giving has been emotionally detached (Hodges, 1996), find that the majority do not show signs of attachment disturbance although they were less likely to develop confiding relationships with peers. In a study by Michael Rutter (2002) of Romanian orphans adopted into Western families following the overthrow of the Ceaucescu regime in 1989, although higher rates of atypical insecure attachment patterns were found for late-adopted children, their histories did not prevent them from forming attachment relationships and 70 per cent of later-adopted children showed no significant attachment difficulties.

Attachment in practice – relevance to safeguarding

Attachment theory emphasises the importance of continuity and sensitivity in care-giving relationships. Research findings suggest that there are benefits to children from the development of secure attachment in infancy. Vivien Prior and Danya Glaser (2006) reviewed both longitudinal and cross-sectional studies of the influence of attachment security on functioning. They summarise the findings as showing clear evidence of an association between secure attachment and good functioning in a number of domains including effective interpersonal relationships, positive mood, and the development of more complex symbolic play in young children. There is evidence that secure attachment acts as a buffer to the physiological stress response. When they were assessed in the Strange Situation Protocol, infants who showed disorganised attachment were found to have elevated cortisol levels (Hertsgaard *et al.*, 1995). Prior and Glaser reported that there are, 'strong associations between early insecure-avoidant attachment and later aggression, anti-social behaviour and negative affect; and between early insecure-resistant attachment and later anxiety and passive withdrawn behaviour. Insecure-disorganised attachment is strongly associated with later hostile and aggressive behaviour as well as with dissociation' (Prior and Glaser, 2006: 179). In the Minnesota longitudinal study of 267 first-time mothers, the strongest single predictor of global pathology in the children at 17½ years of age was disorganised attachment (Sroufe *et al.*, 2005). In order to ensure children's welfare, it follows that assessments of attachment style and care-giving behaviour can make an important contribution to a developing understanding of family dynamics when determining children's futures.

Assessment of attachment

A number of approaches to assessment of a child's attachment and an adult's care-giving are possible. They include exploring a child's developmental history and observed behaviour, observation of the interaction between the child and care-giver, interviews with the child and the care-giver, picture response tasks, narrative story stem approaches, and questionnaire measures. These are listed in full in Appendix 1.

Many of these measures were devised primarily for the purpose of research into attachment rather than as tools for clinical and child protection work, although some are widely used in clinical contexts. Observational methods often require the making of a recording which is evaluated by trained observers with the aim of ensuring reliability and validity. Some of the coding manuals are in unpublished manuscripts, available only after a training course is completed, and in some cases with the requirement for participation in regular training updates. This requirement can make them relatively inaccessible for the purposes of day-to-day practice. It is possible to adapt available materials as I have suggested in Chapter 6, providing that interpretations are made with caution and the findings are combined with information from multiple sources.

I have personally found useful and accessible the Family Relations Test (although availability is restricted to certain professions), which gives an indication of the extent of emotional involvement of the child with family members, Fahlberg checklist, Experiences in Close Relationships-Revised (ECR-R), Story Stems built around family dolls, and informal versions of the Strange Situation protocol. As children grow and develop they are subject to a much wider range of influences than the immediate family. Attachment theory is primarily about what *infants* do. Beyond this stage, caution is advised in giving an attachment style label whilst directing efforts towards understanding the mental models and behaviour patterns through which children and adults negotiate their family relationships.

Interpretation of behaviour

What kind of behaviours in a child might indicate a history of insecure or disorganised attachment? These could range across an entire spectrum from withdrawn, self-sufficient behaviour to extremes of acting out; for this reason, information about the child's behaviour alone is insufficient from which to draw valid conclusions. Some behaviour can be seen as a communication, showing how a child is feeling, but assigning a meaning can be done too hastily. Specific behaviours do not have specific meanings; they occur in the context of relationships and the child may express a different repertoire in different settings.

Rebecca showed global developmental delay and in particular her speech and language were seemingly almost non-existent when she commenced nursery school at age four years. She would not look staff in the eye, spoke no words and presented as extremely shy and withdrawn. Her care-givers said that her behaviour at home differed. There, she was outgoing and funny. She would entertain them with her antics, loved to be cuddled and her language development was 'coming along' despite being delayed. Rebecca's carers were described as neglecting her, failing to provide appropriate stimulation, and as being dishonest when they had reported positive progress to health care professionals involved in routine developmental assessments. The contact supervisor observed that once Rebecca had become familiar with her she had talked at length during the car journey to the contact venue. She showed a great deal of excitement about seeing her mother and when released from her booster seat would run into the venue shouting at the top of her voice. She chattered away freely in her mother's company.

This child showed contrasting behaviours in different settings. A graph plotting data on the files from her regular developmental assessments showed that her progress was following a steady trajectory, somewhat behind the average for a child of her age. For this child it was crucial to observe her behaviour across different settings and with different people in order to avoid drawing erroneous conclusions. Whilst there were issues concerning the standard of cleanliness of the family home, overcrowding, and a previous history of child abuse by one of the mother's earlier partners, there was evidence to suggest a positive emotional bond between the mother and child. Without further information it was not possible to determine the nature of the attachment that Rebecca had developed with her mother. When she moved into a foster placement at first she was silent and withdrawn but within a few weeks she had developed a positive relationship with her substitute care-giver, indicative of a working model of relationships which characterised adults as trustworthy.

When children are placed in substitute care they are likely to replicate relational behaviours learned in their birth family. This is not inevitable but will depend on the age of the child when placed and her or his experience of a range of different care-giving behaviours. Children who have experienced security are more likely to be able successfully to make new interpersonal relationships. The mental state associated with secure attachment is not finite. There is not a fixed quantity of it that has to be shared, but rather an orientation towards and expectations of interpersonal relationships that can be brought to new relationships. When an attachment is severed, there is an experience of loss and grieving that may be shown by the child in all manner of ways. In my experience, some children who are taken from their birth families at age six years or older retain a strong memory of and link with their primary care-givers and are reluctant to develop a secure attachment to a new family, particularly when there is no assurance of placement permanence. I regard this as an adaptive response.

Attachment and contact with birth family

When children have been removed from the care of their birth parents as a result of assessed harm or risk, regular supervised contacts usually take place. Children show a wide spectrum of behaviour in response to such contacts; enthusiasm and affection, reluctance to attend, angry and defiant behaviour, or behaviour which switches between approach and avoidance. I do not think it possible to interpret such behaviour with any degree of confidence because of the unusual circumstances in which it is occurring. It is not naturalistic, the care-givers may be particularly tense under scrutiny, they may not want to discipline a child given the very short period that they are able to spend together, and the venue may not provide suitable conditions for relaxed age-appropriate play. The child may be at any of the stages of separation and loss described by Robertson and Robertson (1971), feeling sadness, apathy and despair; showing withdrawal or anger, crying, clinging and rejection. This is how a five-year-old described the feeling of confusion that she experienced about her birth and foster families:

> It all makes me dizzy. I like my mum and Alfie best. I love everything with my [foster] family here, Dylan, Matty, Sarah and Dave. I just love it. If I had to choose, I'd choose this one [birth family]. I just want to stay here, me [placement]. I want to go back there but they're not letting me. It's real sad. Doing my head in.

One of the other difficulties about observation of contact is that different observers are prone to focus on different matters, take different perspectives on the factors that might indicate a positive relationship, and take different approaches towards helping care-givers to feel relaxed under observation. These contact notes are characteristic of a series involving two different supervisors, the second taking over the role when the first supervisor moved to a new job. The contacts involved a mother and two young children:

> Jack and Kerry ran to their mum when I took them out of the car and she gave them an enthusiastic hug in turn. She had brought fruit snacks and juice for the children. She talked to Jack about his teacher while Kerry ate her snack. When the children became boisterous I suggested finding a game to play. Mum encouraged them to choose a book each and read to them animatedly. She encouraged Jack to read some of the words himself and praised him when he complied. The children started to play football together, kicking the ball too high.

Mum asked Jack repeatedly to keep the ball low, threatening that she would not bring a ball to future contacts. She put the ball away when Jack continued and after a short protest he went over to the toy box to choose a game. Jack went over to his mum and gave her a cuddle, telling her that he loved her. She hugged him back and told him that she loved him too. Mum suggested a game of snakes and ladders. Kerry joined in but struggled to play within the rules. Jack became frustrated and kicked the box onto the floor. Mum told him to pick up the counters and after several times of calmly asking him to do so, Jack did as he was told. His mum praised him and told him that he had earned a star for good behaviour. I gave notice of five minutes remaining. Mum helped the children to put on their coats and shoes and tidied the room. She gave Jack a book to look at while she tidied and encouraged Kerry to help her put some of the toys away. Mum put the children in the car, strapped them in, gave them a hug and said that she would miss them. She waved them out of sight. This was a good quality contact, lots of positive interaction, parenting skills improving and mum was content to take advice.

When mum arrived Jack smiled and gave her a hug. She gave the children a drink and some crisps. Jack said, 'This is rubbish, I want a cake.' His mum opened the crisps, Jack started to eat them, complaining that she had not brought cakes. She explained that she had been told not to bring cakes as he was too full to eat his evening meal when he returned to his placement. He said that he was not coming to contact again if she did not bring cake. She said that she would compromise and bring one cake next time instead of crisps. She asked the children if they wanted to play football. Jack and mum played together while Kerry was left to entertain herself. Jack started to kick the ball too high and hard. His mother told him to stop and he ignored her. I suggested that we do a different activity. Mum told Jack to give her the ball and that they were going to do a different activity. Jack refused to give her the ball so she took it off him and put it away. She suggested a game with the toy kitchen and Jack sat talking to her, explaining all the things that he was making. Mum sat with Kerry on her knee, letting her draw around her hand. Mum changed Kerry's nappy. At the end of contact she tidied the room and took the children to the car. Jack started to run ahead and ignored mum when she told him to come back. I advised that she needed to hold his hand. There were several areas of concern during the contact: mum did not chastise Jack for complaining about the food she brought. She should not have told him that she was not allowed to bring cakes to contact. It was concerning that Jack said that he would not come to contact again if she did not bring cakes and that he ran ahead, ignoring his mum at the end of contact. She needs to set firm boundaries and rules and not let Jack have his own way. She did not follow advice to hold Jack's hand.

Despite my reservations about the impact of the observer's mind-set on what is observed, and about the multiple possible interpretations of children's behaviour if taken alone, I do believe that observations of interaction between children and parents can be fruitful in making a cautious contribution to judgements about the nature of the relationship between them. Observations can be made informally when visiting a child's family home. Teachers and nursery staff can provide useful comments about the interaction between a parent and child at the beginning and end of each school day. Does the child part willingly from the carer, cry and fuss on a regular basis? Do the pair greet each other with enthusiasm or indifference at the end of the school day? Based around the categorisations of attachment devised in research settings the following kinds of behaviour shown in interaction with the care-giver *may*, taken together with other kinds of information, give an indication of problematic attachment styles or mental models of relationship:

- Regularly responds to adult's departure with intense distress or indifference.
- Clings, avoids proximity or effects indifference when reunited with care-giver.
- Little or no eye contact between child and care-giver.
- Behaves in contradictory ways towards carer, veering between clinginess, anger and defiance.
- Freezes in presence of care-giver.
- Appears fearful of care-giver.
- No overt shows of affection or physical contact initiated by child towards carer.
- Child's comments to care-giver give appearance of wishing to humiliate carer in front of other adults.
- Seems very protective towards care-giver and may show unnatural and apparently false cheerfulness on reunion.
- Does not accept comfort offered by care-giver.
- Does not show 'affective sharing' i.e. joining the care-giver into the child's play.
- Does not respond to care-giver signals concerning the level of risk or safety of situations.
- Seems indifferent to the carer's actions and degree of proximity.
- Appears to lack trust and confidence in carer's continued interest in self, e.g. when carer interacts with others in child's presence.
- Does not show a pattern of using the carer as a base from which to explore.

- • Absence of social referencing – child does not refer to carer with eye contact or proximity-seeking when anxious or frightened.
- • Acts as if anticipating interference when adult is trying to help by showing anger, turning away or whining.
- • Indiscriminate with strangers, accepting or seeking physical contact. Does not seem to differentiate between adults.
- • Struggles to regulate own difficult emotions.

Assessment of care-giver sensitivity

Attachment behaviours are developed in the context of relationships with care-givers. An analysis of a child's relationship with an adult care-giver appropriately focuses on the contributions made to the relationship by both parties. A number of methods have been devised with a view to evaluating the contribution made to the developing relationship by the care-giver. Prior and Glaser (2006: 139–155) summarise specific measures for the assessment of care-giving. Information concerning validity and reliability is provided. Observational methods include AMBIANCE (Bronfman *et al.*, 1993), Maternal Sensitivity Scales (Ainsworth, 1969), CARE-Index (Crittenden, 1979–2004), and the Caregiver Behavior Classification System (Marvin and Britner, 1996). Interview methods include the Parent Development Interview (Aber *et al.*, 1985; Slade *et al.*, 2004) and the Experiences of Care-giving Interview (George and Solomon, 1996).

As with measures devised to assess attachment, many of these are relatively inaccessible to practitioners by virtue of being described in unpublished manuscripts. Nevertheless, it is possible to derive ideas from them about the kinds of care-giving behaviours that are thought to enhance the likelihood of the development of secure attachment. An absence of the following may make it difficult for a child to learn functional ways of relating.

Care-giver shows the following:

- • Appears supportive and attuned rather than abrupt and interfering with regard to the child's interests, activities and exploration.
- • Presents neither as unduly fearful and timid, nor as frightening.
- • Largely shows warmth rather than anger and hostility towards child.
- • Appears to accept rather than reject the child's approaches.
- • Shows affection towards child openly.
- • Appears confident rather than uncertain about how to respond to child.
- • Shows good insight into child's-eye view and empathy for child's experiences
- • Typically encourages and praises rather than criticises child's actions.
- • Gives coherent and consistent account of emotionally stressful events in own childhood without undue brevity, excessive length, inability to recall supporting examples, or wandering onto topics irrelevant to the question.

Implications of attachment theory for placement

As attachment theory has gained ground in accounting for children's emotional development, it has carried implications for disputes concerning residence, contact and child custody. The theory implies that secure attachment and continuity of care take precedence over economic factors and birth relationships when making best decisions for children who often have care-providing relationships within the extended birth family and in the wider community. Family courts in the UK have moved considerably towards recognition of the complications of attachment relationships (Rutter and O'Connor, 1999).

The importance of continuity of care when children are unable to remain with their birth families has implications for decisions regarding substitute foster placements. Placement instability reduces the opportunity for children to develop long-term, secure attachments (Leathers, 2002) and may compound existing difficulties and further reinforce dysfunctional mental models of relationships. When children experience frequent changes of placement they are, 'less likely to attempt to establish intimate relationships with future carers and more likely to display behaviour that keeps carers emotionally distant' (Munro and Hardy, 2006: 2).

A study by Ward and Skuse (2001) reported that in the first year of their care episode, 44 per cent of 242 children and young people experienced a single placement, 28 per cent had three or more, including 3 per cent who moved on five or more occasions. Moves of placement were found to be most likely amongst looked-after children and young people in the first 12 months. Sixty nine per cent of this group had moved a year later (Sinclair *et al.*, 2005). Jackson and Thomas (1999: 4) argued that, 'too many children enter a system in which further damage is caused to their social, emotional and cognitive development through its failure to provide a place where the child knows they will remain for any length of time.' Research carried out by Ward *et al.* (2010) reported by Margaret Adcock (2011: 512) included the key finding that,

> By their third birthday, 35% of infants had been permanently separated from parents who had been unable to overcome their difficulties. However, the long term welfare of 60% of these had been doubly jeopardised – by late separation from an abusive family followed by the disruption of a close attachment with an interim carer when they moved to a permanent placement.

Attachment theory reminds us of the importance of trying to ensure that children are not moved repeatedly, particularly during crucial periods for the development of secure attachment (Goldsmith *et al.*, 2004). At times this may mean giving precedence to a marginally satisfactory placement in the extended family where there is evidence of a positive and enduring prior relationship. The issue is discussed further in Chapter 9.

Continuity of attachment

In my experience, most children over the age of four years can be expected to retain a memory of their attachment figures from their birth family, whatever the quality of care-giving that they received, and often anticipate searching for their birth parents when they reach the age of 18 years. At age seven years Luke described the final contact with his birth family which had taken place almost three years earlier:

> The contact centre were good and it were quiet and we all liked to speak and play. I looked forward to it. The last time I saw my mummy it were really really sad. For the last bit I were crying. I wanted them to stay. I wanted to move back but when I'm 18 I'm going to find my mummy. I liked seeing all of them but I was most sad about my mummy. Every time we went to see her she brought us presents. I missed mummy. We might see her when we're 18. I made mummy and daddy cry 'cos I were crying so much. We were all like sad when we left.

This 13-year-old understood the need for cooperation with the local authority, but had plans to take matters into her own hands if her desired outcome did not result from the court proceedings:

> I miss my mum's love. She'd show it in a lot of ways. Sometimes she'd surprise us with things she'd cooked. She'd pretend nothing was ready. Sometimes we said, "We're going to the park," but when we came home we'd go somewhere better: "We'll eat at McDonald's." I like to ring her. If I could I'd ring her every day to talk about what I've been up to and how I'm feeling and that. What I've been up to and stuff; what I've been eating. I just miss being with her. We used to do all the little girly things like straighten her hair and she'd straighten mine and do different hairstyles and talk about what we're doing. Paint my nails and that. My mum helps me when I'm angry. She says, 'Calm down and don't go angry, it's not good.' I loved watching TV quiz shows and soaps with my mum. If someone was trying to bully me at school I'd tell her. My mum always said, 'If there's anything worrying you at school I'll come.' She met all our needs. We all go to mum. I want to go definitely home to my mum. I just want to go home and I feel that I need to be at home. I only stay here 'cos I know if I run off I'll get in trouble and it wouldn't give a good impression for my mum. It wouldn't help so there's no point. They've said to me, 'Wait till September,' so I've been waiting all that time; counting down. If that disappoints me I'll go home anyway.

They're talking about shared care. I don't want to do no shared care. It's just like being passed around really. I'd tell them I'm going home anyway.

Attachment theory is about relationships, the comfort and solace that arise out of closeness, empathy and trust. As a practitioner, I too bring an attachment history to my work, not only to my relationships with friends and family. I need to reflect on my own attachment history, what this means for how I relate to the families I encounter in my practice, and how I can try to create the conditions in which I might provide a secure base from which parents and children may develop confidence in testing their capabilities, in making changes, and in facing their fears. Howe *et al.* (1999) argue that theoretical understanding helps practitioners to bear the insults to their sensibilities encountered in this difficult work, lessening the likelihood of a retreat into procedurally-dominated ways of working. Compassionate practice is the result.

I want to end this chapter by summarising some key points because I believe that attachment theory is sometimes stretched too far in making decisions about children's futures:

- The quality of the child's attachment or the parental bond cannot be judged solely by reference to separation and unification behaviours.
- Assessments of attachment style are impacted by the age of the child. As the child grows older other influences may have a greater impact than early parenting experiences.
- Apparent attachment difficulties may be evoked in response to current stressors but subside once these are resolved.
- Children are able to learn multiple patterns of relating which they reproduce in different settings such as home and school.
- Patterns of parent-child relating developed in childhood may be, to various degrees, 'replicated' or 'corrected'.
- Parents who have experienced poor care histories may have received extensive compensatory care from which they have developed alternative internal models of relationship. People are not invariably at the mercy of their pasts.
- Some children are temperamentally more difficult to parent – they are less able to evoke sensitively responsive care.
- The term 'attachment disorder' can currently only be applied to children who have a significant history of serious neglect through institutionalised care.
- There is no clear one-to-one correspondence between behavioural presentations and specific explanations for their appearance.

8   Risk, safety, protective factors and needs assessment

The concept of risk assessment gained prominence in the UK following a series of child deaths thought to have been preventable. This led to legislative changes and an extension of the notion of child safety from a narrow focus on the protection of the individual to a broader view that includes the wider community (Smith, 2008). I welcome this emphasis because I am sceptical that a mass disorder, in this case that of child maltreatment, can be eradicated by focussing only on specific families. I share George Albee's (1983: 24) view that '… no mass disorder afflicting mankind is ever brought under control or eliminated by attempts at treating the afflicted individual.'

Community interventions emerge out of a wide angle perspective. These are aimed at preventing child maltreatment by ensuring high quality education, good schools, housing and health care for all. Early intervention for all children and families through locally based programmes has been shown to make an impact that resonates throughout children's lives (Department for Children, Schools and Families, 2010; Melhuish *et al.*, 2010). The UK 'Every Child Matters' legislation (Chief Secretary to the Treasury, 2003: 8) recognised the centrality of effective high quality universal services in order to, 'ensure children receive services at the first onset of problems.' Prevention, it could be argued, would imply intervention *before* the first onset of problems.

I find it helpful to remember that assessment of safety and risk in relation to individual children and families takes place within this wider social context. Communities have a crucial role in keeping children safe and governments have a critical role in legislating for universal child welfare. The following illustrations of the 'cake of well-being' and the 'mountain of risk' (Prilleltensky and Prilleltensky, 2006) illustrate the full spectrum of factors associated with child well-being and maltreatment (see Figures 8.1 and 8.2), although in this chapter I will largely be concerned with the assessment of individual children and families.

This chapter focuses on the top two tiers of this cake or mountain, and in particular an exploration of what we are trying to do and how we are trying to do it when faced with the task of determining whether and how the State, and ourselves as its representatives, might decide to intervene in the family lives of others.

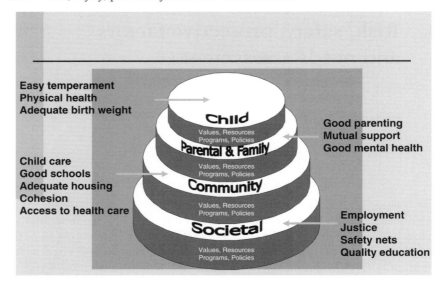

Figure 8.1 Cake of well-being.

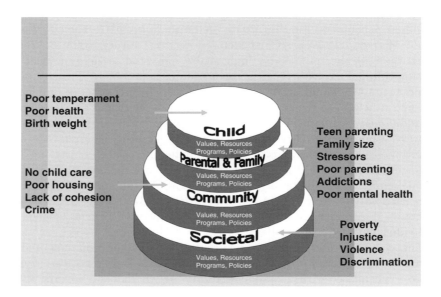

Figure 8.2 Mountain of risk.

Rationale for conducting assessments of risk, safety, protective factors and needs

> The Mexican Sierra has "XVII-15-IX" spines in the dorsal fin. These can easily be counted, but if the sierra strikes hard on the line so that our hands are burned, if the fish sounds and nearly escapes and finally comes in over the rail, his colors pulsing and his tail beating the air, a whole new relational externality has come into being – an entity which is more than the sum of the fish plus the fisherman. The only way to count the spines of the sierra unaffected by this second relational reality is to sit in a laboratory, open an evil-smelling jar, remove a stiff colorless fish from the formalin solution, count the spines and write the truth .... There you have recorded a reality that cannot be assailed – probably the least important reality concerning the fish or yourself.
>
> It is good to know what you are doing. The man with this pickled fish has set down one truth and recorded in his experience many lies. The fish is not that color, that texture, that dead, nor does he smell that way .... The man with his pickled fish has sacrificed a great observation about himself, the fish and the focal point, which is his thought on both the sierra and himself .... We could not observe a completely objective Sea of Cortez, anyway, for in that lonely and uninhabited Gulf our boat and ourselves would change it the moment we entered. By going there, we would bring a new factor to the Gulf. Let us consider that factor and not be betrayed by this myth of permanent objective reality. If it exists at all, it is only available in pickled tatters or in distorted flashes.
>
> (Steinbeck, 2000: 2)

Although I do not fish, I am with John Steinbeck in his preference for the experience of the live creature, even if my hands are scorched as it thrashes on the line. In my professional practice I encounter many situations which do not lend themselves to the counting spines approach, but benefit from immersion together in the murky messy swamp of professional practice where confusing problems defy technical solution (Schön, 1987). 'This is because I experience my work as a relational process in which I aspire to be fully engaged both personally and professionally with other live creatures .... John Steinbeck concluded that the two kinds of 'truth' (derived from the experience of the pickled fish and from the pulsing being on the end of a line, could be complementary and that neither need detract from the evidence provided by the other' (Scaife, 2012: 208). He also drew attention to the need to include ourselves in our observations; once we enter into a relationship, be it with a family or an unknown sea, our very presence changes it. Not only that, but what we bring has been found to assert a significant impact on what we find (or construct): 'a family's chances of having a child taken into custody varies widely according to the person who is assigned to investigate that case' (Rossi *et al.*, 1999).

It has been argued by Sally Holland (2004) that in the social sciences, the contrasting styles of approach that produce Steinbeck's two kinds of 'truth' emerge out of positivist and interpretive traditions. The former emphasises a relatively detached process of scientific data gathering, whilst the latter stresses dialogue and engagement between the participants in the assessment process which take account of the family's own knowledge and expertise and the impact of the worker's values and assumptions. The starting point is the family's strengths.

Jan Horwath (2007) describes two kinds of professional action that arise out of these traditions when she juxtaposes what she calls 'technical-rational' activity (the use of actuarial assessment tools, emphasis on evidence-based practice including empirical research) with 'practice-moral' activity which recognises individuality, the limitations of fitting people into boxes, and the centrality of workers' values to outcomes. She cites evidence from inquiries into child deaths (Morrison, 1996; Reder and Duncan, 1999; Reder et al., 1993) which report that, 'anxiety associated with the assessment task, personal and professional values, feelings about the child and family, perceptions of professional role, the working context and culture and the practitioner's own situation, influence the ways in which professionals make judgements about a case' (Horwath, 2007: 127). We ignore what the assessor contributes to the process at our peril. Lord Laming's (2009) report following the death of baby Peter Connelly commented on the impact of an overemphasis on targets that has led social workers to lose confidence in themselves, and the lack of an outlet through supervision for the, 'severe emotional and psychological stresses that staff involved in child protection often face' (Lord Laming, 2009: 32). This highlights not only what the individual worker brings to the assessment but also the important influence of the employment conditions under which the work is conducted. Different views about what counts as evidence, diversity in what the assessor brings to the task, and the impact of the organisational context, make approaches to the assessment of risk and safety anything but straightforward.

What are we trying to assess?

It has been argued that in assessments relating to child welfare we are trying to undertake multiple tasks which involve assessment of the child's current safety, prediction of future harm (risk assessment), identification of family strengths and needs (needs assessment), the prospects for rehabilitation, and the development of case plans and agreed interventions. This is distilled into seven stages by Bentovim et al. (2009).

- Identification of harm and initial safeguarding
- Full assessment of the child's needs, parenting capacity, family and environmental factors

- Establishing the nature and level of harm
- Assessing prospects for response to professional intervention
- Developing a plan of intervention
- Rehabilitation
- Provision of alternative placement if rehabilitation is not seen as possible

Assessments of safety and risk can aid initial decisions about case priority and where to focus scarce resources, but cannot tell us much about specific individuals (Bolton and Lennings, 2010; Shlonsky and Wagner, 2005). They do not contribute to formulations of causality or illuminate the specific issues with which an individual family is struggling. If, through our initial assessment, we identify that a child is currently unsafe and that there are high levels of risk of future harm, then we are almost certainly going to carry on being involved with these children and their families. Our initial approach sets the tone for the developing relationship between the family and practitioner. If we alienate parents or form unshakeable opinions at this point in the assessment, we disadvantage ourselves in setting about the stages that follow when we try to improve the children's circumstances.

A text produced collectively by the Child Welfare Information Gateway, Children's Bureau, and FRIENDS National Resource Center For Community-Based Child Abuse Prevention (2010) argues that focussing on the promotion of protective factors is a more productive approach than working to reduce risk factors alone because:

- Protective factors are positive attributes that strengthen *all* families. A universal approach helps get needed support to families that may not meet the criteria for "at-risk" services, but who are dealing with stressors that could lead them to abuse or neglect.
- Focusing on protective factors, which are attributes that families themselves often want to build, helps service providers develop positive relationships with parents. Parents then feel more comfortable seeking out extra support if needed. This positive relationship is especially critical for parents who may be reluctant to disclose concerns or identify behaviors or circumstances that may place their families at risk.
- When service providers work with families to increase protective factors, they also help families build and draw on natural support networks within their family and community. These networks are critical to families' long-term success.

(Child Welfare Information Gateway *et al.*, 2010: 8)

This advice from the USA is based on research examining the link between protective factors and *lower* incidence of child abuse and neglect, contrasting with risk assessment approaches that seek to establish relationships between risk factors and *higher* incidence of child abuse and neglect.

How are we to assess? The importance of participation

Front line staff are the first point of contact with families who are struggling. They, 'need to see families as an opportunity and not as a threat to their children' (Tunstill and Atherton, 1996: 43). These authors argue that families are, 'entitled to a generous welcome, not to suspicion': when they ask for help it is because their confidence as parents is wavering. They need a response which builds up rather than undermines their sense of competence, and recognition that it is difficult to ask for or accept help.

My experience of practising in the UK is that, over the course of my career, there has been a cultural shift towards risk aversion. This cultural context makes it difficult to give a generous welcome to care-givers who are suspected of harming their children. It is not so in some other cultures. For French social workers the first task is to build a relationship of trust. 'If this is successful, risks can be taken on the basis that the outcome in the long term will be better' (Hetherington, 1996: 101). Rachael Hetherington reported that it was unheard of in France for a child to be adopted against the wishes of the parents, with a cultural emphasis on the desirability of keeping children in their birth families, or returning them following intervention.

Sarah Borthwick and Barbara Hutchinson (1996: 111) described the Confidential Doctor system which operated in Belgium. The staff employed in this service responded to families in which abuse was confirmed or suspected without recourse to any civil or criminal proceedings. The approach was based on the argument that staff working to protect children could not act both as agents of social control and as therapists because this would lead to conflict and authoritarianism which risked mirroring abusive relationships within families. The approach was seen as resting on a genuine enactment of partnership with parents. Catherine Marneffe (2002) noted that the Belgian approach came under threat as a result of governmental responses to Dutroux (BBC, 2004) and subsequent cases which have prompted a shift towards risk-avoidance, the former confidential system being replaced by 'Advice and Report Centres for Child Abuse' with mandatory reporting. In Sweden, child protection is not effected within a separate system, but is embedded in a wider system of child welfare (Khoo *et al.*, 2002). Authors who have made international comparisons of approaches to child protection have emphasised, 'the need for an approach that combines a focus on child safety with the broader benefits of a focus on child and family welfare' (Gilbert *et al.*, 2009).

In the UK, the Department of Health's Framework for the Assessment of Children in Need and their Families (Department of Health, 2000a: 12) emphasises the importance of partnership with parents although I find it difficult to see how this can be effected in practice without substantial changes to tightly defined procedures in which the investigative role predominates:

> The majority of parents want to do the best for their children. Whatever their circumstances or difficulties, the concept of partnership between the State and the family, in situations where families are in need of assistance in bringing up their children, lies at the heart of child care legislation. The importance of partnership has been further reinforced by a substantial number of research findings, including the child protection studies (Department of Health, 1995) and family support studies (Butt and Box, 1998; Aldgate and Bradley, 1999; Tunstill and Aldgate, 2000). In the process of finding out what is happening to a child, it will be critical to develop a co-operative working relationship, so that parents or caregivers feel respected and informed, that staff are being open and honest with them, and that they in turn are confident about providing vital information about their child, themselves and their circumstances. Working with family members is not an end in itself; the objective must always be to safeguard and promote the welfare of the child. The child, therefore, must be kept in focus.
>
> (Department of Health, 2000: 12)

It has been argued that 'participation' is a more appropriate term than 'partnership' in a child protection context (Shemmings and Shemmings, 1995). They draw on Arnstein's (1969) Ladder of Citizen Participation which conceptualises the notion of participation as having eight levels, ranging from 'manipulation' on the bottom rung to 'citizen control' at the top. The full spectrum also includes 'placation', 'keeping fully informed', 'involvement', 'consultation', 'partnership', and 'delegated power'. The authors argue convincingly that rungs three, four and five (keeping fully informed, involvement and consultation) offer more realistic prospects for encouraging the development of trust and authentic participation. I am attracted by the idea of participation and I aspire towards partnership with care-givers because I know from my experience as a clinician and as a supervisor that the establishment of a working alliance is central to achieving positive outcomes. It is a consistent finding in the literature of supervision, counselling and therapy that the establishment of a working relationship is crucial if the practitioner is to be of assistance or make a difference to the client or supervisee (Beinart, 2004; Hensley reported in Bogo and McKnight, 2005; Kilminster and Jolly, 2000; Ladany *et al.*, 1999; Lizzio *et al.*, 2005; Sweeney *et al.*, 2001). Research findings from social work are no exception (Butler and Williamson, 1994; Thoburn *et al.*, 1995). A focus on the development of respectful relationships free from feelings of shame and stigma are much more highly valued than, 'a partnership that is rights-based but devoid of relationship' (Holland and Scourfield, 2004: 33). When a parent has a grievance, a rights-based approach is to offer information about how to lodge an official complaint; a relationship-based approach is to accept the grievance and work hard to understand how the actions of the practitioner or organisation have produced this effect.

A programme of research commissioned by the Department of Health (1995) in the UK showed that the early stages of child protection enquiries were crucial in creating or destroying a cooperative working relationship between social workers and families. Whether the worker regards the parents, and in particular the mother, to be cooperative has been identified as a key factor in what happens next. 'An uncooperative mother triggered the instigation of a child protection conference even when the concern was relatively minor' (Cleaver *et al.*, 1998: 19). Professionals assessing families have been found to regard the initiative for establishing a cooperative relationship to lie with the family and not with themselves. The importance of the worker's own approach to the family did not seem to be regarded as a primary concern (Department of Health, 1995) and yet, 'when the power relationship is structurally unequal, for trust to be experienced, and then sustained, it must be demonstrated by professionals at all times' (Shemmings and Shemmings, 1995: 53).

In a qualitative study, Gary Dumbrill (2006) found that parents were afraid of the absolute power that they experienced as belonging to investigating agencies, even when abuse or neglect allegations were unfounded. Three ways of responding to intervention emerged: parents fought workers by open opposition, 'played the game' by feigning co-operation, or worked with them in what appeared to be genuine and collaborative relationships. Parents experiencing power being used *over* them tended to fight or 'play the game' while parents experiencing power being used *with* them tended to work with the intervention whilst remaining mindful and cautious of the potential for power to be used over them. No evidence was found linking case type (non-voluntary or voluntary cases) to whether parents perceived power being used by workers over them or with them. The author concluded that dealing with the issue of power imbalance at the outset may be the most crucial issue in developing a relationship between representatives of the State and parents in order to secure the best outcomes for children.

Research examining the views of people who use supportive services in caring for their children graphically illustrates how the relationship with the worker made a difference:

> 'They have all these plans drawn up-but do they ever follow them through? I think not ... They're supposed to be working together – but you'll find that they won't – because it comes under financial funding. And this is where the arguments crop up with these people – not the safety or well-being of the child – but: "We're not paying for that", "Oh, let Social Services do that" and "No, that's not our department – let Education

deal with that". They are trying to pass the buck around and around and around instead of getting to the point and dealing with it.' (Cathy)

'She'll promise us the earth while she's here. But as soon as she gets outside in her car she forgets—because her head's all over the place. She gets at least two phone calls while she's with us—she's always late—she's dizzy! She's nice, but she's dizzy. It's not her fault—they are understaffed.' (John Richardson)

'Dawn (mother): She were great—very pleased with her, she were right calm. She were fair—a very nice person. I could talk to her. Louise (shy teenager): *I* could talk to her!!!' (Pearson family)

'The worst thing? The threats, behaviour, the power they've got. The big words they used frightened me—really frightened me .... Arrogant, very arrogant. Ignorant as well. That person's approach: She didn't ask, she told .... At the time, in my mind I was thinking: "If she's going to be funny, I'm going to be funny ..." ' (Mr Taylor)

'Nothing at all happened after registration—I was disgusted. They are supposedly at risk from me! What's the point of at risk register if they weren't there to back up anything? It feels like my file got stuck in a drawer somewhere .... I just told them that my children being on the at risk register was a waste of time—I could have murdered them and they would have been none the wiser because nobody was ever here. There was nobody to talk to, no back-up. There was: "Oh, we'll assign you a social worker"—but where? They didn't turn up.' (Ms S. Jones)

If we were to ask the involved social workers for their accounts of what took place with these families, I would be very surprised if the narratives matched those of the family members. In order to explain the different accounts given by people who ostensibly have shared an experience, I have found it helpful to draw on a constructivist account which acknowledges that, although we can try, it is not possible to see things exactly as does another. This is because knowledge is built up or constructed, not poured in. People's knowledge is their own construction, based on their life experiences to date and it fits more or less well for them, even if from my perspective I cannot see how this is possible. In most cases this knowledge appears to be fairly stable and unlikely to change unless a misfit is experienced. Misfits are rarely sought because they are emotionally disturbing and tend to generate affective resistance.

This means that the task of meaningfully influencing another person is difficult and that telling is an ineffective lever for change. Constructivism provides a theoretical basis for the finding that the relationship between families and workers needs to be positive if change is to be effected. Workers need to listen and show respect for the knowledge and beliefs of care-givers and this is aided by a professional orientation towards safety, strengths and protective factors. Successful interventions are appropriately focussed on the reduction of risk factors and the promotion of protective factors (Horton, 2003; Pollard *et al.*, 1999). At the same time, it is important to be alert to hazards, dangers and factors that might prove disadvantageous or even fatal to children. Telling parents to change is generally likely to be ineffective, but if a child is in danger, safety must be ensured. The dilemma is that threats may be effective in bringing about cosmetic or surface change, but without a working alliance, deep and meaningful change is unlikely to result. Hostility and resistance may increase.

The UK government in its Framework for the Assessment of Children in Need and Their Families (Department of Health, 2000a) stresses the importance of identifying not only deficits but also the strengths and resources in families which, 'can be mobilised to safeguard and promote the child's welfare' (Department of Health, 2000a: 14). Further advice is offered:

> It is important that an approach to assessment, which is based on a full understanding of what is happening to a child in the context of his or her family and the wider community, examines carefully the nature of the interactions between the child, family and environmental factors and identifies both positive and negative influences. These will vary for each child. Nothing can be assumed; the facts must be sought, the meaning attached to them explored and weighed up with the family. Sometimes assessments have been largely in terms of a child or family's difficulties or problems, or the risks seen to be attached to particular behaviours or situations. What is working well or what may be acting as positive factors for the child and family may be overlooked. For example, a single mother, in crisis over health, financial and housing problems, may still be managing to get her child up in time in the mornings, washed, dressed, breakfasted and off to school each day. An older child, living in a family periodically disrupted by domestic violence, may be provided with welcome respite care on a regular basis by a grandmother living locally. Working with a child or family's strengths may be an important part of a plan to resolve difficulties.
>
> (Department of Health, 2000a: 14)

It has been argued that there are four key conditions necessary in the process of establishing trust (Platt and Shemmings, 1997). The first of these is openness and honesty, which involves professionals being straight with families by sharing what they think, what they write and what they intend to do. The second is 'answerability'; being accountable for their actions. The third is even-handedness, which requires the maintenance of a genuinely open mind and a preparedness to question personal assumptions, values and beliefs. The fourth and final condition is that of sensitivity; an approach in which workers treat people who are subject to investigation with respect, empathy, genuineness and warmth.

What does all this mean for the professional tasked with assessment of families in which children are unsafe or may be at future risk of harm? My summary of the research from different domains suggests:

- The establishment of a positive working alliance with parents is central in generating trust and bringing about effective change.
- This is aided by a focus on protective factors, strengths and efforts to comprehend the parents' understanding of the situation.
- Hazards and risks need to be included in the assessment, and if necessary for the safety of the children, sanctions will need to be imposed even though there is a risk that this will bring about surface compliance rather than deep learning in the care-givers.
- A needs assessment undertaken in conjunction with assessment of safety and risk factors will lead to identification of the interventions required that could bring about change.
- We need to include ourselves and our organisations in the frame because our values, and the imperatives of our employers, influence what we find.
- We need a process for analysing and weighing different kinds of evidence, which involves the integration of best research evidence with clinical expertise and patient values (University of Toronto Libraries, 2000) in reaching decisions about how safe children are with their care-givers.

Breaking bad news

It is one thing to begin an assessment with a family who have presented themselves for help, and quite another when the initial meeting arises out of concerns expressed by someone else to children's services. I have experienced some such initial interviews as emotionally bruising, full of electric tension, and a major challenge to the establishment of a working alliance. If I am able successfully to negotiate the early stages, I may be able to engage the family's strengths in order to have a chance of 'wrestling hope from hell' (Mahoney, 2006: 196). Michael Mahoney draws attention to the impact on practitioners of clients' stories which, 'tell of the worst kinds of human capacities: intentional cruelty, deception, greed, hate, insensitivity, irresponsibility, and violations of human decency' which can challenge the worker's faith in human nature. He urges us to allow these people to touch us rather than just being 'cases' in manila folders full of stacked paper trails. David and Yvonne Shemmings (1995: 54) quote a parent who describes the skill of breaking bad news sensitively as, 'the ability to give people "bad news" while cuddling them at the same time, but without the cuddle masking the "bad news".'

Breaking the news to a care-giver that a child has disclosed abuse, or an adult has reported concerns about the quality of parenting to the authorities, presents a serious challenge. If the professional has a pre-existing functional relationship with the parent this should ease the way but if not, workers are faced with the daunting task of beginning the conversation and explaining the reasons for their investigation. There are hazards in being too blunt whilst undue circumnavigation of the issue can raise anxieties to an even greater pitch. In a study by Harriet Ward and her colleagues (2010: no page numbers) 'Parents particularly appreciated a "straight talking" social worker who was honest about the threat that their children would be removed. Practitioners who found it difficult to break bad news or who encouraged parents to be over-optimistic about their progress were not so highly valued.'

It is helpful to have prepared what to say and to have thought about the best venue and means of introducing the issues. If the issue cannot be introduced face-to-face, then the shorter the period between the identification of the matter to the parent and the initial discussion, the less time there is for anticipatory anxiety to mount. Should the original raising of concerns take place by letter, by telephone, by invitation to a meeting at the child's school or nursery in order to discuss progress, or must the conversation take place with urgency in order to give the parent an opportunity to be present at the hospital where the child is to be examined?

Peter English (2009) argues for gentle movement into the conversation. This might involve a warning of the bad news to come. 'I need to talk to you about a matter that you may find distressing.' The process is likely to involve some 'telling' or information-giving in the first place but can involve asking questions about how the parents have been finding their role or the challenges of the child. At the beginning I have found it helpful just to give the facts using clear and direct statements that I have sometimes rehearsed. The word 'you' is worth avoiding as this tends to be taken as apportioning blame. The 'props of normality' such as a cup of tea may be useful if appropriate to the context. In the aftermath of the initial shock or distress, care can be given by making sure that parents are not left on their own. It is advisable to seek from them information about who might keep them company or to stay yourself and engage them in general conversation about the child and their family. Engagement in practical tasks can move them from a focus which pinpoints only the bad news. It is helpful to introduce the idea of participation at this stage by the use of 'we' where appropriate, and to explain the professional role. 'My job is to work with you to understand what has happened. When I understand more about what has happened we can think together about what to do next.' At this stage it may be helpful to describe the options that will follow; no further involvement, some supportive input for the family and/or the child, a meeting with others to work out a plan for the future, or an immediate plan to ensure the child's safety until a greater understanding has been reached. In order to create more space for the development of positive interaction between parent and practitioner, the introduction of an overseeing third party can help. This can be accomplished with sentences beginning, 'I have been asked to ...' or 'I am required to ...'.

The process requires forethought and planning, and assertiveness in the use of purpose and preference statements (Proctor and Inskipp, 2010: 149). Clarity of purpose is signalled through 'confident enough' communication. It is helpful to discriminate statements of intent or purpose, 'this is what will happen and what I intend to enable and ensure' from statements of preference – 'I would prefer that ... what about you?' The role of the worker in this context is that of leader, or participant manager of the conversation, which benefits from the professional being an authoritative agent (not *the* authority) without being authoritarian or bossy.

After receiving bad news, the recipient will generally appreciate being given time in which to respond. This might include reactions characterised by expressions of anger and distress. In order to foster participation and involvement, I believe that it is crucial to accept these responses with empathy: not by saying, 'I know how you feel', but rather, 'I understand that this is unwelcome news.' Providing sufficient space for parents to process what they have just heard gives an opportunity for their initial reactions to dissipate. The ending of the conversation benefits from planning and is likely to be influenced by the location in which the discussion has been held. People tend to have poor memories for the details of conversations that convey bad news, memory being overwhelmed by emotion (Patterson and Teale, 1997). Recall is aided by the provision of written information. Parents value leaflets that include information about how to get in touch and which explain what will happen next. It can be helpful to agree a time to meet again when parents have had the opportunity to digest the information and reflect on their initial reactions.

Assessments of safety

In the safeguarding and child protection literature, a distinction is made between assessments of safety, which involve making decisions about imminent threats of harm to a child within a family, and assessments of risk which involve the prediction of future harm. 'A child can be considered safe when there is no threat of danger to a child within the family/home or when the protective capacities within the home can manage threats of danger' (Action for Child Protection, 2003a). Immediate threats of danger are regarded as being out-of-control and require some kind of urgent intervention. The focus of the danger is a child, often a vulnerable child such as an infant who cannot take steps to keep safe. When first making contact with a family the practitioner may need to make a judgement about a child's immediate safety. This may be aided by a checklist which allows a focus on a relatively small set of factors that has been established to be of importance in previous assessments of safety. Such checklists (Action for Child Protection, 2003b; Queensland Government, 2010; Wiebush *et al.*, 2001) tend to describe behaviours considered to prejudice a child's safety and might appropriately be termed 'unsafety' assessments. Below I have turned some such factors into statements focussed on safety with a view to aiding the practitioner in facilitating the creation of a constructive climate of assessment when talking to care-givers:

- The care-givers' behaviour is typically calm, not violent, out-of-control or unpredictable.
- The child is not exposed to violence from or between members of the household.
- The care-giver does not appear to find the child's behaviour provocative.
- The care-giver or other household member has not caused or threatened serious physical harm to the child.
- The care-giver is able to give coherent explanations consistent with any injury to the child.
- The care-giver acts warmly and positively towards the child.
- The care-giver has age-appropriate expectations for the child's behaviour.
- The care-giver willingly presents the child to the agency staff and generally cooperates with them.
- The care-giver provides appropriate supervision commensurate with the child's age and development.
- The care-giver meets the child's immediate physical needs including food, clothing, shelter, and medical needs.
- The child's living conditions do not show evidence of presenting serious hazards to the child.
- The care-giver is not known previously to have seriously maltreated a child.
- The child shows no fear or anxiety in the presence of the care-giver.
- There is no behaviour from the child or reports by others to suggest that the child is being sexually abused.
- The child is not presenting with behavioural indicators of emotional harm.
- There is no evidence to suggest that the care-givers' drug or alcohol use is compromising their capability to look after the child.
- There is no evidence to suggest that the care-giver's serious mental health difficulties or learning difficulties are compromising the care of the child.
- The information obtained does not show a pattern of escalating threat to the child's safety.
- The information suggests few significant or multiple current stressful life events.
- There is evidence of social and practical support available to the family.

If any of these factors are judged to be absent a safety plan can be developed, ideally in harmony with the care-givers, even if this requires the child to be moved to a place of safety. Care-givers appreciate their views and opinions being sought. It is helpful for future professional relationships with the family to create an atmosphere that allows parents to show their strengths and enables the practitioner to learn about the parents' own concerns for the safety of their children. This depends on an orientation which does not demonise people who abuse their children, or see them as belonging to a different category of being, but rather recognises the capacity for abuse within us all (Borthwick and Hutchinson, 1996). In the UK, following this phase, most families are diverted from the professional system. In a study by Gibbons *et al.* (1995) only 15 per cent of the original sample became registered and despite pressing needs, the majority of families weeded out at this stage were offered no further services, leaving many children in situations where their needs continued to be neglected.

Having assessed the immediate safety of the child, the worker is tasked with the unenviable job of predicting future harm – the process of risk assessment.

The epidemiology of child abuse and neglect

Risk assessments (particularly the prediction of which children will be killed by their care-givers) present a serious challenge to child protective services because child fatalities arising out of abuse and neglect are relatively rare occurrences. For example, in the UK there are approximately 13 million children, of whom about 450,000 are defined as 'children in need' (Kirton, 2009). Information provided by the Department for Children, Schools and Families (DCSF) showed that on 31 March 2008, 37,000 children in England were the subjects of care orders (of 60,000 children looked-after by local authorities) and 34,000 children became the subject of child protection plans (DCSF, 2008a), a similar number ceasing to be subject to such plans during that fiscal year. The number of children who die from maltreatment has been estimated at between 50 and 100 per year (Creighton and Tissier, 2003; Ofsted, 2008), a figure which is regarded as having remained stable for more than 30 years. In well over half of all cases of children under the age of 16 years killed at the hands of another person, a parent was the principal suspect. Home Office data showed that in 2007/8, 55 children in England and Wales were killed by their parents or by someone known to the child (Povey *et al.*, 2009: 19). A study conducted by Colin Pritchard and Richard Williams (2010) who surveyed the number of child-abuse related deaths of children from birth to 14 years over the period 1974 to 2006 concluded that the results showed a relative 'success story' for England and Wales compared with other major developed countries. The average number of child homicides in 1974–76 was 136 compared with 84 in 2004–06 (reported as a 39 per cent decline). But a report published the same spring stated that there were 186 notifications of death or serious injury resulting from neglect or abuse in England in 2009 compared with 144 in 2008, a 23 per cent rise (Bennett, 2010). I think this difference in reporting reflects the political nature of the issue and how official statistics can be used to support a case that has already been decided.

In the United States of America during the Federal Financial Year (FFY) 2006, an estimated 1,530 children (compared to 1,460 children for FFY 2005) died from abuse or neglect – at a rate of 2.04 deaths per 100,000 children (United States Department of Health and Human Services, 2006). The national estimate was based on data from State child welfare information systems, as well as other data sources available to the States. This is regarded as an underestimate although it suggests a rate of such deaths approximately four times that in England and Wales. The rate has remained stable over the reporting years 2002–6 inclusive. The statistics are very difficult to compare as they are collected in different ways from different professionals and are reported for groups of children in different age ranges, sometimes 0–16 and sometimes 0–18 years.

In addition to the challenge for risk assessment protocols of predicting rare events, fatal child abuse may involve repeated abuse over a period of time or it may involve a single, impulsive incident such as drowning, suffocating, or shaking a baby. In cases of fatal *neglect*, the child's death results not from anything the care-giver does, but from a care-giver's *failure to act*. The neglect may be chronic (e.g. extended malnourishment) or acute (e.g. an infant who drowns after being left unsupervised in the bathtub) (Child Welfare Information Gateway, 2012). A standard process or instrument would be sorely tested to predict the rare result of a number of different causes.

Actuarial and consensual risk assessment tools

Risk assessment tools may be compiled through consensus-based approaches in which selected characteristics are identified by agreement among experts, or through actuarial methods. Consensus-based tools have been found to be better predictors than the individual experts who collected the data for the instrument (Dawes, 1994). But it has been argued that they nevertheless cannot compete with actuarial approaches (Gambrill and Shlonsky, 2000).

Within the risk assessment literature I have encountered a diversity of views regarding the value and place of actuarial risk assessment instruments, the results of which are often contrasted with clinical judgement. These instruments are compiled through a process of retrospective identification of the factors that were present in known examples of repeated child maltreatment. This is known as a regression approach – working backwards from known outcomes. These are weighted on the basis of their correlation with such outcomes, resulting in an index which gives a rating of probability. They aim to predict who will and who will not harm others in the future. The compilers of such instruments are faced with the difficulty of deciding how much weight to give to each factor, and the knowledge that for each factor there are large numbers of people in the general population in whose profile these characteristics were present, but who did not harm their children. The instruments, 'predict an individual's likely behaviour from the behaviour of others in similar circumstances' (Kemshall, 2008: 200). They result in the classification of individuals into groups, typically labelled 'low', 'medium' and 'high' risk. A risk level designation indicates the family's similarity on a range of factors to other families with relatively high or low rates of subsequent maltreatment (Wiebush *et al.*, 2001). There is evidence that they outperform unaided clinical judgement in most forensic fields (Bolton and Lennings, 2010; Shlonsky and Wagner, 2005). Appendix 4 gives a description of some of the available instruments with information, where available, concerning their sensitivity (ability to correctly identify those who will cause harm) and specificity (ability to correctly identify those who will not cause harm).

Although such instruments give an indication of degree of risk they do not say much about specific individuals (Hart, 2003). This is both because in the field of child maltreatment they tend to have been compiled on the basis of limited empirical evidence, and because of the relatively low 'base rate', the rate of occurrence in the population being assessed. With low base rates, risk assessment instruments will identify large numbers of false positives whilst also failing to identify many families who will go on to harm their children again. Eileen Munro gives a very clear account of the latter problem and states, 'researchers face a harder task trying to develop a risk assessment instrument to screen the general population, where the incidence of abuse is relatively low, than if their target population were specifically families known to child protection agencies, where the base rate will be much higher' (Munro, 2004: 875).

Munro (2004: 878) gives an example based on an instrument reported by Susan Zuravin *et al.* (1995) for screening initial referrals. The measure's sensitivity (how many high risk families it will correctly identify – known as 'true positives') is 69 per cent. The specificity of the measure (how many low risk families it will identify accurately – known as 'true negatives') is 74 per cent. In my experience these are relatively high figures for sensitivity and specificity for instruments that have been devised in the field of child abuse and neglect. It has been estimated that the number of referrals substantiated as cases of abuse (the base rate) is about 40 per cent (Besharov, 1990). This would mean that we would expect to substantiate abuse in approximately 400 out of 1000 referrals. If each of the families was assessed using Zuravin's screening measure, of these 400, 276 would screen positive (sensitivity 69 per cent) and of the other 600, 156 would also falsely screen positive (specificity 74 per cent). The distribution of positive and negative results for a hypothetical 1000 referred families would therefore be as shown in Figure 8.3.

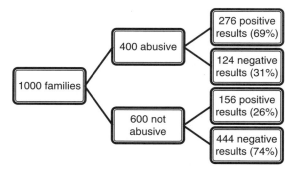

Figure 8.3 Diagnostic tree. Diagnostic value of test with families known to have harmed their children.

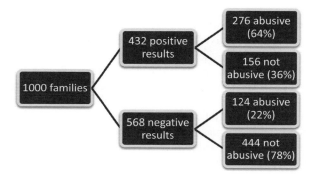

Figure 8.4 Predictive tree. Predictive value of the results of a risk assessment instrument focussing on referred families.

If this measure was used with a view to predicting which referred families would go on to abuse their children, the results shown in Figure 8.4 would, on the basis of the claimed sensitivity and specificity of the instrument, be achieved.

On the basis of this result, much more information would be needed in order to discriminate between the families who obtained positive results. A hundred and twenty four families who went on to abuse their children would have been screened out by the instrument.

If the measure were used to try to predict in which families a child would be killed as a result of abuse or neglect, the predictive capability becomes even more problematic. The task of practitioners is to predict the 55 (2007/8 figure) or so child deaths perpetrated annually in England and Wales by care-givers, from a population of 34,000 children subject to child protection plans (even this assumes that all children who are killed are subject to child protection plans and studies of serious case reviews show that relatively

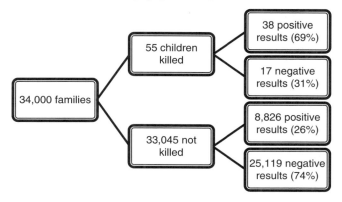

Figure 8.5 Diagnostic tree. Diagnostic value of test projected to parents who kill their children.

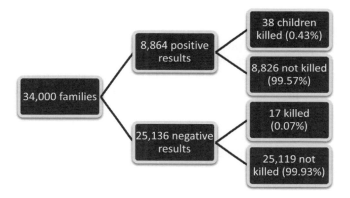

Figure 8.6 Predictive tree. Projected predictive capacity of a risk assessment instrument for child death in children subject to child protection plans in England and Wales.

few of the children who died had been so subject (Reder and Duncan, 1999)). Using Zuravin *et al.*'s measure and making the very big assumption that the same sensitivity and specificity would apply to parents who killed their children as to those who abused, the results are shown in Figure 8.5 and Figure 8.6.

The instrument shows up as quite good at selecting those families whose child will be safe, but the vast majority of parents who obtained a positive score would not go on to kill their child. Almost a third of families in which a child was killed would be screened out by this measure. Even if the sensitivity and specificity of an instrument designed to predict which children would be killed by their parents were both as high as 99 per cent, it would still identify 339 false positives in addition to the 54 or 55 parents who would go on to kill their child. Only 14 per cent of the positive results would be accurate. The difficulty arises because the base rate – the number of child deaths of children on child protection registers – is so low. This is reflected in analyses of serious case reviews. 'Every child's case reveals a multitude of different factors and variables making predictability difficult and leading to a quality of unexpectedness' (Brandon *et al.*, 2009: 40).

These difficulties with prediction have led some authors to suggest that social work as a discipline has subscribed to the fallacy that child abuse can be predicted and therefore prevented (Robinson, 1996: 30). I do not entirely agree, but I am convinced of the futility of trying to predict the deaths of children at the hands of their care-givers solely on the basis of the results of actuarial risk assessment instruments. Such measures may be able to help workers make decisions at the point of intake about how to prioritise the allocation of scarce resources to those families presenting with the highest levels of risk, but many false judgements will nevertheless be made, some of which will result in fatalities. The long-term stability of the statistics concerning the deaths of children through maltreatment gives testament to the problematic nature of prediction in this domain.

One of the reasons given for the difficulties of prediction using actuarial risk assessment instruments is their reliance on static factors (former drug and alcohol misuse, previous incidents of child maltreatment, care-giver abused as a child). These factors are historical in nature and thereby fixed in their risk indication over time. They cannot be undone so are not amenable to intervention and change. 'Dynamic', 'needs', 'protective' and 'responsivity' factors (current substance use, nature of current partnership, availability of social support, quality of parenting skills, bond with the child) are highly pertinent to the evaluation of risk and safety. This has led to a proposal that the most appropriate approach is to complement the results of actuarial risk assessment devices with the clinical assessment of dynamic and individual factors through the use of structured clinical guides. Such guides also allow for the consideration not only of likelihood of an event but also its seriousness or undesirability (Munro, 2002). The Ministry of Justice (n.d.: 1), in its advice to professionals using a risk assessment measure, describes it as, 'an aid to judgement. It is not a substitute for that judgement.'

The representation of individual people by numbers and scores alone is instinctively alien to me. I am not keen on being represented by them myself. Michael Mahoney (2006: 39) suggests that, 'the limitations of numbers to capture important qualities is readily apparent when it comes to the measurement of meaning, particularly personal meaning. Quantifiable measures of persons are plentiful, but meaningful measures are elusive.' He argues that it is facile to imagine that practitioners possess an 'errorless psychic dipstick', capable of capturing clients' personalities, their problems and possible risks associated with people like them. Psychological measures were originally developed to document individual differences, not, as often now used, to diminish those differences. Categorisations of individuals can become obstacles to the change process when scores or diagnoses are regarded as a capsule summary of who the person is or is capable of becoming.

I believe that formal measures, procedural manuals and protocols can contribute, but cannot substitute for personal knowledge and experience (Gordon, 2001). The reductionism of formal models can obscure or exclude important dimensions of a situation in which individual understanding is needed. This has been likened to 'broken leg' cues whereby a current factor can override historical factors in terms of relevance to risk. In the short term, a broken leg would hinder an individual's opportunity to engage in violent behaviour (Murray and Thomson, 2010). It has also been argued that government guidance has sometimes been, 'followed mechanistically and used as a check list, without any differentiation according to the child's or family's circumstances' (Department of Health, 2000a: xi). This cannot be in children's best interests.

These problems have begun to be acknowledged in recent literature by a range of authors who are trying to unite actuarial risk assessment approaches with clinical judgement using evidence from a range of sources (Bolton and Lennings, 2010; Cash, 2001; Schwalbe, 2008; Shlonsky and Wagner, 2005). Instead of working backwards from factors associated with known offences, tree-based methods of decision-making allow that the factors relevant to risk assessment for one individual may differ from those that are relevant for another. The particular questions asked depend on answers given to prior questions. Some authors have adopted a process by which the 'lead' variable of the classification tree is altered and the process repeated, adjusting estimates of risk according to the number of classification trees upon which high risk was estimated.

Decision tree methods – HCR-20

One of the widely used classification tree methods is the Historical-Clinical-Risk-Management-20 (HCR-20) (Douglas *et al.*, 2006; Webster *et al.*, 2002). It was devised with a view to evaluating violence risk in people known or suspected to have mental or personality disorder, and as such its applicability to other populations needs to be treated with circumspection. Ten of the assessed factors are historical, and to this extent it has characteristics in common with actuarial instruments, whilst five factors are dynamic, applying to the present time, and five are dynamic referring to the future. The method is not seen as 'fixed' but constantly evolving in light of professional experience arising out of use of the method. Christopher Webster and colleagues (2002) urge much caution in its use, including recognition that it is a guide not a test, that assessments of its reliability and validity are in progress and that it should be used as a first step in an assessment process rather than as an end in itself. It is based on the idea that local as well as general conditions are relevant in evaluating risk, much as in attempting to forecast the weather. The focus is towards the management of risk rather than accurate prediction of future behaviour with an orientation towards assessment of risk as an ongoing process and not a single one-off event (Murray and Thomson, 2010). HCR-20 items are listed at: http://www.psychology.heacademy.ac.uk/mini-projects/riskassessment/Violence%20RA/hcr20_items.html. Each risk item is coded 2 if definitely present, 1 if possibly present or present to a limited degree, 0 if the item is not present or does not apply, and omitted if there is insufficient information available to make a judgement.

The MacArthur Violence Risk Assessment study, led by John Monahan (Monahan *et al.*, 2005), has developed a decision-tree-based method for assessing risk for people who have been diagnosed with a mental health difficulty, and employs cut-offs for both high and low risk. Their method integrates five tree-based prediction models, making manual scoring unwieldy. Risk assessment software has been developed and is available from Psychological Assessment Resources Inc. Details can be found at: http://www.macarthur.virginia.edu/risk.html.

A wide range of risk assessment tools has been evaluated in terms of validation history, empirical grounding, inter-rater reliability, identification of risk of re-offending level and identification of risk factors by the Scottish Risk Management Authority (RMA). Recommended tools are required to have been peer reviewed by authors other than those who constructed the test. The RMA publishes a directory of these measures which can be accessed at: www.rmascotland.gov.uk/index.php/download_file/view/169/.

Aims of risk assessment

I like the aims proposed by Anne Hollows for any model of risk assessment. Her aims are pertinent both to assessment of current safety and future risk of harm. She says that a useful model would enable the assessor to say:

- This was my starting point. I am aware of other potential starting points and I have borne these in mind as the assessment has proceeded.
- These were the actions I took to ensure that the child was safe while I gathered all the relevant information. I endeavoured to avoid actions that would prejudice future decisions.
- I formed the judgement that the issues causing concern in the case included these elements, and my view on the available evidence was that in these circumstances there could be harm to this degree.
- I therefore developed the following strategies to intervene, manage and reduce the risks in the case. These were the outcomes of the strategies.
- I can therefore now say that concerns identified have changed in the following ways and the level of risk to the child is now as follows.

(Hollows, 2008: 58)

It is also worth bearing in mind that it is in the nature of risk that no matter how scrupulous has been a process of risk assessment, poor outcomes will still on occasion result:

> If a decision involves risk, then even when one can demonstrate that one has chosen the unarguably optimal course of action, some proportion of the time the outcome will be suboptimal. It follows that a bad outcome in and of itself does not constitute evidence that the decision was mistaken. The hindsight fallacy is to assume that it does.
>
> (Macdonald and Macdonald, 1999: 22)

Approaches to assessing strengths, needs and protective factors

Evidence from a study by Hedy Cleaver and colleagues (1998: 24) suggests that, 'social workers could be channelled into perceptions of the family as needing *either* a child protection route *or* a family support route, rather than taking an overview of the situation and seeing child protection concerns within the context of the family's broader characteristics or needs.' A focus on strengths and protective factors can serve to remind families of the positive qualities which have sometimes become invisible as they attempt to cope with the stresses of their daily lives. Joan Robinson argues that:

> If the initial emphasis is on investigating, evidence-gathering and critical analysis of parental performance, it is likely to undermine the parent. If it is directed towards finding out what can give the child a safer, happier, more fulfilled life, then it can open up a process which will enable the family to use help, and also protect the child. This means accepting that social workers cannot contain every risk, and that abuse is often unpredictable.
>
> (Robinson, 1996: 32)

Assessments in children's proceedings can inappropriately emphasise the summative, a judgement of fitness to parent, right from the off, but assessments in children's proceedings are diagnostic. I need to learn about what is going on in this particular family and which of their needs my agency may be able to fulfil. I am not trying to see if this family can pass a test which has been designed to assess *the* correct way to bring up children.

An orientation towards strengths and protective factors can begin with diagnostic assessment and progress to a formative role in which intervention is designed to encourage learning and development, often through the judicious use of questions rather than through telling and information-giving which tend to imply that something happening now is wrong. Even if the worker believes this to be the case, learning can be encouraged without directly challenging or confronting care-givers with their weaknesses.

Assessing strengths

A focus on strengths has been operationalised by Dennis Saleebey (2006: 87) who proposes a number of categories of question, informed by a narrative approach, which encourage parents to give both to themselves and the worker a constructive account of their experiences.

1   Survival questions: How have you managed to overcome/survive the challenges that you have faced? What have you learned about yourself and your world during those struggles?
2   Support questions: Who are the people that you can rely on? Who has made you feel understood, supported, or encouraged?
3   Exception questions: When things were going well in life, what was different? Possibility questions: What do you want to accomplish in your life? What are your hopes for your future, or the future of your family?
4   Esteem questions: What makes you proud about yourself? What positive things do people say about you?
5   Perspective questions: What are your ideas about your current situation?
6   Change questions: What do you think is necessary for things to change? What could you do to make that happen?

This approach is termed 'assessment as conversational inquiry' by Clay Graybeal and Shelley Conrad (2008: 190). They provide an example of a report on the same child conducted through a 'traditional' approach contrasted with a report produced on the basis of assessment as conversational inquiry. In Table 8.1 I represent some of the differences between the two reports.

To my mind, the second column in Table 8.1 indicates an orientation towards assessment which does not ignore problems and deficits, but seeks explanations which give pointers for beneficial intervention, and notes family strengths and indications of resilience despite adverse historical circumstances. The descriptions manifest an orientation towards benevolent explanations for presenting problems, the portrayal of which are more likely to engage rather than alienate parents who are involved in such difficult processes. When I apply a strengths-based assessment to myself I know that I prefer to think in terms of developing what I am able to do now rather than focussing on my deficits, which can be disheartening. When I dwell on my own children I can get bogged down by thinking about all the things I would like them to be able to do but I have failed to teach them such as playing a musical instrument, being highly accomplished at a sport or achieving outstanding grades. Instead, I find it helpful to challenge these ideas by reassuring myself that they are generally reasonably contented, have valued friendships and good health. I also like to think that I have in some way been responsible for the strengths that they have developed, and not for those areas in which I would like them to do better. I enjoy relationships with others who

Table 8.1 Comparison of Traditional and Conversational Assessments

Traditional Assessment	Assessment as Conversation
Little exploration of mother's view that child 'does bad real good' and that this will serve him well in standing up for himself.	Greater depth of exploration reveals that her view is based on fear that other children will make fun of her son because he has scarring from earlier cleft palate repair.
Child has limited peer contact, no explanation provided.	Mother explains that she works long hours so enjoys one-to-one contact with her son and he has social contact with his cousins on a regular basis.
Mother said to describe child as 'a problem from birth'.	Mother said to describe child as 'having feeding difficulties from birth in consequence of his cleft palate.'
Mother says that father loves his son but does not like him because Doug does not listen.	Greater depth of exploration produces information that father is uncomfortable around his children and has not had the opportunity to get to know them.
Mother says that she gets along well with everyone unless they mess with her family.	When asked about family losses and separations mother says that the reason she works nights and stays 'straight' is to make sure her kids have better options in life. 'Family comes first.'
Doug acclimated quickly to the playroom but could not settle on one toy to play with.	Doug showed great curiosity and energy when surveying the playroom.
Doug initiated perseverative play with a series of trucks, putting them neatly in a row and then running through them at full speed. Doug got frustrated when it was time to end the truck play. He was difficult to redirect and refused to settle down to draw a picture or identify letters, numbers or shapes.	Doug placed the trucks neatly in a row and then crashed through them enthusiastically. He repeated this activity many times. Doug was so involved with this activity that ending it proved challenging. He showed less interest in sitting still and participating in visual-spatial activities than he had in larger motor play.
Because of his non-compliance an assessment of his cognitive development could not be completed.	Assessing Doug's cognitive abilities will take creative planning and patience.
Doug's mother acknowledges Doug's problems with attention and hyperactivity but has not sought help for any of these behaviours.	Doug has thus far not received any early services addressing his attention and behaviour. His mother shares the paediatrician's concerns about his attention and is committed to investigating the possibilities of intervention that can help Doug with his development.
Family history is significant for substance abuse and antisocial behaviour on both sides of the family.	Mother has strengths evidenced by her capacity to reliably financially support her young family. She is well aware that substance abuse has been an issue in her family and as a response she chooses not to use alcohol.

encourage my positive thoughts but I am likely to avoid those who remind me of my deficits or failures. If this is what *I* prefer, why not apply this to my thinking about the families I am tasked to assess? This is the approach proposed by Bob Lonne and colleagues (2009: 110) in their arguments for the reform of child protection: 'We need a reorientation of thinking about what works to keep children safe and foster their well-being; to move from being risk-based and deficit-oriented to strengths- and capacity-centred.'

I also generally wish to be self-directed. I may need help at times, and I want that help to be offered to me in a form that, as far as possible, respects my autonomy and encourages me to build on my strengths. Sally Holland and Jonathan Scourfield (2004) drew my attention to the views of Isaiah Berlin about freedom to act:

> I wish to be somebody, not nobody; a doer-deciding, not being decided for, self-directed and not acted upon by external nature or by other men as if I were a thing, or an animal, or a slave incapable of playing a human role, that is, of conceiving goals and policies of my own and realizing them.
>
> (Berlin, 1969: 131)

Holland and Scourfield acknowledge that all societies will place some restrictions on the lives of individuals, and parents are not free to bring up their children at will. But they explore whether there is room within the UK child protection system to promote positive freedoms in the lives of those affected by systems directed at safeguarding children.

Needs assessment

Considered the 'father of needs assessment', Roger Kaufman defined 'needs' as 'a gap in results'. Needs assessment involves comparison of current performance with a statement of desired outcomes. The gap between these is the development need. Intervention is targeted at closing the gap (Kaufman and English, 1979). Bringing up children is a challenging task, whether this is soothing a constantly crying baby, managing a defiant toddler or engaging with a stroppy teenager. It is normal for families to experience problems from time to time and this may result in them turning to the State for help (Ward and Rose, 2002).

> Parents are individuals with needs of their own. Even though services may be offered primarily on behalf of their children, parents are entitled to help and consideration in their own right. Their parenting capacity may be limited temporarily or permanently by poverty, racism, poor housing or unemployment or by personal or marital problems, sensory of physical disability, mental illness or past life experiences.
>
> (Department of Health, 1990: 8)

In my view, the needs of children and their parents are inseparably inter-twined. Calm, self-confident, well organised parents may still have some difficulties with their parental role but for those experiencing symptoms of anxiety and depression, marital difficulties which may include domestic violence, poor physical home conditions and poverty, disability and multiple stressful life events, it is only when these factors are addressed that parents will be able to focus sufficiently on meeting the needs of their child. If parents are unable effectively to organise their own daily lives, the children are at risk of experiencing neglect, exposure to uncontrolled intense emotion, insensi-tivity, unresponsiveness and hostility from their care-givers. When financial resources are insufficient children may feel ashamed of their appearance and find it difficult to sustain friendships. Paul, aged 14, told ChildLine, 'They spend all the money on drink. There's no soap in the house and all my clothes are too small. I lost my girlfriend because she said I smell. Others call me names and make fun of me. It hurts' (ChildLine, 1997: 37).

As I see it, a needs assessment begins with observations which result in factual data about a child's appearance and behaviour. Professionals keep in mind a global notion of age-appropriate development, behaviour and of appearance that suggests adequate levels of care. If there is a gap between these desired states and the child's current presentation, explanatory accounts or causal relationships are sought. If the quality of parental care is thought to be wanting, the focus turns to the care-givers. Care-givers are more likely to struggle to meet their child's needs if their own needs remain unmet. Intervention directed towards the care-givers indirectly addresses the child's needs by attending to critical influences within the care-giving system.

In the UK, Dorset County Council and Adult Social Care Services suggest a number of general questions that can be used to assess needs:

- What can you do for yourself?
- What can you do if given some help?
- What needs to be done for you?
- What help do you feel you need?
- Who helps you at the moment?
- What is the best way of meeting your needs?

Karl Dunst and colleagues (1988), in a description of their Support Functions Scale, suggest a number of questions designed to explore the extent to which families feel the need for different kinds of assistance, including, 'someone to encourage you when you are down,' 'someone to talk to about problems with raising your child,' 'someone to hassle with agencies or businesses when you can't,' 'someone to lend you money,' 'someone who accepts your child regardless of how he or she acts,' and 'someone to fix things around the house.' These authors tie together strengths and needs. This leads into an approach in which the worker challenges strengths in the context of a positive frame. In my experience this is much more likely to lead to learning and development than a focus on weaknesses which frequently prompts defensiveness and the likelihood of confrontation, argument and hinders learning. This kind of challenge is intended as an invitation to test capabilities to the full. Affirmative comments can effectively be paired with suggestions for further development using the connecting word 'and' rather than the 'but' that detracts from the initial affirmation. 'I can see the efforts you have been making to keep the house tidy despite having three little ones to mess it up *and* what do you think about getting a new belt to fix the vacuum cleaner?' 'Look how Kirsty reacted to the tone of your voice. What a lovely smile. Do you think she would like you to sing some nursery rhymes?' 'Your community nurse tells me that you've been managing your drinking really well recently. What kinds of things are helping?'

Children with special needs

The Framework for the Assessment of Children in Need and their Families (Department of Health, 2000a) outlines the universal needs of children. Beyond these needs, some children are born with genetic or other congenital impairments that make even greater demands on care-givers. Infants may need to be tube fed or require assisted ventilation. Children may have hearing or visual impairments or restricted mobility that requires the use a powered wheelchair. When impairments or disruptions to development are identified beyond infancy, reaching a plausible causal account is sometimes beyond the scope of current professional knowledge. One such example is the condition of foetal alcohol syndrome which can be very difficult to identify with any degree of certainty.

Ruth Marchant (2001) argues that when a child's needs are complex, assessments of parenting can be particularly challenging because some children need intensive or particularly skilled parenting for much longer than others. (I prefer this terminology to the use of 'better than good enough parenting' since performance as a parent can vary over time between adequate, good and poor. My own experience of being a parent suggests that 'good enough' is quite sufficient a challenge.) The challenge of parenting children with complex needs extends to apparently simple expectations of parents such as keeping appointments. Marchant cites the example of a four-year-old who had already attended more than 300 medical appointments. Not only are there likely to be high levels of practical demands on parents caring for children with special needs, but also emotional demands as they face disappointments, distressing procedures to which their child is subjected, multiple meetings with different specialists, and always the spectre of impending bad news:

> When I first had Kim he was my son. A year later he was epileptic and developmentally delayed. At eighteen months he had special needs and he was a special child. He had a mild to moderate learning difficulty.

He was mentally handicapped ... I was told not to think about his future .... By the time he was four he had special education needs. He was a statemented child. He was dyspraxic, epileptic, developmentally delayed and he had complex communication problems .... At eight he had severe intractable epilepsy with associated communication problems. He was showing a marked developmental regression. He had severe learning difficulties. At nine he came out of segregated schooling and he slowly became my son again. Never again will he be anything else but Kim – a son, a brother, a friend, a pupil, a teacher, a person.

(Murray and Penman, 1996: 6)

Untangling concerns about a child's developmental progress is no easy task and may benefit from an interprofessional approach, providing this does not subject a family to the even greater pressure of intense scrutiny by multiple professional strangers. In my view, when a child is developmentally delayed or presenting with physical impairments, it is essential always to keep in mind that multiple causal factors may be implicated. Whether a parent is able to provide the necessary intensity of care or learn the special skills to manage a child with an impairment is an appropriate question, the answer to which may rely on the kinds of support that may be provided by the State.

Structured decision making

Recent literature suggests that attempts are being made to design interventions from assessments that link findings concerning safety, risk, strengths and needs (Bolton and Lennings, 2010; Schwalbe, 2008; Shlonsky and Wagner, 2005). 'Risk and needs assessments, for example, should be linked directly to service plans. In the aggregate, assessment data also will help indicate the range and extent of service resources needed in a community' (Wiebush *et al.*, 2001). This linking process is sometimes known as Structured Decision Making, which is a set of principles that guides the decision-making process, rather than a rigidly defined procedure (Spain, 2004). In this chapter I have endeavoured to link different stages and approaches to assessment, beginning with attention to issues of current safety and prediction of future harm, whilst advocating a focus on strengths, protective factors and needs, an analysis of which should lead to a plan for intervention built around existing resources within the family. For the involved agencies the process of investigation and intervention eventually reaches a conclusion. However, the shock waves may continue indefinitely for the family who may live with their own 'case' for the rest of their lives.

The challenge to parents' shortcomings undermines their sense of reality and control. It is as if the door has been opened to a room in which everything said and done assumes sinister significance. At the end of the investigation the door stays ajar; the contents still spill out. Irrespective of the outcome, parents must struggle to integrate what happened into their normal understanding of the world ...

(Cleaver and Freeman, 1995: 72)

Placement, residence and
contact arrangements

I'm happy 'cos I'm safe here. My mam's happy 'cos I'm safe being with carers what love me. Being safe with people that I know and not being moved. I like it. I get upset when my mam cancels contact. I think something's happened to her like she might be ill or Dave punched her and she's in hospital or she might have been killed. She has a cold, a problem with her stomach and she has asthma. You can't blame my mam for everything. Lots of times I worry about my sisters that they'll get hurt. I cry all the time when I'm sad and I always cry when contacts get cancelled. Sally and Pete help me when I'm sad. They give me a love and talk to me. I get really worried when I phone my mam and I can hear shouting.

In this short extract, a looked-after 10-year-old expressed many of the dilemmas faced by children accommodated by the local authority on either a voluntary or statutory basis. Is it permissible to love and be loved by another family? What frightening things might be happening at home in the child's absence? Why has she been placed away from her birth family when her siblings remain? What does it mean when a parent fails to turn up for or cancels contact? Whose fault is it that there are such profound difficulties in the birth family that the child cannot safely live there? What guarantees are there that this placement will be stable and the child will not be moved again?

Issues in deciding placement

Permanence

In care proceedings the issue of 'permanence' is typically at the centre of considerations for the care of the child, with recognition that repeated changes of care-giver undermine the process of development of secure attachment and can generate feelings of rejection and self-blame. June Thoburn (1988: 31) points out that, 'it is a *sense* of permanence which is crucial, rather than a particular legal permanence option such as adoption.' In my own practice I have found this of special importance for young children whose sense of security emerges out of their day-to-day experience of predictable and reliable care-giving and not from the formal legal status. For some children, their beloved pets effectively constitute family members from whom they cannot bear to be parted. A placement may be contraindicated if carers will provide a home for the child but not for their pet.

Sense of identity

The popularity of research into family history is testament to the importance for people of knowledge about their ancestry and cultural heritage. For children who are unable to live with their birth families, developing a sense of identity and of place in a family, in their culture and social group cannot readily be accomplished through the regular channels of shared memories, celebrations, story-telling and a photographic record. Children who have moved a great deal as a result of family instability or repeated changes of placement often lose important possessions that help define their identity. In the following example, along with her younger sister, Matilda had been in a temporary placement for three years. The plan had been for both children to be adopted together but when an adoptive family could not be found, Kiera was adopted and Matilda remained in her 'short-term' foster placement. When I arrived to meet with her she immediately asked if I would like to see her life story book and as she turned the pages described some of the photographs:

> This is me when it was my fifth birthday. My daddy Michael and my nana Evie gave me a pink fairy dress and wings. When I got dressed I loved asking my mummy to put nail varnish on. This is grandma Davies (maternal great grandmother). I used to go and see her a lot. I slept once. When I left my mummy I was living with Anita (two years earlier). She's got my care bear teddies. She's still got everything of mine. I feel sad because I love my care bears. There's one giant one up in the loft. She's got my Bratz spinner thing. I want everything of mine back. I have thousands of care bears and lots of them's at Anita's.

Matilda was eventually returned to the care of her mother who had made significant changes to her lifestyle in the intervening period. When I saw her after a few weeks living with her birth family and asked if she would like to show me her life story book she said told me firmly that she did not like it any more. I took it that her sense of identity was now being confirmed by her day-to-day experience so she had no need of a transitional object to do this work for her. The life story book had contained some negative (and inaccurate) information about her mother, which it appeared that she would rather forget in light of her own first-hand experience.

The acknowledged importance of information about birth families for people who have been adopted has led to the opening up of previously closed adoption records and has been a factor in changes to legislation concerning children born through assisted conception.

> It just makes you feel that you belong to something because I used to very much feel as I was growing up, especially when I was going through traumatic times, like I'd just been plonked on the earth – a mystery – no past at all that you can relate to – I'd constantly think, 'why do I think this way, surely there is something else, someone who understand about this or that?' So you feel isolated and cut off. I'm sure that's one of the reasons why wanting to find birth parents is so important, because it makes you feel you have a beginning, a middle and an end.
>
> (Howe and Feast, 2000: 140)

June Thoburn (1988: 31) argued that, 'a sense of identity can best be achieved by continued contact with parents and other members of the natural family and with other people who have cared for or about a youngster in the past.' In the absence of direct contact some children become preoccupied by fantasies concerning their birth families.

Identity is seen as a particular issue in the UK for children who are of black and ethnic minority heritage. I have found some authorities to adopt a very simplistic view of this: if a child is black the carer must be black, even if this involves the child being placed miles away and out of the authority. In one such instance from my experience, a child of African-Caribbean heritage was placed with an African carer. As we walked together to collect the child from school, the carer told me that she experienced Jamaican men as purveyors of sexual abuse and pornography, and in this she included the child's grandfather. There was no suggestion that the child had been sexually abused but it became clear that the carer was hyper-vigilant about any behaviours which might be seen as sequelae. I would have said that she was prejudiced against Jamaican men but this factor had not been addressed in the 'matching'.

In a review of the literature addressed to placement stability, Emily Munro and Ainsley Hardy reported that, 'Interviews with carers revealed some concerns that matching was based upon 'colour coding' and that authorities did not always fully consider culture and religion (Holland *et al.*, 2005). Ward and colleagues (2006) found that in certain authorities social workers and family placement workers felt that, 'policies on placing minority groups had been over simplified and matching on this criteria [sic] was prioritised over other needs' (Munro and Hardy, 2006: 9). What ethnicity is a child born of a father whose mother was Chinese and father Jamaican, and of a mother whose father was from Pakistan and mother from the UK? We live in a contemporary ethnic melting pot and it becomes increasingly difficult to specify ethnicity whilst it is incumbent on us to be aware of racism and the impact of belonging to a minority group. In my view, it is the carers' awareness of this and their willingness to help the child understand their ethnicity that matters, rather than superficial ill-conceived 'matching'.

Reciprocal roles

Children learn survival strategies in their birth families which they bring to new placements where the same behaviours and mental models of relationships will be maladaptive. Substitute carers may be drawn into responding to the child in similar ways to the birth parents with difficult results and outcomes for everyone. A number of psychological theories bear on this process. In psychodynamic theories, the process of transferring feelings and behavioural patterns to new relationships is known as 'transference' and the other's response as 'counter-transference'. Feelings arise from substitute carers finding themselves inadvertently playing out the reciprocal role to the child's transference (e.g. playing the role of the child's angry parent). The carer may try to counter the transference of the child by steadfastly refusing to adopt this role. Cognitive Analytic Psychotherapy (CAT) focuses on such reciprocal role relationships. Systemic approaches aim to bring these habitual patterns of interaction into awareness, describing them from multiple perspectives. These models are useful in locating the 'problem' in the interactional process, thereby avoiding the attribution of blame or responsibility to a single participant. Knowledge of a child's relationship patterns may be helpful in the matching process.

Known outcomes of different kinds of placement

In seeking to establish permanence for children it follows that outcomes of the different arrangements for alternative care are particularly material to the decision. It has been argued, and there is some evidence to support the view, that long-term fostering offers less permanence than adoption (Selwyn and Quinton, 2004), although in this study, children whose adoptive placement broke down and who were subsequently fostered were included in the foster care group.

Age at placement is often cited as a powerful factor predicting disruption (Holloway, 1997). John Triseliotis (2002) explored this issue through a large-scale review of evidence reported in studies from the UK and USA. Placements of children under the age of one year rarely broke down. When the results of studies from an earlier period were included in his analysis, breakdowns amongst the adopted group of children, placed at 4–6 years of age, were significantly lower than for the fostered group. However, if only those studies carried out between 1990 and 2000 were included, hardly any differences between the two groups were found. Triseliotis attributed this to the likelihood of improved policies and practices in the intervening period. For children placed between the ages of 5–12 years, long-term fostering showed significantly higher placement breakdowns for fostered children but with the gap narrowing in studies carried out after 1990. Adolescents are far more likely to be fostered than adopted and overall breakdown rates are quite high with between a third and a half of placements disrupting within a 3–5 year period. Although the breakdown rate suggested a slight advantage for adoption, Triseliotis pointed out that this disguises the fact that a proportion of older children are adopted by their foster carers if the placement has stabilised. His overall conclusions were:

> Allowing for all the methodological difficulties in contrasting data from different studies, two broad conclusions can be drawn from this paper. First, because of the type of child currently being adopted or fostered, differences in breakdown rates and in adjustment between these two forms of substitute parenting are diminishing and in some age groups evening out. Yet at least one recent study reported that foster care rarely offers permanence. Its placements are too liable to break down (Sinclair *et al.*, 2000). Second, compared with long-term fostering, adoption still provides higher levels of emotional security, a stronger sense of belonging and a more enduring psychosocial base in life for those who cannot live with their birth families. The main limitation of long-term fostering is its unpredictability and the uncertain and ambiguous position in which the children find themselves. Taken together these conditions appear to generate long-standing feelings of insecurity and anxiety in children.
>
> (Triseliotis, 2002: 31)

A note of caution regarding these findings is sounded by Sellick *et al.* (2004). Their review of the literature concluded that, 'When age at placement and other variables are held constant, there are no differences in breakdown rates between adoptive placements and placements with permanent foster families' (Sellick *et al.*, 2004: 4). Similar findings have been reported by Holloway (1997) and Thoburn (1991).

Triseliotis argued that the best predictor of placement stability was, where children are old enough, consulting with them and responding to their views. The results of outcome studies show a number of factors which are associated with differences in outcomes for children, whatever the nature of the substitute care:

- 'Long-term placement with relatives or friends ("kinship care"), and short-term placements that become permanent, have been found to be more successful for the full range of children than placement with families not previously known to the child ("stranger care")' (Sellick *et al.*, 2004).
- Older age at placement accounts for higher disruption rates. In a study by Holloway (1997) the higher disruption rates for children who were fostered as opposed to adopted was due to the older age of the children at placement. The disruption rate for children placed for fostering aged seven or over was 56 per cent as opposed to only 1.6 per cent for children under seven placed for adoption.
- Being placed alone has emerged as a risk factor even when other variables have been held constant (Fratter *et al.*, 1991; Sinclair, 2005; Thoburn and

Rowe, 1988; Wedge and Mantle, 1991). Sibling groups have typically fared better than individual children in terms of reduced risk of placement breakdown.

- Outcomes for children are more positive when carers are 'child-oriented', practise responsive parenting, and are rated as 'authoritative' (warm, encouraging, sensitive to the child's needs, willing to listen and being clear in terms of boundaries and expectations for the child's behaviour) (Sinclair *et al.*, 2007; Wilson, 2006).
- The 'chemistry' between the child and carers is a factor that may be difficult to define or predict. Some children and carers take to each other whilst others struggle (Sinclair and Wilson, 2009).
- Commitment of the care-giver to providing a permanent family and home irrespective of the level of difficulty presented by the child is a positive indicator (Sinclair and Wilson, 2009) which is often a factor in successful kinship placements. Such placements have been particularly successful for children placed between the ages of 5 and 10 years (Farmer and Moyers, 2008).
- The presence of a large total of previous challenging behaviours or a child who was out-of-control have been correlated with poorer outcomes, particularly for foster care placements with strangers (Farmer and Moyes, 2008).
- Ward and Skuse (2001) found emotional abuse to be strongly associated with disruption. The exclusive rejection of one child in the family ('preferential rejection' or 'scapegoating') has been found to be associated with less settled placements (Dance *et al.*, 2002).
- Providing information to new parents in advance of placement about sexual abuse and behaviour problems can help to lessen the problems that may arise for new families (Sellick *et al.*, 2004).
- Positive relationships between the child and the carer's own children are crucial. Carers may accept challenging behaviour towards themselves but are much less tolerant of difficult behaviour directed towards their birth children (Farmer *et al.*, 2004; Quinton *et al.*, 1998). In a survey of 160 adoption agencies in England and Wales on placing siblings permanently, the main reasons for placement disruption and poor outcome for siblings was stated to be, 'a child's violent or sexually abusive behaviour towards other children' (Lowe *et al.*, 1999). This was the apparent cause of *all* placement disruptions in 226 adoptive families.
- Many studies of the placement of infants and of older children have found that placement breakdown was associated with the existence of a birth child close in age to the child being placed (Sellick *et al.*, 2004).
- It is important for new parents to feel comfortable about integrating a child's early history into their family life (Sellick *et al.*, 2004).
- Some studies have found that children who have physical or learning disabilities generally do as well or better, when placed with new parents, than children who are in all other respects similar (Sellick *et al.*, 2004).

• When children are sufficiently mature, consulting with them about their wishes and feelings is the best predictor of placement stability (Sellick and Thoburn, 1996; Triseliotis *et al.*, 1995).

Types of alternative placement – factors related to outcomes

When children cannot live with birth parents either because they have been relinquished voluntarily, as a result of their challenging behaviour, or because the quality of care has been judged inadequate or harmful, the State is faced with a range of options for providing alternative care. 'The trend since the mid-1990s has been for younger children to enter care, increasingly for reasons of abuse or neglect, and to remain longer due to the seriousness of their difficulties' (Biehal, 2007). As a professional who discovers a child living in a sorry state with carers whose functioning is compromised and who may have caused a child significant harm, it can be difficult to keep an open mind about future placement, especially when the alternative care that the child is receiving presents such a profound contrast. Having 'rescued' the child, who is now flourishing, workers often cannot bear to contemplate reunification, even when the conditions that led to the child's accommodation or reception into care no longer pertain. People who become substitute carers are frequently child-centred, positively motivated to provide high quality care for the children placed with them, and have passed the tests and detailed scrutiny of the local authority. It is not surprising that the quality of care that they are able to provide surpasses that of birth families, but this is not the basis on which a decision concerning the child's long-term placement can be made. The philosophy underlying the Children Act 1989 (CA89) and the Human Rights Act 1998 (HRA) is that individuals have a right to respect for private and family life, home and correspondence. Local authority inter-vention is required to be proportionate. Hedley J[1] (cited in Davis, 2009) explained these requirements as follows:

> Basically it is the tradition of the UK, recognised in law, that children are best brought up within natural families …. It follows inexorably that society must be willing to tolerate very diverse standards of parenting, including the eccentric, the barely adequate and the inconsistent. It fol-lows too that children will inevitably have both very different experi-ences of parenting and very unequal consequences flowing from it. It means that some children will experience disadvantage and harm, while others flourish in atmospheres of loving security and emotional stability. These are the consequences of our fallible humanity and it is not the

---

1   *Re L (Care: Threshold Criteria)* [2007] IFLR 2050 High Court, at paragraphs 50–51.

provenance of the state to spare children all the consequences of defective parenting. In any event, it simply could not be done.

(Davis, 2009: 175)

Reunification

In the quest for permanency for children, a move which began in the USA, rehabilitation with families was the placement of first choice. In England, the emphasis has tended towards finding permanent substitute families for children rather than on planned work to return them to their families of origin (Biehal, 2007). On the other hand, 'Birth parents may have harmed children and had children removed and yet are entitled to our concern and support' (Schofield and Simmonds, 2009: 6). The result of professionals' concern and support may be that the child *is* able to return to parents who have made significant and enduring changes such that the safety of a child is now assured. Or a family crisis may have passed with the result that parents have returned to a previous adequate level of functioning. Many of the children in the care system will at some date seek out their birth parent; children who are older are likely to return sooner. Elaine Farmer (2009) identified four different groups of children in terms of the relationship between the initial care plan and reunification. There was a group of children who absconded or were removed from care by their parents before initial care plans could be made. A second group comprised voluntarily accommodated adolescents who returned within an average of six months. Younger children stayed in care for longer prior to reunification and a fourth small group returned to the care of their birth family after an average of three years because the permanence plans made for them had not materialised. In the UK, children accommodated voluntarily under section 20 of the Children Act, 1989 are three times as likely to be returned to their families as those placed under care orders (Cleaver, 2000).

Research findings have suggested that one of the crucial factors in the success or otherwise of reunification is the extent to which the return has been purposeful and planned (Biehal, 2006, 2007; Thoburn, 2009). Nina Biehal argues the need for greater attention to assessment, a written agreement with the parents, forward planning and follow-up support (Farmer *et al.*, 2008; Harwin *et al.*, 2003). When reunification was subject to scrutiny by the courts, local authorities provided higher levels of assessment, monitoring and service provision. These placements were more likely to succeed (Farmer *et al.*, 2008). The birth family's readiness to resume care of the child through having resolved their original difficulties and addressed subsequent emergent needs is crucial (National Family Preservation Network, 2003; Thoburn, 2009). It follows that re-assessment needs to be thorough and as searching as the original process that led to the child's removal. Resolution of previously problematic issues is achieved through provision of, 'targeted services to address parents' and children's difficulties; involving [substitute] caregivers in assisting returns and their aftermath; marshalling parents' informal support systems; and involving schools and other agencies in monitoring and assisting children during reunification' (Farmer, 2009: 95).

Parental motivation and willingness to change feature strongly in positive reunification outcomes (Thoburn, 2009). Ambivalence and poor motivation are associated with professional reluctance to attempt reunification (Harwin *et al.*, 2003) and a higher probability of disruption if children are returned (Farmer *et al.*, 2008). Re-entry to care following reunion has been associated with parental substance misuse (Courtney *et al.*, 1997; Terling, 1999), mental health problems (Packman and Hall, 1998), social isolation and a lack of support networks (Terling, 1999). 'The evidence suggests a need for adequate support to both children and parents to ensure positive outcomes on return. Yet, the research indicates that this is rarely provided, despite the fact that there may have been little change in the problems that led to placement and that readjustment to family life may be difficult when family membership has changed during the child's absence, as is often the case' (Biehal, 2007: 820).

I agree with the findings of Nina Biehal. In my experience, parents with mental health difficulties or who are misusing drugs or alcohol are often required to access therapeutic intervention unaided, the capability to do so being regarded as a required positive indicator. The pathways to such help are often beset with hurdles and the requirement to meet very specific referral criteria. I have known parents to pursue a number of routes by which to access treatment for mental health difficulties that have been diagnosed during the course of the proceedings, only to be turned away when a different professional tells them that they do not have the symptoms that would open the door to the service. Whether appropriate input can be accessed varies enormously by location. Some voluntary services provide excellent input to parents who are struggling, including out-of-hours support, accompaniment and introduction to staff in mainstream services. When I hear the voices of their children explaining the meaning of 'home' it is clear to me that concerted effort to improve the lot and functioning of struggling parents is worthwhile:

She drank, yes. She went in hospital and the doctor said to her, 'You can't drink,' and she doesn't drink any more and my mum wouldn't because the doctors told her she'll get ill. She's back to normal, especially at contact. No one told me about her drinking. You just know. I'm really really glad she's got off it because hearing about George Best; because most people can't do it. I didn't really see her drunk. To me, drunk is where you see them on the telly falling over and tipsy topsy. She was never like that I don't think, falling over. She definitely got things done around the house. Mum always tried her best. If I asked, 'Do you think I'm getting fat?' and all that. She'd say, 'No, you're just ... I love you just how you are.' Mum cheers me up because she tells me stuff; a joke, or sometimes mum just cheers me up with a cuddle, a love.

She says, 'I'll always be there for you. I always love you. When you're happy I'm happy.' She'd show it in a lot of ways. I cry when I'm alone but no one notices, mostly at night.

Kinship care

In England, the white paper, Care Matters: Time for Change, provided a new framework for family and friends care, with a view to ensuring that this is considered as an option at the first and each subsequent stage of decision making for children (Department for Education and Skills, 2007). The potential advantages of kinship care are that placements tend to be of longer duration than those with unrelated carers (Farmer and Moyers, 2008), children are often going to carers with whom they are already acquainted (including placement within a familiar community or ethnic group), and they experience a greater sense of belonging and less stigma (Mosek and Adler, 2001). When consulted, children themselves have expressed preferences for care within the extended family (Department for Education and Skills, 2007).

In a study of children living with extended family members and with unrelated foster carers in four different local authorities (Farmer and Moyers, 2008), the level of placement disruption in kinship placements varied between 8 per cent and 49 per cent from authority to authority. The local authority with 49 per cent disruptions had the highest level of deprivation, the largest number of drug-using parents and more frequently placed children with family and friends than the other authorities. The authors proposed that the disparity could have arisen from the fact that in the local authority with high levels of disruption the majority of the social workers were employed by an agency rather than the authority, kinship care approval may have been granted at lower thresholds, and monitoring could have been less vigilant.

Among the risks of kinship care are the potential for problematic contact and the possibility of conflict within the wider family when birth parents resent the child being looked after by other family members. It can be a considerable challenge for extended family members to protect children from their birth parents although Elaine Farmer and Sue Moyers (2008) found that in most cases relatives, 'managed the tricky business of putting the children's needs first very well' (Farmer and Moyers, 2008: 223). Nevertheless over half of the family and friends carers had difficult relationships with the children's parents:

> Some parents were resentful that a relative had taken over the care of their children, other parents were actively hostile to the kin carers and a few made threats or actually attacked them, whilst others made false allegations against the carers or undermined the placement in other ways. Occasionally, two sides of the extended family were in conflict about who should be caring for the children.
>
> (Farmer and Moyers, 2008: 223)

The following factors have been found to be associated with successful outcomes for kinship care (Hunt *et al.*, 2008):

- When the child was relatively young at the point of placement.
- When the child was presenting few emotional and behavioural difficulties.
- When the child had previously lived with the carer.
- When the carer had instigated the arrangement.
- When the carer was a grandparent.
- When the carer was a lone carer.
- When there were no children other than siblings of the placed child/children in the household.
- When carers had been assessed for suitability as foster parents.

(Farmer and Moyers, 2008)

Joan Hunt and colleagues (2008) argue that practitioners are quite poor at predicting which kinship placements will present difficulties and should not become overly preoccupied by concerns such as age of the relatives, contact with birth parents or child protection issues. The main factor to be assessed is the carers' functioning in the role of parent. Carers themselves have expressed resentment at the focus on risk assessment and instead would prefer acknowledgement of their knowledge and skills in the parenting role (Doolan *et al.*, 2004). Hunt (2009) points out that kinship care presents unique challenges and significant costs to family and friends carers in terms of overcrowding, low incomes, chronic health conditions, having to give up their jobs, which affects not only carers' current but future retirement income, coupled with the emotional roller coaster of adapting to what was often the sudden arrival of their relatives' children in their homes and the changes that this imparted to other relationships within the wider family. Although they are likely to need support, the evidence suggests that kinship carers typically receive less support than unrelated carers. The need for financial assistance is a major theme, as is the desirability of respite care and advice on how to navigate the various legal, education and social services systems.

Some children have birth relatives living overseas who could offer a home to a child, or at least offer a link with the family's country of origin, culture, language and lifestyle. In the UK, an organisation known as Children and Families Across Borders (CFAB) can make arrangements to trace such relatives, and for the establishment of contact between the extended family and children in local authority care. An assessment of the home environment overseas can be requested from partner organisations and arrangements made for the child to be received, supported and protected there. Such assessments may also conclude that it is unsafe for the child to be placed with their relatives overseas. Details are available from: http://www.cfab.uk.net/what_we_do/state_care.php.

Fostering

Approximately 70 per cent of looked-after children in England are in foster care (Department for Children, Schools and Families, 2007). Fostering plays a key part for these children, with a number of different roles and functions including short-term emergency or assessment placements; shared care with birth parents through the provision of regular short breaks; task-centred placements of intermediate duration, which may serve as a bridge to a longer term placement or are termed 'therapeutic', 'professional', or 'specialist', often for adolescents who are presenting with very challenging behaviour, for children with learning difficulties or those who have been sexually abused. Long-term foster care – the provision of a substitute family for children who are unable to live with their birth families – is the most common, although the relative permanency may not have been planned, as when a match for a child with an adoptive family cannot be found and the child lingers in what was intended to be a short-term placement. In such circumstances I have generally found foster carers to do a superb job. When they struggle it is often because workers, short of resources and faced with a pressing need for urgent placements, make matches that are clearly unsuitable at the outset. Not infrequently in my experience, the number of children for whom the carer is approved is exceeded, children of inappropriate ages are placed, the child arrives accompanied by a stranger after traumatic separation from the birth parents and from their siblings who have been dropped at different placements en route, or they arrive carrying a dustbin liner into which their precious possessions have been hastily packed.

Assessments of suitability for the role of foster carer are important because there is evidence that some foster carers have fewer placement breakdowns than others (Sinclair and Wilson, 2009). In addition to the factors associated with differences in outcomes for children whatever the nature of the substitute care, the following criteria have emerged as influential in the success of foster placements:

- Taking into account the child's wishes and feelings, including preferences such as wanting to be the only child in a placement or in a placement with a baby, where there is no conflict of loyalty with their family of origin, where they feel they belong, where they have a room of their own, where there is support for their interests and hobbies and where there are clear plans for their future (Sinclair *et al.*, 2007).
- Placements made in a rush are more susceptible to breakdown (Farmer *et al.*, 2004; Sinclair *et al.*, 2005).
- Placements work better when the carer's preferences are taken into account.
- Sometimes placements are less susceptible to breakdown when the school is seen as supporting the child effectively (Sinclair *et al.*, 2005).

One of the complications of fostering, apparent in day-to-day decision making, is that the foster carer must share parental responsibility with the local authority and, to some extent, with birth parent/s. Whilst this can have a positive impact through support provided for issues associated with schooling and relationships with the birth family, there can be a negative impact over delays associated with gaining approval for matters such as haircuts, school trips and staying over with friends. This can lead to children having the sense that they are not part of a 'normal' family (Timms and Thoburn, 2003) and carers feeling as if they are being undermined (Schofield, 2009).

> Sleep-overs, a very important part of children's lives, were impossible to arrange as SSDs [social services departments] needed weeks to make decisions and do police checks. Consequently, carers were faced with the dilemma of either denying the young person the opportunity to lead a 'normal life' or lying to social services.
>
> (Selwyn and Quinton, 2004: 12)

Julie Selwyn and David Quinton reported that needing permission for sleep-overs was a fallacy as there has never been a statutory requirement for Criminal Records Bureau (CRB) checks which had been introduced by some very cautious local authorities. They concluded that children in long-term foster care might be provided with greater security through the delegation of many more decisions to the carers.

Foster carers are a remarkable resource. They take into their homes children who often present serious challenges to family functioning, not infrequently under conditions that violate their original agreements with local authorities about the characteristics of children they want to foster, at very short notice and with minimal background information. They tolerate being kicked and punched, being accused of abuse, damage to or theft of their possessions, being woken repeatedly in the night when a child cannot settle or has disturbed sleep, and temper tantrums to the point of vomiting. They develop understanding and management skills in caring for children who present with sexualised and sexually provocative behaviour, they cope with children's distress at missing their birth family, with management of contact or failed contacts with birth parents, and defending the child against threats to well-being that can emanate from multiple sources. Their commitment to children is reflected in the detail with which they can often describe those in their care:

> Michael has a lot of trouble with understanding. If he wants to read a book I sit with him and it takes him ages to settle and he gets fed up and bored. Everything has to be turned off so there are no distractions and if I persist and encourage him, he will get it. I've bought him a mobile phone and taught him to text and that's really helping his reading and writing. He's always in trouble at school because he'll say things like 'dickhead' to a teacher but he can't tell you what it means.

He's just copied what other kids say and doesn't understand why he's in trouble. It's very frustrating for him. He'll laugh at something on TV but he won't know what he's laughing at and even if you explain he often doesn't remember. He's really really slow in a morning and I have to 'myther' him. I set out his uniform and wake him at half seven with a cup of tea but he's still in his bedroom getting ready at half past eight. He'll walk to school using the pelican crossing but if he's distracted he just goes off. If a friend comes by he'll forget to go. He wouldn't do it deliberately and he's so sorry even if he's five minutes late. He struggles to make judgements and needs a set of rules or else he becomes totally confused. He always asks me if I want any help and he knows how to dust and vacuum and put on a duvet cover. He knows how to make cakes but I have to supervise him in the kitchen so we do it together. I really enjoy Michael's company and we have lots of laughs together. He loves food and eats anything. He knows what's good for him and he's a lovely lad, a great kid.

Twenty-first century policy initiatives in England have made it clear that long-term fostering should be regarded as a credible alternative form of permanent care for children, with no disincentives attached to this option over any other (*Every Child Matters*, Department for Education and Skills, 2003 and *Care Matters: Time for Change*, Department for Education and Skills, 2007).

Special guardianship

In the UK, the Adoption and Children Act 2002 introduced special guardianship and special guardianship orders. It does not remove parental responsibility from birth parents but is intended to secure long-term stability of placements, allow for continuing links with the birth family and enable the special guardian to exercise parental responsibility without reference to others. Special guardianship occupies a role between adoption and long-term fostering. The differences between special guardianship, residence orders and adoption are explained fully at: http://www.thecustodyminefield.com/25.html.

Adoption

In England, when seeking permanence for a child whom it is thought cannot return to the care of the birth family, adoption has come to be seen as a positive route to securing a child's future. However, adoption against the parents' wishes is a highly radical intervention, and in the rest of Europe dispensing with the consent of parents and severing the legal link between children and their birth parents is more typically regarded as an infringement of human rights (Simmonds, 2009). Adoption cannot be justified on the grounds that it will improve a child's lot. It either requires informed consent or it must be demonstrated that there is a significant risk of harm resulting from inadequate parenting which cannot be ameliorated by intervention and professional help.

Although children adopted in infancy appear to do very well (Juffer and van Ijzendoorn, 2005, 2007) outcomes for children adopted from care when aged between 5 and 11 years are less clear cut. A study by Rushton and Dance (2006) provided evidence that children adopted at this age have typically experienced a number of prior foster placements and previous attempts at reunification with birth families. Despite the impact of so many transitions, about half of these children had formed strong and positive relationships with their adoptive carers. Just over a quarter were intact but struggling with the challenges presented, and the final quarter of placements had disrupted when the difficulties had become insurmountable. Risk factors included the following and accounted for 83 per cent of the disruptions in the Rushton and Dance study:

- Being older when placed
- Having been preferentially rejected by the birth family
- Having been in local authority care for a longer period prior to matching
- Having experienced a high number of moves of placement
- Having experienced repeated failed attempts at reunification
- After a year in placement, continuing to show challenging behaviour, over activity, and a lack of attachment to adoptive female carers

Adopters have autonomy to make best interest decisions for children. Although adopters sometimes struggle with a lack of support from the local authority, they can turn to other agencies for help or purchase private sector services when they are in difficulty. They are able to make free choices about how best to meet the needs of the child and can act independently of social services. Where benefits accrue from adoption this may in part result from the greater security that adopters experience in acting autonomously in the best interests of the children for whom they provide a home (Selwyn and Quinton, 2004). Children's sense of security is built on that of the carers. On this dimension, adopters are in a privileged position compared with foster carers.

Residential care

As a young professional I worked for a while in a residential facility for young people and in an Observation and Assessment Centre. For the purposes of research I visited many other residential establishments. I am still haunted from time to time by the experience of observing young people standing in line in their underwear in the cold to use the primitive washing facilities available, and of young teenagers sitting rapt as I read their first bedtime story for many months. Working there gave me an experience of being punched by a child (I quickly learned not to prioritise 'getting results' over sensitivity to the child's experience) and of taking children out without the faintest idea of how to retrieve them if they took it upon themselves to abscond. I agree with Roger Bullock (2009) when he argues that congregating adolescents who are presenting with challenging behaviour creates a potential for disaster.

I also participated in a study aimed at exploring outcomes for children and young people who were placed in such facilities and also being cared for in alternative ways (Vobe *et al.*, 1978). I gained a great deal of respect for pioneers who were trying new ways of helping children with histories of trauma, abuse and neglect. Whatever their nature and form, the success of these alternatives seemed largely to depend on the vision and commitment of the leadership and staff.

Nowadays there are far fewer children in residential care where, despite the good intentions of well motivated, empathic and concerned staff, unlike other forms of care-giving, they go on and off duty and cannot be available to young people on a 24-hour-a-day basis, unlike their counterparts in families. Roger Bullock (2009) concluded that residential placements are suitable only for adolescents exhibiting challenging behaviour who are presenting dangers to themselves and/or others or where specialised treatment is needed. I concur; these are the criteria by which to judge whether residential care is the only option for this young person at this time.

The decision to place siblings together or apart

> Sometimes when Zoe comes in my bedroom in the night or in the morning when I'm watching telly having a bit of peace she keeps on coming in. I'm just sad because I say, 'Go out,' and she says, 'No', then she goes out and comes back in again. She messes with my telly, makes it go to a silly noise but when I switch it off and on again it's OK. I do like having a bit of peace but I wouldn't want to leave her. She is kind of naughty but I wouldn't want to leave her. She does bite me. I tell her off and then she asks to go in her bed. I'll miss her if I leave her. I'll start crying. I'll definitely put a sad. I just want to play on my bike because every time she crashes into me I crash her back. She doesn't like me playing that.

This five-year-old was struggling with some of his younger sister's behaviour but was very clear that separation from her would distress him. An international overview of sibling studies (Hegar, 2005) concluded that joint sibling placements are as stable as, or more stable than, placements of single children or separated siblings. Rushton *et al.* (2001) concluded that sibling placements are associated with greater stability, although this was not to say that the disruption to single placements would have been ameliorated had they been placed with siblings. Separation of children who have lived together has lifelong implications in that they stand to lose a shared identity and a sense of belonging to the same family. Marjut Kosonen (1999) argued that children placed with siblings valued the presence of their sisters and brothers and whilst acknowledging conflict, nevertheless wanted to live close to them.

In my own experience of assessing parents who have been brought up in the care system, siblings placed on their own sometimes have experienced limited opportunities to confer about their shared experiences and can feel in some way responsible for having been unable to remain in their birth family. I agree with Jennifer Lord and Sarah Borthwick (BAAF)'s (2008) view that the decision to separate siblings who have lived together, or who are currently living together, should be treated with the same seriousness as the decision to separate children permanently from their parents. These authors take the view that there should be a presumption that siblings will grow up together despite, 'episodes of intense conflict as well as ones of joy, sharing and support' (Lord and Borthwick, 2008: 1).

In order to assess sibling relationships I have found it illuminating to talk to the children themselves about their own relationships with siblings, and about their observations of relationships between other siblings in the birth family. Observation of their relationships in action is also helpful. Particularly for young children, it can be quite challenging just to establish who the siblings are in an extensive and ever-changing family group. Some of the individuals described by the child being interviewed may be cousins; children of similar ages may be nephews or nieces; some older siblings may have children of similar age to the child I am interviewing; some siblings may live at a distance and visit infrequently. Some may be children of a parent's earlier partner of whom the child is aware but has never met. Determining the relative importance of sibling relationships may present a challenge in itself, let alone making recommendations about single or joint placements. It can be helpful to make a distinction between 'core' siblings and 'kin' siblings (Kosonen, 1999). Core siblings are those with whom a child has lived and kin siblings are those who live elsewhere and with whom there has been a more distant relationship. It is appropriate to ask children whom they regard as their brothers and sisters because, 'the significance of sibling relationships is personal and interpersonal rather than biological or legal' (Burnell *et al.*, 2009).

When assessing the child's relationship with specific siblings, I have found some of the materials described in Chapter 6 to be of use since they offer the opportunity for the child to show as well as tell. Story Stem approaches can be particularly illuminating, providing an opportunity for the child to enact how they envisage a sibling responding in situations where they are hurt or proud to show some work that they have accomplished. Reports from carers, teachers and other involved professionals who have seen or looked after the children together are essential since they are familiar with the mutual impact of the siblings on each other and the degree of strain that this might put upon future substitute carers.

Lord and Borthwick (2008: 38) provide a Sibling Relationship Checklist that I have found very helpful in thinking about sibling placements. The dimensions included are:

- Defends or protects
- Recognises sibling's distress and offers comfort
- Accepts comfort from sibling
- Teaches or helps
- Initiates play
- Responds to overtures to play
- Openly shows affection
- Misses sibling when apart
- Resolves conflict through age-appropriate reasoning
- Annoys, teases or irritates
- Shows hostility or aggression
- Blames or attempts to get sibling into trouble
- Behaviour sabotages care-giver efforts to meet the other sibling's needs
- Evidence of sharing with other sibling (boisterous play, imaginative play, rituals at bed or bath time, jokes and fun, secrets)
- Differences and similarities between the siblings (roles, activities and interests, behaviour, personality)
- Evidence of reciprocity (pride in each other, praise and criticism, mutual help)
- Evidence of modelling on each other (think they look alike, imitate each other, copy qualities they like, unite in the face of problems)

Proposals to place apart siblings who have previously lived together typically arise when there are concerns that together their challenging behaviour will provide too great a test of the parenting skills of the substitute care-givers, hence increasing the risk of placement breakdown. A second circumstance is in the case of large sibling groups for whom it has not been possible to find a single adoptive home or foster placement. Third, proposals for separate placements are often made when there are plans for a young infant to be adopted and it is thought that the older sibling/s will be unable to integrate fully into a family with the commitment needed to join an adoptive family. Fourth, one of the siblings may have made a secure attachment to another carer during the period that the children have been placed separately, and this may take precedence over reunification. Fifth, siblings may be separated because one of the children is placed with a member of the extended family with whom the other child has no birth relationship. In the latter instance, it is important not to make assumptions that one child's birth family will not offer a home to an unrelated sibling as not infrequently I have encountered willingness to extend a permanent home to an unrelated child in recognition of the strength of the sibling relationship by members of the extended family. There was initial reluctance to place an unrelated sibling with the father below but he was able to show empathy, sophisticated and sensitive thinking about how his daughter's younger half-brother might experience the placement:

> To help build an attachment I'd spend time with Kyle watching television and playing. I try to now but we haven't had the right weather to play out. He's got an attachment to me. He's come up to me and loves me. It just needs that bond. He'll copy off Emma. He calls me dad and five minutes later calls me John. I think it'll just come natural in time because I think he's a bit unsettled because Angie (foster carer) has told him that he won't be staying there. Secure attachment gives you a lot of confidence. I've had a lot of support. There were always somebody there and it were my choice I stayed with my dad because we had a good bond until the day he died. It's given me everything. If you're not attached, especially as a teenager, I see a lot of difficulties. I still have a good bond with my mum. I'd be happy to adopt Kyle because if he's going to be here till he's 18, 19, 20 .... He's Emma's brother and if I were to adopt him then Kyle would have our surname and that might make it easier for him. Whether he's adopted or not Moira will always be his mum. Moira always used to say I wouldn't be able to be Emma's dad and mum but I'm doing my best. She's calmed down a bit now and if she wants to see the kids and it's properly supervised than that's fine with me. I never bad mouth her to them. I just want them to be safe and to grow up happy together.

Developing a secure attachment to the adoptive or foster parent is seen as a priority when making placement decisions for previously traumatised children (Burnell *et al.*, 2007). If placement together were to inhibit this process then there is an argument for separate placements. However, it is important not to make assumptions that prior experience of trauma will make a child unsuited to a shared placement. Children who have a common experience can help each other to make sense of their history, as can others who have borne witness to the abusive treatment of children. In my clinical practice, a child who was referred and received treatment after being rejected by his adoptive family continued to visit the staff team long after the intervention ceased. He had made a success of his long-term foster placement with the care and tolerance provided by his foster carers, but still recalled the way in which he had been scapegoated within his former adoptive family. He said, 'You saw how they treated me.' The staff team could provide important validation of his own experiences that helped him to recognise and develop his sense of self-worth, despite the experience of rejection both by his birth family and his adoptive family who, in both instances, continued to look after his younger siblings.

When the concerns are that placement together will be too challenging for the long-term carers, it has been proposed (Lord and Borthwick, 2008) that a judgement needs to be made concerning the intransigence of the dysfunctional patterns of sibling interaction developed in the birth family. These may

include intense sibling rivalry to the extent that each child is unable to tolerate attention paid to the other, exploitation when one child has been encouraged to dominate another, chronic scapegoating of one child that is perpetuated
by a sibling, highly sexualised interaction between siblings or when each child
acts as a trigger to the other's traumatic memories, repeatedly re-traumatising
in the process. This may be unintentional and carried out unconsciously.

For very needy children who are to be placed together, whilst the permanent carers need to be fully conversant with the challenges that this will
present by having met with the siblings together, it may be helpful for the
children to be placed in sequence rather than simultaneously. These are
known as 'staggered' placements (Head and Elgar, 1999). This is how children usually arrive in families. Eldest children have the experience of being a
lone child before the birth of younger siblings. For a very demanding older
child, providing an opportunity for the child to have the undivided attention
of the new carers may help them to create an attachment relationship which
is less threatened when the younger sibling later joins the new family. Such
arrangements may be particularly suited to circumstances in which children
have been sexually abused in their birth families and are continuing to show
sexualised behaviour, possibly with each other.

Contact with birth families

It can be a puzzle to work out the best arrangements for contact between
looked-after children and their birth parents. It is tempting to see the capacity
for attachment as of finite quantity; if children are to become attached to one
family or carer they will have 'used up' their given amount and will be unable
to make or sustain additional attachment relationships, although there is
substantial evidence to the contrary. 'There is no evidence to support the view
held by many that continued contact with birth parents prevents children
from becoming attached to new parents, other than in a minority of cases
where parents deliberately set out to wreck a placement' (Thoburn, 1988: 50).
When substantial contact amounting to shared care between a foster carer and
birth parent is proposed, this may be seen as having the potential to confuse
children about the identity of their primary carer. And yet children of divorced
or separated parents frequently find themselves in this position. Unless they
are under pressure to take sides, such children appear to be capable of sustain-
ing a relationship with both birth parents and are also able in due course to
develop positive relationships with their parents' new partners.

Whilst proceedings are ongoing, a variety of arrangements are made for
contact with birth families. Following a judgement by Mr (now Lord) Justice
Munby in 2003[2], the widely-accepted practice in regard to infants under a

---

2 Re M (Care Proceedings: Judicial Review) [2003] EWHC 850 (Admin), [2003] 2FLR 171).

year in age has been for frequent contact with the birth parent/s. He has subsequently welcomed further discussion of the issue in terms of the need to prioritise the welfare of the individual infant (Schofield and Simmonds, 2011). These authors stress the importance of giving due consideration to the purpose of contact: that of enabling the infant and parent to develop or sustain a positive and enjoyable relationship with each other. This requires practical arrangements that support the infant's need for developing security, and regular routines through consistency of escort and supervisor, stress-free travel arrangements, appropriate frequency, duration and timing, emotional and practical support for parents, and understanding on the part of foster carers of the critical role that they are playing in the infant's developing sense of security.

What is made of the child's behaviour immediately following or prior to contact? It is quite natural for children to feel hurt, upset and angry when they meet with their birth families, because they feel rejected, confused or in turmoil that they are separated from someone to whom they had an attachment, however dysfunctional the relationship may have been. Recognition of children's distress on separation was highlighted by research carried out in relation to hospitalised children by James and Joyce Robertson in the early 1970s to which I have referred earlier. Despair, apathy, listlessness and eventual detachment and withdrawal from birth parents, are 'normal' responses to separation.

June Thoburn (1988) argued that ongoing contact is beneficial, unless parents of young children request adoption, where children are totally rejected by parents, or where badly-treated children reject the parents. Only rarely did contact with parents contribute to placement breakdown yet fear of placement breakdown was a significant factor leading workers to put barriers in the way of such arrangements (Berridge and Cleaver, 1987).

The stipulations of the Children Act (1989) have led to a statutory 'presumption of reasonable contact' with birth parents for children who are accommodated or looked-after. The specification is worded to signify that contact is a right of the child, although parents' views are usually taken into account in decision-making forums (Schofield and Stevenson, 2009). The definition of what is 'reasonable' remains an area of some dispute (Schofield and Stevenson, 2009). The same presumption is not made for contact with siblings or extended family members such as grandparents, although they are typically included in the care plan for looked-after children.

> For some birth parents, contact visits were emotionally difficult and stressful, particularly when contact sessions were regulated, highly supervised, in awkward and hard-to-reach places, and fairly short in duration. They felt that this often put restrictions on the communication between themselves and their children, and they felt intimidated by the continual surveillance.
>
> (McSherry *et al.*, 2009: no page numbers)

If the quality of ongoing contact is going to be positive, then discomfort with the arrangements needs to be acknowledged and adjustments made in discussion with birth parents and the child's current carers. Contact centres are often unsuited to older children's needs. Activity-based meetings in the community can be more relaxed, harmonious and less forced. Often there is appropriate reluctance for contact to take place in the birth parent's family home, backed by valid arguments that the child may take it as a false indicator of permanency plans. But this can be managed and I would not rule it out, on the grounds that it may give children the opportunity to see that they have not been displaced from their family of origin. Such arrangements would be contra-indicated if the parent were to give children the false impression that they will be coming home to the bedroom that has been preserved or redecorated especially for them.

Ongoing contact with at least one birth parent is most likely to take place when children are looked after by other members of the family or by friends (Hunt, 2009). This is despite the fact that the contact was not infrequently problematic by virtue of hostility, resentment and behaviours from the birth parents which could have had an undermining impact on the placement. However, contact that was detrimental to the child was more likely in non-kin care (Farmer and Moyers, 2008). For children who are fostered, contact with birth families is the norm (Sinclair and Wilson, 2009). Sinclair and Wilson reported that contact is usually encouraged, children would like more rather than less and contact is regarded as beneficial to a developing sense of identity. In a series of studies reported by Neil *et al.* (2011) adoptive parents listed the benefits of contact being the facilitation of an ongoing exchange of information between children and their birth families, that it helped children to make sense of the key people in their lives and could reduce feelings of abandonment.

Families have become increasingly complex, as parents (sometimes repeatedly) sever relationships with partners and reconstitute their families. Consideration needs to be given to the nature, frequency and duration of contact not only with parents, but also with siblings and extended family members. Children enjoy relationships with birth siblings, half-siblings, step-siblings and a variety of grandparents, aunts, uncles and cousins. The logistics of the practical arrangements alone can present a serious challenge to professionals and carers who are trying to establish purposeful and positive contacts for children. When determining the frequency and nature of contact with birth family members I regard the following issues as central to the decision-making process:

- Clarity about the purpose of the contact in terms of its contribution to the child's developing sense of identity, self-esteem, clarity of life narrative and general well-being. The primary purpose of benefit to the child is best held in mind.
- To what extent the contact exposes the child to further risk of harm through poor care-giving, abuse, rejection or parental hostility to the child or substitute carers.

- To what extent ongoing contact generates risks to the permanency of the child's long-term placement. In my experience it is important that the child's behaviour, be it emotional distress or increases in challenging behaviour, immediately preceding or following contact, are not taken as evidence supporting arguments to reduce or terminate contact, since they are normally associated with separation from attachment figures for all children.
- For adopted children it has been argued both that ongoing contact may interfere with the establishment of secure attachment to the new family and also the opposite: that the pain associated with the loss of birth family members may interfere with the development of attachment to the adoptive family (Young and Neil, 2009). A judgement of this issue needs to be made for each individual child.
- To what extent the contact interferes with the child's experience of 'normality'. If the arrangements for contact prevent the child from fully enjoying friendships, engaging in hobbies and leisure interests, or involve frequent lengthy journeys with associated tiredness then alternative arrangements need to be considered.
- To what extent the arrangements cause confusion to children about the future arrangements for their care. If contact is frequent but reunification is not an option this needs to be apparent to the child through conversation and explanation, through their day-to-day experience and by ensuring that the parent does not give counter-messages and false hope of a return home.
- The importance of the established relationships between the child and birth family prior to placement. Pre-verbal infants are unable to code relationships in language which means that their memory for birth parents will be very limited. Once a decision has been made for permanent substitute care, arguments in favour of contact, other than with the purpose of aiding the development of a secure identity, may be less persuasive.

With regard to contact following adoption, Tony Baker identifies a number of prerequisites:

- the birth relative supports the care plan of permanent substitute care (adoption);
- the birth relative accepts the child will have a new place to call 'home' and new people to call 'mummy' and 'daddy';
- the birth relative and new parents can establish a respectful and harmonious relationship around the contact issue;
- there is a common understanding about the reasons for the child not living with the birth family;
- all parties accept that any contact will take place between the child and birth relatives in the context of the child's new family rather than exclusively with his or her birth relatives.

(Baker, 1995: 257)

Although the findings may be counter-intuitive, for a group of adopted children who were placed at a mean age of 21 months, face-to-face contact was appreciated by all parties (Young and Neil, 2009). It was generally preferred to letter-box contact which posed greater challenges to the achievement of helpful information exchange (Neil, 2004). Elsbeth Neil reported that both adoptive parents and birth relatives found it difficult to know what to write to people with whom they were not acquainted, and communications were easily misunderstood. Photographs were valued. She reported that contact venues varied from family centres to neutral venues where there was less pressure to make conversation. Some families enjoyed frequent meetings in each other's homes. Annual time-restricted meetings with undisclosed personal information about the adoptive family were vital in some cases. Contact worked better when the adoptive parents were able to show the children that they were there with them in spirit in their dual family connections, rather than leaving the child physically and emotionally to manage the issues and feelings that arose (Schofield and Beek, 2006).

There is evidence that less attention is paid to the arrangement of ongoing contact between siblings in long-term placements, than to decisions regarding contact with birth parents. This is unsurprising given the complex logistics of scheduling, arranging venues, providing supervisory staff, transport and financial costs. In a study by Cherilyn Dance and Alan Rushton (1999), nearly half of the placements in the sample had been made without any definite plan for contact and when there was a plan, this rarely involved all siblings. Foster children often have more complex constellations of siblings than other children in the community (Kosonen, 1999) and social workers naturally struggle to keep track. Worryingly, a complete lack of contact most often signified that the other siblings had remained with the birth family (Dance and Rushton, 2005). This is a recipe for the development of a sense of rejection and self-blame for the child who has been removed.

Strong feelings in favour of contact with siblings were expressed by children in a study by Macaskill (2002) and the vast majority of contacts with grandparents work well (Neil, 2004). Elsbeth Neil concludes her chapter by inviting professionals to be open-minded about contact arrangements, not allowing prior experiences to prejudice judgements regarding contact with the family in question, and helping all parties to understand their roles in supporting positive arrangements for the benefit of the child. This may involve phone calls, adult-only meetings, exchange of recorded material and modifications to contact arrangements which may promote improved communication between the birth family members and substitute caregivers. The quality of the contact experience for the child is central to decisions about nature and frequency. 'Children usually look forward to contact, commonly want more contact than they get, but are nevertheless commonly upset by it' (Sinclair, 2005: 91). The role of professionals and the child's carers is to help children to understand and make sense of these feelings, rather than terminate birth family links because the workers cannot bear the child's distress.

Contact with birth parents when there has been prior domestic violence

In my experience, allegations of domestic violence are common both in contested public and private law. It has been raised as a reason for restricting contact in 22 per cent of private law disputes reaching the courts (Smart *et al.*, 2003). The Practice Direction (President of the Family Division, 2008) on this matter advises that where allegations are made, a fact finding hearing should be held at the earliest opportunity whilst in the meantime arrangements are put in place to safeguard the child. Giving priority to establishment of the facts is crucial in minimising the risks of creating a rift between child and carer when allegations are adjudicated as unfounded.

The outstanding concerns regarding the advisability of contact with a parent against whom an allegation has been substantiated are the nature and extent of the risks to the child and the parent-victim of further physical and/ or emotional harm, set against the value of contact to the child's well-being. Potential negative impacts of contact are the child's continuing fear of a parent who has perpetrated violence, the arousal of post-traumatic anxieties through proximity to the perpetrator, continuing awareness of the fear engendered in the child's main carer, and the potential impact on the child's developing attitudes towards violence (Sturge and Glaser, 2000). These authors argued that there should be no automatic assumption that contact with a violent parent was in the child's best interests. They argue that the balance is tipped against contact without evidence of the following:

- Some (preferably full) acknowledgement of the violence;
- Some acceptance (preferably full if appropriate, i.e. the sole instigator of violence) of responsibility for that violence;
- Full acceptance of the inappropriateness of the violence particularly in respect of the domestic and parenting context and of the likely ill-effects on the child;
- A genuine interest in the child's welfare and full commitment to the child, i.e. a wish for contact in which he [sic] is not making the conditions;
- A wish to make reparation to the child and work towards the child recognising the inappropriateness of the violence and the attitude to and treatment of the mother [sic], and helping the child to develop appropriate values and attitudes;
- An expression of regret and the showing of some understanding of the impact of their behaviour on their ex-partner in the past and currently;

- Indications that the parent seeking contact can reliably sustain contact in all senses.

(Sturge and Glaser, 2000: 624)

This analysis carries the assumption that domestic violence is about male perpetrators and female victims, whereas the accounts that I hear from families are sometimes about a process of interaction specific to a particular relationship, not infrequently involve female perpetrators, or are shown to have been very convincingly fabricated. The literature cited in Chapter 3 makes clear that there are many women who assault their partners yet I rarely encounter proscriptions, on the basis of domestic violence, against contact for mothers. I also fear that the requirements proposed by Claire Sturge and Danya Glaser could generate merely surface compliance. At the same time, I meet women who have overwhelming and authentic fears of a partner who has almost killed them, and cannot understand how contact with their father could benefit the children.

Sturge and Glaser do propose some creative solutions to the resolution of contact difficulties, such as enabling a child to see a parent in a safe context in which the child is able to experience a sense of control, such as through use of a one-way screen with the child prompting an interviewer regarding topics they want to explore with the parent. They also propose the usefulness of proxy contact with a 'go-between' meeting each party separately and conveying individual concerns. Such interventions are designed to establish a sense of safety and ease which may allow contact to progress in a manner that secures benefit to the child. Whilst in my experience this approach has 'worked' for some children who have been resistant to contact as a result of their experience of domestic violence, an overly cautious approach can also serve to impress upon children that their fears are grounded.

In my view, assessment of the wisdom of and arrangements for contact between children and a parent when domestic violence has been established requires a wide-angle view. I like to hear from each parent, the children and any professionals who have been involved, particularly when they are able to provide a perspective over time. I want to know about the following:

- What is the evidence for change in the parent's attitude towards and use of force in relationships?
- What is the evidence for the child's attachment and the parent's bond?
- To what extent has the parent shown commitment to the child through indirect contact/keeping informed about the child's progress even if the child has failed to respond?
- How much empathy does the parent show for the child's experience?
- How does the parent describe and prioritise their various motivations for contact?

- To what extent has the parent complied with professional prescriptions/contracts of expectation/existing arrangements for contact?
- To what extent does the parent support the child in relationships with the current carers and family members who are important to them?
- What are the child's expressed wishes and feelings (both overt and shown indirectly in her or his behaviour)?
- To what extent has the child's development been vulnerable or resilient to the experience of the domestic violence?
- How would the contact impact on the child's current stability or lack of it?
- To what extent would contact put the child in a 'double-bind' (compliance with contact would serve to alienate the other parent even if the child is looked-after)?

We would do a great disservice to children if we failed to recognise the human potential for change. Neither can I see the value of demanding that their parents prostrate themselves before professionals in order to be assessed as safe to see their children.

Private law

Residence and contact arrangements

> Everything can be tolerable until the children are taken from you. I cannot begin to describe the pain, the awful eviscerating pain of being handed a note, sanctioned by your (still) wife with whom you had made these little things, with whom you had been present at their birth and previously had felt grow and kick and tumble and turn and watched the scans and felt intense manly pride and profound love before they were even born, had changed them, taught them to talk, read and add, wrestled and played with, walked them to school, picked them up, made tea with, bathed and dressed, put them to bed, cuddled and lay with in your arms and sang to sleep, felt them and smelt them around you at all times, alert even in sleep to the slightest shift in their breathing ... a note that will ALLOW you ACCESS to these things who are the best of you ... ALLOW mark you, REASONABLE!!!! ACCESS?!?!!! to those whom two weeks ago you couldn't wait for to walk in the door at home.
>
> (Bob Geldof, 2003: 182)

Residence and contact (formerly known as custody and access in the UK, and referred to as custody and visitation in the USA) is at the centre of disputes in private law proceedings. When separated parents cannot negotiate future arrangements for the care of the children themselves, the force of law may be brought to bear and professionals are faced with the need to make assessments in the best interests of the children. When couples separate, the role of the court is not to prescribe where children will live and how they will spend time with the non-resident parent, but only to resolve disputes when parents are unable to reach agreements themselves. In my experience such disputes are fearsome things. Positions are entrenched by the time the dispute comes to court, and the well-being of the children has often become lost in the intensity of the warfare between the parents as each tries to 'prove' the unsuitability of the other to the role of care-giver. The rage that parents often feel in these situations is clear from Bob Geldof's exposition above.

One of the most distressing experiences for professionals can arise from the parents' involvement of the children in their battles. The pressure on children to take sides can be enormous and I have known the sustained tension to result in children's developmental regression, with the loss of skills formerly accomplished. I have seen children squirm in extreme discomfort when pressured by a parent to fabricate an incident involving the other parent. In a phone-in on BBC Radio Five (BBC, 2009), people in late middle age spoke in tears about the continuing impact of their parents' battles which had caused them problems throughout their entire lives.

There is an extensive literature, especially from the USA, providing advice on assessment of parents in child custody determinations to which I have referred in earlier chapters. Assessments of risk, of parenting, and of adults in their own right have been discussed there and I will not repeat them here. What I do want to emphasise is the emotional damage that can be caused to children by the inability of parents to extricate themselves from the emotional tangles of failed relationships and, at their extreme, such children may warrant becoming the focus of intervention by the authorities on the basis of being subject to significant harm. I think that in the case of contested residence and contact after parental separation, the courts too often take a 'softly softly' approach that unintentionally serves to consolidate the position, typically of non-resident parents losing touch with their children through the obstructive strategies of the resident parent. There are, in some cases, very good reasons for such obstructiveness, as when a parent has been subjected to extremes of domestic violence and fears that the perpetrator will harm the child. It is understandable that such parents will question the benefits that could accrue to a child from direct contact with a former partner who has had such a long-term negative impact on them. But with a clear positive purpose to contact, this situation can be managed with orders that specify the detail of the arrangements and ensure that contact is properly supervised.

Where they are made, residence orders typically follow a relationship breakdown and the court's concern is with whom, not where, the child lives, although location can be ordered if a parent, for example, plans to move in order to thwart contact with the non-resident parent.

When, following a conflicted separation, parents engage in private law proceedings about arrangements for the care of the children, there is no statutory presumption of contact (Davis, 2009) but the English courts work on the basis expressed by Ward LJ[3] that, 'every child is entitled to know its parents and to have contact with them unless there are cogent reasons to refuse it.' It is assumed that contact will be face-to-face and only if this is considered impossible will indirect contact in the form of letters, emails, cards, photographs, school reports and presents be prescribed. Neither is there a presumption that children should have equal amounts of contact with separated parents. Although parents have equal rights before the court the best interests of the children will vary greatly according to individual circumstances. Particularly as children grow older it becomes increasingly challenging for them to maintain friendships, keep clothing and possessions, and transfer homework and materials needed for school between households in two locations. On the other hand, when separated and warring parents live in very close proximity, children can readily be engaged by the parents on a daily basis in the front line of hostilities.

'The longer that a child goes without having contact, the harder it is to re-establish a relationship' (Davis, 2009: 97). Davis cites an example of a case that had been in court for five years over 43 hearings conducted by 16 different judges with 950 pages of evidence. I have been involved in similar 'cases' myself. Parents repeatedly defy contact orders without any consequence, on the basis of arguments that disposals such as a custodial sentence for the resident parent will harm the child. Children are coached against the other parent. This allows the resident parent to take the position that he or she supports contact but the child resists. False (or genuine) allegations of abuse can kick-start the termination of contact. It is appropriate for such allegations to be investigated but in the meantime, contact is often suspended. I can understand the need for supervision whilst the investigations proceed but when it is suspended, re-establishment becomes problematic and the longer the situation pertains, the more difficult re-introduction becomes. It is not even necessary for allegations to be made in order for a child who enjoys contact to begin to refuse to go. Sensitive to a resident parent's feelings about the former partner, children can feel a great deal of pressure to protect the adult, who is after all their primary care-giver, from the stresses involved in sustained contact. Whilst empathic and child-centred parents will protect a child from the intensity of their own anguish, others expose their children to their sadness, anger, feelings and thoughts about the other parent in a manner which distorts the non-resident parent in the mind of the child.

In a study by Liz Trinder *et al.* (2005), contact was regarded as 'working' when it took place without risk of harm to any of the parties, all were committed to it, all were broadly satisfied with the prevailing arrangements and on balance it was a positive experience for all. There was an implicit agreement between the parents about their respective roles and

3   *Re L (Special Guardianship: Surname)* [2007] EWCA Civ 196 [2007] 2FLR 50 Court of Appeal, paragraph 58.

neither challenged the status of the other, denigrated or threatened the resident parent. Resident parents actively supported contact and gave children permission through their actions and expression of feelings, to enjoy the continuing relationship with the other parent. When contact was successful, parents had a realistic and balanced appraisal of each other and managed conflict on the basis of an assumption that the other parent was well-intentioned.

When contact was not working, there was typically either a lack of commitment or high levels of parental conflict. In some families that were studied, no regular pattern of contact had ever been established. Some children were apparently indifferent to a lack of contact whilst others were distressed by the unpredictability or absence of the non-resident parent:

> We don't know what she looks like anymore. Every time when she's promised to come round, she keeps on lying which makes me sad ... ever since she kept on lying I just kept on getting annoyed and then getting annoyed at school, disrupting my education and that lot. (Child 13–15).
> (Trinder *et al.*, 2005: 5)

Whilst some parents do disappoint children by failing to honour commitments to contact, a caller to the BBC phone-in (BBC, 2009), after re-connecting with her father as an adult, discovered that on the days he was due to visit her mother would take the children out, and on days when contact was not scheduled, she would dress them up in coats and shoes when they would sit on the stairs futilely awaiting his arrival. When contact is not working, unravelling the complexities of parental feelings, thoughts and actions can be a serious challenge for the professionals involved.

Various motivations drive the contest between parents over their children. Affection, a long-standing bond, and deeply felt love make it very difficult for a parent to give up a child or to bear a change to the living arrangements which prevent the unconstrained daily access to which they are used. This can be especially difficult when the non-resident parent fears for the safety of the child in the care of a former partner whom they know drinks to excess, shouts at or hurts the child. Where there is economic disparity between the former partners, fear and insecurity that the child will prefer the materially superior household abound. Most problematic are circumstances of continuing hostility where the contest over residence and contact becomes a strategy for gaining ground in the battle or represents a way of staying in control of the other parent. No account is taken of the child's wishes and feelings as the intensity of emotions takes over, sometimes putting the child in serious danger:

> Once, when I was about seven, mum followed me and dad in the car, because my dad said that he wasn't going to bring me home on time. My dad drove off with me and I started crying because I knew I should be coming back and he said, 'Calm down Harry.' I tried to stop crying. Then mum quickly got in her car and zoomed right down and there was

a bit of a fight between both cars. They both pulled in front of each other so none of the cars could actually go, and then they went on the main road and started having a race and I was going to take the risk of jumping and walking back home but I decided not to. My dad drove to the police station. Mum showed them the paper that said about when I should see my dad, and this policewoman speaks to me, trying to calm me down. It was really scary. I didn't think I'd be going back home for about a year but it turned out I came back on Sunday.

Whether valid or not, accusations against the other parent can be highly convincing and in systems where there are such high levels of conflict it is easy for professionals unwittingly to become attached to one or other side of the dispute. As the conflict escalates, so each parent seeks to add weight to their case by bringing in more witnesses. Family violence allegations are the norm (Jaffe *et al.*, 2006). Trinder *et al.* (2005) found that as parents became increasingly angry and frustrated with each other, they could only portray the former partner in all-or-nothing terms. Neither was able to show understanding of the behaviour of the other. If, in their own childhood, parents have been valued for their accomplishments rather than for themselves, or have been treated as pawns in their own parents' battles, then their underlying insecurity can feed into the contest, which becomes 'no holds barred'.

Child and parental alienation

I have undoubtedly encountered families in which children have been coached by parents into making false allegations against the non-resident parent and into implacable hostility and abject refusal to have any contact. The resident parent assures me that the child is being encouraged to enjoy contact but endorses the child's refusal. I have found such positions to be intractable. Although some parents may deliberately coach children, alienation can arise as a result of the manner in which the wider family interacts without any explicit intent on the part of the resident parent. There are many other reasons why children resist contact or visitation which do not warrant the label 'alienation':

> These reasons include resistance rooted in normal developmental process-es (e.g., normal separation anxieties in the very young child), resistance rooted primarily in the high-conflict marriage and divorce (e.g., fear or inability to cope with the high-conflict transition), resistance in response to a parent's parenting style (e.g., rigidity, anger, or insensitivity to the child), resistance arising from the child's concern about an emotionally fragile custodial parent (e.g., fear of leaving this parent alone), and resistance arising from the remarriage of a parent (e.g., behaviors of the parent or stepparent that alter willingness to visit).
> (Kelly and Johnston, 2001: 251)

The term 'alienation' is only warranted when there is a severe distortion on the child's part of the previous parent–child relationship (Kelly and Johnston, 2001). It most often arises in high-conflict residence or custody disputes. The kinds of behaviours shown by alienated children include unremitting negativity towards the targeted parent, poor rationale for the negativity, strong assertions that they have come to their views independently, use of mimicked 'adult' phrases, the description of scenarios of which they could not have memories or for which they are unable to provide any detail, and extension of negativity to the targeted parent's extended family and friendship network. Joan Kelly and Janet Johnston (2001) state that both empirical research and clinical observation suggest the presence of pathology and anger in parents who encourage the alienation of the child, including problems with boundaries and differentiation from the child, and severe separation anxieties (Dunne and Hedrick, 1994; Lampel, 1996).

There is controversy as to whether the alienation comprises a sufficiently discrete pattern of behaviours that would warrant it being labelled as a syndrome (either child alienation syndrome or parental alienation syndrome/ disorder). These 'diagnoses' are not accepted by the court or mental health professionals. The controversy over the issue parallels the conflict between parents who continue to enact their battles following separation. In my experience, a diagnostic label is unnecessary as a description of the dynamics in individual families has been sufficient to inform judgements. It has been argued that children younger than age seven or eight rarely show consistently alienated behaviours towards a parent (Kelly and Johnston, 2001) but this is not my experience, particularly in the presence of attachment difficulties and intense anxiety at separation from the resident parent. However, young children who have been deliberately coached often reveal this insouciantly during interviews because their cognitive skills limit their capability for consistent deceit. Children cannot help but be aware of conflict between parents:

"So before you see your dad, do you know how you feel?"

"Well the whole family usually gets well, not upset, but they all feel uptight with it. I feel that I have to make the most of mum before I leave the house, before I leave to go with dad. I feel a bit more sad than happy because every time I go with my dad then when I come back dad and mum always have an argument when mum comes to pick me up or something like that." (Child, 7–9).

(Trinder *et al.*, 2005: 6)

Children under pressure will often align with one or other parent. Non-resident parents become *persona non grata* and the child may refuse to see them. When children are struggling to manage the internal tension and anxiety that they feel, the psychological process of 'splitting' may result, in which children tend to view their world in an 'all or nothing' way. Splitting is common in early childhood but when there has been a predominance of frustrating experiences early in development, Kernberg (1975, reported in Gould *et al.*, 1996) argued that there is an interference in the process of normal integration of good and bad representations of self and others into more realistic and balanced perceptions. Instead, splitting becomes entrenched and utilized defensively in an effort to maintain psychological stability and cohesion. It is at this juncture that splitting becomes the hallmark defence that many authors have observed in borderline, narcissistic and other severe personality disorders. It readily leads to chaotic and unstable interpersonal relationship patterns, identity diffusion and mood swings.

Under these circumstances, ascertaining children's wishes and feelings can be very tricky. Particularly as they grow older, children can be very guarded and may have learned that above all they need to protect the resident parent from distress. Even when it is possible clearly to establish the child's wishes and feelings, when these run counter to the parent's view they are inclined to take no notice and find reasons to dismiss the professionals' findings. When parents sought court assistance in the study by Trinder *et al.* (2005) there was little improvement. '[A]pplications for court orders appeared to exacerbate rather than resolve parental disputes' (Trinder *et al.*, 2005: 6). These authors concluded that resources should be redirected towards more creative work to improve parental relationships and towards mediation rather than towards repeated attempts to impose a solution. From my experience, a contrasting but potentially effective intervention can be to take more radical court action at an early stage, for example by switching the child's residence. This averts the process by which parents learn that if they fail to comply with court orders nothing will happen and would prevent the establishment of long periods during which children do not see the non-resident parent. During these times they are open only to the picture being painted by, and influence of, the resident parent. The longer the duration of a pattern of non-contact, the more difficult it becomes to reintroduce parent and child. In a case heard *Re D* by Munby J[4] the previous two years of litigation were described as, 'an exercise in absolute futility .... The system has failed him .... I feel desperately, desperately sorry for him. I am very sad that the system is as it is.'

It is the role of the court to make judgements about allegations and counter-allegations. It is the role of professionals to assist the court in reaching its judgements. A Finding of Fact hearing that *follows* the lodging of a report may determine that an injury to a child was or was not caused by a parent. This may mean that the professional needs to reach two different sets of conclusions that will follow from the judgement yet to be made.

When professionals set out to ascertain a child's wishes and feelings in contested residence and contact, I have found it helpful to try and establish these using the approaches described in Chapter 6. I find the 'Bag of Feelings' particularly helpful as it aids children in talking about their feelings in

---

4   *Re D (Intractable Contact Dispute: Publicity)* [2004] 1FLR 1226 High Court.

general without necessarily focussing on the court process. I regard it as important not to put pressure on children by asking direct questions such as, 'Who do you want to live with?' 'How often do you want to see your father?' Even then, if they are so minded, children will provide answers to these questions in response to indirect queries. I regard it as important that children do not feel under pressure to make decisions about residence and contact, thereby risking feelings of guilt in relation to having hurt a parent's feelings.

> I'm angry that my dad really applied for all of this because it's just been really difficult to deal with it. When I was seeing my dad for a day it was difficult to keep being happy just in case he said anything about the court because I didn't want him to because it makes me frightened. It makes me think I might have to leave my mum and my sister. Once, he asked if I wanted to live with him and I said yes just so I didn't upset him and then he told everyone about what I'd said. And sometimes I said I wanted to live with both of them because it was too difficult to say I just wanted to live with him. It would make my mum cry if she thought that. I just want it all to stop.

Children need to know that what they share is not confidential and what they have said will be reported and seen by both parents. Sometimes assessment reports can serve interventive functions when children express their wishes and feelings in ways that can move a recalcitrant parent or provide insights about the child's experience of parental disputes or domestic violence.

Although assessments in private law disputes pose a challenge to practitioners, the children of angry and mutually hostile parents are sometimes at just as much risk of harm as children in public law proceedings and the State must intervene. Decisions about who will care for the children of separated or divorced parents are based on values which are often contested in a changing, pluralistic society. 'Custody laws once did take a clear and strong stand favoring fathers as property holders, and later, mothers as nurturers. Today, there is no social consensus about the appropriate family roles for men and women' (Emery *et al.*, 2005: 24).

> Deciding what is best for a child poses a question no less ultimate than the purposes and values of life itself. Should the judge be primarily concerned with the child's happiness? Or with the child's spiritual and religious training? Should the judge be concerned with the economic "productivity" of the child when he grows up? Are the primary values of life in warm interpersonal relationships, or in discipline and self-sacrifice? Is stability and security for a child more desirable than intellectual stimulation? These questions could be elaborated endlessly.
>
> (Mnookin, 1975: 260)

Although the judicial system struggles to assist families where parents are locked in battle, assessment of the collateral damage to the child can inform best interest decisions and needs the same care and commitment from professionals as assessments conducted in public law. Wherever possible, disputes between parents are best settled through cooperation and agreement. This is reflected through the introduction of a requirement, in the Family Procedure Rules (2010) for England and Wales, of confirmation of attendance at a Mediation Information and Assessment meeting or the provision of reasons for not having attended such a meeting prior to commencement of proceedings (Redley, 2011). This acknowledges that an adversarial court process is not well suited to the resolution of family disputes relating to children.

10 Theoretical considerations, data synthesis and formulation

In a study by Eileen Munro (1999), in which she analysed all child abuse inquiry reports published in Britain between 1973 and 1994 (45 inquiries in total), she concluded that, 'Errors in professional reasoning in child protection work are not random but predictable on the basis of research on how people intuitively simplify reasoning processes in making complex judgements.' Decision making may also inadvertently be simplified by the tendency first to make a decision and later to seek its justification (Klein, 2000). Munro summarised her findings thus:

> It was found that professionals based assessments of risk on a narrow range of evidence. It was biased towards the information readily available to them, overlooking significant data known to other professionals. The range was also biased towards the more memorable data, that is, towards evidence that was vivid, concrete, arousing emotion and either the first or last information received. The evidence was also often faulty, due, in the main, to biased or dishonest reporting or errors in communication. A critical attitude to evidence was found to correlate with whether or not the new information supported the existing [professional] view of the family. A major problem was that professionals were slow to revise their judgements despite a mounting body of evidence against them.
>
> (Munro, 1999: 745)

She took the view that intuitive reasoning has a central role in evaluation of the evidence in child protection, but that the judgements made need to be more rigorously and systematically reviewed against a wide range of evidence from multiple sources.

The meaning of information

As an assessment of a family proceeds, more and more information is collected. This can amount to a row of lever arch files. Meaning does not lie within this data but in the mind of the assessor who constructs meaning from the array. The array itself comprises only what we have constructed from interviews, what we have collected of other people's constructions, various documents and the results of any tests or questionnaires that have been completed. The meaning-making process occurs in people's heads and is transformed into language which can be communicated. Listeners construct their own meaning from the received language. By the time the assessment report is written, multiple translations have taken place between the 'raw' data and the black squiggles on the page.

Peter Choate (2009) argues that information obtained from medical and school records, from professionals who have provided counselling and treatment to the parent, and police and probation records all contribute to a deeper understanding of the family and the ways in which family members have interacted with the community. I agree with his proposition that parents should have an opportunity to comment upon and correct misleading or inaccurate entries within the records because it cannot be assumed that records are unerringly accurate. They contain not only matters of fact but also professional opinion, sometimes expressed in a pejorative and unjustified manner. Caution is also urged regarding over-reliance on formal test or questionnaire results since they can create the unwarranted impression of scientific validity.

> In our work we have access to all sorts of 'information'. Rumour, fantasies, hopes, hearsay, slander, scandal, chatter, defamation, wishes, aspirations, overheard conversations, miscommunication, false leads, speculation, hypotheses, projections, unfinished business, idle gossip, scapegoating, fuzzy thinking, grudges, half truths, personal opinions, misunderstandings, misquotations and dishonest statements collectively have the potential to mutate into fact as professionals consult with one another, conduct assessments, make records and compile client files and reports.
> (Michael Pomerantz, personal communication, July 2011)

Assembling, generating and organising information about a family for the purposes of assessing whether child and parents can safely live together are not neutral acts. I do not think that it can be accomplished dispassionately. As a professional I bring my whole self to work, as feeler, thinker and actor. The way in which I construct meaning from the data will be influenced by my values, my prior experiences, my profession, my working context and history. People are objects of fellow feeling and I may be just as influenced by growing affection for the people I am assessing as by a sense of distaste at the actions I hear tell that they have committed. Quentin Dobshansky, an attendant in a mental hospital in Joanne Greenberg's (1989) *I Never Promised You a Rose Garden* experienced the dilemma that this can pose.

He was beset by anxiety because he began to feel kindly towards someone he knew was 'crazy', although he had been encouraged to think of her as mentally ill. He was worried that he might make her sicker if he said the wrong things and this meant that he should be tentative, calm and should not show strong feelings. He should be cheerful and supportive. But he had learned that by what he said and how he acted he could move her, which led him to try to do so. He connected with her as a fellow human being and someone whom he might in time come to love.

Because the stakes are so high, the assessment process requires a commitment to developing awareness of what I bring to the task. The desirability of self-knowledge and ongoing personal and professional development throughout a practitioner's lifetime constitutes the reflective practice described in Donald Schön's seminal 1983 and 1987 texts *The Reflective Practitioner* and *Educating the Reflective Practitioner*.

> Reflective practice involves thinking from a 'birds-eye' view about an event and/or aspects of my practice. The perspective includes myself; encompassing my behaviour, thoughts and/or feelings in relation to my practice, with the implication that the reflection will impact on, although not necessarily alter, my practice. Gillie Bolton (2005) refers to this orientation as 'the hawk in your mind'. Such a distanced perspective may also include an analysis of social, ethical and cultural issues. This dimension arises particularly in health, social care and education settings because the worker is discharging a moral responsibility to care for the feelings of the student, client or patient. The practical actions of these professionals have wider and potentially more enduring consequences than is likely to be the case in occupations that deal with inanimate material although consideration of value positions is still relevant .... Reflection that involves analysis and/or synthesis is sometimes called critical reflection in the literature. The term implies that the reflection involves making discriminations, evaluating, judging, assessing, and weighing up options. This is the kind of reflection that I think is involved in reflective practice and which can result in more elegant, integrated and useful know-how ... [It] involves an attitude of open-minded curiosity oriented towards ongoing learning based on any of our experiences that are capable of informing professional practice.
>
> (Scaife, 2010: 3)

I do not take the view that this is the only kind of thinking that appropriately informs practice. If I were to reflect so widely (or deeply) on all of my professional actions I wouldn't get much done. 'Not only is reflective practice impractical and potentially dangerous in situations where judgements need to be made in an instant and on the basis of well-established routines, but it is also unsuited to learning that takes place through "osmosis" unconsciously in what Guy Claxton (1998) calls "the undermind"'

(Scaife, 2010: 4). But there can be danger in relying on what we seem to know without subjecting it to critical tests:

> ... very often we find that we have reached some kind of a conclusion in our thinking without having recorded or noted any actual instances: they have occurred, but the separate incidents have disappeared into a general sense of knowing ... we often find that we are acting from a value position which is not actually based upon the facts. We then need to examine our practice for data that will confirm, modify or challenge our existing value position.
>
> (Tripp, 1993: 39)

In my experience this creation of 'facts' to fit a belief position is not at all unusual. I have encountered it in narratives from children and parents in family proceedings, from my friends and family, and it has featured in some high profile cases such as that of Professor Sir Roy Meadow who created a 'fact', later shown to be erroneous, that the chances of two deaths which could be classified as 'SIDS' (Sudden Infant Death Syndrome) in a family like Mrs Clark's were one in 73 million. I have no doubt that this was created in good faith and that I must have been guilty of inadvertently creating inaccurate 'facts' myself at times over the course of my professional lifetime. I suspect that such errors are much easier to identify in others than in oneself.

I believe that several kinds of thinking are needed when carrying out assessments in family proceedings. Eileen Munro (1999) draws attention to the terms 'analytic' and 'intuitive'. Analytic reasoning is characterized as, 'a step-by-step, conscious, logically defensible process' (Hammond, 1996: 60). Intuitive reasoning is, 'a cognitive process that somehow produces an answer, solution or idea without the use of a conscious, logically defensible, step-by-step process' (Hammond, 1996: 60). Gregory Bateson (1972) gave these two kinds of thinking the terms 'strict' and 'loose'.

> I want to emphasise that whenever we pride ourselves upon finding a newer, stricter way of thought or exposition; whenever we start insisting too hard upon 'operationalism' or symbolic logic or any other of these very essential systems of tramlines, we lose something of the ability to think new thoughts. And equally, of course, whenever we rebel against the sterile rigidity of formal thought and exposition and let our ideas run wild, we likewise lose. As I see it, the advances in scientific thought come from a *combination of loose and strict thinking*, and this combination is the most precious tool of science.
>
> (Bateson, 1972: 75)

An attitude of open-minded curiosity and a combination of loose and strict thinking requires tolerance of ambiguity and the accompanying feelings of uncertainty. These were seen by Carl Jung as a function of the nature of work with people. He argued in favour of individual understanding which can only be achieved within a flexible and mutable framework. Methods (and the users of them) need to be adaptable, and theories open to challenge:

> Naturally, a doctor must be familiar with so-called 'methods'. But he must guard against falling into any specific, routine approach. In general one must guard against theoretical assumptions. Today they may be valid, tomorrow it may be the turn of other assumptions. In my analyses they play no part. I am unsystematic very much by intention. To my mind, in dealing with individuals, only individual understanding will do. We need different language for every patient.
>
> (Jung, 1963: 153)

Eileen Munro's review of child protection (2011) concluded that such flexibility has been suppressed in a, 'system that has become over-bureaucratised and focused on meeting targets' (Munro, 2011: 15).

> The focus of reforms has been on providing detailed assessment forms, telling the social worker what data about families to collect and, how quickly to collect it. Less attention has been given to helping frontline staff acquire the skills to analyse the information collected .... In some cases, formulaic responses have been developed, for example specifying when a certain number of reports of domestic violence have been received trigger a visit. The rational-technical approach has fed into a view that a good enough picture of practice can be gained from procedural manuals and from the written record where the results of the cognitive work are displayed.
>
> (Munro, 2011: 36)

Jan Horwath (2007) distinguishes between technical-rational activity, which emphasises traditional views of knowledge, standard procedures and empirical research, and personal-moral activity, which recognises that individuals do not fit neatly into boxes and that personal and professional values and beliefs influence judgements. Contemporary professional contexts of pluralism, diversity and contestability encourage a reflective approach and openness to a range of interpretations. This runs counter to a human tendency towards 'verificationism' (Scott, 1998) through which practitioners' initial impressions of a family tend to shape their subsequent thinking, and the ensuing process of assessment acts to confirm original explanations (Holland, 2004). I recognise in myself a tendency to notice information that fits with my current understanding but ignore that which is disconfirmatory. Jean Piaget (1972) offered an explanation for this reluctance, using the term 'dis-equilibration' (a sense of being off balance) to describe the unsettling process of having to modify current understanding in order to achieve a better fit between it and the new material. It has been proposed that in order to counter this tendency workers need to aim *not* for neutrality, but to use processes that force consideration of a range of different ways of understanding the people we meet in family proceedings (Holland, 2004).

If we do create multiple explanatory accounts which presage different solutions, we are faced with the dilemma of selecting amongst them. This is the place for an intervention, responses to which will provide evidence in support of or counter to each of the provisional accounts. This might involve modifications to contact arrangements for a time-limited period in order to assess the impact on parent and child behaviour, or therapeutic sessions aimed to assess the impact on parenting of improvements in the parent's mental health. The intervention constitutes a 'test' of provisional hypotheses.

In my assessments of families I have found it helpful to try to think in different ways at different stages of the process. Three ways of thinking, known as 'domains of action', were described by Peter Lang and colleagues (1990). In the 'domain of explanation' the focus is on understanding and the style is non-judgmental. In the 'domain of production' the position is one of evaluation in a world of rights and wrongs. When operating in either of these domains the authors argue that the process can be accomplished with taste and sensitivity through the third 'domain of aesthetics'. As a member of a helping profession I want to work within the domain of explanation with a primary focus on learning about and understanding a family. When I prepare a report for court it is with the knowledge that the process will result in judgements of right and wrong within the domain of production. I see the first assessment task to be the development of understanding. Judgements of right, wrong, need, risk and harm follow from this initial stage.

Theoretical considerations

Theories offer a way of looking at, viewing, or considering the available material about a family in its contexts. Theories attempt to provide explanations about the causes or nature of the matter under consideration and enable predictions to be made. Different theories can be used to frame the same dataset and generate a range of accounts for the findings which may be more or less plausible. Theories rise into and fall out of fashion. In the past, Freud's psychodynamic ideas about individual development dominated professional discourse. Psychodynamic theories incorporate the notion of persistence of *unconscious* patterns of relating through the concept of '*transference*', ideas which continue to have relevance today. This school of thought was subsequently impacted by the tenets of behaviourism, by cognitive-behavioural accounts, and currently by the popularity of attachment theory. This is reflected in questions addressed by the courts to expert witnesses. 'What is the nature and quality of the attachment between the child and the parent?'

is common. I have yet to be asked, 'What kinds of reinforcement has the child been exposed to in the birth family?' or 'What issues of transference are impacting on the relationship between Mr French and his children?' For me, attachment theory (described in Chapter 7) offers a coherent account of infants' developing repertoire of behaviours in response to the care-giving that they experience, whilst additional theories of learning become increasingly relevant to an account of older children's behaviour and development.

Ecological, community and systemic perspectives

I experience a serious challenge when attempting to balance a focus on broader systems in which families are but one element, with a narrow focus on the individuals who comprise a specific family. Both I and the families I assess are impacted by political, social, professional and personal imperatives which are time and place dependent. Whilst provision of housing may represent a useful intervention for *this* homeless family, ensuring through political action that good quality housing is provided as a universal service would take it out of the negative equation for *all* families.

The United Nations Convention on the Rights of the Child (UNCRC) makes clear that the child's right to protection from harm places a duty on the State not just to react to incidents of maltreatment but to take action to reduce their incidence in the first place. This includes effective preventive procedures such as the provision of social programmes which support the child and those who care for the child. It involves an overview of the systems within which individual families function. A systemic or community perspective identifies the person-environment fit as the appropriate focus of assessment and action rather than the spotlight being on a 'problem' individual or family. From such a perspective, problems are defined as gaps between available resources (personal, social or material) and environmental demands. Community and systemic approaches promote prevention and interventions designed to enable those who have been labelled as 'deviant' to live with respect and self-determination. There is acknowledgement of the effects of stress on individuals arising from the demands of society, and the impact of historical and structural factors. The approach emphasises personal strengths and competency, as opposed to weaknesses and pathology. Systemic theories stress the desirability of staying open to many and different ideas about families and their situation. Problems may represent the struggles of the system and the individuals within it to adapt to a transition or change of circumstance. Habitual patterns of interaction may no longer fit the new situation.

These ideas do not negate the gate-keeping task of professionals. Contemporary society does not tolerate children being harmed. What these ideas do influence is the manner and mind-set within which the assessment task is conducted. An open-minded emphasis on strengths can help to minimise the demoralisation that readily results from being the focus of professional concerns. Within this wider frame, I find the need to draw on theories of individual development and learning when carrying out assessments in family proceedings.

Social learning theories

Social learning theories (Bandura, 1977) account for development in terms of the impact on the child of other people. These theories emphasise the importance of the developing child's observation of others' behaviour, imitation and modelling. If a child experiences the attempted resolution of differences between people through aggression, physical or verbal violence, then this may be replicated in the child's behaviour towards adults and/or peers. The learning process requires that the child has paid attention to the actions, has remembered them through mental organisation, mental and practical rehearsal, has a reason or motivation to imitate and is capable of reproducing the behaviour. Albert Bandura argued that the development of aggressive behaviour could not be explained through a simple mechanism of imitation, but that it is necessary to invoke the cognitions of the learner in order to explain why aggression may sometimes be replicated but also shunned. Bandura (1995) has also argued that the observation of others is important in the development of self-efficacy – the experience of a sense of agency in bringing about desired outcomes. He argues that self-efficacy can be learned through personal mastery of a skill, and also through seeing how others persevere in times of hardship and are able to rebound from setbacks. Observation of others' failures can have a converse effect. Positive mood states are viewed as related to perceived self-efficacy and low mood to a sense of helplessness.

Lev Vygotsky (1978) argued that 'higher mental functioning' emerges from participation in social processes, processes which are cultural-historical in origin. Adults have a crucial role to play in a child's development, by providing help that allows the child to move beyond current knowledge and skills to the next level through providing experiences within the Zone of Proximal Development (ZPD). Parents and peers have an important function in providing children with experiences which stretch them, but not beyond the point whereby they become demoralised by too challenging a level of difficulty. I see a link here with attachment theory's focus on parental sensitive responsiveness which is not only to the child's affective state but also to the level of cognitive development.

Cognitive theories

Cognitive theories present the view that people's emotions and behaviour are mediated by individuals' mental constructions of their experiential worlds. The therapies that were devised from this position encourage people to identify these cognitions or thoughts and to test them through practical assignments. The approaches involve the identification of underlying schemas or core beliefs such as, 'I am an unlovable person' (Padesky, 1994) or philosophies (Woods and Ellis, 1997) that play a causal role in the person's emotions and behaviour.

It can be tempting to assume that parents who experienced maltreatment and abuse in their own childhoods will necessarily replicate this in their own parenting. The research literature suggests that this is not the case and that, 'painful childhood experiences with regard to attachment may have become resolved, insecurity in childhood becoming "earned security" in adulthood' (Prior and Glaser, 2006: 49). Such parents' action schemas or internal working models of relationship have accommodated to contrasting experiences.

Erikson's stage theory of ego development

Erik Erikson (1994) was regarded as a neo-Freudian who devised a stage theory of development across the lifespan. He focussed on the development of the ego or sense of self. He argued that in the first year of life it is important for infants to learn to trust that their carers are reliable. This is followed by the toddler stage in which parents need to achieve a balance through which the child's explorations are neither smothered nor neglected. As the child grows older, experiences that generate a sense of accomplishment gain in importance. In adolescence there is a questioning of self which is best explored without undue demands for conformity from parents in order to prevent the development of identity confusion. During this and following stages the young person tests out loving and intimate relationships with others. Those who struggle to form enduring relationships may feel isolated and lonely. Erikson points to the importance of the development of personal identity and self-esteem, a subjective conviction of continuity of self and of a sense of being valued within a social setting. Other people recognise this stability of identity and interact in ways that are experienced as affirming.

'Nature' theories

The theories thus far mentioned are 'nurture' theories in that they ascribe aspects of development to the impact of the environment. Congenital factors (present at birth or very shortly afterwards, of which genetic accounts are one type) give precedence to the inherited or early acquired 'nature' of the being and these can be highly relevant when trying to account for disruptions to a child's developmental pattern. Detailed developmental histories are of great assistance when trying to answer questions about whether a child's disrupted or delayed development can be accounted for by biological factors and/or by adverse parenting. There may be complex interactions between nature and nurture which require both to be taken into consideration in creating a coherent causal account. I return to theoretical considerations in a number of examples that follow later in this chapter.

Organisation of material

Because there is often a great deal of information arising in assessments, a storage and retrieval system can be useful. The formal structure used to file papers in court bundles can be helpful whilst I also like to organise data using a more personal structure. Knowing in which section to find material saves time and effort. I am often tempted, in my haste, to adopt a 'carrier bag' approach in which more and more information is stuffed into an already burgeoning file either on my desk or in my head, whilst I am fully aware that a sorting process and structure is less demanding on my memory.

Although the input process is time-consuming, the storage of data electronically can aid retrieval since key words can be found in the text. Notes can be made electronically in the text, or by hand in margins of a hard copy. Providing that they do not become dislodged, sticky notes are useful to mark on pages in the file the location of particular information and ideas to which I think I will want to return. Electronic bookmarks may also be used in this way. These notes can record provisional explanations that may contribute to my emerging narratives about and understanding of the family. In addition, I choose to make notes of my developing ideas, understandings and themes in a separate document as they unfurl. I use headings and make short summaries of key points relating to each of the individuals in the family. If I am unsure where to 'park' an idea I have a 'miscellaneous' category which includes some outstanding queries for myself or which I need to investigate with other parties. Once I have created a first draft of my overall thinking I turn back to these 'misfits' and try to understand what they might mean in light of this. Every now and then a radical restructuring is necessary when a new piece of information challenges my provisional understanding.

Strategies for data analysis and synthesis

Analytic induction

His way of attacking the cello problem is to produce the maximum amount of data possible, to do as many things as he can, to use his hands and the bow in as many ways as possible. Then as he goes along, he begins to notice regularities and patterns. He begins to ask questions – that is to make deliberate experiments. But it is vital to note that until he has a great deal of data, he has no idea what questions to ask, or what questions there are to be asked.

(Holt, 1991: 75)

The above analogy does not quite map onto assessments for the family court because some questions may already have been posed at the outset, but it is likely that more will arise as the process unfolds. The quote illustrates inductive methods which are associated with qualitative research. Inductive methods of research involve a close examination of the available data, with a view to seeking patterns, consistencies, and inconsistencies, out of which tentative explanations and understandings are developed. Further data is used to test these tentative ideas in a circular process of ongoing refinement. Where there is a lack of fit, the initial ideas may need to be discarded altogether, and replaced by understandings that are more consistent with the data. At this stage I need to grasp the nettle and be prepared to give up what may already have become a cherished idea. This is the point at which I need to challenge my tendency towards verification lest I otherwise confirm my original ideas through selective assessment and blinkered, or even 'tunnel' vision. Supervision can be particularly helpful at this time where I can tell interim 'stories' about a family in order to hear myself summarising my current ideas and to receive helpful questions that assist me in clarifying my thoughts.

Focussing only on one way of understanding the data is always likely to miss critical influences. For example, if a car engine overheats, an immediate conclusion may be that the radiator lacks water. This hypothesis is based on well-established understandings that are documented in the literature about how the cooling system in a car works and what happens if it malfunctions. Understanding what has caused the radiator to lack water requires a wider view of the system and the creation of a greater number of potential explanations. Whilst my prior experience may lead me hastily to conclude that the most probable explanation is a leaking hose, investigation leading to negative results will mean that I need to explore further and create alternative hypotheses to explain what is going on in this unique circumstance. What's more, understanding a problem with a vehicle is typically going to be much less taxing than understanding my fellow human beings, all of whom are unique models for whom explanatory manuals are unavailable.

The next part of the process involves using the ideas and understandings that have been constructed to devise 'experiments' or tests. For example, I might have developed an understanding that suggests, despite assertions to the contrary, that this parent is misusing alcohol. This can be tested with a fair degree of reliability by hair strand analysis. If the results do not conform to my expectations I will need to revise my developing understanding. The process of testing a hypothesis is a hallmark of the hypothetico-deductive scientific method. There are very few satisfactorily reliable tests that can be carried out in the assessment of families. Even such 'hard' data as medical records can contain information that is inaccurate and contestable. And so 'tests' in this context are more likely to be carried out as part of a process of 'triangulation'.

Triangulation

Triangulation is a way of trying to assess or establish the credibility of developed understandings or conclusions by using more than one approach or coming at the process from different angles. The term derives from the use of a series of triangles to map out a geographical area in an ecological survey. The process of looking for data in different sections of the area surveyed gives greater credibility to the results than looking in only one place. What is found is likely to be more representative of the fauna and flora of the area than what would be recorded from examination of a single site.

Triangulation, in its broader sense, can involve different kinds of data, different respondents, more than one investigator; it can draw on more than one theory or use different methods. If there is consistency between the inferences that are drawn from information obtained from different individuals, that is obtained from different sources, or that is of different types (documents, interviews, 'tests', questionnaire measures, historical records) then more confidence can be placed in these understandings than if they are based on a single source, single individual or obtained through a single method. It has also been argued that triangulation of data helps to counter the 'hierarchy of credibility' in which the evidence provided by people of higher social rank or job status is typically afforded greater authority (Altrichter *et al.*, 2007). Triangulation may lead to convergent or competing constructions of meaning. The task of the assessor is to report the degree of convergence, to make a case for the conclusions reached from the analysis, whilst being prepared to entertain and express multiple understandings where the evidence could support two or more cases. Even though a triangulation process may result in a convergence of ideas, this does not mean that these are unquestionable since the understandings reached by drawing from the different sources may still be flawed.

In one case example, I reached a tentative conclusion that a five-year-old had formerly developed an insecure attachment pattern in her relationship with her mother. She had been placed with her father for a year but the evidence suggested that there was limited emotional investment from the child in her relationship with him. I argued that a securely attached child will typically have the skills to make a secure attachment to new care-givers, but that an insecurely attached child brings an insecure pattern to new relationships. A second alternative explanation was that the child's attachment insecurity may have arisen from the experience of a series of losses arising out of her separation from her mother and mother's extended family. A third potential explanation was that the relatively high frequency of contact with her birth mother was interfering with the establishment of secure attachments to her father and his family. Each of these hypotheses suggests different courses of action or intervention. Sometimes it is not possible to reach a clear view on such matters although, in my experience, there can be a great deal of pressure on professionals to express certainty. In this case example, I suggested an intervention (a contact 'holiday'), the results of which would provide further evidence in support of or counter to each of these accounts.

Actuarial methods

Actuarial methods for making predictions from multiple types of data have been developed in many settings. These involve giving a numerical value to factors that have been found to correlate with the behaviour or outcome in question, and combining them in a formula. Numerical values can be allocated to very vague and impressionistic data so that qualitative information is not lost. Research suggests that such formulae are generally more dependable than clinical judgment when combining and weighing different kinds of information. In a review of 135 studies, William Grove and Paul Meehl (1996) found only eight studies in which predictions using 'clinical judgment' were more reliable than actuarial instruments. Grove and Meehl suggest that staff in departments conducting assessments might routinely collect data about their decisions and outcomes in order to create a locally derived actuarial tool.

Such methods are also said to help improve the practices of individual professionals by providing actuarial information allowing them to evaluate their track records. Actuarial approaches aim to improve consistency between practitioners, across the decisions of individual practitioners, and to increase the likelihood that particular data will not be overlooked or over-emphasised. However, the method of data combination needs to be continually reviewed and tested against outcomes in order to refine the process. In addition, 'Clinician judgments, for which statistical predictions were available as cues, can and should be studied to learn whether they are more accurate than clinical predictions made in the absence of such cues' (Grove and Lloyd, 2006).

The family's understanding and explanations

Whatever the worker's developing understanding of what is happening in families, family members themselves will have explanations. Sally Holland (2004) makes a strong case for starting with this because unless the family members feel heard and experience their ideas as being treated with respect, the process of engagement will be hindered, and it may become impossible for them to move forward in the ways that are being required of them. Even when there is denial of abuse or harm to children it may still be possible to help care-givers to recognise that they must change if they are to keep their children. I have sometimes begun work with a family with a contract to 'get the authorities off our backs'. Whilst this would be an inadequate basis for the overall intervention, it can unite the family and professional in a common aim and acts as a starting point from which an influencing relationship can be established. The care-givers' construction of the issues in question cannot be demolished with facts:

> Supposing you're the therapist and I'm the client and I say that I want some therapy because I'm grossly obese. You're looking at someone who clearly isn't grossly obese and yet is reporting this as a perception. It is the client's reality but not that of the therapist. You would have to have measurements and a set of norms in order to define whether the client is obese or not. That could be done. But in a way it doesn't matter what the facts are, it only matters whether I *think* I'm obese. The interesting thing is that the therapist's instruments don't see the pink elephants that are flying all around the room. I can see the pink elephants.
>
> (Scaife, 1995: 69)

Within some specialties, such as pain management, it is almost exclusively the subjective experience of the client which provides meaningful data for comparison. Constructivists would argue that subjective experience is all we have.

Case formulation

The process of creating a provisional account of, 'how things seem to be, how they got this way and why they are continuing to be this way' is known as a case formulation or re-formulation. Case formulation aims to create a description of a person's concerns, issues and problems, and by reference to theory and research findings make explanatory inferences about causes and maintaining factors so as to inform interventions. It is a narrative which goes beyond description and includes provisional attempts to explain how problems have developed and are being maintained with a view to devising interventions that have the potential to impact on the predisposing and maintaining mechanisms. Formulation is the crucible, where the individual particularities of a given case, relevant theory and research synthesise into an understanding of the presenting issues (Kuyken, 2006). It involves several elements which I have adapted and developed from Persons (2008):

- A *description* of the material arising from the assessment process that describes the problematic aspects of child care.
- Hypotheses or provisional explanations about the *mechanisms* that account for the difficulties.
- Proposals concerning the *origins* of the difficulties including historical and more recent *precipitating* factors.
- A focus on *strengths* which provide anchors from which positive developments may be made and around which interventions may be devised.

The following is an example of a formulation offered by Jacqueline Persons (2008: 128–9), which could be a description of some parents who find themselves in care proceedings. As I have added the dimension 'strengths' to the elements, it does not appear in the example below:

> Maria grew up in an abusive home in which she was punished or ignored when she expressed distress in a reasonable way and only received attention when she dramatically and intensely communicated distress (e.g., by punching a wall). Her father appeared to have untreated bipolar disorder and her parents "fought like cats and dogs". They modeled maladaptive emotion regulation strategies and did not teach or model adaptive ones, and Maria may have inherited a biological predisposition to bipolar disorder (ORIGINS). As a result, Maria had high emotional sensitivity and used maladaptive emotion regulation strategies. Maria tended to invalidate, minimize, ignore, and suppress her emotional reactions until they were so extreme that she lost control of her behaviour (MECHANISM). For example, she ignored disrespectful or mean behaviour from her friends until she became overwhelmed with rage and broke off the relationship. She experienced emotional reactivity (PROBLEM), especially outbursts of rage and anger (PROBLEM), and had chaotic intense relationships with all the important people in her life (PROBLEM), including her husband, girlfriends, and dissertation chairperson. Her tendency to invalidate and ignore her emotional experiences also blocked her from getting the information she needed to identify her career interests and goals. She felt truly lost about whether to pursue a career as a biologist or an actress (PROBLEM). These mechanisms were chronically present but had been triggered more intensely by her upcoming comprehensive exams and by her husband's increasing unhappiness with her emotionality (PRECIPITANTS). Both of these events tended to push Maria to try even harder to suppress her feelings, which had led to increased volatility. She felt out of control. The accumulation of all these problems and her failed efforts to solve them made her miserable and depressed (PROBLEM).

Although the author explains that this formulation is based on ideas from Dialectical Behaviour Therapy (Linehan, 1993) she has adapted the theory to accommodate the details of the individual presentation of this client.

Another way of representing these elements has been described variously as the 'Four Ps' (Weerasekera, 1996) and 'Five Ps' approach. The origins of the difficulties are termed 'Predisposing Factors' which include inherited or congenital predispositions, early history and attachment patterns; the values, beliefs and assumptions that these have generated; physical and mental health vulnerabilities; learning difficulties and environmental factors such as poverty. The second P is 'Precipitating Factors', those more recent events which may have contributed to the onset of the difficulties. These typically occur at times of transition such as births and deaths, new partnerships or separations, moves of house, changes of employment or unemployment, or traumatic experiences. They may include the onset of drug or alcohol misuse. Precipitating factors may be environmental but include internal changes in the person's ways of experiencing. The third P represents the 'Presenting Problems' which may include thoughts, feelings and behaviours. 'Perpetuating Factors' (the fourth P) are those which maintain the problems. They may include a care-giver's struggle to manage and face up to difficult feelings, which results in denial of the concerns of the authorities, being in thrall to a partner whose behaviour is characterised by violence, or habitual self-defeating patterns of behaviour. Fifthly, there are 'Protective Factors' which comprise helpful beliefs, positive relationships, functional coping skills and other strengths.

The following examples illustrate the process of formulation using information obtained from multiple sources:

Mr Jennings presents a somewhat complex picture. In his childhood Mr Jennings experienced two distinct models of parenting. His step-father was physically and emotionally abusive and involved in crime (PREDISPOSING/ORIGINS). His mother and her family were well-to-do and he was doted on by his maternal grandparents and their house-keepers with whom he spent much of his childhood. He was regarded with envy by his friends and extended family, and felt very different from his peers. His grandparents were strict in an old-fashioned way. He has thus experienced being the centre of an adult's attention to the point of being 'spoiled' whilst also being subject to abuse and observation of domestic violence perpetrated by his step-father towards his mother. He thus has multiple and conflicting internal models of relationship (PREDISPOSING/ORIGINS). He can present as charming and considerate (POTENTIAL PROTECTIVE FACTOR/STRENGTH) but also as threatening (PRESENTING PROBLEM). I suspect that his beginning involvement in crime when he went to live with his father was a strategy to try and escape his feeling of being different (MECHANISM/PERPETUATING). It is often important to adolescents to feel the same as everyone else. He has a long history of offending which includes five offences resulting in conviction for threatening and verbally abusive behaviour and three of assault (PROBLEM). He has had no convictions for such offences in the last five years (PROTECTIVE FACTOR/STRENGTH) although there have been more recent driving offences. Such a record creates a reputation which is difficult to escape (MECHANISM/PERPETUATING). Having recognised this (PROTECTIVE FACTOR/STRENGTH) he moved away from Bedford and ultimately from a relationship which appeared to have been mutually destructive. He says that he is trying to keep out of trouble and this was validated by PC Barley at the pre-birth child protection conference (PROTECTIVE FACTOR/STRENGTH).

I think that the contrasting experiences of care-giving have produced some confusion about his identity and a great sense of loss since the deaths of his mother and grandparents (MECHANISM/PERPETUATING). He is too ashamed, embarrassed and lacks the courage to reconnect with the side of his family in which the members have loving and affectionate relationships with each other (MECHANISM/PERPETUATING). Interview material and questionnaire results did not suggest that Mr Jennings suffers with anxiety, depression, feelings of worthlessness or low self esteem (PROTECTIVE FACTOR/STRENGTH). He has at times been unable to contain his distress which has led him to shout, make derogatory comments and hit inanimate objects (PROBLEM). This is a model of adult male behaviour that he experienced from his stepfather (PREDISPOSING/ ORIGINS). His anger expression probably acts as a front for his feelings of vulnerability (MECHANISM/PERPETUATING). Most children are very frightened by the observation of domestic violence and he probably learned to be fearful of his step-father's violence towards him as well (PREDISPOSING FACTOR/ORIGINS). This would leave him suscepti- ble to feelings of vulnerability to anticipated attacks (MECHANISM/ PERPETUATING). He appears to be developing more adaptive self- soothing strategies for dealing with his distress and anger (PROTECTIVE FACTOR/STRENGTH). The chair of the pre-birth child protection conference commented that she had expected the meeting to be difficult but that Mr Jennings was able to contain his feelings when under pressure (PROTECTIVE FACTOR/STRENGTH).

This formulation is centred upon the particular individual, whilst drawing on a number of theories and research literature. It refers to theories of attachment and the formation of internal working models of relationship (John Bowlby and Mary Ainsworth), the process of identity formation in adolescence (Erik Erikson), biologically-based theories of shame (Paul Gilbert) and the research literature which tells us that children who have been exposed to domestic violence experience increased arousal, fear and tend towards the reproduction of violence in their own relationships (social learn- ing theory). Mention is also made in the account of theories of loss.

The mother described next was seriously abused in her own childhood but has been able to internalise compensatory experiences. Even so, she has struggled to meet the standards of child care that would secure the well-being of her daughter:

One of the most formative experiences of Ms McKechnie's childhood was the hurt and humiliation that she experienced in consequence of the harm that she suffered from her father's sexual abuse from infancy

(PREDISPOSING/ORIGINS). She staunchly defends herself against such feelings of humiliation in her adulthood since she observed first-hand the potential devastating consequences of this for her mother's mental health (MECHANISM/PERPETUATING). This is one of the reasons why she struggles to acknowledge and express her sad feelings as this makes her feel weak and ashamed (MECHANISM/PERPETUATING). She presents a 'hard' front. She finds it difficult to respond positively to instructions, advice and overt criticism, since this implies that what she is doing is incorrect and she defends herself relentlessly against such difficult feelings (MECHANISM/PERPETUATING). Ms McKechnie has a number of secure and long-standing attachments in her life to people whom she trusts (PROTECTIVE FACTOR/STRENGTH). Throughout her life a number of adults have been prepared to make an effort to understand her, like her, and have been able to accept the more difficult aspects of behaviour (PROTECTIVE FACTOR/STRENGTH and PROBLEM). Ms McKechnie showed a great deal of intelligent insight into the events of her life. She has been able to integrate these into a coherent and intelligible account, a feat which often takes much longer and is sometimes not achieved at all by people who have been abused so early in their childhoods (PROTECTIVE FACTOR/STRENGTH). She has been aided in this by life-story work, therapy, and through being accepted and valued by a number of adults. Ms McKechnie accepts what happened to her in her childhood as an integral part of the person she has become. She is clear that none of it was her fault and that her parents should have been responsible adults. She does not feel that she can entirely put matters behind her until such time as her father either confesses or dies (PROBLEM). However, she does not blame him but believes that there will be an explanation in his own history for how he behaved towards his family (PROTECTIVE FACTOR/STRENGTH).

Ms McKechnie continues to experience high levels of arousal (PROBLEM). She gives a coherent explanation for this in that despite telling the extended family of her abuse no-one took any notice of her unless she 'upped the ante' (PERPETUATING FACTOR/MECHANISM and ORIGINS). The results of the STAXI-2 suggested that she often experiences angry feelings associated with perceptions of being treated unfairly by others (PRECIPITANT) and that she is quick-tempered and readily expresses anger with little provocation (PROBLEM). There are indications that she is often impulsive and lacking some self-control (PROBLEM). There is no evidence that she expresses her anger in physical violence but rather loses her temper in a somewhat random way and has learned to manage it without undue suppression or expression of hostility to others.

Ms McKechnie suffered profound hurt in her childhood in consequence of the abuse she experienced, through her mother's failure to protect her and refusal to acknowledge that she even had a daughter (PREDISPOSING FACTOR/ORIGINS). As a child Ms McKechnie took responsibility way beyond her years in an effort to protect her younger siblings and this has given her some major strengths such as the capability to manage her finances effectively and her determination to make something of her life (PROTECTIVE FACTOR/STRENGTH). Ms McKechnie's high degree of insight means that she knows when her healthy defences are at risk of being breached (PROTECTIVE FACTOR/STRENGTH). This has led her to have been cautious about forming an attachment with her infant daughter as she fears a total psychological breakdown were she to commit herself totally only to lose her daughter (PERPETUATING FACTOR/MECHANISM). She does not recognise the negative impact that this is having upon her daughter's developing attachment pattern. Questionnaire results suggest that Ms McKechnie is experiencing a moderate degree of depression. Her depressed mood does not appear to result from low self-esteem or feelings of worthlessness. It appears to be reactive to the current proceedings, rather than illustrative of a more general mood state (PRECIPITATING FACTOR/MECHANISM). Ms McKechnie has struggled to understand the degree of concern of professionals involved. The quality of care that she has given to her daughter, whilst judged as not good enough, has been much in excess of that which she received herself at her age and yet she was repeatedly returned to the care of her parents (PERPETUATING FACTOR/MECHANISM). She has not well understood the needs of a small child or been able to interact in ways which would have ensured healthy development. This has been though a lack of knowledge and a desire to follow her own counsel, both factors which are explicable in terms of her history (PERPETUATING FACTOR/MECHANISM and PREDISPOSING/ORIGINS).

This formulation is based around theories concerning the mechanisms by which the development of children who have been sexually abused is impacted (David Finkelhor), uses the notion of defence mechanisms originally propounded by Freud, draws from attachment theory and the underpinning theories of cognitive behaviour therapy (Aaron Beck).

This process of gathering together, sorting among and organising data, looking for patterns and discrepancies and hypothesising about the mechanisms that may account for client difficulties, is the skill of formulation. Whilst it takes place at the centre of the initial assessment process, it is continuously evolving, updated in light of further information and evidence. It is sometimes known as 're-formulation', a reminder for the practitioner to remain open to changing perspectives and understandings. The formulation or conceptualisation of the difficulties draws together material from and about the child and care-giver, linking with relevant theory and the research literature. The research process links theory and research with the personal story and idiosyncratic needs of each individual family member (Corrie and Lane, 2006).

Persons (1989: 55) proposed five tests of a formulation which, although they derive from the world of therapy, can readily be translated to the requirements of the family court:

- Try to account for each problem/symptom in the light of the case formulation.
- Try to account for current (including new) precipitants of problems.
- Make predictions/retrodictions about how the client is likely to behave, feel, think, or have behaved, felt, thought, in specific circumstances.
- Check whether the client feels that the formulation 'fits' them.
- Evaluate treatment success/failure; this may not always be due to the accuracy/inaccuracy of the formulation, but there is at least a strong possibility that it is.

Whilst formulations can be created in text, diagrams can be a useful aid. These encourage more distant perspectives and support the creation of provisional accounts. Figure 10.1 is taken from a presentation made under

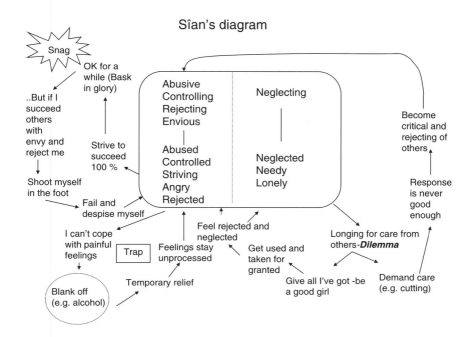

Figure 10.1 Diagrammatic formulation.

the auspices of the British Psychological Society Faculty of Eating Disorders (Beglin and Bassra, 2007) and is based on the theory underpinning cognitive analytic therapy.

Such diagrams may be created cooperatively together with a parent or family. I have found them to be a useful way of reflecting together on a lifetime of the client's experiences in order to develop a coherent and empathic understanding on which the future directions of the work can be built.

Re-formulation

One of the critical features of a case formulation is the centrality of a mind-set oriented towards empirical disconfirmation and re-formulation. When new information comes along, the practitioner has to be prepared repeatedly to modify or abandon altogether the ever-provisional account of the difficulties being assessed. The continuous process involves proposing, testing, re-evaluating, revising, rejecting and creating new accounts. In her review of child abuse public inquiry reports, Eileen Munro (1999) highlighted the impact of the issue of failure to revise judgements, especially when new information was provided by members of the general public rather than by professionals. 'Inquiries argue that it is not only with hindsight that the judgement can be faulted but the error could have been rectified if professionals had checked their views against a wider range of evidence' (Munro, 1999: 750). Amongst the 45 cases of child deaths reviewed, the following failures were identified:

Problematic issues with assessment process	Number of cases
Not using evidence from past history	26
Not using research on risk factors	25
Not using written evidence (files, reports)	16
Known to others but not collated	12
Persisting influence of first impression	11

The failure to revise initial assessments was particularly pertinent for the families in Munro's study in which low levels of risk had been determined. In all of these cases, subsequent repeated allegations were made but were poorly investigated. One tragic example was the death of Jasmine Beckford (London Borough of Brent, 1985), when the parents' claim that all was well was accepted and no attempt was made to check this by reference to her school or by seeing Jasmine herself. Another was the death of three-year-old Leanne White. Investigation of the first allegations of abuse led to the conclusion that there were no grounds for concern. The initial assessment stood despite subsequent allegations received from her grandmother and two sets of neighbours which were ignored (Nottinghamshire Area Child Protection Committee, 1994). I imagine that both of these workers were under enormous case-load pressure and focussed on the needs of children who may otherwise have met similar fates. I also doubt whether they were receiving sufficient formative and restorative supervision to help them manage the relentless emotional impact of working in stressful circumstances.

Inquiries into child deaths in the UK have repeatedly made reference to the natural tendency to be drawn into closeness with a family, making it difficult to stand back in order to gain a more distant perspective. This has not been helped by a shift of supervisory focus towards managerial oversight and monitoring of procedural imperatives (Rushton and Nathan, 1996). In my first-hand experience, front line work has been suspended in a social work department whilst practitioners organised files to an unnecessarily exacting standard for the purposes of an inspection.

> Memory is a key factor in producing bias in the evidence used in making judgements. Strategies are needed to compensate for the way some data are far more easily retrieved than others. Vivid details, data that are concrete, easily imagined, emotionally charged and recent, spring to mind more readily than the by-gone, pallid, abstract, or statistical. In terms of child protection work, this means past history, written records, abstract theory and research findings tend to be under-used compared with the current, often emotionally charged, factual information gained in interviews.
>
> (Munro, 1999: 754)

It behoves professionals to subject their conclusions to critical scrutiny. Re-formulation benefits professional understanding not only in revisions which suggest greater risk, but also towards reduced risk when carers have made substantive and lasting changes to their lives, resulting in a better fit for the role and tasks of parenting. Case studies are *post hoc* explanations for the data and alternative interpretations are almost invariably possible. Open-mindedness to alternative explanations and hypotheses is an appropriate mind-set, particularly when the stakes are so high.

Jon Scaife (2004) suggests that claims made and conclusions reached in the process of formulation can be categorised as 'unproblematic or self-evident' (almost everyone within the community of practice would be expected to agree with the claim), 'personal' ('*I* think' or 'on the basis of my experience'), and 'other' which, for purposes of credibility, need to be substantiated with evidence. In the last case, support may come from the strength of argument that can be made from the practitioner's data, or from academic books or papers that have been refereed prior to publication.

Munro argues also for the development of strategies that increase practitioners' readiness to change their views. One method is to keep in mind and document the provisional nature of the professional narrative. Another is to purposefully adopt an opposite perspective and create an account from a hypothetical alternative view. This was found to be an effective strategy in a study by Koriat *et al.* (1980). The process entails seeking information to support an opposing view rather than posing a challenge to the worker's current thinking, a strategy likely to evoke defensiveness and consolidation of an existing position. The crucial aspect of strategies and methods to counteract bias and aid further understanding is that they involve considering alternative perspectives and creating distance. Many such methods can be found in Scaife (2010). They can be particularly salient when adopted in supervision and offered in a manner that allows the worker to feel supported and constructively challenged rather than inspected with a view to being found wanting.

It has been argued that the analysis and synthesis of data in a formulation process is difficult or problematic (Frick *et al.*, 2010) but I don't agree. Like any skill it requires practice and can be aided by consultation with a colleague, especially one who is prepared to ask open-ended questions. It is the part of the assessment process that involves creativity and detective work. It is like putting together the pieces of a jigsaw, trying to find the best fit, matching shapes and colours, setting some pieces aside until greater clarity can be found, and disassembling the work in progress when too much material is left over. Unlike a jigsaw, there is no one correct solution. Providing that this is kept in mind at the outset the emerging picture serves as a provisional map to action, giving a sense of direction and purpose to interventions and judgements that follow and enabling us better to keep children safe.

In conclusion

I hope that in this book you have found some ideas to help you with the challenge of assessing families who are in trouble. I believe that those of us who are tasked with such roles will not go too far wrong if we remember that our main aim is to help families who are struggling to do better, and in the process treat them how we would like to be treated ourselves in such testing circumstances: the 'good' practitioner is described by a client as follows:

> [One] who in your first acquaintance lets you know by his or her expression that he's in your home to be of service to you if possible, and to show trust because most people are trustworthy if one shows trust in them; to be able to understand reasonably well problems concerning the family as a whole; not to criticize but to analyze why a person or a family is in unfavourable circumstances; to give helpful advice in a way that isn't demanding but that lets a person feel that it's his own idea; one who has a sincere desire to help people, feeling that it might have been

her as well as they but for the grace of God; one who encourages you to go above the capabilities that you thought you possess; one who guides you and makes the way possible but insists that you do for yourself what you're capable of doing.

(Overton, 1959: 12 cited in Kadushin and Kadushin, 1997: 396)

Postscript

My initial plan for this book was to write for expert witnesses, and in particular for clinical psychologists, but as it took shape I was struck by the many commonalities in the roles and tasks of different disciplines involved in the assessment processes, and I have therefore written with a view to the text having relevance to a much wider group of people than I originally envisaged.

In particular, social workers are in a strong position to make comprehensive assessments of children and families, inhibited by shortage of time, heavy case-loads and in some cases lack of confidence. I have seen some excellent social work reports about families to which I have felt my own assessment and analysis added little. I hope that this book will help to give social work readers more confidence in their skills in assessing children and families for the family courts.

I also hope that the book will act as a reference text for lawyers, barristers and judges in terms of the kinds of measures that may be used in such assessments, and the information that they might be expected to contribute. In particular, I would encourage a degree of scepticism about the relevance, reliability and predictive validity of many of the measures used in assessments, most of which have been devised for different purposes. They are a valuable adjunct to the assessment process but cannot replace sensitive responsiveness to a family's predicament and well-honed listening skills that evoke both reporting of a family's strengths coupled with an acute sensitivity to danger for the child and to parental attempts to deceive.

I had hoped, in conjunction with colleagues in the legal profession, to write about giving evidence and how to prepare for cross examination but did not have the space. For anyone facing this potentially nerve-racking experience for the first time I would recommend discussing the issues with experienced colleagues, reading the advice available from different professions, and attending a course in preparation for the conventions and processes of the court room. Sources for some of these are listed in Appendix 6. Ongoing clinical supervision is mandatory for clinical psychologists and applies to all aspects of work. It can be particularly helpful to novice 'experts', although opinions expressed are the responsibility of the instructed individual and not the individual's supervisor.

I also hope that some parents involved in proceedings may find the book useful as an aid to understanding: that it helps them to feel that they are not alone in their predicament, but belong to a community of parents whose children, despite our love for them, regularly, and sometimes relentlessly, test our patience and resolve.

References

Aber, J., Slade, A., Berger, B., Bresgi, I. and Kaplan, M. (1985). *The Parent Development Interview*. Unpublished manuscript, Barnard College, Columbia University, New York.

Abidin, R.R. (1990). *Parenting Stress Index/Short Form*. Lutz, FL: Psychological Assessment Resources, Inc.

Abidin, R.R. (1995). *Parenting Stress Index: professional manual* (3rd edition) Odessa, FL: Psychological Assessment Resources, Inc.

Accardo, P.J. and Whitman, B.Y. (1990). Children of parents with mental retardation. In B.Y. Whitman and P.J. Accardo (eds.) *When a parent is mentally retarded*. Baltimore, MD: Brookes.

Achenbach, T.M. (1991). *Manual for the Youth Self-Report and 1991 profile*. Burlington, VT: University of Vermont, Department of Psychiatry.

Achenbach, T.M. and Rescorla, L.A. (2001). *Manual for the ASEBA school-age forms and profiles*. Burlington, VT: University of Vermont, Research Center for Children, Youth and Families. Retrieved 1 September 2011 from: http://www.aseba.org/

Ackerman, M.J. (2005). The Ackerman–Schoendorf Scales for Parent Evaluation of Custody (ASPECT): a review of research and update. *Journal of Child Custody*, 2(1/2), 179–93.

Action for Child Protection (2003a). *The difference between risk and safety*. Retrieved 21 July 2010 from: http://www.actionchildprotection.org/archive/article0103.htm

Action for Child Protection (2003b). *The foundation of safety assessment*. Retrieved 25 July 2010 from: www.actionchildprotection.org/archive/article0403.htm

Adcock, M. (2011). The likelihood of rehabilitation for young children in care. *Family Law*, 41, 508–13.

Ahmed, A.A. (2000). Health and disease: an Islamic framework. In A. Sheikh and A.R. Gatrad (eds.) *Caring for muslim patients*. Abingdon: Radcliffe Medical Press.

Ainsworth, M. (1969). *Maternal Sensitivity Scales: revised*. Johns Hopkins University, Baltimore, MD: Retrieved 26 June 2011 from: www.psychology.sunysb.edu/attachment/measures/content/ainsworth_scales.html

Ainsworth, M.D.S. (1973). The development of infant-mother attachment. In B.M. Caldwell and H.N. Ricciuti (eds.) *Review of child development research* (Volume 3) Chicago, IL: University of Chicago Press.

Ainsworth, M.D.S., Blehar, M.C., Waters, E. and Wall, S. (1978). Patterns of attachment: a psychological study of the Strange Situation. Hillsdale, NJ: Lawrence Erlbaum.

Albee G.W. (1983). Psychopathology, prevention, and the just society. *Journal of Primary Prevention*, 4(1), 5–40.

Alden, L.E., Wiggins, J.S. and Pincus, A.L. (1990). Construction of circumplex scales for the Inventory of Interpersonal Problems. *Journal of Personality Assessment*, 55, 521–36.

Aldgate, J. and Bradley, M. (1999). *Supporting families through short term fostering.* London: The Stationery Office.

Aldridge, M. and Wood, J. (1998). *Interviewing children: a guide for child care and forensic practitioners.* Chichester: John Wiley and Sons Ltd.

Altrichter, H., Feldman, A., Posch, P. and Somekh, B. (2007). *Teachers investigate their work: an introduction to action research across the professions* (2nd edition). London: Routledge.

American Psychiatric Association (2000). *The Diagnostic and Statistical Manual of Mental Disorders, Fourth Edition, Text Revision (DSM-IV-TR).* Washington, DC: American Psychiatric Association.

Ammaniti, M., Candelori, C., Dazzi, N., De Coro, A., Muscetta, S., Ortu, F., Pola, M., Speranza, A., Tambelli, R. and Zampino, F. (1990). *Intervista sull'attaccamento nella latenza (Attachment interview for childhood and adolescence).* Unpublished protocol, University of Rome.

Andersen, P.A. and Guerrero, L.K. (1998). *Handbook of communication and emotion: research, theory, applications, and contexts.* San Diego, CA: Academic Press.

Archer, J. (2002). Sex differences in physically aggressive acts between heterosexual partners: a meta-analytic review. *Aggression and Violent Behavior,* 7(4), 313–51.

Arnstein, S.R. (1969). A Ladder of Citizen Participation. *Journal of the American Institute of Planners,* 35(4), 216–24.

Astell, A.W. (2004). Saintly mimesis, contagion, and empathy in the thought of René Girard, Edith Stein and Simone Weil. *SHOFAR: an interdisciplinary journal of Jewish studies,* 22(2), 116–31.

Aunos, M., Pacheco, L. and Moxness, K. (2010). Turning rights into realities in Quebec, Canada. In G. Llewellyn, R. Traustadóttir, D. McConnell and H.B. Sigurjónsdóttir (eds.) *Parents with intellectual disabilities: past, present, futures.* Chichester: John Wiley and Sons Ltd.

Averill, P.M., Diefenbach, G.J., Stanley, M.A., Breckenridge, J.K. and Lusby, B. (2002). Assessment of shame and guilt in a psychiatric sample: a comparison of two measures. *Personality and Individual Differences,* 32, 1365–76.

Azar, S.T. and Cote, L.R. (2002). Sociocultural issues in the evaluation of the needs of children in custody decision making: what do our current frameworks for evaluating parenting practices have to offer? *International Journal of Law and Psychiatry,* 25, 193–217.

Azar, S.T., Lauretti, A.F. and Loding, B.V. (1998). The evaluation of parental fitness in termination of parental rights cases: a functional-contextual perspective. *Clinical Child and Family Psychology Review,* 1, 77–100.

Babor, T.F., Higgins-Biddle, J.C., Saunders, J.B. and Monteiro, M.G. (2001). Audit. The Alcohol Use Disorders Identification Test: guidelines for use in primary care (2nd edition). World Health Organization, Department of Health and Substance Dependence. Retrieved 4 December 2010 from: http://www.who.int/substance_abuse/publications/alcohol/en/

Baird, C. and Wagner, D. (2000). The relative validity of actuarial and consensus-based risk assessment systems. *Children and Youth Services Review,* 22(11–12), 839–71.

Baker, T. (1995). What constitutes reasonable contact? In P. Reder and C. Lucey (eds.) *Assessment of parenting: psychiatric and psychological contributions.* London: Routledge.

Bandura, A. (1977). *Social learning theory.* New York: General Learning Press.

Bandura, A. (1995). Exercise of personal and collective efficacy in changing societies. In A. Bandura (ed.) *Self-efficacy in changing societies.* Cambridge: Cambridge University Press.

Barrera, M.J., Sandler, I.N. and Ramsay, T.B. (1981). Preliminary development of a scale of social support: studies on college students. *American Journal of Community Psychology,* 9, 435–47.

Bartholomew, K. and Horowitz, L.M. (1991). Attachment styles among young adults: a test of a four-category model. *Journal of Personality and Social Psychology*, *61*, 226–44.

Bates, P. and Brophy, J. (1996). *The appliance of science? The use of experts in care proceedings: a court-based study*. Report to the Department of Health. London: Stationery Office.

Bateson, G. (1972). *Steps to an ecology of mind*. New York: Chandler.

Baum, S., Gray, G. and Stevens, S. (2011). *Good practice guidance for clinical psychologists when assessing parents with learning disabilities*. Leicester: British Psychological Society.

Baumrind, D. (1978). Parental disciplinary patterns and social competence in children. *Youth and Society*, *9*, 239–76.

BBC (2004, 17 June). *Profile: Marc Dutroux*. Retrieved 12 December 2011 from: http://news.bbc.co.uk/2/hi/europe/3522367.stm

BBC (2009, 16 November). *Have you lost your father?* Radio 5 live phone-in.

BBC (2011, 13 April). *All domestic abuse deaths to have multi-agency review*. Retrieved 14 April 2011 from: http://www.bbc.co.uk/news/uk-13058300

Beck, A.T. and Steer, R.A. (1993). *Beck Anxiety Inventory Manual*. San Antonio, TX: The Psychological Corporation, Harcourt Brace and Company.

Beck, A.T., Steer, R.A. and Brown, G.K. (1996). *Manual for the Beck Depression Inventory-II*. San Antonio, TX: Psychological Corporation.

Becker-Weidman, A. and Hughes, D. (2008). Dyadic Developmental Psychotherapy: an evidence-based treatment for children with complex trauma and disorders of attachment. *Child and Family Social Work*, *13*, 329–37.

Beglin, S. and Bassra, P. (2007). Managing complex eating disorder cases using a Cognitive Analytical Therapy (CAT) approach. Retrieved 5 May 2009 from: www.bps.org.uk/downloadfile.cfm?file_uuid=26D76984-1143-DFD0-7E8B-80F0BD2968EF&ext=ppt

Behrens, K.Y., Hesse, E., and Main, M. (2007). Mothers' attachment status as determined by the Adult Attachment Interview predicts their 6-year-olds' reunion responses: a study conducted in Japan. *Developmental Psychology*, *43*(6), 1553–67.

Beinart, H. (2004). Models of supervision and the supervisory relationship and their evidence base. In I. Fleming and L. Steen (eds.) *Supervision and clinical psychology*. Hove: Brunner-Routledge.

Beitchman, J.H. (1996). The FAB-C: Feelings, Attitudes and Behaviour Checklist: a manual for users. Toronto, Ontario: Multi-Health Systems.

Belsky, J. and Cassidy, J. (1994). Attachment: theory and practice. In M. Rutter and D. Hay (eds.) *Development through life: a handbook for clinicians*. Oxford: Blackwell Science.

Belsky, J., Campbell, S., Cohn, J. and Moore, G. (1996). Instability of infant-parent attachment security. *Developmental Psychology*, *32*, 921–24.

Bené, E. and Anthony, J. (1957). Family Relations Test: children's version. London: nferNelson.

Bennett, R. (2010, 1 February). Child abuse deaths still rising despite action after Baby P. *The Times* [online]. Retrieved 25 June 2011 from: www.timesonline.co.uk/tol/news/uk/crime/article7010408.ece

Bennett S., Plint, A. and Clifford, T.J. (2005). Burnout, psychological morbidity, job satisfaction, and stress: a survey of Canadian hospital based child protection professionals. *Archives of Diseases in Childhood*, *90*, 1112–16.

Benoit, D., Parker, K.C.H. and Zeanah, C.H. (1997). Mothers' representations of their infants assessed prenatally: stability and association with infants' attachment classifications. *Journal of Child Psychology and Psychiatry*, *38*, 307–13.

Bentall, R. (2010). Psychology . . . there's no future in it. *The Psychologist*, *23*(2), 148–51.

Bentovim, A. (2009). Therapeutic intervention with children living with trauma and family violence. In A. Bentovim, A. Cox, L. Bingley Miller and S. Pizzey (eds.) *Safeguarding children living with trauma and family violence.* London: Jessica Kingsley.

Bentovim, A., Cox, A., Bingley Miller, L. and Pizzey, S. (2009). *Safeguarding children living with trauma and family violence.* London: Jessica Kingsley.

Berlin, I. (1969). *Four essays on liberty.* Oxford: Oxford University Press.

Berridge, D. and Cleaver, H. (1987). *Foster home breakdown.* Oxford: Basil Blackwell.

Besharov, D. (1990). *Recognising child abuse: a guide for the concerned.* New York: The Free Press.

Bettmann, J.E. and Lundahl, B.W. (2007). Tell me a story: a review of narrative assessments for preschoolers. *Child and Adolescent Social Work Journal*, 24, 455–75.

Beutler, L.E. and Harwood, M.T. (2000). *Prescriptive therapy: a practical guide to systematic treatment selection.* New York: Oxford University Press.

Beutler, L.E., Moleiro, C.M. and Talebi, H. (2002). Resistance. In J.C. Norcross (ed.) *Psychotherapy relationships that work.* Oxford: Oxford University Press.

Beutler, L.E., Groth-Marnat, G. and Rosner, R. (2003). Introduction to integrative assessment of adult personality. In L.E. Beutler and G. Groth-Marnat (eds.) *Integrative assessment of adult personality.* New York: Guilford Press.

Biehal, N. (2006). *Reuniting looked after children with their families: a review of the research.* London: National Children's Bureau.

Biehal, N. (2007). Reuniting children with their families: reconsidering the evidence on timing, contact and outcomes. *British Journal of Social Work*, 37, 807–23.

Bifulco, A., Lillie, A., Ball, B. and Moran, P. (1998). *Attachment Style Interview (ASI). Training manual.* Unpublished manuscript, Royal Holloway, University of London.

Bifulco, A., Jacobs, C., Bunn, A., Thomas, G. and Irving, K. (2008). The Attachment Style Interview (ASI): a support-based adult assessment tool for adoption and fostering practice. *Adoption and Fostering*, 32(3), 33–45.

Bifulco, A., Moran, P., Ball, C. and Bernazzani, O. (2002). Adult attachment style. I: its relationship to clinical depression. *Social Psychiatry and Psychiatric Epidemiology*, 37, 50–9.

Bifulco, A., Mahon, J., Kwon, J.-H., Moran, P.M. and Jacobs, C. (2003). The Vulnerable Attachment Style Questionnaire (VASQ): an interview-based measure of attachment styles that predicts depressive disorder. *Psychological Medicine*, 33(6), 1099–110.

Binks, C.A., Fenton, M., McCarthy, L., Lee, T., Adams, C.E. and Duggan, C. (2006). Psychological therapies for people with borderline personality disorder. *Cochrane Database of Systematic Reviews*, 1, CD005652.

Binney, V. and Wright, J. (1997). The bag of feelings: an ideographic technique for the assessment and exploration of feelings in children and adolescents. *Clinical Child Psychology and Psychiatry*, 2(3), 449–62.

Binney, V.A., McKnight, I. and Broughton, S. (1994). Relationship play therapy for attachment disturbances in 4- to 7-year-old children. In J. Richer (ed.) *Clinical applications of ethology and attachment theory.* London: Association for Child Psychology and Psychiatry.

Black, P.J. and Wiliam, D. (1998). Assessment and classroom learning. *Assessment in Education*, 5(1), 7–74.

Blow, A.J. and Sprenkle, D. (2001). Common factors across theories of marriage and family therapy: a modified Delphi study. *Journal of Marital and Family Therapy*, 27, 385–401.

Bogo, M. and McKnight, K. (2005). Clinical supervision in social work: a review of the research literature. *Clinical Supervisor*, 24(1–2), 49–67.

Bohart, A.C. and Tallman, K. (1999). *How clients make therapy work: the process of active self-healing.* Washington: American Psychological Association.

Bolling, K., Grant, C., Hamlyn, B. and Thornton, A. (2007). *Infant feeding survey 2005.* The Information Centre, 2007. Retrieved 3 September 2011 from: http://www.ic.nhs.uk/webfiles/publications/ifs06/2005%20Infant%20Feeding%20Surv ey%20%28final%20version%29.pdf

Bolton, A. and Lennings, C. (2010). Clinical opinions of structured risk assessments for forensic child protection: the development of a clinically relevant device. *Children and Youth Services Review, 32*(10), 1300–1310.

Bolton, G. (2005). *Reflective practice* (2nd edition). London: Sage.

Bonanno, G.A. (2004). Loss, trauma, and human resilience: have we underestimated the human capacity to thrive after extremely adverse events? *American Psychologist, 59,* 20–28.

Bools, C. (2007). *Fabricated or induced illness in a child by a carer: a reader.* Oxford: Radcliffe Publishing Ltd.

Booth, P.B. and Jernberg, A.M. (2010). *Theraplay: helping parents and children build better relationships through attachment-based play.* San Fancisco, CA: Jossey-Bass.

Booth, T. (2000). Parents with learning difficulties, child protection and the courts. *Representing Children, 13*(3), 175–88.

Booth, T. and Booth, W. (1993). Parenting with learning difficulties: lessons for practitioners. *British Journal of Social Work, 23,* 459–80.

Booth, T. and Booth, W. (1994). *Parenting under pressure.* Buckingham: Open University Press.

Booth, T. and Booth, W. (2003). Self-advocacy and supported learning for mothers with learning difficulties. *Journal of Learning Disabilities, 7*(2), 165–93.

Booth, T., Booth, W. and McConnell, D. (2005). The prevalence and outcomes of care proceedings involving parents with learning difficulties in the Family Courts. *Journal of Applied Research in Intellectual Disabilities, 18,* 7–17.

Borthwick, S. and Hutchinson, B. (1996). The Confidential Doctor system: an appraisal. In D. Batty and D. Cullen (eds.) *Child protection: the therapeutic option.* London: British Agencies for Adoption and Fostering (BAAF).

Boud, D. (2001). Using journal writing to enhance reflective practice. In L.M. English and M.A. Gillen (eds.) *Promoting journal writing in adult education.* San Francisco, CA: Jossey Bass.

Bowlby, J. (1969). *Attachment and loss. Volume I. Attachment.* London: Hogarth Press and the Institute of Psycho-analysis.

Bowlby, J. (1982). Attachment and loss: retrospect and prospect. *American Journal of Orthopsychiatry, 52,* 664–78.

Brand, H.J. (1996). The diagnostic value of the Bené–Anthony Family Relations Test. *Perceptual and Motor Skills, 83,* 1299–303.

Brandon, M., Bailey, S., Belderson, P., Gardner, R., Sidebotham, P., Dodsworth, J., Warren, C. and Black, J. (2009). *Understanding serious case reviews and their impact: a biennial analysis of serious case reviews 2005–07.* DCSF research report number DCSF-RR129. Retrieved 6 September 2011 from: https://www.education.gov.uk/publications/standard/publicationdetail/page1/DCSF-RR129

Bretherton, I. and Oppenheim, D. (2003). The MacArthur Story Stem Battery: development, directions for administration, reliability, validity and reflections about meaning. In R.N. Emde, D.P. Wolf and D. Oppenheim (eds.) *Revealing the inner worlds of young children: the MacArthur Story Stem Battery and parent-child narratives.* New York: Oxford University Press.

Bretherton, I., Ridgeway, D. and Cassidy, J. (1990). Assessing internal working models of the attachment relationship: an attachment story completion task for 3-year-olds. In M. Greenberg, D. Cicchetti and M. Cummings (eds.) *Attachment in the preschool years: theory, research and intervention*. Chicago, IL: University of Chicago Press.

Bricklin, B. and Halbert, M.H. (2004). Perception-of-Relationships Test and Bricklin Perceptual Scales: validity and reliability issues, Part II. *The American Journal of Family Therapy*, 32(3), 189–203.

Bronfman, E., Parsons, E. and Lyons-Ruth, K. (1993). *Atypical Maternal Behaviour Instrument for Assessment and Classification (AMBIANCE): manual for coding disrupted affective communication*. Unpublished manuscript. Available from K. Lyons-Ruth, Department of Psychiatry, Cambridge Hospital, 1493 Cambridge Street, Cambridge, MA 02139. karlen_lyons-ruth@hms.harvard.edu

Brooke, S.L. (2004). Critical review of play therapy assessments. *International Journal of Play Therapy*, 13(2), 119–42.

Brophy, J. (2006). *Research review: child care proceedings under the Children Act 1989*. London: Department for Constitutional Affairs. Retrieved 29 April 2011 from: http://webarchive.nationalarchives.gov.uk/+/http://www.dca.gov.uk/research/2006/05_2006.pdf

Brophy, J., Bates, P., Brown, L., Cohen, S., Radcliffe, P. and Wale, C.J. (1999). *Expert evidence in child protection litigation: where do we go from here?* London: The Stationery Office.

Brophy, J., Jhutti-Johal, J. and Owen, C. (2003) Significant harm in a multi-cultural setting. Research Series 1/03. London: Department for Constitutional Affairs.

Brown, A.L. (1985). Mental orthopedics, the training of cognitive skills: an interview with Alfred Binet. In J.W. Segal, S.F. Chipman and R. Glaser (eds.). *Thinking and learning skills: research and open questions, Volume 2*. Hillsdale, NJ: Lawrence Erlbaum Associates Inc.

Brown, G.W., Andrews, B., Harris, T.O., Adler, Z. and Bridge, I. (1986). Social support, self-esteem and depression. *Psychological Medicine*, 16, 813–31.

Budd, K.S. and Holdsworth, M.J. (1996). Issues in clinical assessment of minimal parenting competence. *Journal of Clinical Child Psychology*, 25(1), 2–14.

Bullock, R. (2009). Residential care. In G. Schofield and J. Simmonds (eds.) *The child placement handbook: research, policy and practice*. London: British Agencies for Adoption and Fostering (BAAF).

Burnell, A., Vaughan, J. and Williams, L. (2007). *Family futures assessment handbook: framework for assessing children who have experienced developmental trauma*. London: Family Futures.

Burnell, A., Castell, K. and Cousins, K. (2009). *Siblings together or apart*. London: Family Futures.

Burns, D.D. (1997). *Therapist's toolkit*. Retrieved 20 June 2011 from: http://www.feelinggood.com/therapist%27s_toolkit.htm

Busby, D.M., Christensen, C., Crane, D.R. and Larson, J.H. (1995). A revision of the Dyadic Adjustment Scale for use with distressed and nondistressed couples: construct hierarchy and multidimensional scales. *Journal of Marital and Family Therapy*, 21(3), 289–308.

Butcher, J.N. and Beutler, L.E. (2003). The MMPI-2. In L.E. Beutler and G.Groth-Marnat (eds.) *Integrative assessment of adult personality*. New York: The Guilford Press.

Butler, I. and Williamson, H. (1994). *Children speak: children, trauma and social work*. Harlow: Longman.

Butler, R.J. and Green, D. (2001). *The Self Image Profiles for Children (SIP-C) and Adolescents (SIP-A)*. Manual. London: The Psychological Corporation Limited.

Butler, R.J. and Gasson, S.L. (2006). Development of the Self-Image Profile for Adults (SIP-AD). *European Journal of Psychological Assessment*, 22(1), 52–58.

Butt, J. and Box, C. (1998). *Family centred. A study of the use of family centres by black families*. REU: London.

Byng-Hall, J. (1995). *Rewriting family scripts*. New York: Guilford Press.

Calam, R.M., Cox, A.D., Glasgow, D.V., Jimmieson, P. and Groth Larsen, S. (2000). Assessment and therapy with children: can computers help? *Clinical Child Psychology and Psychiatry*, 5(3), 329–43.

Caldwell, B.M. and Bradley, R.H. (2001). *HOME inventory and administration manual* (3rd edition). University of Arkansas for Medical Sciences and University of Arkansas at Little Rock.

Camasso, M.J. and Jagannathan, R. (2000). Modeling the reliability and predictive validity of risk assessment in child protective services. *Children and Youth Services Review*, 22, 873–96.

Campbell, D.T. (1957). A typology of tests, projective and otherwise. *Journal of Consulting Psychology*, 21, 207–210.

Canty-Mitchell, J. and Zimet, G.D. (2000). Psychometric properties of the Multidimensional Scale of Perceived Social Support in urban adolescents. *American Journal of Community Psychology*, 28, 391–400.

Carlson, E.A. (1998). A prospective longitudinal study of attachment disorganisation/disorientation. *Child Development*, 69, 1107–29.

Carr, G.D., Moretti, M.M. and Cue, B.J.H. (2005). Evaluating parenting capacity: validity problems with the MMPI-2, PAI, CAPI, and ratings of child adjustment. *Professional Psychology: Research and Practice*, 36(2), 188–96.

Cash, S.J. (2001). Risk assessment in child welfare: the art and science. *Children and Youth Services Review*, 23(11), 811–30.

Cassidy, J., Marvin, R. and the MacArthur Working Group (1992). *Attachment organization in three- and four-year-olds: coding guidelines*. Unpublished manuscript, University of Virginia, Charlottesville.

Cavell, T.A. and Malcolm, K.T. (2007). *Anger, aggression and interventions for interpersonal violence*. Mahwah, NJ: Lawrence Erlbaum Associates Inc.

Cedar, R.B. and Levant, R.F. (1990). A meta-analysis of the effects of Parent Effectiveness Training. *American Journal of Family Therapy*, 18(4), 373–84.

Cheek, J.M. (1983). *The Revised Cheek and Buss Shyness Scale*. Unpublished manuscript, Wellesley College, Wellesley MA 02181. Available from: http://www.wellesley.edu/Psychology/Cheek/research.html

Cheek, J.M. and Buss, A.H. (1981). Shyness and sociability. *Journal of Personality and Social Psychology*, 41, 330–39. Retrieved 12 December 2010 from: http://www.wellesley.edu/Psychology/Cheek/research.html

Chess, S. and Thomas, A. (1986). *Temperament in clinical practice*. New York: Guilford Press.

Chief Secretary to the Treasury (2003). *Every child matters*. London: The Stationery Office.

Child Welfare Information Gateway (2012). *Child abuse and neglect fatalities 2010: statistics and interventions*. Retrieved 3 June 2012 from: http://www.childwelfare.gov/pubs/factsheets/fatality.pdf

Child Welfare Information Gateway (n.d.). *Searching for birth relatives*. Retrieved 1 July 2011 from: http://www.childwelfare.gov/pubs/f_search.cfm

Child Welfare Information Gateway, Children's Bureau, and FRIENDS National Resource Center for Community-Based Child Abuse Prevention (2010). *Strengthening families and communities: 2010 resource guide*. Washington, DC: Department of Health and Human Services. Retrieved 25 June 2010 from: http://www.childwelfare.gov/preventing/

ChildLine (1997). *Beyond the limit: children who live with parental alcohol misuse*. London: ChildLine.

Children and Family Court Advisory and Support Service (CAFCASS) (2007). *Domestic violence toolkit*. Retrieved 1 May 2011 from: http://www.cafcass.gov.uk/pdf/Domestic_Violence_toolkit_%28Version_2_-_August_2007%29.pdf

Children and Family Court Advisory and Support Service (CAFCASS) (n.d.). *My needs, wishes and feelings pack*. Retrieved 14 June 2010 from: http://www.cafcass.gov.uk/publications/my_needs_wishes_and_feelings.aspx

Children's Workforce Development Council (2009). *The common assessment framework for children and young people: a guide for practitioners*. Retrieved 20 February 2011 from: http://education.gov.uk/publications/standard/publicationDetail/Page1/IW91/0709

Choate, P.W. (2009). Parenting capacity assessments in child protection cases. *The Forensic Examiner* [online]. Retrieved 5 April 2011 from: http://findarticles.com/p/articles/mi_go1613/is_1_18/ai_n31636820/

Chorpita, B.F., Moffitt, C.E. and Gray, J. (2005). Psychometric properties of the Revised Child Anxiety and Depression Scale in a clinical sample. *Behavior Research and Therapy*, *43*(3), 309–22.

Cicchetti, D. and Toth, S.L. (1995). A developmental psychopathology perspective on child abuse and neglect. *Journal of the American Academy of Child and Adolescent Psychiatry*, *34*, 541–65.

Claxton, G. (1998). *Hare brain tortoise mind*. London: Fourth Estate.

Cleaver, H. (2000). *Fostering family contact*. London: The Stationery Office.

Cleaver, H. (2002). Assessing children's needs and parents' responses. In H. Ward and W. Rose (eds.) *Approaches to needs assessment in children's services*. London: Jessica Kingsley.

Cleaver, H. and Freeman, P. (1995). *Parental perspectives in cases of suspected child abuse*. Dartington Social Research Unit. London: HMSO.

Cleaver, H., Wattam, C. and Cawson, P. (1998). *Assessing risk in child protection*. London: NSPCC.

Cleaver, H., Walker, S. and Meadows, P. (2004). *Assessing children's needs and circumstances: the impact of the Assessment Framework*. London: Jessica Kingsley.

Coffman, J.K., Guerin, D.W. and Gottfried, A.W. (2006). Reliability and validity of the Parent-Child Relationship Inventory (PCRI): evidence from a longitudinal cross-informant investigation. *Psychological Assessment*, *18*(2), 209–14.

Connor, K.M. and Davidson, J.R.T. (2003). Development of a new resilience scale: the Connor–Davidson Resilience Scale (CD-RISC). *Depression and Anxiety*, *18*, 76–82.

Coohey, C. (1996). Child maltreatment: testing the social isolation hypothesis. *Child Abuse and Neglect*, *20*(3), 241–54.

Cook, D.R. (1994). *Internalized Shame Scale: professional manual*. Menomonie, WI: Channel Press.

Cook, D.R. (2001). *Internalized Shame Scale: technical manual*. Toronto: Multi-Health Systems.

Cooper, M. (2008). *Essential research findings in counselling and psychotherapy*. London: Sage.

Corby, B., Miller, M. and Pope, A. (2002). Out of the frame. *Community Care*, 12–18 September. Retrieved 14 December 2011 from: http://www.communitycare.co.uk/Articles/12/09/2002/37991/Out-of-the-frame.htm

Cordess, C. (2003). Can personality-disordered parents adequately care? In P. Reder, S. Duncan and C. Lucey (eds.) *Studies in the assessment of parenting*. Hove: Brunner-Routledge.

Corrie, S. and Lane, D.A. (2006). Constructing stories about clients' needs: developing skills in formulation. In R. Bor and M. Watts (eds). *The trainee handbook* (2nd edition). London: Sage.

Costa, A. and Kallick, B. (1993). Through the lens of a critical friend. *Educational Leadership*, *51*(2), 49–51.

Cotson, D., Friend, J., Hollins, S. and James, H. (2001). Implementing the Framework for the Assessment of Children in Need and their Families when the parent has a learning disability. In J. Horwath (ed.) *The child's world: assessing children in need.* London: Jessica Kingsley.

Courtney, M., Piliavin, I. and Wright, B. (1997). Note on research: transitions from and returns to out of home care. *Social Service Review, 71*, 652–67.

Cox, A. (2008). *The HOME Inventory: a guide for practitioners—the UK approach.* York: Child and Family Training.

Cox, A. and Bentovim, A. (2000). *Framework for the assessment of children in need and their families: the family pack of questionnaires and scales.* London: The Stationery Office. Retrieved 20 February 2011 from: http://www.dh.gov.uk/en/Publicationsandstatistics/Publications/PublicationsPolicyAndGuidance/DH_4008144

Cox, J.L., Holden, J.M. and Sagovsky, R. (1987). Detection of postnatal depression: development of the 10-item Edinburgh Postnatal Depression Scale. *British Journal of Psychiatry, 150*, 782–86.

Creighton, S. and Tissier, G. (2003). *Child killings in England and Wales.* London: NSPCC.

Crittenden, P.M. (1979–2004). *CARE-Index: coding manual.* Unpublished manuscript, Miami, FL.

Crittenden, P.M. (1988–1994). *Preschool Assessment of Attachment Manual.* Unpublished manuscript available from the author.

Crittenden, P.M. (1988). Family and dyadic patterns of functioning in maltreating families. In K. Browne, C. Davies and P. Stratton (eds.) *Early prediction and prevention of child abuse.* New York: Wiley.

Crittenden, P., Kozlowska, K. and Landini, A. (2010). Assessing attachment in school-age children. *Clinical Child Psychology and Psychiatry, 15*(2), 185–208.

Cross, R.M. (2005). Exploring attitudes: the case for Q methodology. *Health Education Research, 20*(2), 206–13.

Crowell, J. and Owens, G. (1998). *Manual for the Current Relationship Interview and scoring system.* Version 4. Retrieved 29 August 2010 from: http://ww.psychology.sunysb.edu/attachment/measures/content/cri_manual.pdf

Crowell, J. and Treboux, D. (n.d.) *Reminders about interviewing.* Retrieved 5 January 2010 from: http://www.psychology.sunysb.edu/attachment/measures/content/aai_interviewing.pdf

Crozier, M., Rokutani, L., Russett, J.L., Godwin, E. and Banks, G.E. (2010). A multisite program evaluation of Families and Schools Together (FAST): continued evidence of a successful multifamily community-based prevention program. *The School Community Journal, 20*(1), 187–208.

Cummings, J.A. (2003). Projective drawings. In H.M. Knoff (ed.) *The assessment of child and adolescent personality.* New York: Guilford Press.

Cutrona, C.E. and Russell, D.W. (1987). The provisions of social relationships and adaptation to stress. In W.H. Jones and D. Perlman (eds.) *Advances in personal relationships: volume 1.* Greenwich, CT: JAI Press.

Cutrona, C.E. and Russell, D.W. (1990). Type of social support and specific stress: toward a theory of optimal matching. In B.R. Sarason, I.G. Sarason and G.R. Pierce (eds). *Social support: an interactional view.* New York: Wiley.

Dale, P. (2004). Parents' perceptions of child protection services. *Child Abuse Review, 13*, 137–57.

Dale, P. and Allen, J. (1998). On memories of childhood abuse: a phenomenological study. *Child Abuse and Neglect, 22*(8), 799–812.

Dale, P., Green, R. and Fellows, R. (2005). *Child protection assessment following serious injuries to infants.* Chichester: John Wiley and Sons Ltd.

Dance, C. and Rushton, A. (1999). Sibling separation and contact in permanent placement. In A. Mullender (ed.) *We are family: sibling relationships in placement and beyond.* London: British Agencies for Adoption and Fostering (BAAF).

Dance, C. and Rushton, A. (2005). Predictors of outcome for unrelated adoptive placements made during middle childhood. *Child and Family Social Work*, 10(4), 269–80.

Dance, C., Rushton, A. and Quinton, D. (2002). Emotional abuse in early childhood: relationships with progress in subsequent family placement. *Journal of Child Psychology and Psychiatry*, 43, 395–407.

Davie, C.E., Hutt, S.J., Vincent, E. and Mason, M. (1984). *The young child at home.* Windsor: NFER-Nelson.

Davies, P. (2011). The impact of a child protection investigation: a personal reflective account. *Child and Family Social Work*, 16, 201–9.

Davis, L. (2009). *The social worker's guide to children and family law.* London: Jessica Kingsley.

Dawes, R.M. (1994). *House of cards: psychology and psychotherapy built on myth.* New York: Free Press.

de Graaf, I., Speetjens, P., Smit, F., de Wolff, M. and Tavecchio, L. (2008). Effectiveness of the Triple P Positive Parenting Program on behavioral problems in children: a meta-analysis. *Behaviour Modification*, 32(5), 714–35.

Dennett, D.C. (1991) *Consciousness explained.* London: Penguin.

Department for Children, Schools and Families (DCSF) (2007). *Children looked after in England (including adoption and care leavers) year ending 31 March 2007.* Retrieved 26 June 2011 from: http://www.education.gov.uk/rsgateway/DB/SFR/s000741/sfr27-2007v2.pdf

Department for Children, Schools and Families (DCSF) (2008a). *Child protection and research 3 (CPR3) data collection 31 March 2008.* Retrieved 1 September 2011 from: http://www.education.gov.uk/rsgateway/DB/SFR/s000811/index.shtml

Department for Children, Schools and Families (DCSF) (2008b). *Safeguarding children in whom illness is fabricated or induced.* Retrieved 14 July 2011 from: https://www.education.gov.uk/publications/standard/publicationDetail/Page1/DCSF-00277-2008

Department for Children, Schools and Families (2010). *Early intervention: securing good outcomes for all children and young people.* Retrieved 1 September 2011 from: https://www.education.gov.uk/publications/standard/publicationDetail/Page1/DCSF-00349-2010

Department for Education and Skills (2003). *Every child matters.* London: The Stationery Office.

Department for Education and Skills (2007). *Care matters: time for change.* London: The Stationery Office.

Department of Health (1990). *The care of children: principles and practice in regulations and guidance.* London: The Stationery Office.

Department of Health (1995). *Child protection: messages from research.* London: HMSO.

Department of Health (2000a). *Framework for the assessment of children in need and their families.* London: The Stationery Office.

Department of Health (2000b). *Psychiatric morbidity among adults living in private households, 2000.* London: Office for National Statistics. Retrieved 15 December 2010 from: http://www.dh.gov.uk/en/Publicationsandstatistics/Publications/PublicationsStatistics/DH_4019414

Department of Health (2010). Maternal and infant nutrition. Retrieved 22 February 2011 from: http://webarchive.nationalarchives.gov.uk/+/www.dh.gov.uk/en/Healthcare/Children/Maternity/Maternalandinfantnutrition/index.htm

Department of Health, Home Office and Department for Education and Employment (1999). *Working together to safeguard children: a guide to inter-agency working to safeguard and promote the welfare of children.* London: Stationery Office.

Derogatis, L.R. (1993). *BSI Brief Symptom Inventory: administration, scoring, and procedures manual* (4th edition). Minneapolis, MN: National Computer Systems.

Retrieved 26 June 2011 from: http://brown2.alliant.wikispaces.net/file/view/BSI+Article.pdf

Derogatis, L.R. (1994). *Symptom Checklist-90-R: administrative scoring and procedures manual.* Minneapolis, MN: NCS Pearson.

Devani, I. (2007). Successful wheelchair parenting. *Disability, Pregnancy and Parenthood International*, 59, 4–5. Retrieved 18 December 2010 from: http://www.dppi.org.uk/journal/59/index.html

De Wolff, M.S. and van Ijzendoorn, M.H. (1997). Sensitivity and attachment: a meta-analysis on parental antecedents of infant attachment. *Child Development*, 68, 571–91.

Dingwall, R., Eekelaar, J. and Murray, T. (1983). *The protection of children: state intervention and family life.* Basil Blackwell: Oxford.

Domestic Abuse Intervention Programs (2008). *Wheel gallery.* Retrieved 1 May 2011 from: http://www.theduluthmodel.org/documents/PhyVio.pdf

Donald, T. and Jureidini, J. (2004). Parenting capacity. *Child Abuse Review*, 13, 5–17.

Doolan, P., Nixon, P. and Lawrence, P. (2004). *Growing up in the care of relatives or friends: delivering best practice for children in family and friends care.* London: Family Rights Group.

Dorset County Council and Adult Social Care Services (n.d.). *Needs assessment by social services.* Retrieved 29 July 2010 from: http://www.dorsetforyou.com/161282

Doueck, H.J., Levine, M. and Bronson, D.E. (1993). Risk assessment in child protective services: an evaluation of the Child at Risk Field System. *Journal of Interpersonal Violence*, 8(4), 446–67.

Douglas, K.S., Guy, L.S. and Weir, M.S. (2006). HCR-20 violence risk assessment scheme: overview and annotated bibliography. Retrieved 25 June 2011 from: kdouglas.files.wordpress.com/2006/04/annotate10-24nov2008.pdf

Dowdney, L. and Skuse, D. (1993). Parenting provided by adults with mental retardation. *Journal of Child Psychology and Psychiatry*, 34, 25–47.

Dozier, M. and Stovall, K.C. (1997). *Parents' Attachment Diary.* Unpublished manuscript, University of Delaware. Retrieved 23 June 2011 from: http://icp.psych.udel.edu/Publications.html

Dumbrill, G.C. (2006). Parental experience of child protection intervention: a qualitative study. *Child Abuse and Neglect*, 30, 27–37.

DuMont, K.A., Widom, C.S. and Czaja, S.J. (2007). Predictors of resilience in abused and neglected children grown-up: the role of individual and neighbourhood characteristics. *Child Abuse and Neglect*, 31, 255–74.

Dunbar, G. (2005). *Evaluating research methods in psychology: a case study approach.* Oxford: Blackwell Publishing.

Duncan, B.L., Miller, S.D., Walpold, B.E. and Hubble, M.A. (2009). *The heart and soul of change: delivering what works in therapy* (2nd edition). Washington, DC: American Psychological Association.

Dunne, J. and Hedrick, M. (1994). The Parental Alienation Sydrome: an analysis of sixteen selected cases. *Journal of Divorce and Remarriage*, 21, 21–38.

Dunst, C.J., Trivette, C.M. and Deal, A.G. (1988). *Enabling and empowering families: principles and guidelines for practice.* Cambridge, MA: Brookline Books.

Dunst, C.J., Trivette, C.M. and Jodry, W. (1997). Influences of social support on children with disabilities and their families. In M.J. Guralnick (ed.) *The effectiveness of early intervention.* Baltimore, MD: Paul H. Brookes.

Easton, J.A. and Turner, S.W. (1991). Detention of British citizens in the Gulf—health, psychological, and family consequences. *British Medical Journal*, 303, 1231–34.

Eckermann, A., Dowd, T., Chong, E., Nixon, L., Gray, R. and Johnson, S. (2006). *Binan Goonj: bridging cultures in Aboriginal health.* Sydney: Elsevier Australia.

Egan, G. (2002). *The skilled helper* (7th edition). Monterey: Brooks/Cole.

Eleftheriadou, Z. (1994). *Transcultural counselling*. London: Central Book Publishing.

Emery, R.E., Otto, R.K. and O'Donohue, W.T. (2005). A critical assessment of child custody evaluations. *Psychological Science in the Public Interest*, 6(1), 1–29. Retrieved 29 April 2011 from: http://www.psychologicalscience.org/pdf/pspi/pspi6_1.pdf

English, D. and Pecora, P. (1994). Risk assessment as a practice method in child protective services. *Journal of Child Welfare*, 73(5), 451–73.

English, P. (2009). *Tackling difficult conversations*. Alresford: Management Pocketbooks Ltd.

English, R. (2011). *The adoption dilemma: the rights of parents v child's interests*. Retrieved 15 December 2011 from: http://ukhumanrightsblog.com/2011/06/02/the-adoption-dilemma-the-rights-of-parents-v-childs-interests/

Erikson, E.H. (1994). *Identity and the life cycle*. New York: W.W. Norton and Co. Ltd.

Evans, M.A. (1987). Discourse characteristics of reticent children. *Applied Psycholinguistics*, 8, 171–84.

Fahlberg, V. (1991). *A child's journey through placement*. London: British Agencies for Adoption and Fostering (BAAF).

Farmer, A. and Tiefenthaler, J. (2003). Explaining the recent decline in domestic violence. *Contemporary Economic Policy*, 21, 158–72.

Farmer, E. (2009). Reunification with birth families. In G. Schofield and J. Simmonds (eds.) *The child placement handbook: research, policy and practice*. London: British Agencies for Adoption and Fostering (BAAF).

Farmer, E. and Moyers, S. (2008). *Kinship care: fostering effective family and friends placements*. London: Jessica Kingsley.

Farmer, E., Moyers, S. and Lipscombe, J. (2004). *Fostering adolescents*. London: Jessica Kingsley.

Farmer, E., Sturgess, W. and O'Neill, T. (2008). *The reunification of looked after children with their parents: patterns, interventions and outcomes*. Report to the Department for Children, Schools and Families, School for Policy Studies, University of Bristol.

Feeney, J., Noller, P. and Hanrahan, M. (1995). Assessing adult attachment. In M. Sperling, M. Berman and W. Berman (eds.) *Attachment in adults: theory, assessment, and treatment*. New York: Guilford Press.

Feldman, M.A. and Walton-Allen, N. (1997). Effects of maternal mental retardation and poverty on intellectual, academic, and behavioral status of school-age children. *American Journal on Mental Retardation*, 101(4), 352–64.

Feldman, M.A., Varghese, J., Ramsay, J. and Rajska, D. (2002). Relationship between social support, stress and mother-child interactions in mothers with intellectual disabilities. *Journal of Applied Research in Intellectual Disabilities*, 15(4), 314–23.

Fewtrell, M., Wilson, D.C., Booth, I. and Lucas, A. (2011). Six months of exclusive breast feeding: how good is the evidence? *British Medical Journal*, 342, 209–12.

Figley, C.R. (1995). *Compassion fatigue: coping with secondary traumatic stress disorder in those who treat the traumatized*. New York: Brunner-Mazel.

Figley, C.R. (ed.) (2002). *Treating compassion fatigue*. New York: Brunner-Routledge.

Finzi, R., Har-Even, D., Weizman, A., Tyano, S. and Shnit, D. (1996). The adaptation of the attachment styles questionnaire for latency-aged children. *Psychologia: Israel Journal of Psychology*, 5(2), 167–77. Reviewed on the National Child Traumatic Stress Network. Retrieved from: http://www.nctsnet.org/nctsn_assets/pdfs/measure/Attachment_Style_Classification_Questionnaire.pdf

Fitzpatrick, G., Reder, P. and Lucey, C. (1995). The child's perspective. In P. Reder and C. Lucey (eds.) *Assessment of parenting: psychiatric and psychological contributions*. London: Routledge.

Fivaz-Depeursinge, E., and Corboz-Warnery, A. (1999). *The primary triangle: a developmental systems view of mothers, fathers, and infants.* New York: Basic Books.

Flanagan, O. (1992). *Consciousness reconsidered.* London: Bradford Books.

Flynn, M.C. (1989). *Independent living for adults with mental handicap: 'a place of my own'.* London: Cassell.

Fonagy, P. and Bateman, A. (2006). Mechanism of change in mentalization based treatment of borderline personality disorder. *Journal of Clinical Psychology, 62,* 411–30.

Fonagy, P. and Target, M. (1997). Attachment and reflective function: their role in self-organization. *Development and Psychopathology, 9,* 677–99.

Fonagy, P., Gergely, G., Jurist, E.L. and Target, M. (2002). *Affect regulation, mentalization and the development of the self.* New York: Other Press.

Foucault, M. (1977). *Discipline and punish: the birth of the prison.* Translated by Alan Sheridan. New York: Pantheon.

Fowler, J. (2003). *A practitioner's tool for child protection and the assessment of parents.* London: Jessica Kingsley.

Fraley, C. (2002). Attachment stability from infancy to adulthood: meta-analysis and dynamic modeling of developmental mechanisms. *Personality and Social Psychology Review, 6,* 123–51.

Fraley, R.C., and Spieker, S.J. (2003). Are infant attachment patterns continuously or categorically distributed? A taxometric analysis of Strange Situation behavior. *Developmental Psychology 39*(3), 387–404.

Fraley, R.C., Waller, N.G. and Brennan, K.G. (2000). An item response theory analysis of self-report measures of adult attachment. *Journal of Personality and Social Psychology, 78,* 350–65.

Frances, C. and Guzzo, S. (2009). Review of the Dyadic Adjustment Scale. Retrieved 24 June 2011 from: http://www.scribd.com/doc/21571203/Review-of-the-Dyadic-Adjustment-Scale

Fratter, J., Rowe, J., Sapsford, D. and Thoburn, J. (1991). *Permanent family placement: a decade of experience.* London: British Agencies for Adoption and Fostering (BAAF).

Freeman, M. (2007). *Understanding family law.* London: Sweet and Maxwell Ltd.

Frick, P.J., Barry, C.T. and Kamphaus, R.W. (2010). *Clinical assessment of child and adolescent personality and behaviour* (3rd edition). New York: Springer Science and Business Media, LLC.

Fuller, T.L., Wells, S.J. and Cotton, E.E. (2001). Predictors of maltreatment recurrence at two milestones in the life of a case. *Children and Youth Services Review, 23*(1), 49–78.

Furnham, A. and Taylor, J. (2011). *Bad apples: identify, prevent and manage negative behavior at work.* Basingstoke: Palgrave MacMillan.

Gair, S. (2010). Social work students' thoughts on their (in)ability to empathise with a birth mother's story: pondering the need for a deeper focus on empathy. *Adoption and Fostering, 34*(4), 39–49.

Gallo, L.C., Bogart, L.M. and Vranceanu, A.M. (2005). Socioeconomic status, resources, psychological experiences, and emotional responses: a test of the Reserve Capacity Model. *Journal of Personality and Social Psychology, 88,* 386–99.

Gambrill, E. and Shlonsky, A. (2000). Risk assessment in context. *Children and Youth Services Review, 22,* 813–37.

Gath, A. (1988). Mentally handicapped people as parents. *Journal of Child Psychology and Psychiatry, 29*(6), 739–44.

Gath, A. (1995). Parents with a learning disability. In P. Reder and C. Lucey (eds.) *Assessment of parenting.* London: Routledge.

Gavin, D.R., Ross, H.E. and Skinner, H.A. (1989). Diagnostic validity of the Drug Abuse Screening Test in the assessment of DSM-III drug disorders. *British Journal of Addiction 84*(3), 301–307.

Geldof, B. (2003). The real love that dare not speak its name. In A. Bainham, B. Lindley, M. Richards, and L. Trinder (eds.) *Children and their families: contact, rights and welfare.* Oxford and Portland, OR: Hart Publishing.

George, C. and Solomon, J. (1996). Representational models of relationships: links between caregiving and attachment. *Infant Mental Health Journal*, *17*(3), 198–216.

George, C., Kaplan, N. and Main, M. (1984). *Adult Attachment Interview Protocol.* Unpublished manuscript, University of California, Berkeley.

George, C., Kaplan, N. and Main, M. (1996). *Adult Attachment Interview Protocol* (3rd edition). Unpublished manuscript, University of California, Berkeley.

Gerard, A.B. (1994). *Parent-Child Relationship Inventory Manual.* Los Angeles, CA: Western Psychological Services.

Gershoff, E.T. (2002). Corporal punishment by parents and associated child behaviors and experiences: a meta-analytic and theoretical review. *Psychological Bulletin*, *128*(4), 539–79.

Gibbons, J., Conroy, S. and Bell, C. (1995). *Operating the child protection system.* London: HMSO.

Gibbs, J., Underdown, A., Stevens, M., Newbery, J. and Liabo, K. (2003). *Group-based parenting programmes can reduce behaviour problems of children aged 3–12 years.* What Works for Children Group Evidence Nugget April 2003. Retrieved 3 January 2011 from: http://www.whatworksforchildren.org.uk/docs/Nuggets/pdfs/parenting%20nugget.pdf

Gilbert, P. (2010). *The compassionate mind.* London: Constable and Robinson Ltd.

Gilbert, R., Kemp, A., Thoburn, J., Sidebotham, P., Radford, L., Glaser, D. and MacMillan, H.L. (2009). Child maltreatment 2: recognising and responding to child maltreatment. *The Lancet*, *373*(9658), 167–80.

Gitterman, A. (1991). Creative connections between practice and theory. In M. Weil, K.L. Chau and D. Southerland (eds.) *Theory and practice in social group work: creative connections.* Binghampton, NY: The Haworth Press Inc.

Glasersfeld, E. von. (1995). *Radical constructivism.* London: Falmer.

Glasgow, D. and Crossley, R. (2004). Achieving best evidence: a comparison of three interview strategies for investigative interviews in a forensic sample with mild learning disabilities. In C. Dale and L. Storey (eds.) *Learning disability and offending behaviour.* Proceedings of the 2nd international conference on the 'Care and Treatment of Offenders with a Learning Disability' held in Preston, United Kingdom 9–11 April 2003. Retrieved 7 June 2012 from: http://www.ldoffenders.co.uk/conferences/2ndCon2003/2ndConDocuments/03main.doc

Glasser, M., Kolvin, I., Campbell, D., Glasser, A., Leitch, I. and Farrelly, S. (2001). Cycle of child sexual abuse: links between being a victim and becoming a perpetrator. *British Journal of Psychiatry*, *179*, 482–94.

Goldberg, D.P. and Hillier, V.F. (1979). A scaled version of the General Health Questionnaire. *Psychological Medicine*, *9*(1), 139–45.

Goldberg, D.P., Gater, R., Sartorius, N., Ustun, T.B., Piccinelli, M., Gureje, O. and Rutter, C. (1997). The validity of two versions of the GHQ in the WHO study of mental illness in general health care. *Psychological Medicine*, *27*, 191–97.

Goldberg, S. (2000). *Attachment and development.* London: Arnold.

Goldman, J., Salus, M.K., Wolcott, D. and Kennedy, K.Y. (2003). *A coordinated response to child abuse and neglect: the foundation for practice.* Washington, DC: Office on Child Abuse and Neglect. Retrieved 1 May 2011 from: http://www.childwelfare.gov/pubs/usermanuals/foundation/index.cfm

Goldsmith, D.F., Oppenheim, D. and Wanlass, J. (2004). Separation and reunification: using attachment theory and research to inform decisions affecting the placements of children in foster care. *Juvenile and Family Court Journal*, *55*(2), 1–13. Retrieved 1 May 2011 from: http://www.zerotothree.org/site/DocServer/AttachmentandFosterCare.pdf?docID=2542

Goldstein, W.M. and Hogarth, R.M. (1997). Judgement and decision research: some historical context. In W.M. Goldstein and R.M. Hogarth (eds.) *Research on judgement and decision making: current, connections and controversies.* Cambridge: Cambridge University Press.

Golombok, S. (2000). *Parenting: what really counts?* London: Routledge.

Goodinge S. (2000). *A jigsaw of services: inspection of services to support disabled adults in their parenting role.* London: Department of Health. Retrieved 16 December 2010 from: http://webarchive.nationalarchives.gov.uk/+/www.dh.gov.uk/en/Publicationsandstatistics/Lettersandcirculars/Chiefinspectorletters/DH_4003041

Goodman, R. (1997). The Strengths and Difficulties Questionnaire: a research note, *Journal of Child Psychology and Psychiatry, 38,* 581–86.

Goodman, R., Meltzer, H. and Bailey, V. (1998). The Strengths and Difficulties Questionnaire: a pilot study on the validity of the self-report version. *European Journal of Child and Adolescent Psychiatry, 7,* 125–30.

Gordon, D.R. (2001). Research application: identifying the use and misuse of formal models in nursing practice. In P. Benner (ed.) *From novice to expert: excellence and power in clinical nursing practice.* Upper Saddle River, NJ: Prentice Hall Health.

Gottleib, B.H. and Bergen, A.E. (2010). Social support concepts and measures. *Journal of psychosomatic research, 69,* 511–20.

Gould, J.R., Prentice, N.M. and Ainslie, R.C. (1996). The Splitting Index: construction of a scale measuring the defense mechanism of splitting. *Journal of Personality Assessment, 66,* 414–30.

Gould, J.W. and Martindale, D.A. (2009). *The art and science of child custody investigations.* New York: Guilford Press.

Gould, S.J. (1996). *The mismeasure of man* (revised and extended edition). New York: W.W. Norton and Company Inc.

Graham, J., Liu, Y. and Jeziorski, J. (2006). The Dyadic Adjustment Scale: a reliability generalization meta-analysis. *Journal of Marriage and Family, 68*(3), 701–17.

Graham, M.H. (1999–2000). The expert witness predicament: determining 'reliable' under the gatekeeping test of *Daubert, Kumho,* and proposed amended rule 702 of the Federal Rules of Evidence. *University of Miami Law Review, 318,* 317–57.

Graybeal, C.T. and Konrad, S.C. (2008). Strengths-based child assessment: locating possibility and transforming the paradigm. In M.C. Calder (ed.) *Contemporary risk assessment in safeguarding children.* Lyme Regis: Russell House Publishing Ltd.

Green, J., Stanley, C., Smith, V. and Goldwyn, R. (2000). A new method of evaluating attachment representations in young school-age children: the Manchester Child Attachment Story Task. *Attachment and Human Development, 2*(1), 48–70.

Greenberg, J. (1989). *I never promised you a rose garden.* New York: Signet.

Grossmann, K., Grossmann, K. and Kindler, H. (2005). Early care and the roots of attachment and partnership representations. In K. Grossmann, K. Grossmann and E. Waters (eds.) *Attachment from infancy to adulthood: the major longitudinal studies.* New York: Guilford Press.

Grove, W.M. and Lloyd, M. (2006). Meehl's contribution to clinical versus statistical prediction. *Journal of Abnormal Psychology, 115*(2), 192–94.

Grove, W.M. and Meehl, P.E. (1996). Comparative efficiency of informal (subjective, impressionistic) and formal (mechanical, algorithmic) prediction procedures: the clinical-statistical controversy. *Psychology, Public Policy, and Law, 2*(2), 293–323.

Grue L. and Laerum K.T. (2002). 'Doing motherhood': some experiences of mothers with physical disabilities. *Disability and Society, 17*(6), 671–83.

Haakens, J. (2011). The school of hard knocks. *The Psychologist, 24*(7), 512–15.

Haavik, S.F. and Menninger, K.A. (1981). *Sexuality, law and the developmentally disabled person: legal and clinical aspects of marriage, parenthood, and sterilization.* Baltimore, MD: Paul H. Brookes.

Haley, J. (1987). *Problem-solving therapy.* New York: Harper and Row.

Hamilton, M. (1980). Rating depressive patients. *Journal of Clinical Psychiatry, 41,* 21–24.

Hammond, K. (1996). *Human judgement and social policy: irreducible uncertainty, inevitable error, unavoidable injustice.* Oxford: Oxford University Press.

Hammond, K.R., Hamm, R.M., Grassia, J. and Pearson, T. (1987). Direct comparison of the efficiency of intuitive and analytical cognition in expert judgment. *IEEE Transactions on Systems, Man and Cybernetics, 17,* 753–70.

Hansburg, H.G. (1972). *Separation Anxiety Test.* Huntington, NY: Krieger.

Hanson, K., Helmus, L. and Bourgon, G. (2007). *The validity of risk assessments for intimate partner violence: a meta-analysis.* Corrections User Report No. 2007-07. Ottawa: Public Safety Canada.

Harder, D.W. and Zalma, A. (1990). Two promising shame and guilt scales: a construct validity comparison. *Journal of Personality Assessment, 55,* 729–45.

Harlen, W. (2003). How high stakes testing impacts on motivation for learning. *Science Teacher Education, 37,* 2–6.

Harlen, W. (2009). Assessment for learning: research that is convincing (Part 1). *Education in Science, 231,* 30–31.

Harlow, H. (1958). The nature of love. *American Psychologist, 13,* 673–85.

Harmon, S.C., Lambert, M.J., Smart, D.M., Hawkins, E., Nielson, S.L., Slade, K. and Lutz, W. (2007). Enhancing outcome for potential treatment failures: therapist-client feedback and clinical support tools. *Psychotherapy Research, 17*(4), 379–92.

Harré, R. (1998). When the knower is also the known. In T. May and M. Williams (eds.) *Knowing the social world.* Buckingham: Open University Press.

Harrison, P.L. and Oakland, T. (2003). *Adaptive Behaviour Assessment System* (2nd edition). Minneapolis, MN: Pearson Assessment.

Hart, D.H. (2003). The sentence completion techniques. In H.M. Knoff (ed.) *The assessment of child and adolescent personality.* New York: Guilford Press.

Hartnett, P.H. (2007). A procedure for assessing parents' capacity for change in child protection cases. *Children and Youth Services Review, 29,* 1179–88.

Harwin, J., Owen, M., Locke, R. and Forrester, D. (2003). *Making care orders work: a study of care plans and their implementation.* London: The Stationery Office.

Hawkins, P. and Shohet, R. (2006) *Supervision in the helping profession* (3rd edition). Maidenhead: Open University Press.

Hayes, J.A. and Gelso, C.J. (1991). Effects of therapist-trainees' anxiety and empathy on countertransference behaviour. *Journal of Clinical Psychology, 47,* 284–90.

Hayman, R.L. Jr (1990). Presumptions of justice: law, politics, and the mentally retarded parent. *Harvard Law Review, 103*(6), 1205–68.

Hazan, C. and Shaver, P. (1987). Romantic love conceptualized as an attachment process. *Journal of Personality and Social Psychology, 52,* 511–24.

Head, A. and Elgar, M. (1999). The placement of sexually abused and abusing siblings. In A. Mullender (ed.) *We are family: sibling relationships in placement and beyond.* London: British Agencies for Adoption and Fostering (BAAF).

Hegar, R.L. (2005). Sibling placement in foster care and adoption: an overview of international research. *Children and Youth Services Review, 27*(7), 717–39.

Hertsgaard, L., Gunnar, M., Erickson, M. and Nachmias, M. (1995). Adrenocortical responses to the Strange Situation in infants with disorganised/disoriented attachment relationships. *Child Development, 66,* 1100–106.

Hetherington, R. (1996). Prevention and education in work with children and families. In D. Batty and D. Cullen (eds.) *Child protection: the therapeutic option.* London: British Agencies for Adoption and Fostering (BAAF).

Higgins, D.J. and McCabe, M.P. (2000). Multi-type maltreatment and the long-term adjustment of adults. *Child Abuse Review, 9,* 6–18.

Hill, M., Lambert, L., Triseliotis, J. and Buist, M. (1992). Making judgements about parenting: the example of freeing for adoption. *British Journal of Social Work*, 22, 373–89.

Hitchings, P. (1999). Supervision and sexual orientation. In M. Carroll and E. Holloway (eds.) *Counselling supervision in context*. London: Sage.

HM Government (2004). *Every Child Matters: change for children*. London: The Stationery Office.

HM Government (2006). *Working together to safeguard children: a guide to inter-agency working to safeguard and promote the welfare of children*. London: The Stationery Office.

HM Government (DCSF) (2007). *The Children's Plan: building brighter futures*. London: The Stationery Office.

HM Government (2008). *Information sharing: guidance for practitioners and managers*. London: The Stationery Office. Retrieved 6 July 2011 from: https://www.education.gov.uk/publications/eOrderingDownload/00807-2008BKT-EN-March09.pdf

Hodges, J. (1996). The natural history of early non-attachment. In J. Brannen and B. Bernstein (eds.) *Children, research and policy: essays for Barbara Tizard*. Philadelphia, PA: Taylor & Francis.

Hodges, J., Steele, M., Hillman, S., Henderson, K. and Kaniuk, J. (2003). Changes in attachment representations over the first year of adoptive placement: narratives of maltreated children. *Clinical Child Psychology and Psychiatry*, 8, 351–67.

Hodges, J., Hillman, S., Steele, M. and Henderson, K. (2004). *Story stem assessment rating manual*. Unpublished manuscript. The Anna Freud Centre, London.

Hodges, J., Steele, M., Kaniuk, J., Hillman, S. and Asquith, K. (2009). Narratives in assessment and research on the development of attachments in maltreated children. In N. Midgley, J. Anderson, E. Grainger, T. Nesic and C. Urwin (eds.) *Child psychotherapy and research: new approaches, emerging findings*. London: Routledge.

Hoghughi, M. and Speight, A.N.P. (1998). Good enough parenting for all children—a strategy for a healthier society. *Archives of Disease in Childhood*, 78, 293–300.

Holaday, M., Smith, D.A. and Sherry, A. (2000). Sentence completion tests: a review of the literature and results of a survey of members of the Society for Personality Assessment. *Journal of Personality Assessment*, 74(3), 371–83.

Holland, S. (2004). *Child and family assessment in social work practice*. London: Sage.

Holland, S. and Scourfield, J. (2004). Liberty and respect in child protection. *British Journal of Social Work*, 34, 21–36.

Holland, S., Faulkner, A. and Perez-del-Aguila, R. (2005). Promoting stability and continuity of care for looked after children: a survey and critical review. *Child and Family Social Work*, 10, 29–41.

Holloway, J.S. (1997). Outcome in placements for adoption or long term fostering. *Archives of Disease in Childhood*, 76, 227–30.

Hollows, A. (2008). Professional judgement and the risk assessment process. In M.C. Calder (ed.) *Contemporary risk assessment in safeguarding children*. Lyme Regis: Russell House Publishing Ltd.

Hollows, A. and Nelson, P. (n.d.) Submission to the third seminar of the Victoria Climbie enquiry: determining requirements. '*Getting it right—turning theory into practice*'. Retrieved 3 June 2010 from: http://www.nationalarchives.gov.uk/ERORecords/VC/2/2/Evidence/p2subs/pdfs/Sem3/public/Peter%20Nelson%20-%20Sheffield%20Hallam%20University.pdf

Holt, J. (1969). *How children fail*. Harmondsworth: Penguin Education.

Holt, J. (1991). *How children learn*. Harmondsworth: Penguin Education.

Hopwood, C.J., Pincus, A.L., DeMoor, R.M. and Koonce, E.A. (2008). Psychometric characteristics of the Inventory of Interpersonal Problems-Short Circumplex (IIP-SC) with college students. *Journal of Personality Assessment*, 90(6), 615–18.

Horton, C. (2003). *Protective factors literature review: early care and education programs and the prevention of child abuse and neglect*. Washington, DC: Center for the Study of Social Policy. Retrieved 21 June 2010 from: www.cssp.org/uploadsFiles/horton. pdf

Horwath, J. (2007). *Child neglect: identification and assessment.* Basingstoke: Palgrave Macmillan.

Howe, D. (2003). Attachment disorders: disinhibited attachment behaviours and secure base distortions with special reference to adopted children. *Attachment and Human Development, 5*(3), 265–70.

Howe, D. and Feast, J. (2000). *Adoption, search and reunion: the long term experience of adopted adults.* London: Children's Society.

Howe, D., Brandon, M., Hinings, D. and Schofield, G. (1999). *Attachment theory, child maltreatment and family support.* London: Palgrave.

Howes, N. (2010). Here to listen! Communicating with children and methods for communicating with children and young people as part of the assessment process. In J. Horwath (ed.) *The child's world: the comprehensive guide to assessing children in need* (2nd edition). London: Jessica Kingsley.

Hughes, C. (2003). Making and breaking relationships. In A. Bainham, B. Lindley, M.P.M. Richards and E. Trinder (eds.) *Parent child relationships and contact: a socio-legal analyis.* Oxford: Hart.

Hughes, D. (2009). *Attachment focused parenting: effective strategies to care for children.* New York: W.W. Norton Inc.

Humphreys, C., Thiara, R.K. and Skamballis, A. (2011). Readiness to change: mother-child relationship and domestic violence intervention. *British Journal of Social Work, 41*(1), 166–84.

Hunt, J. (2009). Family and friends care. In G. Schofield and J. Simmonds (eds.) *The child placement handbook: research, policy and practice.* London: British Agencies for Adoption and Fostering (BAAF).

Hunt, J., Waterhouse, S. and Lutman, E. (2008). *Keeping them in the family: outcomes for children placed in kinship care through care proceedings.* London: British Agencies for Adoption and Fostering (BAAF).

Hynan, D.J. (2003). Parent-child observations in custody evaluations. *Family Court Review, 41,* 214–23.

Hynan, D.J. (2006). Scientific considerations in observing how children interact with their parents. *The Forensic Examiner, 15*(4), 42–47. Retrieved 5 April 2011 from: http://findarticles.com/p/articles/mi_go1613/is_4_15/ai_n29310477/ pg_3/?tag=content;col1

Jack, G. (2001). Ecological perspectives in assessing children and families. In J. Horwath (ed.) *The child's world: assessing children in need.* London: Jessica Kingsley.

Jackson, S. and Thomas, N. (1999). *On the move again? What works in creating stability for looked after children.* Ilford: Barnardo's.

Jacobsen, T., Edelstein, W. and Hofmann, V. (1994). A longitudinal study of the relation between representations of attachment in childhood and cognitive func-tioning in childhood and adolescence. *Developmental Psychology, 30,* 112–24.

Jacobson, N.S. and Gottman, J.M. (1998). *When men batter women: new insights into ending abusive relationships.* New York: Simon and Schuster.

Jaffe, P.G., Crooks, C.V. and Bala, N. (2006). *Making appropriate parenting arrange-ments in family violence cases: applying the literature to identify promising practices.* Canada: Family, Children and Youth Section, Department of Justice. Retrieved 29 June 2011 from: http://www.justice.gc.ca/eng/pi/fcy-fea/lib-bib/rep-rap/2006/ 2005_3/pdf/2005_3.pdf

Jampolsky, G.G. (2011). *Love is letting go of fear* (3rd edition). Berkeley, CA: Celestial Arts.

Jenkins, J.M. and Smith, M.A. (1990). Factors protecting children living in dishar-monious homes: maternal reports. *Journal of the American Academy of Child and Adolescent Psychiatry, 29,* 60–69.

Jenner, S. (1997). Assessment of parenting in the context of child protection using the Parent/Child Game. *Child and Adolescent Mental Health*, 2(2), 58–62.

Johnson, B. (1996). Feeling the fear. In D. Boud and N. Miller (eds.) *Working with experience: animating learning*. London: Routledge.

Jones, D.P.H. (2003). *Communicating with vulnerable children*. London: Royal College of Psychiatrists.

Johnson, K., Wagner, D. and Wiebush, R. (2000). *Risk assessment revalidation study*. South Australia Department of Family and Community Services. Retrieved 18 August 2012 from: http://www.nccdglobal.org/sites/default/files/publication_pdf/so_aus_2000_risk_reval.pdf

Johnson, W. (2004). *Effectiveness of California's child welfare Structured Decision-Making (SDM) model: a prospective study of the validity of the California Family Risk Assessment*. Retrieved 17 August 2012 from: http://www.nccdglobal.org/sites/default/files/publication_pdf/ca_sdm_model_feb04.pdf

Jory, B. (2004). The Intimate Justice Scale: an instrument to screen for psychological abuse and physical violence in clinical practice. *Journal of Marital and Family Therapy*, 30(1), 29–44.

Jory, B. and Anderson, D. (2000). Intimate justice III: healing the anguish of abuse and embracing the anguish of accountability. *Journal of Marital and Family Therapy*, 26, 349–64.

Juffer, F. and van Ijzendoorn, M.H. (2005). Behaviour problems and mental health referrals of international adoptees: a meta-analysis. *Journal of the American Medical Association*, 293(20), 2501–15.

Juffer, F. and van Ijzendoorn, M.H. (2007). Adoptees do not lack self-esteem: a meta-analysis of studies on self-esteem of transracial, international, and domestic adoptees. *Psychological Bulletin*, 133(6), 1067–83.

Jung, C.J. (1963). *Memories, dreams, reflections*. London: Collins and Routledge and Kegan Paul.

Kadushin, A. and Kadushin, G. (1997). *The social work interview: a guide for human service professionals* (4th edition). New York: Columbia University Press.

Kağıtçıbaşı, C. (2006). Theoretical perspectives on family change. In J. Georgas, J.W. Berry, F.J.R. van de Vijver, C. Kağıtçıbaşı and Y.H. Poortinga (eds.) *Families across cultures: a 30-nation psychological study*. Cambridge: Cambridge University Press.

Kallianes, V. and Rubenfeld, P. (1997). Disabled women and reproductive rights. *Disability and Society*, 12, 203–21.

Katz, S., Ford, A.B., Moskowitz, R.W., Jackson, B.A. and Jaffe, M.W. (1963). Studies of illness in the aged. The Index of ADL: a standardized measure of biological and psychosocial function. *JAMA*, 185(12), 914–919.

Kaufman, J. and Zigler, E. (1993). The intergenerational transmission of abuse is overstated. In R.J. Gelles and D.R. Loseke (ed.) *Current controversies on family violence*. Newbury Park, CA: Sage.

Kaufman, R. and English, F.W. (1979). *Needs assessment: concept and application*. Englewood Cliffs, NJ: Educational Technology Publications.

Kay Hall, S.E. and Geher, G. (2003). Behavioural and personality characteristics of children with reactive attachment disorder. *Journal of Psychology: Interdisciplinary and Applied*, 137, 145–62.

Kellett, J. and Apps, J. (2009). *Assessments of parenting and parenting support needs*. York: Joseph Rowntree Foundation. Retrieved 20 February 2011 from: www.jrf.org.uk

Kelly, G. (1955). *Principles of personal construct psychology*. New York: Norton.

Kelly, J. and Johnston, J. (2001). The alienated child: a reformulation of parental alienation. *Family Court Review*, 39, 249–66.

Keltner, B., Wise, L., and Taylor, G. (1999). Mothers with intellectual limitations and their 2-year-old children's developmental outcomes. *Journal of Intellectual and Developmental Disability*, 24(1), 45–57.

Kemshall, H. (2008). Actuarial and clinical risk assessment: contrasts, comparisons and collective usages. In M.C. Calder (ed.) *Contemporary risk assessment in safeguarding children*. Lyme Regis: Russell House Publishing.

Kennedy, H., Landor, M. and Todd, L. (2011). *Video interaction guidance: a relationship-based intervention to promote attunement, empathy and wellbeing*. London: Jessica Kingsley Publishers.

Keyzer, P., Carney, T. and Tait, D. (1997). *Against the odds: parents with intellectual disability. Report to the Disability Services Sub-Committee*. Sydney: Commonwealth Department of Health and Family Services.

Khoo, E., Nygren, L. and Hyvönen, U. (2002). Child welfare or child protection. A comparative study of social intervention in child maltreatment in Canada and Sweden. In M. Hill, A. Stafford and P.G. Lister (eds.) *International perspectives on child protection: report of a seminar held on 20 March 2002*. Retrieved 12 December 2011 from: http://www.scotland.gov.uk/Resource/Doc/1181/0009926.pdf

Kilminster, S.M. and Jolly, B.C. (2000). Effective supervision in clinical practice settings: a literature review. *Medical Education*, 34(10), 827–40.

Kilpatrick, K.L. (2005). The parental empathy measure: a new approach to assessing child maltreatment risk. *American Journal of Orthopsychiatry*, 75(4), 608–20.

Kilpatrick, K.L. and Hine, D. (2005). *Parental empathy, personality disorders and child maltreatment*. Final Report for Industry Partner: New South Wales Department of Community Services. Summary retrieved 1 July 2011 from: http://www.community.nsw.gov.au/docswr/_assets/main/documents/researchnotes_parental_empathy.pdf

Kirkbride, L. and Piper, R. (n.d.). *You go first*. London: Children's Society.

Kirmayer, L.J. (1990). Resistance, reactance and reluctance to change: a cognitive attributional approach to strategic interventions. *Journal of Cognitive Psychotherapy: An International Quarterly*, 4, 83–103.

Kirshbaum, M. and Olkin, R. (2002). Parents with physical, systemic or visual disabilities. *Sexuality and Disability*, 20(1), 29–52.

Kirton, D. (2009). *Child social work policy and practice*. London: Sage.

Klein, G. (2000). *Sources of power: how people make decisions*. Cambridge, MA: MIT Press.

Koriat, A., Lichenstein, S. and Fischoff, B. (1980). Reasons for confidence. *Journal of Experimental Psychology: Human Learning and Memory*, 6, 107–18.

Kosonen, M. (1999). 'Core' and 'kin' siblings: foster children's changing families. In A. Mullender (ed.) *We are family*. London: British Agencies for Adoption and Fostering (BAAF).

Kroese, B.S., Hussein, H., Clifford, C. and Ahmed, N. (2002). Social support networks and psychological well-being of mothers with intellectual disabilities. *Journal of Applied Research in Intellectual Disabilities*, 15(4), 324–40.

Kropp, P., Hart, S., Webster, C. and Eaves, D. (1995). *Manual for the Spousal Assault Risk Assessment Guide* (2nd edition). Vancouver, Canada: British Columbia Institute on Family Violence.

Kuehnle, K. and Connell, M. (2009). *The evaluation of child sexual abuse allegations: a comprehensive guide to assessment and testimony*. Hoboken, NJ: Wiley.

Kuyken, W. (2006). Evidence-based case formulation: is the emperor clothed? In N. Tarrier (ed.) *Case formulation in cognitive behavior therapy: the treatment of challenging and complex cases*. New York: Routledge.

Lacharité, C., Ethier, L. and Couture, G. (1996). The influence of partners on parental stress of neglectful mothers. *Child Abuse Review*, 5, 18–33.

Ladany, N., Ellis, M.V. and Friedlander, M.L. (1999). The supervisory working alliance, trainee self-efficacy, and satisfaction. *Journal of Counseling and Development*, 77(4), 447–55.

Lakey, B. and Drew, J. (1997). A social-cognitive perspective on social support. In G.R. Pierce, B. Lakey, I.B. Sarason and B.R. Sarason (eds.) *Sourcebook of social support and personality*. New York: Plenum.

Lamb, H. (2010). *Hair strand testing for alcohol: hair today, gone tomorrow*. Retrieved 12 December 2010 from: http://www.familylawweek.co.uk/site.aspx?i=ed71707

Lamb, M.E., Hershkowitz, I., Orbach, Y. and Esplin, P.W. (2008). *Tell me what happened: structured investigative interviews of child victims and witnesses*. Chichester: John Wiley and Sons Ltd.

Lambert, M.J. (2007). Presidential address: what we have learned from a decade of research aimed at improving psychotherapy outcome in routine care. *Psychotherapy Research*, 17(1), 1–14.

Lambert, M.J. and Ogles, B.M. (2004). The efficacy and effectiveness of psychotherapy. In M.J. Lambert (ed.) *Bergin and Garfield's handbook of psychotherapy and behaviour change* (5th edition). Chicago, IL: Wiley.

Lambert, M.J., Harmon, C., Slade, K., Whipple, J.L. and Hawkins, E.J. (2005). Providing feedback to therapists on their patients' progress: clinical results and practice suggestions. *Journal of Clinical Psychology*, 61(2), 165–74.

Lampel, A.K. (1996). Children's alignments with parents in highly conflicted custody cases. *Family and Conciliation Court Review*, 39(3), 282–98.

Lang, W.P., Little, M. and Cronen, V. (1990). The systemic professional: domains of action and the question of neutrality. *Human Systems*, 1 (1), 39–55.

Lanyon, R. and Carle, A. (2007). Internal and external validity of scores on the Balanced Inventory of Desirable Responding and the Paulhus Deception Scales. *Educational and Psychological Measurement*, 67(5), 859–76.

Larsson, I. (2000). *Child sexuality and sexual behaviour*. Translated by Kate Lambert and Stuart Tudball (2001). Swedish National Board of Health and Welfare. Retrieved 8 June 2010 from: http://www.socialstyrelsen.se/publikationer2001/2001-123-20

Lasher, L.J. and Sheridan, M.S. (2004). *Munchausen by Proxy: identification, intervention, and case management*. Binghamton, NY: Howarth Press.

Lassiter, F.D., Geers, A.L., Munhall, P.J., Ploutz-Snyder, R.J. and Breitenbecher, D.L. (2002). Illusory causation: why it occurs. *Psychological Sciences*, 13, 299–305.

Lawton M.P. and Brody, E.M. (1969). Assessment of older people: self-maintaining and instrumental activities of daily living. *Gerontologist*, 9(3), 179–86.

Lazowski, L.E., Miller, F.G., Boye, M.W. and Miller, G.A. (1998). Efficacy of the Substance Abuse Subtle Screening Inventory-3 (SASSI-3) in identifying substance dependence disorders in clinical settings. *Journal of Personality Assessment*, 71(1), 114–28.

Leach, P. (1979). *Baby and child*. Harmondsworth: Penguin.

Leathers, S.J. (2002). Foster children's behavioural disturbance and detachment from caregivers and community institutions. *Children and Youth Services Review*, 24(4), 239–68.

Lee, R.M. (1993). *Doing research on sensitive topics*. London: Sage.

Lester, S. (1999). *An introduction to phenomenological research* [online]. Retrieved 9 January 2010 from: http://www.sld.demon.co.uk/resmethy.pdf

Levesque, R. (1996). Maintaining children's relations with mentally disabled parents: recognizing difference and the difference it makes. *Children's Legal Rights Journal*, 16(2), 14–22.

Lewak, R.W. and Hogan, R.S. (2003). Integrating and applying assessment information. In L.E. Beutler and G. Groth-Marnat (eds.) *Integrative assessment of adult personality.* New York: Guilford Press.

Lewin, C. (2005). Elementary quantitative methods. In B. Somekh and C. Lewin (eds.) *Research methods in the social sciences.* London: Sage.

Lindaman, S.L., Booth, P.B. and Chambers, C.L. (2000). Assessing parent-child interactions with the Marschak Interaction Method (MIM). In K. Gitlin-Wiener, A. Sangrund and C. Schaefer (eds.) *Play diagnosis and assessment.* New York: Wiley.

Lindley, B. (1994). *On the receiving end: families' experiences of the court process.* London: Family Rights Group.

Linehan, M.M. (1993). *Cognitive-behavioral treatment of borderline personality disorder.* New York: Guilford Press.

Linehan, M.M. (2007). Dialectical behavior therapy for individuals with borderline personality disorder and substance dependence. In L.A. Dimeff, K. Koerner, M.M. Linehan (eds.) *Dialectical behavior therapy in clinical practice: applications across disorders and settings.* New York: Guilford Press.

Lizzio, A., Stokes, L. and Wilson, K. (2005). Approaches to learning in professional supervision: supervisee perceptions of processes and outcome. *Studies in Continuing Education,* 27(3), 239–56.

Llewellyn, G. (1995). Relationships and social support: views of parents with mental retardation/intellectual disability. *Mental Retardation,* 33, 349–63.

Llewellyn, G. and McConnell, D. (2002). Mothers with learning disabilities and their support networks. *Journal of Intellectual Disability Research,* 46(1), 17–34.

Llewellyn, G. and McConnell, D. (2005). You have to prove yourself all the time: people with learning disabilities as parents. In G. Grant, P. Goward, M. Richardson and P. Ramcharan (eds.) *Learning disability: a life cycle approach to valuing people.* Maidenhead: Open University Press, McGraw-Hill Education.

Llewellyn, G., McConnell, D., Honey, A., Mayes, R. and Russo, D. (2003). Promoting health and home safety for children of parents with intellectual disability: a randomised controlled trial. *Research in Developmental Disabilities,* 24(6), 405–31.

Llewellyn, G., Trasutadóttir, R., McConnell, D. and Sigurjónsdóttir, H.B. (2010). Introduction. In G. Llewellyn, R. Traustadóttir, D. McConnell and H.B. Sigurjónsdóttir (eds.) *Parents with intellectual disabilities: past, present, futures.* Chichester: John Wiley and Sons Ltd.

Loman, A.L. and Siegel, G.L. (2005). *An evaluation of the Minnesota SDM Family Risk Assessment: final report.* St Louis, MO: Institute of Applied Research. Retrieved 10 July 2011 from: http://www.iarstl.org/papers/FinalFRAReport.pdf

London Borough of Brent (1985). *A child in trust: the report of the panel of inquiry into the circumstances surrounding the death of Jasmine Beckford.* London: London Borough of Brent.

Lonne, B., Parton, N., Thomson, J. and Harries, M. (2009). *Reforming child protection.* Abingdon: Routledge.

Lord, J. and Borthwick, S. (2008). *Good practice guide: together or apart?* London: British Agencies for Adoption and Fostering (BAAF).

Lord Laming (2009). *The protection of children in England: a progress report.* London: The Stationery Office.

Lowe, N., Murch, M., Borkowski, M., Weaver, A., Beckford, V. and Thomas, C. (1999). *Supporting adoption: reframing the approach.* London: British Agencies for Adoption and Fostering (BAAF).

Lundahl, B.W., Nimer, J. and Parsons, B. (2006). Preventing child abuse: a meta-analysis of parent training programs. *Research on Social Work Practice,* 16, 251–62.

Macaskill, C. (2002). *Safe contact? Children in permanent placement and contact with their birth relatives.* Lyme Regis: Russell House Publishing.

McCarty, C.A., Lau, A.S., Valeri, S.M. and Weisz J.R. (2004). Parent-child interactions in relation to critical and emotionally overinvolved expressed emotion (EE): is EE a proxy for behavior? *Journal of Abnormal Child Psychology*, 32(1), 83–93.

McConnell, D. and Llewellyn, G. (2000). Disability, discrimination and statutory child protection proceedings. *Disability and Society*, 15(6), 883–95.

McConnell, D., Feldman, M. and Aunos, M. (2008). Child welfare investigation outcomes for parents with cognitive impairment and their children in Canada. *Journal of Intellectual Disability Research*, 52, 722.

McConnell, D., Feldman, M., Aunos, M. and Prasad, N. (2011). Child maltreatment investigations involving parents with cognitive impairments in Canada. *Child Maltreatment*, 16(1), 21–32.

McCracken, G. (1988). *The long interview.* Newbury Park, CA: Sage.

Macdonald, K.I. and Macdonald, G.M. (1999). Perceptions of risk. In P. Parsloe (ed.) *Risk assessment in social care and social work: research highlights.* London: Jessica Kingsley.

McGaw, S. (1996). Services for parents with learning disabilities. *Tizard Learning Disability Review*, 1(1), 21–32.

McGaw, S. (2012). Working with parents who happen to have intellectual disabilities. In E. Emerson, C. Hatton, J. Bromley and A. Caine (eds.) *Clinical psychology and people with intellectual disabilities* (2nd edition). London: John Wiley and Sons Ltd.

McGaw, S. and Newman, T. (2005). *What works for parents with learning disabilities?* Ilford: Barnardo's.

McGaw, S. and Sturmey, P. (1994). Assessing parents with learning disabilities: the Parental Skills Model. *Child Abuse Review*, 3(1), 27–35.

McGaw, S., Beckley, K., Connolly, N., and Ball, K. (1998). *Parent Assessment Manual.* Truro: Trecare NHS Trust.

McGaw, S., Ball, K. and Clark, A. (2002). The effect of group intervention on the relationships of parents with intellectual disabilities. *Journal of Applied Research in Intellectual Disabilities*, 15(4), 354–66.

McGaw, S., Scully, T. and Pritchard, C. (2010). Predicting the unpredictable? Identifying high-risk versus low-risk parents with intellectual disabilities. *Child Abuse and Neglect*, 34, 699–710.

McHale, J.P. (2007). When infants grow up in multiperson relationship systems. *Infant Mental Health Journal*, 28(4), 370–92.

McLoyd, V.C. and Smith, J. (2002). Physical discipline and behaviour problems in African American, European American and Hispanic children: emotional support as a moderator. *Journal of Marriage and Family*, 64(1), 40–53.

McSherry, D., Larkin, E., Fargas, M., Kelly, G. and Robinson, C. (2009). *From care to where: summary report.* Retrieved 26 April 2011 from: http://www.qub.ac.uk/research-centres/TheCarePathwaysandOutcomesStudy/Publications/

Macur, J. (2005). Factitious illness by proxy: where are we now? *Family Law Week.* Retrieved 14 December 2010 from: http://www.familylawweek.co.uk/site.aspx?i=ed205

Mahoney, M.J. (2006). *Constructive psychotherapy.* New York: Guilford Press.

Main, M. (n.d.). *Avoiding common errors in conducting the Adult Attachment Interview.* Retrieved 5 January 2010 from: http://www.psychology.sunysb.edu/attachment/measures/content/aai_interviewing.pdf

Main, M. and Cassidy, J. (1988). Categories of response to reunion with the parent at age six: predictable from infant attachment classifications and stable over a 1-month period. *Developmental Psychology*, 24, 415–26.

Main, M. and Solomon, J. (1986). Discovery of an insecure disorganized/disoriented attachment pattern: procedures, findings and implications for the classification of behavior. In T. Braxelton and M. Yogman (eds.) *Affective development in infancy.* Norwood, NJ: Ablex.

Main, M. and Soloman, J. (1990). Procedures for identifying infants as disorganized/ disoriented during the Ainsworth Strange Situation. In M. Greenberg, D. Cicchetti and E.M. Cummings (eds.) *Attachment in the preschool years: theory, research and intervention.* Chicago, IL: University of Chicago Press.

Main, M., Kaplan, N. and Cassidy, J. (1985). Security in infancy, childhood, and adulthood: a move to the level of representation. In I. Bretherton and E. Waters (eds.) Growing points of attachment theory and research. *Monographs of the Society for Research in Child Development, 50,* Serial no. 209(1–2), 66–104.

Mankowski, E.S. and Wyer, R.S. Jr (1997). Cognitive causes and consequences of perceived social support. In G.R. Pierce, B. Lakey, I.B. Sarason and B.R. Sarason (eds.) *Sourcebook of social support and personality.* New York: Plenum.

Mantle, G., Moules, T., Johnson, K., Leslie, J., Parsons, S. and Shaffer, R. (2007). Whose wishes and feelings? Children's autonomy and parental influence in family court enquiries. *British Journal of Social Work, 37,* 785–805.

Marchant, R. (2001). The assessment of children with complex needs. In J. Horwath (ed.) *The child's world: assessing children in need.* London: Jessica Kingsley.

Marcus, G.E. and Fischer, M.M.J. (1986). *Anthropology as cultural critique: an experimental moment in the human sciences.* Chicago, IL: University of Chicago Press.

Marneffe, C. (2002). Voluntary child protection work in Belgium. In M. Hill, A. Stafford and P.G. Lister (eds.) *International perspectives on child protection: report of a seminar held on 20 March 2002.* Retrieved 12 December 2011 from: http://www.scotland.gov.uk/Resource/Doc/1181/0009926.pdf

Marshall, P.J. and Fox, N.A. (2005). Relationship between behavioral reactivity at 4 months and attachment classification at 14 months in a selected sample. *Infant Behavior and Development, 28,* 492–502.

Martindale, D.A. (2005). Confirmatory bias and confirmatory distortion. In J.R. Flens and L. Drozd (eds.) *Psychological testing in child custody evaluations.* Binghampton, NY: The Haworth Press Inc.

Marvin, R. and Britner, P. (1996). *Classification system for parental caregiving patterns in the preschool Strange Situation.* Unpublished manuscript, University of Virginia.

Masson, J., Winn Oakley, M. and Pick, K. (2004). *Emergency protection orders: court orders for child protection crises.* Unpublished report: Warwick University. Retrieved 27 June 2011 from: http://www.nspcc.org.uk/Inform/publications/downloads/EPO_wdf48137.pdf. Also available from: http://www2.warwick.ac.uk/fac/soc/law/about/staff/masson/

Masten, A.S. (2001). Ordinary magic: resilience processes in development. *American Psychologist, 56,* 227–38.

Maugham, A. and Cicchetti, D. (2002). Impact of child maltreatment and interadult violence on children's emotion, regulatory abilities and socioemotional adjustment. *Child Development, 73,* 1525–42.

Megginson, D. and Clutterbuck, D. (2005). *Techniques of coaching and mentoring.* Oxford: Elsevier Butterworth-Heinemann.

Melhuish, E., Belsky, J. and Barnes, J. (2010). Evaluation and value of Sure Start. *Archives of Disease in Childhood, 95,* 159–61.

Merrell, K.W. (2003). *Behavioral, social and emotional assessment of children and adolescents.* Mahwah, NJ: Lawrence Erlbaum Associates.

Mickelson, P. (1949). Can mentally deficient parents be helped to give their children better care? *American Journal of Mental Deficiency, 53*(3), 516–34.

Miller, J.G. (1984). Culture and the development of everyday social explanation. *Journal of Personality and Social Psychology, 46,* 961–78.

Miller, W.R. and Rollnick, S. (1991). *Motivational interviewing: preparing people to change addictive behaviour*. New York: Guilford Press.

Miller, W.R. and Rollnick, S. (2002). *Motivational interviewing: preparing people for change* (2nd edition). New York: Guilford Press.

Millichamp, J., Martin, J. and Langely, J. (2006). On the receiving end: young adults describe their parents' use of physical punishment and other disciplinary measures during childhood. *The New Zealand Medical Journal, 119*, no. 1228. Retrieved 19 February 2011 from: https://www.nzma.org.nz/journal/119-1228/1818/

Milner, J.S. (1986). *The Child Abuse Potential Inventory: Manual* (2nd edition). Webster, NC: Psytec.

Milner, J.S. (1995). Physical child abuse assessment: perpetrator evaluation. In J.C. Campbell (ed.) *Assessing dangerousness: violence by sexual offenders, batterers, and child abusers*. Thousand Oaks, CA: Sage Publications Inc.

Milner, J. and O'Byrne, P. (2002). *Assessment in social work* (2nd edition). Basingstoke: Palgrave Macmillan.

Ministry of Justice (2008). *Practice direction: experts in family proceedings relating to children*. Retrieved 3 July 2011 from: http://www.justice.gov.uk/guidance/docs/Experts-PD-flagB-final-version-14-01-08.pdf

Ministry of Justice (n.d.) *Offender group reconviction scale version 3. Guidance*. Retrieved 6 June 2010 from: http://www.probation.homeoffice.gov.uk/files/pdf/Offender%20Group%20Reconviction%20Scale%20v3%20Guidance.pdf

Minnis, H., Putter, S., Read, W., Green, J. and Schumm, T-S. (2008). *The computerised Manchester Attachment Story Task: a novel medium for a measure of attachment patterns*. CHI Workshop on Technology in Mental Health. Retrieved 15 June 2010 from: www.scss.tcd.ie/conferences/TIMH/12-Minnis.pdf

Mnookin, R. (1975). Child custody adjudication: judicial functions in the face of indeterminacy. *Law and Contemporary Problems, 39*, 226–93.

Mohr, D. and Beutler, L.E. (2003). The integrative clinical interview. In L.E. Beutler and G. Groth-Marnat (eds.) *Integrative assessment of adult personality*. New York: The Guilford Press.

Mollon, P. (1989). Anxiety, supervision and a space for thinking: some narcissistic perils for clinical psychologists in learning psychotherapy. *British Journal of Medical Psychology, 62*, 113–22.

Monahan, J., Steadman, H., Robbins, P., Appelbaum, P., Banks, S., Grisso, T., Heilbrun, K., Mulvey, E., Roth, L. and Silver, E. (2005). An actuarial model of violence risk assessment for persons with mental disorders. *Psychiatric Services, 56*, 810–15.

Moos, R.H. (1990). Conceptual and empirical approaches to developing family-based assessment procedures: resolving the case of the Family Environment Scale. *Family Process, 29*(2), 199–208.

Moos, R. and Moos, B. (1994). *Family Environment Scale manual: development, applications, research* (3rd edition). Palo Alto, CA: Consulting Psychologist Press.

Morgan, P. and Goff, A. (2004). *Learning curves: the assessment of parents with a learning disability*. Norfolk Area Child Protection Committee. Retrieved 22 December 2010 from: http://www.lscb.norfolk.gov.uk/

Morris, J. and Wates, M. (2006). *Supporting disabled parents and parents with additional support needs*. Bristol: Social Care Institute for Excellence.

Morrison, T. (1996). Partnership and collaboration: rhetoric and reality. *Child Abuse and Neglect, 20*(2), 127–40.

Morrison, T. (2010). Assessing parental motivation for change. In J. Horwath (ed.) *The child's world: the comprehensive guide to assessing children in need* (2nd edition). London: Jessica Kingsley.

Mosek, A. and Adler, L. (2001). The self-concept of adolescent girls in non-relative versus kin foster care. *International Social Work, 44*(2), 149–62.

Munro, E. (1999). Common errors of reasoning in child protection work. *Child Abuse and Neglect*, 23(8), 745–58.

Munro, E. (2002). *Effective Child Protection*. London: Sage.

Munro, E. (2004). A simpler way to understand the results of risk assessment instruments. *Children and Youth Services Review*, 26, 873–83.

Munro, E. (2011). *The Munro review of child protection interim report: the child's journey*. Crown Copyright. Retrieved 1 May 2011 from: www.education.gov.uk

Munro, E. and Hardy, A. (2006). *Placement stability—a review of the literature*. Report to the Department for Education and Skills. Retrieved 27 June 2011 from: http://www.lboro.ac.uk/research/ccfr/Publications/placementstabilitylitreview.pdf

Murray, P. and Penman, G. (1996). *Let our children be: a collection of stories*. Sheffield: Parents with Attitude.

Murray, J. and Thomson, M.E. (2010). Clinical judgement in violence risk assessment. *Europe's Journal of Psychology*, 6(1), 128–49. Retrieved 25 June 2011 from: http://www.ejop.org/archives/2010/02/clinical-judgement-in-violence-risk-assessment.html

Myers, D. and Wee, D. (2005). *Disaster mental health services: a primer for practitioners*. New York: Routledge.

Myers, M.G., Stewart, D.G. and Brown, S.A. (1998). Progression from conduct disorder to antisocial personality disorder following treatment for adolescent substance abuse. *American Journal of Psychiatry*, 155, 479–85.

National Family Preservation Network (2003). *Intensive family reunification services protocol*. Retrieved 4 June 2012 from: http://www.hunter.cuny.edu/socwork/nrcfcpp/downloads/teleconferences/IFRS-Protocol.pdf

Neil, E. (2004). The 'contact after adoption' study: indirect contact and adoptive parents' communication about adoption. In E. Neil and D. Howe (eds.) *Contact in adoption and permanent foster care: research, theory and practice*. London: British Agencies for Adoption and Fostering (BAAF).

Neil, E., Cossar, J., Jones, C., Lorgelly, P. and Young J. (2011). *Supporting direct contact after adoption*. London: British Agencies for Adoption and Fostering (BAAF).

Nieto, M. and Jung, D. (2006). *The impact of residency restrictions on sex offenders and correctional management practices: a literature review*. California Research Bureau: California State Library. Retrieved 6 June 2010 from: http://www.library.ca.gov/crb/06/08/06-008.pdf

Nobes, G., Smith, M., Upton, P. and Heverin, A. (1999). Physical punishment by mothers and fathers in British homes. *Journal of Interpersonal Violence*, 14, 887–902.

Nottinghamshire Area Child Protection Committee (1994). *Report of overview group into the circumstances surrounding the death of Leanne White*. Nottingham: Nottinghamshire County Council.

Novaco, R.W. (1994). Anger as a risk factor for violence among the mentally disordered. In J. Monahan and H. Steadman (eds.) *Violence and mental disorder: developments in risk assessment*. Chicago, IL: University of Chicago Press.

Novaco, R.W. (2000). Anger. In A.E. Kazdin (ed.) *Encyclopedia of psychology*. Washington, DC: American Psychological Association and Oxford University Press.

Novaco, R.W. (2007). Anger dysregulation. In T.A. Cavell and K.T. Malcolm (eds.) *Anger, aggression and interventions for interpersonal violence*. Mahwah, NJ: Lawrence Erlbaum Associates Inc.

Novaco, R.W. and Chemtob, C.M. (2002). Anger and combat-related posttraumatic stress disorder. *Journal of Traumatic Stress*, 15, 123–32.

Nowicki, S. and Strickland, B.R. (1973). A locus of control scale for children. *Journal of Consulting and Clinical Psychology*, 40, 148–55.

Office of the Deputy Prime Minister (ODPM) (2004). *Mental health and social exclusion*. Social Exclusion Unit Report. London: ODPM.

Ofsted (2008). *The annual report of Her Majesty's Chief Inspector of Education, children's services and skills 2007/08.* London: The Stationery Office.

Olkin, F. (1999). *What psychotherapists should know about disability.* New York: Guilford Press.

Olsen, R. (1996). Young carers: challenging the facts and politics of research into children and caring. *Disability and Society, 11*(1), 41–54.

Olsen, R. and Clarke, H. (2003). *Parenting and disability: disabled parents' experience of raising children.* Bristol: The Policy Press.

Oster, G.D. and Crone, P.G. (2004). *Using drawings in assessment and therapy: a guide for mental health professionals.* New York: Brunner-Routledge.

Otto, R.K. and Edens, J.F. (2003). Parenting capacity. In T. Grisso (ed.) *Evaluating competencies: forensic assessments and instruments* (2nd edition). New York: Kluwer.

Otto, R.K., Edens, J.F. and Barcus, E.H. (2000). The use of psychological testing in child custody evaluations. *Family and Conciliation Courts Review, 38*(3), 312–40.

Packman, J. and Hall, C. (1998). *From care to accommodation: support, protection and control in child care services.* London: The Stationery Office.

Padesky, C.A. (1994). Schema change processes in cognitive therapy. *Clinical Psychology and Psychotherapy, 1,* 267–78.

Painz, F. (1993). *Parents with a learning disability.* Norwich: University of East Anglia.

Parnell, T.F. and Day, D.O. (1998). *Munchausen by Proxy Syndrome: misunderstood child abuse.* Thousand Oaks, CA: Sage.

Parsloe, P. (1999). *Risk assessment in social care and social work.* London: Jessica Kingsley Publishers.

Parton, N. (1996). Social work, risk and 'the Blaming System'. In N. Parton (ed.) *Social theory, social change and social work.* London: Routledge and Kegan Paul.

Pascalis, O., de Schonen, S., Morton, J., Deruelle, C. and Fabre-Grenet, M. (1995). Mother's face recognition in neonates: a replication and an extension. *Infant Behavior and Development, 17,* 79–85.

Patterson, C. and Teale, C. (1997). Influence of written information on patients' knowledge of their diagnosis. *Age and Ageing, 26,* 41–42.

Persons, J.B. (1989). *Cognitive therapy in practice: a case formulation approach.* New York: W.W. Norton.

Persons, J.B. (2008). *The case formulation approach to cognitive-behavior therapy.* New York: The Guilford Press.

Piaget, J. (1972). *The principles of genetic epistemology,* Translated by W. Mays. London: Routledge.

Pierce, G.R., Lakey, B., Sarason, I.G., Sarason, B.R. and Joseph, H.J. (1997). Personality and social support processes: a conceptual overview. In G.R. Pierce, B. Lakey, I.G. Sarason and B.R. Sarason (eds.) *Sourcebook of social support and personality.* New York: Plenum Press.

Platt, D. and Shemmings, D. (1997). *Making enquiries into alleged child abuse and neglect.* Chichester: John Wiley and Sons Ltd.

Plomin, R. and Dunn, J. (1986).*The study of temperament: changes, continuities and challenges.* Hillsdale, NJ: Lawrence Erlbaum Associates.

Polansky, N.A. (1985). Determinants of loneliness among neglectful and other low income mothers. *Journal of Social Service Research, 8,* 1–15.

Polansky, N.A., Chalmers M.A., Buttenwieser, E. and Williams, D.P. (1981). *Damaged parents.* Chicago, IL: The University of Chicago Press.

Polansky, N.A., Ammons, P.W. and Gaudin, J.M. (1985). Loneliness and isolation in child neglect. *Social Casework: The Journal of Contemporary Social Work, 6,* 38–47.

Pollard, J., Hawkins, J. and Arthur, M. (1999). Risk and protection: are both necessary to understand diverse behavioral outcomes in adolescence? *Social Work Research, 23*(3), 145–58.

Poortinga, Y.H. (1995). Cultural bias in assessment—historical and thematic issues. *European Journal of Psychological Assessment*, *11*, 140–46.

Povey, D., Coleman, K., Kaiza, P. and Roe, S. (2009). *Homicides, firearm offences and intimate violence 2007/08 (Supplementary volume 2 to crime in England and Wales 2007/08)*. London: Home Office. Retrieved 14 July 2010 from: http://rds.home-office.gov.uk/rds/pdfs09/hosb0209.pdf

President of the Family Division (2008). *Practice direction: residence and contact orders: domestic violence and harm*. Retrieved 5 July 2011 from: http://www.judiciary.gov.uk/Resources/JCO/Documents/Practice%20Directions/pd-domestic-violence.pdf

Preston, P. (2010). Parents with disabilities. In J.H. Stone and M. Blouin (eds.) *International Encyclopedia of Rehabilitation*. Retrieved 15 December 2010 from: http://cirrie.buffalo.edu/encyclopedia/en/article/36/

Prilleltensky, I. and Prilleltensky, O. (2006, November). *Promoting child and family well-being and preventing child abuse*. Speaking tour in five Australian cities (Melbourne, Canberra, Sydney, Brisbane and Perth). Retrieved 24 July 2010 from: www.melissainstitute.org/documents/Prilleltensky-1.ppt

Prince-Embury, S. (2007). *Resiliency Scales for Children and Adolescents: Profiles of Personal Strength*. San Antonio, TX: Harcourt Assessment, Inc.

Prior, V. and Glaser, D. (2006). *Understanding attachment and attachment disorders: theory, evidence and practice*. London: Jessica Kingsley.

Pritchard, C. and Williams, R. (2010). Comparing possible 'child-abuse-related-deaths' in England and Wales with the major developed countries 1974–2006: signs of progress? *British Journal of Social Work*, *40*, 1700–1718.

Prochaska, J.O. and DiClemente, C.C. (1982). Transtheoretical therapy: toward a more integrative model of change. *Psychotherapy: Theory, Research and Practice*, *19*(3), 276–88.

Prochaska, J.O., DiClemente, C.C. and Norcross, J.C. (1992). In search of how people change: applications to addictive behavior. *American Psychologist*, *47*, 1102–14.

Proctor, B. and Inskipp, F. (2009). Group supervision. In J. Scaife (ed.) *Supervision in clinical practice: a practitioner's guide* (2nd edition). London: Routledge.

Proctor, P. and Ditton, A. (1989). How counselling can add value to organisations. *Journal of Workplace Learning*, *1*(2), 3–6.

Puckering, C., Rogers, J., Mills, M., Cox, A.D. and Mattsson-Graff, M. (1994). Progress and evaluation of a group intervention for mothers with parenting difficulties. *Child Abuse Review*, *3*, 299–310.

Queensland Government (2010). *Child safety practice manual*. Retrieved 25 July 2010 from: http://www.childsafety.qld.gov.au/practice-manual/investigation-assessment/gather.html

Quinton, D., Rushton, A., Dance, C. and Mayes, D. (1998). *Joining new families: adoption and fostering in middle childhood*. Chichester: John Wiley and Sons Ltd.

Rassool, G.H. (2009). *Alcohol and drug misuse: a handbook for students and health professionals*. Abingdon: Routledge.

Ray, N.K., Rubenstein, H. and Russo, N.J. (1994). Understanding the parents who are mentally retarded: guidelines for Family Preservation Programs. *Child Welfare League of America*, *73*(6), 725–43.

Reder, P. and Duncan, S. (1999). *Lost innocents? A follow-up study of fatal child abuse*. London: Routledge.

Reder, P. and Lucey, C. (1995). Significant issues in the assessment of parenting. In P. Reder and C. Lucey (eds.) *Assessment of parenting: psychiatric and psychological contributions*. London: Routledge.

Reder, P., Duncan, S. and Gray, M. (1993). *Beyond blame—child abuse tragedies revisited*. London: Routledge.

Reder, P., Duncan, S. and Lucey, C. (2003a). *Studies in the assessment of parenting*. Hove: Brunner-Routledge.

Reder, P., Duncan, S. and Lucey, C. (2003b). What principles guide parenting assessments? In P. Reder, S. Duncan and C. Lucey (eds.) *Studies in the assessment of parenting*. Hove: Brunner-Routledge.

Redley, C. (2011). *Family Procedure Rules 2010: a guide to private and public law family proceedings concerning children*. Retrieved 5 April 2011 from: http://www.familylaw-week.co.uk/site.aspx?i=ed81936

Reich, J.W., Zautra, A.J. and Hall, J.S. (2010). *Handbook of adult resilience*. New York: Guilford Press.

Robbie, C. (2009). *Examining methods and techniques for eliciting the wishes and feelings of children (aged 5–11) in the middle of parental disputes in the family courts*. Paper presented at the CAFCASS research conference. What do children need? Working with families involved with the family court. Retrieved 15 June 2010 from: http://www.cafcass.gov.uk/research/research_conference_2009.aspx

Robertson, J. and Bowlby, J. (1952). Reponses of young children to separation from their mothers. *Courier du Centre Internationale de l'Enfance, Paris*, 2, 131–40.

Robertson, J. and Robertson, J. (1971). Young children in brief separations: a fresh look. *Psycho-analytic Study of the Child*, 26, 264–315.

Robins, R.W., Noftle, E.E. and Tracy, J.L. (2007). Assessing self-conscious emotions: a review of self-report and nonverbal measures. In J.L. Tracy, R.W. Robins and J.M. Tangney (eds.) *The self-conscious emotions: theory and research*. New York: Guilford.

Robinson, J. (1996). Social workers—investigators or enablers. In D. Batty and D. Cullen (eds.) *Child protection: the therapeutic option*. London: British Agencies for Adoption and Fostering (BAAF).

Robinson, J.P., Shaver, P.R. and Wrightsman, L.S. (1991). *Measures of personality and social psychological attitudes*. San Diego, CA: Academic Press, Elsevier Science.

Rogers, C.R., Gendlin, E.T., Kiesler, D.J. and Truax, C.B. (eds.) (1967). *The therapeutic relationship and its impact: a study of psychotherapy with schizophrenics*. Madison, WI: University of Wisconsin Press.

Roggman, L.A., Boyce, L. and Newland, L. (2000). Assessing mother-infant interaction in play. In K. Gitlin-Wiener, A. Sangrund and C. Schaefer (eds.) *Play diagnosis and assessment*. New York: Wiley.

Rohner, R.P. and Khaleque, A. (eds.) (2005). *Handbook for the study of parental acceptance and rejection* (4th edition). Storrs, CT: Rohner Research Publications.

Rohner, R. and Pettengill, S. (1985). Perceived parental acceptance-rejection and parental control among Korean adolescents. *Child Development*, 56, 524–28.

Rohner, R.P., Bourque, S.L. and Elordi, C.A. (1996). Children's perceptions of corporal punishment, caretaker acceptance, and psychological adjustment in a poor, biracial southern community. *Journal of Marriage and Family Therapy*, 58, 842–52.

Rosenberg, M. (1989). *Society and the adolescent self-image* (2nd edition). Middletown, CT: Wesleyan University Press.

Rosenberg, S.A. and McTate, G.A. (1982). Intellectually handicapped mothers: problems and prospects. *Children Today*, 11(1), 24–26.

Rossi, P.H., Schuerman, J. and Budde, S. (1999). Understanding decisions about child maltreatment. *Evaluation Review*, 23, 579–98.

Rothschild, B. and Rand, M. (2006). *Help for the helper: the psychophysiology of compassion fatigue and vicarious trauma*. New York: W.W. Norton and Co. Ltd.

Rotter, J.B., Lah, M.I. and Rafferty, J.E. (1992). *Rotter Incomplete Sentences Blank Second Edition manual*. New York: Psychological Corporation.

Rush, A.J., Trivedi, M.H., Ibrahim, H.M., Carmody, T.J., Anrow, B., Klein, D.N., Markowitz, J.C., Ninan, P.T., Kornstein, S., Manber, R., Thaase, M.E., Kocsis, J.H. and Keller, M.B. (2003). The 16-item Quick Inventory of Depressive Symptomatology (QUIDS), clinician rating (QUIDS-C) and self-report (QUIDS-SR): a psychometric evaluation in patients with chronic major depression. *Biological Psychiatry*, 54, 573–83.

Rushton, A. and Dance, C. (2006). The adoption of children from public care: a prospective study of outcome in adolescence. *Journal of the American Academy of Child and Adolescent Psychiatry*, 45(7), 877–83.

Rushton, A. and Nathan, J. (1996). The supervision of child protection work. *British Journal of Social Work*, 26, 357–74.

Rushton, A., Dance, C., Quinton, D. and Mayes, D. (2001). *Siblings in late permanent placements*. London: British Agencies for Adoption and Fostering (BAAF).

Russell, D. and Cutrona, C.E. (1984). *The Social Provisions Scale*. Unpublished manuscript. Iowa City: University of Iowa, College of Medicine. Retrieved 7 June 2012 from: http://www.iprc.unc.edu/longscan/pages/measures/Ages5to11/Social%20 Provisions%20Scale.pdf. Contact author: ccutrona@iastate.edu

Russell, M. (1994). New assessment tools for drinking in pregnancy: T-ACE, TWEAK, and others. *Alcohol Health and Research World*, 18(1), 55–61.

Russell, R.J.H. and Wells, P.A. (1993). *Marriage and Relationship Questionnaire Handbook*. Sevenoaks: Hodder and Stoughton.

Rutgers, A., Bakermans-Kranenburg, M., van Ijzendoorn, M. and van Berckelaer-Onnes, I.A. (2004). Autism and attachment: a meta-analytic review. *Journal of Child Psychology and Psychiatry*, 45, 1123–34.

Rutter, M. (1995). Clinical implications of attachment concepts: retrospect and prospect. *Journal of Child Psychology and Psychiatry and Allied Disciplines*, 36(4), 549–71.

Rutter, M. (2002). Nature, nurture, and development: from evangelism through science toward policy and practice. *Child Development*, 73(1), 1–21.

Rutter, M. and O'Connor, T.G. (1999). Implications of attachment theory for child care policies. In J. Cassidy and P.R. Shaver (eds.) *Handbook of attachment: theory, research and clinical applications*. New York: Guilford Press.

Safran, J.D., Muran, J.C., Samstag, L.W. and Stevens, C. (2002). Repairing alliance ruptures. In J.C. Norcross (ed.) *Psychotherapy relationships that work*. Oxford: Oxford University Press.

Saleebey, D. (ed.) (2006). *The strengths perspective in social work practice* (4th edition). Boston, MA: Allyn and Bacon.

Salzberger-Wittenberg, I. (1983). Part 1: beginnings. In I. Salzberger-Wittenberg, G. Henry and E. Osborne (eds.) *The emotional experience of teaching and learning*. London: Routledge and Kegan Paul.

Sarason, B.R., Sarason, I.G. and Pierce, G.R. (1990). *Social support: an interactional view*. New York: Wiley.

Sargent, K. (1999). Assessing risk for children. In P. Parsloe (ed.) *Risk assessment in social care and social work: research highlights*. London: Jessica Kingsley.

Sawyer, G.K., Di Loreto, A.R., Flood, M.F., DiLillo, D. and Hansen, D.J. (2002, November). *Parent-child relationship and family variables as predictors of child abuse potential: implications for assessment and early intervention*. Poster presented at the 36th Annual Convention of the Association for the Advancement of Behavioral Therapy, Reno, Nevada. Retrieved 5 April 2011 from: http://www.unl.edu/ psypage/maltreatment/documents/P-crelationshipandfamilyvariablesaspredictors ofCAP.pdf

Scaife, J.A. (2004). Reliability, validity and credibility. In C. Opie (ed.) *Doing educational research*. London: Sage.

Scaife, J. (1995). *Training to help: a survival guide*. Sheffield: Riding Press.

Scaife, J. (2009). *Supervision in clinical practice: a practitioner's guide* (2nd edition). London: Routledge.

Scaife, J. (2010). *Supervising the reflective practitioner*. London: Routledge.

Scaife, J. (2012). Soapbox. Reflections on evidence and the place of reflective practice. *Clinical Child Psychology and Psychiatry*, 17(2), 208–11.

Scaife, J.A. and Wellington, J. (2010). Varying perspectives and practices in formative and diagnostic assessment: a case study. *Journal of Education for Teaching*, 36(2), 137–51.

Schaffer, H.R. (2000). Early experience and the parent-child relationship: genetic and environmental interactions as development determinants. In B. Tizard and V. Varma (eds.) *Vulnerability and resilience in human development: a festschrift for Ann and Alan Clarke.* London: Jessica Kingsley.

Schilling, R.F., Schinke, S.P., Blythe, B.J. and Barth, R.P. (1982). Child maltreatment and mentally retarded parents: is there a relationship? *Mental Retardation*, 20(5), 201–09.

Schmidt, F., Cuttress, L.J., Land, J., Lewandowski, M.J. and Rawana, J.S. (2007). Assessing the parent-child relationship in parenting capacity evaluations: clinical applications of attachment research. *Family Court Review*, 45(2), 247–59.

Schofield, G. (2009). Permanence in foster care. In G. Schofield and J. Simmonds (eds.) *The child placement handbook: research, policy and practice.* London: British Agencies for Adoption and Fostering (BAAF).

Schofield, G. and Beek, M. (2006). *Attachment handbook for foster care and adoption.* London: British Agencies for Adoption and Fostering (BAAF).

Schofield, G. and Simmonds, J. (2009). *The child placement handbook: research, policy and practice.* London: British Agencies for Adoption and Fostering (BAAF).

Schofield, G. and Simmonds, J. (2011). Contact for infants subject to care proceedings. *Family Law*, 41, 617–22.

Schofield, G. and Stevenson, O. (2009). Contact and relationships between fostered children and their birth families. In G. Schofield and J. Simmonds (eds.) *The child placement handbook: research, policy and practice.* London: British Agencies for Adoption and Fostering (BAAF).

Schofield, G. and Thoburn, J. (1996). *Child protection: the voice of the child in decision-making.* London: Institute for Public Policy Research.

Schön, D.A. (1983). *The reflective practitioner: how professionals think in action.* New York: Basic Books.

Schön, D.A. (1987). *Educating the reflective practitioner.* San Francisco, CA: Jossey Bass.

Schuckit, M.A. (2000). *Drug and alcohol abuse: a clinical guide to diagnosis and treatment* (5th edition). New York: Kluwer Academic/Plenum Publishers.

Schwalbe, C.S. (2008). Strengthening the integration of actuarial risk assessment with clinical judgement in an evidence based practice framework. *Children and Youth Services Review*, 30, 1458–64.

Scott, D. (1998). A qualitative study of social work assessment in cases of alleged child abuse. *British Journal of Social Work*, 28(1), 73–88.

Seligman, M.E.P. (1995). The effectiveness of psychotherapy: the Consumer Reports study. *American Psychologist*, 50(12), 965–74.

Sellick, C. and Thoburn, J. (1996). *What works in family placement?* London: Barnardo's.

Sellick, C., Thoburn, J. and Philpot, T. (2004). *What works in adoption and foster care?* London: Barnardo's. Summary retrieved 2 July 2011 from: http://www.barnardos.org.uk/what_works_in_adoption_and_foster_care__-_summary_1_.pdf

Selwyn, J. and Quinton, D. (2004). Stability, permanence, outcomes and support: foster care and adoption compared. *Adoption and Fostering*, 28(4), 6–15.

Sheldon, B. (1995). *Cognitive-behavioural therapy: research, practice and philosophy.* London and New York: Routledge.

Shemmings, D. and Shemmings, Y. (1995). Defining participative practice in health and welfare. In R. Jack (ed.) *Empowerment in community care.* London: Chapman and Hall.

Shlonsky, A. and Wagner, D. (2005). The next step: integrating actuarial risk assessment and clinical judgement into an evidence-based practice framework in CPS case management. *Children and Youth Services Review*, 27, 409–27.

Shmueli-Goetz, Y., Target, M., Fonagy, P. and Datta, A. (2008). The Child Attachment Interview: a psychometric study of reliability and discriminant validity. *Developmental Psychology*, 44(4), 939–56.

Simmonds, J. (2009). Adoption: developmental perspectives within an ethical, legal and policy framework. In G. Schofield and J. Simmonds (eds.) *The child placement handbook: research, policy and practice.* London: British Agencies for Adoption and Fostering (BAAF).

Sinclair, I. (2005). *Fostering now: messages from research.* London: Jessica Kingsley.

Sinclair, I. and Wilson, K. (2009). Foster care in England. In G. Schofield and J. Simmonds (eds.) *The child placement handbook: research, policy and practice.* London: British Agencies for Adoption and Fostering (BAAF).

Sinclair, I., Wilson, K. and Gibbs, I. (2000). *Supporting foster placements.* London: Interim Report to the Department of Health.

Sinclair, I., Wilson, K. and Gibbs, I. (2005). *Foster placements: why they succeed and why they fail.* London: Jessica Kingsley.

Sinclair, I., Baker, C., Lee, J. and Gibbs, I. (2007). *The pursuit of permanence: a study of the English care system.* London: Jessica Kingsley.

Slade, A., Aber, L., Bresgi, I., Berger, B. and Kaplan, M. (2004). *The Parent Development Interview-Revised.* Unpublished protocol, the City University of New York.

Slough, N.M. and Greenberg, M.T. (1990). Five-year-olds' representations of separation from parents: responses from the perspective of self and other. In I. Bretherton and M.W. Watson (eds.) *Children's perspectives on the family.* San Francisco: Jossey Bass.

Smart, C., May, V., Wade, A. and Furniss, C. (2003). *Residence and contact disputes in court (Volume 1).* London: LCD.

Smeeton, J. and Boxall, K. (2011). Birth parents' perceptions of professional practice in child care and adoption proceedings: implications for practice. *Child and Family Social Work,* 16(4), 444–53.

Smith, E.J. (1981). Cultural and historical perspectives in counseling blacks. In D.W. Sue (ed.) *Counseling the culturally different.* New York: Wiley.

Smith, R. (2008). From child protection to child safety: locating risk assessment in a changing landscape. In M.C. Calder (ed.) *Contemporary risk assessment in safeguarding children.* Lyme Regis: Russell House Publishing Ltd.

Smyke, A. and Zeanah, C. (1999). Disturbances of Attachment Interview (DAI) Unpublished manuscript. Retrieved 27 June 2011 from: http://download.lww.com/wolterskluwer_vitalstream_com/PermaLink/CHI/A/00004583-920020800-00014.doc

Sobsey, D. (2000). Faces of violence against women with developmental disabilities. *Impact,* 13(3), 2–27.

Social Care Institute for Excellence (2005). *SCIE research briefing 13: helping parents with a physical or sensory impairment in their role as parents.* Retrieved 16 December 2010 from: http://www.scie.org.uk/publications/briefings/briefing13/index.asp#key

Spain, A. (2004). *Structured decision making: an overview.* National Evaluation and TA Center for the Education of Children and Youth Who Are Neglected, Delinquent, or At-Risk. Retrieved 31 July 2010 from: http://www.neglected-delinquent.org/nd/events/2004oct/Presentations/DCRWaughstruc.doc

Spanier, G.B. (1976). Measuring dyadic adjustment: new scales for assessing the quality of marriage and similar dyads. *Journal of Marriage and the Family,* 38, 15–28.

Sparrow, S.S., Cicchetti, D.V. and Balla, D.D. (2005). *Vineland Adaptive Behaviour Scales* (2nd edition). Minneapolis, MN: Pearson.

Spielberger, C.D., Gorsuch, R.L. and Lushene. R.E. (1970). *Manual for the State-Trait Anxiety Inventory.* Palo Alto, CA: Consulting Psychologists Press.

Spielberger, C.D., Johnson, E.H., Russell, S.F., Crane, R.J., Jacobs, G.A. and Worden, T.J. (1985). The experience and expression of anger: construction and validation of an anger expression scale. In M.A. Chesney and R.H. Rosenman (eds.) *Anger and hostility in cardiovascular and behavioural disorders.* New York: Hemisphere/McGraw-Hill.

Spitzer, R., Kroenke, K., Williams, J. and Lowe, B. (2006). *A brief measure for assessing generalized anxiety disorder: the GAD-7. Archives of Internal Medicine, 166*(10), 1092–97.

Spoth, R.L., Redmond, C. and Shin, C. (2001). Randomized trial of brief family interventions for general populations: adolescent substance use outcomes 4 years following baseline. *Journal of Consulting and Clinical Psychology, 69*(4), 627–42.

Spoth, R., Randall, G.K. and Shin, C. (2008). Increasing school success through partnership-based family competency training: experimental study of long-term outcomes. *School Psychology Quarterly, 23*(1), 70–89.

Spradley J. (1989). *The ethnographic interview.* New York: Holt, Rinehart and Winston.

Sroufe, A., Egeland, B., Carlson, E. and Collins, A. (2005). *The development of the person: the Minnesota study of risk and adaptation from birth to adulthood.* New York: Guilford Press.

Steele, H. and Steele, M. (2003). *Friends and family interview coding.* Unpublished manuscript, University College London.

Steele, H. and Steele, M. (2005). The construct of coherence as an indicator of attachment security in middle childhood: the Friends and Family Interview. In K. Kerns and R. Richardson (eds.) *Attachment in middle childhood.* New York: Guilford Press.

Steele, H., Steele, M. and Fonagy, P. (1996). Associations among attachment classifications of mother, fathers, and their infants. *Child Development, 57*, 541–55.

Steinbeck, J. (2000). *The log from the Sea of Cortez.* London: Penguin Classics.

Stickland, H. and Olsen, R. (2005). Children with disabled parents. In G. Preston (ed.) *At greatest risk: the children most likely to be poor.* London: Child Poverty Action Group.

Straus, M.A. (1994). *Beating the devil out of them: corporal punishment in American families.* New York: Lexington Books.

Straus, M.A. (2007). Conflict Tactics Scales. In N.A. Jackson (ed.) *Encyclopedia of domestic violence.* New York: Routledge.

Straus, M.A. and Gelles, R.J. (1995). *Physical violence in American families: risk factors and adaptations to violence in 8,145 families.* New Brunswick, NJ: Transaction Publishers.

Strohmer, D.C., Shivy, V.A. and Chiodo, A.L. (1990). Information processing strategies in counselor hypothesis testing: the role of selective memory and expectancy. *Journal of Counseling Psychology, 37*, 465–72.

Strong, S.R. and Matross, R.P. (1973). Change processes in counseling and psychotherapy. *Journal of Counseling Psychology, 20*(1), 25–37.

Sturge, C. and Glaser, D. (2000). Contact and domestic violence—the experts' court report. *Family Law, 30*, 615–29.

Substance Abuse and Mental Health Services Administration, Office of Applied Studies (1998). *National Household Survey on drug abuse: population estimates 1997.* Rockville, MD: US Department of Health and Human Services.

Sunderland, M. and Engleheart, P. (2005). *Draw on your emotions.* Milton Keynes: Speechmark Publishing.

Sutherland, S. (2007). *Irrationality* (2nd edition). London: Pinter and Martin.

Swain, P.A. and Cameron, N. (2003). 'Good enough parenting': parental disability and child protection. *Disability and Society, 18*(2), 165–77.

Sweeney, G., Webley, P. and Treacher, A. (2001). Supervision in occupational therapy. Part 1: the supervisor's anxieties. *British Journal of Occupational Therapy Special Issue, 64*(7), 337–45.

Tangney, J.P. and Dearing, R.L. (2002). *Shame and guilt.* New York: Guilford Press.

Target, M., Fonagy, P. and Shmueli-Goetz, Y. (2003). Attachment representations in school-age children: the development of the Child Attachment Interview (CAI). *Journal of Child Psychotherapy*, 29(2), 171–86.

Tarleton, B., Ward, L. and Howarth, J. (2006). *Finding the right support?* London: Baring Foundation.

Taylor, J., Spencer, N. and Baldwin, N. (2000). Social, economic and political context of parenting. *Archives of Disease in Childhood*, 82, 113–20.

Taylor, J., Lauder, W., Moy, M. and Corlett, J. (2009). Practitioner assessments of 'good enough' parenting: factorial survey. *Journal of Clinical Nursing*, 18, 1180–89.

Terling, T. (1999). The efficacy of family reunification practices: reentry rates and correlates of reentry for abused and neglected children reunited with their families. *Child Abuse and Neglect*, 23, 1359–70.

Thoburn, J. (1988). *Child placement: principles and practice.* London: Wildwood House.

Thoburn, J. (1991). Evaluating placements and survey findings and conclusions. In J. Fratter (Ed.) *Permanent family placement: a decade of experience.* London: BAAF.

Thoburn, J. (2009). Reunification of children in out-of-home care to birth parents or relatives: a synthesis of the evidence on processes, practice and outcomes. Deutsches Jugendinstitu (DJI). Retrieved 27 April 2011 from: www.dji.de/pkh/ expertise_dji_thoburn_reunification.pdf

Thoburn, J. and Rowe, J. (1988). A snapshot of permanent family placement. *Adoption and Fostering*, 12(3), 29–34.

Thoburn, J., Lewis, A. and Shemmings, D. (1995). *Paternalism or partnership? Family involvement in the child protection process.* London: HMSO.

Thomas, A., Chess, S. and Birch, H.G. (1968). *Temperament and behaviour disorders in children.* New York: New York University Press.

Timms, J. and Thoburn, J. (2003). *Your shout! A survey of the views of 706 children and young people in care.* London: NSPCC.

Tomison, A.M. (1996). Intergenerational transmission of maltreatment. *Issues in Child Abuse Prevention, 6, Winter.* Retrieved 3 June 2012 from: http://www.aifs. gov.au/nch/pubs/issues/issues6/issues6.html

Toneatto, T. (1995). Review of the SAQ—Adult Probation (Substance Abuse Questionnaire). In J.C. Conoley and J.C. Impara (eds.) *The twelfth mental measurements yearbook.* Lincoln, NE: Buros Institute of Mental Measurements.

Totsika, V. and Sylva, K. (2004). The Home Observation for Measurement of the Environment revisited. *Child and Adolescent Mental Health*, 9(1), 25–35.

Trinder, L., Beek, M. and Connolly, J. (2005). *Making contact: how parents and children negotiate and experience contact after divorce.* York: Joseph Rowntree Foundation. Retrieved 14 January 2006 from: http://www.jrf.org.uk/knowledge/findings/ socialpolicy/092.asp

Tripp, D. (1993). *Critical incidents in teaching.* London: Routledge.

Triseliotis, J. (2002). Long-term foster care or adoption? The evidence examined. *Child and Family Social Work*, 7, 23–33.

Triseliotis, J., Borland, M., Hill, M. and Lambert, L. (1995). *Teenagers and the social work services.* London: HMSO.

Trivette, C.M. and Dunst, C.J. (1990). Assessing family strengths and family functioning style. *Topics in Early Childhood Special Education*, 10(1), 16–35.

Trommsdorf, G. (1985). Some comparative aspects of socialization in Japan and Germany. In I.R. Lagunes and Y.H. Poortinga (eds.) *From a different perspective.* Lisse: Swets and Zeitlinger.

Trotter, C., Sheehan, R. and Oliaro, L. (2001). *Decision making, case planning and case management in child protection: a review of the literature.* Melbourne: Monash University.

Tsui, M.S., Ho, W.S., and Lam, C.M. (2005). The use of supervisory authority in Chinese cultural context. *Administration in Social Work*, 29(4), 51–68.

Tunstill, J. and Aldgate, J. (2000). *From policy to practice: services for children in need.* London: The Stationery Office.

Tunstill, J. and Atherton, C. (1996). Family support and partnership: the law demands—does practice respond? In D. Batty and D. Cullen (eds.) *Child protection: the therapeutic option.* London: British Agencies for Adoption and Fostering (BAAF).

Turner, S. (2001). Resilience and social work practice: three case studies. *Families in Society* 82(5), 441–50.

Turney, D., Platt, D., Selwyn, J. and Farmer, E. (2011). *Social work assessment of children in need: what do we know? Messages from research.* Bristol: University of Bristol, School for Policy Studies.

Tymchuk, A.J. (1990). Assessing emergency responses of people with mental handicaps: an assessment instrument. *Journal of the British Institute of Mental Handicap*, 18(4), 136–42.

Tymchuk, A.J. (1991). Assessing home dangers and safety precautions. *Mental Handicap*, 19(1), 4–10.

Tymchuk, A.J. (1999). Moving toward integration of services for parents with intellectual disabilities. *Journal of Intellectual and Developmental Disability*, 24(1), 59–74.

Tymchuk, A.J. and Feldman, M.A. (1991). Parents with mental retardation and their children: a review of research relevant to professional practice. *Canadian Psychology/ Psychologie Canadienne*, 32, 486–96.

Uba, L. (1994). *Asian Americans: personality patterns, identity, and mental health.* New York: Guilford Press.

UCLA Center for Human Nutrition (n.d.). *Prochaska and DiClemente's Stages of Change Model.* Retrieved 31 January 2012 from: http://www.cellinteractive.com/ucla/physcian_ed/stages_change.html

United Nations (1989). *The United Nations Convention on the Rights of the Child.* Retrieved 23 August 2011 from: http://www2.ohchr.org/english/law/crc.htm

United States Department of Health and Human Services (2006). *Child maltreatment 2006.* Retrieved 14 July 2010 from: http://www.acf.hhs.gov/programs/cb/pubs/cm06/index.htm

University of Toronto Libraries (2000). *Introduction to EBM: what is EBM?* [online]. Toronto: University of Toronto Libraries. Retrieved 16 September 2002 from: http://www.cebm.utoronto.ca/intro/whatis/.htm

van Ijzendoorn, M. (1995). Adult attachment representations, parental responsiveness, and infant attachment: a meta-analysis on the predictive validity of the Adult Attachment Interview. *Psychological Bulletin*, 117, 387–403.

van Ijzendoorn, M., Schuengel, C. and Bakermans-Kranenburg, M. (1999). Disorganized attachment in early childhood: meta-analysis of precursors, concomitants, and sequelae. *Development and Psychopathology*, 11, 225–49.

Van Oudenhoven, J.P., Hofstra, J. and Bakker, W. (2003). Ontwikkeling en evaluatie van de hechtingstijlvragenlijst (HSL) [Development and evaluation of the Attachment Styles Questionnaire (ASQ)]. *Nederlands Tijdschrift voor de Psychologie*, 58, 95–102. Retrieved 3 July 2011 from: http://dissertations.ub.rug.nl/FILES/faculties/gmw/2009/j.hofstra/thesis.pdf

Vaughn, B.E. and Waters, E. (1990). Attachment behavior at home and in the laboratory: Q-sort observations and the Strange Situation classifications of one-year-olds. *Child Development*, 61(6), 1965–73.

Velicer, W.F., Prochaska, J.O., Fava, J.L., Norman, G.J. and Redding, C.A. (1998). Smoking cessation and stress management: applications of the Transtheoretical Model of behavior change. *Homeostasis*, 38, 216–33.

Verstegen, S., van de Goor, L. and de Zeeuw, J. (2005). *The stability assessment framework: designing integrated responses for security, governance and development.* Clingendael Institute for the Netherlands Ministry of Foreign Affairs.

Vobe, R., Bakewell, S., Collinge, C., Craig, G., Croucher, D., Gorman, T. and Scaife, J.M. (1978). *Child care task group: final report.* Nottingham: Nottinghamshire County Council.

Vygotsky, L.S. (1978). *Mind in society: the development of higher psychological processes.* Collected essays edited by M. Cole, V. John-Steiner, S. Scribner, and E. Souberman. Cambridge, MA: Harvard University Press.

Wade, C., Llewellyn, G. and Matthews, J. (2008). Review of parent training interventions for parents with intellectual disability. *Journal of Applied Research in Intellectual Disabilities, 21*(4), 351–66.

Wagnild, G.M. and Young, H.M. (1993). Development and psychometric evaluation of the Resilience Scale. *Journal of Nursing Measurement, 1,* 165–78.

Walby, S. and Allen, J. (2004). *Domestic violence, sexual assault and stalking: findings from the British Crime Survey.* London: Home Office Research. Retrieved 1 May 2011 from: http://www.broken-rainbow.org.uk/research/Dv%20crime%20survey.pdf

Wan, M.W. and Green, J. (2010). Negative and atypical story content themes depicted by children with behaviour problems. *Journal of Child Psychology and Psychiatry, 51, 1125–31.*

Ward, H. and Rose, W. (2002). *Approaches to needs assessment in children's services.* London: Jessica Kingsley.

Ward, H. and Skuse, T. (2001). Performance targets and stability of placements for children long looked after away from home. *Children and Society, 15,* 333–46.

Ward, H., Munro, E.R. and Dearden, C. (2006). *Babies and young children in care: life pathways, decision-making and practice.* London: Jessica Kingsley.

Ward, H., Brown, R., Westlake, D. and Munro, E.R. (2010). *Infants suffering, or likely to suffer, significant harm: a prospective longitudinal study.* Retrieved 5 September 2011 from: https://www.education.gov.uk/publications/eOrderingDownload/DFE-RB053.pdf

Waters, E. (1987). *Attachment Q-set (Version 3).* Retrieved 30 August 2010 from: http://www.johnbowlby.com

Waters, E. (2002). *Comments on Strange Situation classification.* Retrieved 29 August 2010 from http://www.johnbowlby.com

Waters, E. and Deane, K. (1985). Defining and assessing individual differences in attachment relationships: Q methodology and the organization of behaviour in infancy and early childhood. In I. Bretherton and E. Waters (eds.) Growing points of attachment theory and research. *Monographs of the Society for Research in Child Development, 50,* Serial no. 209 (1–2), 66–104.

Waters, E., Merrick, S., Treboux, D., Crowell, J. and Albersheim, L. (2000). Attachment security in infancy and early adulthood: a twenty-year longitudinal study. *Child Development, 71,* 684–89.

Webb, E., Ashton, C.H., Kelly, P. and Kamali, F. (1996). Alcohol and drug use in UK university students. *Lancet, 348,* 922–25.

Webster, C.D., Müller-Isberner, R. and Fransson, G. (2002). Violence risk assessment: using structured clinical guides professionally. *International Journal of Forensic Mental Health, 1*(2), 185–93.

Webster-Stratton, C. (1990). Long-term follow-up of families with young conduct-problem children: from pre-school to grade school. *Journal of Clinical Child Psychology, 19*(2), 144–49.

Webster-Stratton, C., Reid, M. and Hammond, M. (2004). Treating children with early-onset conduct problems: intervention outcomes for parent, child, and teacher training. *Journal of Clinical Child and Adolescent Psychology, 33,* 105–24.

Wedge, P. and Mantle, G. (1991). *Sibling groups and social work: a study of children referred for permanent substitute family placement.* Aldershot: Avebury.

Weerasekera, P. (1996). *Multiperspective case formulation: a step towards treatment integration.* Melbourne: Krieger Publishing.

Weinfield, N., Whaley, G. and Egeland, B. (2004). Continuity, discontinuity, and coherence in attachment from infancy to late adolescence: sequelae of organization and disorganization. *Attachment and Human Development*, 6, 73–97.

Werner, E. and Smith, R. (1992). *Overcoming the odds: high-risk children from birth to adulthood.* New York: Cornell University Press.

Westcott, H., Davies, G.M. and Bull, R.H.C. (2002). *Children's testimony: a handbook of psychological research and forensic practice.* Chichester: John Wiley and Sons Ltd.

Whitehead, A.N. (1978). *Process and reality.* New York: The Free Press.

Whitman, B. and Accardo, P. (1990). *When a parent is mentally retarded.* Baltimore, MD: Paul H. Brookes.

Whitman, B., Graves, B. and Accardo, P. (1989). Training in parenting skills for adults with mental retardation. *Social Work*, 34(5), 431–34.

Wiebush, R., Freitag, R. and Baird, C. (2001). *Preventing delinquency through improved child protection services.* Washington, DC: Office of Juvenile Justice and Delinquency Prevention. Retrieved 18 July 2010 from: www.ncjrs.gov/pdffiles1/ojjdp/187759.pdf

Wilson, K. (2006). Can foster carers help children resolve their emotional and behavioural difficulties? *Clinical Child Psychology and Psychiatry*, 11(4), 495–511.

Winnicott, D.W. (1964). *The child, the family and the outside world.* London: Penguin.

Winters, K. (1991). *Manual for the Personal Experience Screening Questionnaire (PESQ).* Los Angeles, CA: Western Psychological Services.

Winters, K.C. (1992). Development of an adolescent alcohol and other drug abuse screening scale: Personal Experiences Screening Questionnaire. *Addictive Behaviors*, 17, 479–90.

Wolin, S.J. and Wolin, S. (1993). *The resilient self: how survivors of troubled families rise above adversity.* New York: Villard Books.

Wood, C.D. and Davidson, J.A. (2002). Emotional skills and stress: parents' stress reduction following PET training in empathic listening, non-antagonistic assertiveness and family conflict resolution. *Australian Journal of Psychology*, 54 (Suppl.), 64.

Wood, J., McClure, K. and Birch, R. (1996). Suggestions for improving interviews in child protection agencies. *Child Maltreatment*, 1, 223–30.

Woods, P.J. and Ellis, A. (1997). Supervision in rational emotive behaviour therapy. In C.E. Watkins Jr (ed.) *Handbook of psychotherapy supervision.* New York: Wiley.

World Health Organization (1992). *International Statistical Classification of Diseases and Related Health Problems, Tenth Revision (ICD-10).* Geneva: World Health Organization.

World Health Organization (2002). 55th World Health Assembly. *Infant and young child nutrition.* (WHA55.25). Retrieved 22 February 2011 from: http://apps.who.int/gb/archive/pdf_files/WHA55/ewha5525.pdf

World Health Organization (2010a). *Mental health: definition: intellectual disability.* Retrieved 22 December 2010 from: http://www.euro.who.int/en/what-we-do/health-topics/diseases-and-conditions/mental-health/news2/news/2010/15/childrens-right-to-family-life/definition-intellectual-disability

World Health Organization (2010b). *Lexicon of alcohol and drug terms.* Retrieved 15 December 2010 from: http://www.who.int/substance_abuse/terminology/who_lexicon/en/index.html

World Health Organization (2011). The World Health Organization's infant feeding recommendation. Retrieved 22 February 2011 from: http://www.who.int/nutrition/topics/infantfeeding_recommendation/en/index.html

World Health Organization (n.d.). *Mastering depression in primary care*. Retrieved 3 December 2010 from: http://www.gp-training.net/protocol/psychiatry/who/whodep.htm#Scoring

Wright, J.C., Binney, V. and Smith, P.K. (1995). Security of attachment in 8- to 12-year-olds: a revised version of the Separation Anxiety Test, its psychometric properties, and clinical interpretation. *Journal of Child Psychology and Psychiatry*, *36*, 757–74.

Young, J. and Neil, E. (2009). Contact after adoption. In G. Schofield and J. Simmonds (eds.) *The child placement handbook: research, policy and practice*. London: British Agencies for Adoption and Fostering (BAAF).

Young, P. (2000). 'I might as well give up': self esteem and mature students' feelings about feedback on assignments. *Journal of Further and Higher Education*, *24*(3), 409–418.

Young, S., Young, B. and Ford, D. (1997). Parents with a learning disability: research issues and informed practice. *Disability and Society 12*, 57–68.

Zeanah, C.H. and Benoit, D. (1995). Clinical applications of a parent perception interview in infant mental health. *Child and Adolescent Psychiatric Clinics of North America*, *4*, 539–54.

Zeanah, C.H., Benoit, D. and Barton, M. (1993). *Working Model of the Child Interview*. Retrieved 3 April 2011 from: http://www.oaimh.org/newsFiles/Working_Model_of_the_Child_Interview.pdf

Zeanah, C.H., Scheeringa, M., Boris, N.W., Heller, S.S., Smyke, A.T. and Trapani, J. (2004). Reactive attachment disorder in maltreated toddlers. *Child Abuse and Neglect*, *28*, 877–88.

Zigmond, A.S. and Snaith, R.P. (1983). The Hospital Anxiety and Depression Scale. *Acta Psychiatrica Scandinavica*, *67*, 361–70.

Zimet, G.D., Dahlem, N.W., Zimet, S.G. and Farley, G.K. (1988). The Multidimensional Scale of Perceived Social Support. *Journal of Personality Assessment*, *52*, 30–41.

Zuravin, S., McMillen, C., DePanfilis, D., and Risley-Curtiss, C. (1996). The intergenerational cycle of child maltreatment. *Journal of Interpersonal Violence*, *11*(3), 315–34.

Zuravin, S., Orme, J. and Hegar, R. (1995). Disposition of child physical abuse reports: review of the literature and test of a predictive model. *Children and Youth Services Review*, *17*, 547–66.

Glossary

This glossary defines terms used in the UK. USA terms follow in brackets. It is a glossary of terms used in family proceedings with which readers may need to be familiar, rather than a reference for terms used in the text.

Addressing judges

In the county court, district judges, recorders and assistant recorders are addressed as 'sir' or 'madam' and circuit judges as 'your honour'. In all higher courts they are addressed as 'my lord' and 'my lady', but the same person may hear cases in different levels of court and is addressed differently according to the level of the court, i.e. 'my lady' in a higher court or 'your honour' in a lower court.

Adoption order

An adoption order can be sought once a child has been living with prospective adopters for a period of time (from 10 weeks to one year depending on circumstances). An adoption order gives Parental Responsibility (PR) to the adopters and extinguishes the PR which any person or local authority has for the child.

Affirming and being under oath

Witnesses are asked by the court usher to swear on the bible or affirm that they will tell the truth. The usher provides a card from which to read the statement of truth. Once under oath, witnesses are required not to discuss the matter with any of the parties. If the examination goes on over a lunch break or over several days, this pertains throughout.

CAFCASS: Child and family court advisory and support service

The organisation which employs children's guardians who are appointed to represent the child's view, and family reporters who provide welfare reports to the court and may set up mediation sessions to help separating and divorcing parents reach agreement on plans for the future care of the children.

CAMHS: Child and adolescent mental health services

The multi-disciplinary service to children, young people and their families which is provided in the UK by the National Health Service. The team typically comprises the disciplines of psychiatry, psychology, social work, nursing and possibly a range of therapies. Referral to the multi-disciplinary team is usually through the family general practitioner.

Capacity assessments

Psychologists and psychiatrists may be asked to ascertain the extent of parents' understanding of the proceedings and give an opinion as to whether they have the capacity effectively to instruct a solicitor. If not, and parents have no friends or family who are prepared to undertake the role, the official solicitor may be asked to act in the best interests of the parent.

Care order

An Order of the Court under Section 31 of the Children Act 1989. An Interim Order allows the local authority to share parental responsibility for a child and determine (after consultation) important issues affecting a child. This would include where a child should live and with whom. This can only be made when the child concerned is suffering, or is likely to suffer significant harm, that the harm, or likelihood of harm is attributable to the care given to the child or likely to be given to him if the Order were not made, not being what it would be reasonable to expect a parent to give; or the child's being beyond parental control. Care Orders may be Interim, whilst investigations are carried out, or Full. A Full Care Order lasts until a child is 18 years old or earlier married. Applications can be made for its discharge.

Care plan

A plan drawn up by the local authority for each child for the final hearing in care proceedings. It will contain details of residence and contact and how the child's welfare will be secured.

Child in need assessment

An initial assessment carried out at the point of referral and conducted under section 17 of the Children Act 1989. A Child in Need is one who is unlikely to experience a reasonable standard of health or development without assistance, or their health or development is likely to be significantly impaired without assistance, or they have a disability. A Child in Need Plan outlines the support that the child and family need and how it will be provided in order for the child to experience adequate health and development. Such assessments also seek evidence as to whether a child is suffering, or is likely to suffer, 'significant harm' due to parental actions or omissions.

Children act 1989

With subsequent modifications this still comprises the basis for decisions in the care of children in the UK.

Children's guardian (Guardian ad litem)

An experienced social worker employed by the Child and Family Court Advisory and Support Service (CAFCASS) to ensure that the child's welfare is paramount. The guardian appoints a legal representative for the child who is usually the lead solicitor.

Confidentiality

In family proceedings nothing can be 'off the record' and if respondents ask that something they are about to say be kept confidential they need to be assured that this is not possible. Expert reports are the property of the court and copies cannot be given to anyone else without the consent of the court. In practice the report is sent to the lead solicitor who lodges it with the court and ensures its distribution to the advocates for the other parties.

Consent

Expert witnesses cannot assume that they have permission to see children or to see them without the presence of the care-giver. This needs to be established with the lead solicitor and a case may need to be made for the child being seen alone. Although parents do not need to give consent for children to be assessed, it may work to their disadvantage if they refuse.

Contact order (Visitation order)

An order requiring the individual with whom a child lives (or is to live) to visit or stay with the individual named in the order. Contact Orders often specify details of times and days.

Contemporaneous notes

A note needs to be kept of all conversations, any test results and question-naires. They need to be kept for a minimum of 6 years after the conclusion of the case and if they pertain to children, until the child reaches the age of majority or much longer if the child has been in the care of the local authority.

Core assessment

In the UK the Core Assessment is an in-depth assessment addressing the needs of a child and the capacity of her or his care-givers to meet them in the context of the wider family and community. It commences following an initial assessment when a child is thought to have been harmed or at risk of harm. The assessment is then carried out under section 47 of the Children Act, 1989.

Core group

A Core Group of professionals is identified at the initial child protection conference to develop, oversee, manage and implement the child protection plan. The Core Group at a minimum should meet to review the plan on a monthly basis. The Initial Review Child Protection Case Conference takes place after three months with subsequent conferences taking place a minimum of every six months.

Court levels

The lowest tier of the family court is the Family Proceedings Court (Magistrates' Court), presided over by either lay magistrates supported by legal advisors, or district judges. More complex cases may at any point be transferred to the nearest County Court that is a designated Care Centre. The Care Centres are presided over by district judges or circuit judges. Each Care Centre has a designated family judge presiding over more complex cases. The Family Division of the High Court, presided over by high court judges and led by the president of the family division, may be referred complicated family cases.

Covert video surveillance (CVS)

Can be ordered if medical information suggests harm to the child as in suspected Fabricated and Induced Illness (FII).

Criminal records bureau (CRB)

People working with children are exempt from the Rehabilitation of Offenders Act and must declare any prior or pending offences in an application to the Criminal Records Bureau. This check needs to be made before being allowed unsupervised access to children.

Cross examination

After the Examination in Chief by the solicitor who called the practitioner as a witness, cross examination is carried out by each of the other parties' advocates. They do so with the aim of progressing their party's case and undermining the case of the other parties. Re-examination may follow.

Diagnostic and statistical manual (DSM-IV)

The official classification system used in the USA by psychiatrists. It contains a description of mental health disorders.

Emergency protection order (Emergency custody order)

Introduced in the Children Act 1989 to replace the Place of Safety Order. It provides for a quick but temporary response to a child protection crisis, using limited court procedures which require less preparation than care proceedings and empowers the applicant to remove or detain a child for up to eight days.

Every child matters

A set of reforms supported by the Children Act 2004. Its aim is for every child, whatever their background or circumstances, to have the support they need to:

- be healthy
- stay safe
- enjoy and achieve
- make a positive contribution
- achieve economic well-being

It requires local authorities to work with its partners, through Children's Trust Partnerships, to find out what works best for children and young people in its area and to act on this, involving children and young people in the process.

Examination in Chief

At the start of giving their evidence, experts are asked to outline their full name, qualifications, experience, and professional address. It may be helpful to have a written concise summary available to read out. The solicitor who called the witness (usually the lead solicitor) asks questions. This stage is called Examination in Chief.

Expert immunity

For 400 years, expert witnesses had immunity from being sued for negligence in the civil courts. This was overturned by a decision of the Supreme Court in March 2011. Professional indemnity insurance covers experts in the event of such claims.

Expertise

It is important for practitioners to remain within their area of expertise and refuse to be drawn into answering questions that are outside their knowledge and experience.

Family assistance order

Allows for the provision of assistance to families following parental separation or divorce.

Final hearing

When the investigation is complete, the judge makes a decision on the case. If the parties agree, there is no need for a full hearing. If there is still disagreement, the hearing is contested and each party gives evidence. The witnesses can be questioned. The hearing concludes with a judgement.

Finding of fact hearing

This is heard in the civil court rather than the criminal court. The standard of proof is 'on the balance of probabilities' rather than 'beyond reasonable doubt'. Once a judgement has determined the Facts practitioners must not 'go behind the Facts' in their assessments and evidence. The Facts are unassailable and equivalent to a conviction in a criminal court.

Framework for the assessment of children and their families

Introduced in the UK in 2000 in order to promote a systematic approach to assessment of families. A triangle is used to represent the three inter-related dimensions of the child's developmental needs, parenting capacity and the family in its wider environment.

Human rights

Article 8 of the European Convention on Human Rights guarantees the right of respect for family life. It is a qualified, not an absolute right. This article underpins decisions about the placement of children since placement away from the birth family, unless absolutely necessary, is a violation of human rights and local authority intervention must be proportionate.

Initial assessment

Used in the UK to denote an assessment of a Child in Need under section 17 of the Children Act 1989.

International classification of disease (ICD-10)

The official diagnostic classification system used in the UK by psychiatrists. Contains a description of mental health disorders.

Issues resolution hearing

A hearing involving care-givers and their advocates, the social worker, children's guardian and judge with a view to determining the issues about which decisions will need to be made at the final hearing.

Lead solicitor

This is normally the solicitor for the child who has been instructed by the Children's Guardian. The lead solicitor is generally the person to whom an expert witness will direct questions on matters about which they are unsure.

Local safeguarding children board (LSCB)

In the UK the LSCB replaced the Area Child Protection Committee as the key statutory mechanism for promoting cooperation between agencies to safeguard and promote the welfare of children in a particular locality (HM Government (2006) *Working together to safeguard children*).

Official solicitor

The official solicitor may be asked to act for parents who have been determined as lacking capacity. The role involves acting in the best interest of the parents, taking all measures necessary on behalf of the parents, taking full account of all the evidence, ensuring that appropriate assessments have been conducted bearing in mind the lack of capacity. The role of the Official Solicitor is to mitigate disadvantage resulting from disability or age and vulnerability to social exclusion.

Paramountcy principle (Best interests of the child standard)

A legal imperative that in family proceedings the welfare of the child is paramount.

Parental responsibility (PR)

Mothers have this automatically as do fathers if the parents were married at the time of the child's birth or conception. Since 1st December 2003, any father who registers the child's birth with the mother or makes a statutory declaration of paternity also automatically has parental responsibility.

If a child is looked-after by the local authority the local authority shares parental responsibility. Only people with parental responsibility can make certain decisions, e.g. about medical and dental treatment, trips abroad.

Placement order

An order authorising a local authority to place a child with prospective adopters where there is no parental consent, or where consent should be dispensed with. Placement by consent is the free unconditional agreement of the parent or guardian of a child to that child's adoption. The consent can be withdrawn at any time up and until an adoption order is made. Parental consent is not valid if given in the first six weeks following the child's birth. Placement Orders can be made at the same time as a Care Order, to allow the local authority to place a child with adopters.

Practice direction for expert witnesses

This lays out the requirements of the expert in terms of issues such as absence of conflict of interest, compliance to offer opinions only within areas of expertise, the requirement to lay out the strength of evidence in support of the expert's opinion and any counter-evidence, the degree of certainty with which the opinion is held, capability to comply with the timescale etc. Experts are required to make a statement of compliance with the practice direction in their reports.

Professional indemnity insurance

Professional indemnity (PI) insurance protects professionals against claims made against them by a past or present client. It covers the legal defence costs, as well as any damages payable if a client suffers a loss that could be attributed to an expert's failure to uphold professional standards. A client's loss can be material, financial or physical.

Professionals' meeting

These are arranged in advance of final hearings in order to establish areas of agreement and disagreement between the parties. They are intended to reduce the amount of time needed to debate these issues in court and to minimise contested areas.

Prohibited steps order

An order that prevents a parent from an action relating to their child such as taking the child abroad without the agreement of the other parent, or preventing a change of surname.

Public and private law

Public law applies to care proceedings. Private law applies when a case is contested between divorcing or separated parents.

Public law outline

This is a framework which prescribes the functioning of the court. It has replaced the 'protocol' and its aim is to make cases run more smoothly, thus avoiding delays. It emphasises consistency, judicial continuity and active case management. It can be downloaded from: http://www.judiciary.gov.uk/

NR/rdonlyres/A61353A8-AD84-491F-9614-5A95F1A90837/0/public_
law_outline.pdf

Residence and contact (Custody and visitation)

The terms used to describe with whom a child lives and whom they see. In the UK these have replaced the terms 'custody' and 'access'.

Residence order

This sets out where and with whom a child should live. It confers parental responsibility on the holder if it is not already held (e.g. grandparent) but can only be made in exceptional circumstances after the child is sixteen. Under this order parents share PR.

Special guardianship order (SGO)

These are intended to secure a child's long-term future when adoption would be inappropriate, for example in the case of unaccompanied asylum seekers and when it is considered in the child's interests to retain a significant link with the birth family. A Special Guardian obtains parental responsibility (PR) and permission to exercise it without consultation with others who have PR. There are specific rules about who can apply.

Specific issue order

This determines a particular issue about which parents have been unable to agree, such as preventing contact with a particular person, the type of school the child should attend, or a decision regarding medical treatment.

Strategy meeting

Convened by the local authority when there is reasonable cause to believe that a child may be suffering or likely to suffer significant harm.

Threshold criteria

The conditions that must be met if a care order is to be granted. The test is of whether the child is suffering or likely to suffer significant harm as a result of the care being provided.

Welfare checklist

A list of the factors that the court must consider in deciding what is in the child's interests. It includes the ascertainable wishes and feelings of the child, the child's physical, emotional and educational needs, the likely effect of the change of circumstances on the child, age, sex and background, any harm suffered or the risk thereof, capability of care-givers to meet the child's needs and the range of the court's powers.

Appendix 1   Assessment methods for children's attachment and adult romantic relationships

Method	Reference	Age	Accessibility for Clinical Assessment
Observational Methods			
Strange Situation	Main and Soloman (1990)	9–20 months	Requires trained coders. Informal observations of separation and reunion of child and care-giver may provide useful information. Scoring guidance available from: Waters (2002) at http://www.johnbowlby.com
Preschool Strange Situation	Cassidy et al. (1992)	3–4 years	Unpublished coding guidelines.
Attachment classification system for kindergarten-age children	Main and Cassidy (1988)	6-year-olds	Requires extensive training for the coding process.
Preschool Assessment of Attachment (PAA)	Crittenden (1988–1994)	18 months–5 years	Categorises into Secure/Balanced, Defended and Coercive. Details can be accessed at: http://www.patcrittenden.com/include/preschool_assessment.htm
Attachment Q-set Version 3	Waters and Deane (1985) Waters (1987)	1–5 years	Q-set items are sorted by an observer (or a care-giver) into a number of piles based on how accurately the statements characterise a child's behaviour. Results in scores on 'Security' and 'Dependency' continua. Q-set items and sorting guidance may be downloaded from the measurement library at: http://www.johnbowlby.com. A method is described in Vaughn and Waters (1990).

(Continued)

Method	Reference	Age	Accessibility for Clinical Assessment
Attachment Observation Checklist	Fahlberg (1991)		A set of guidelines for observation of parents and children in different age ranges, listing those behaviours from the parent towards the child which would give an indication of the quality of the parent-child relationship.
Marschak Interaction Method (MIM)	Lindaman *et al.* (2000)	Pre-natal to adolescent versions	Assesses relationship in the categories 'Structure', 'Engagement', 'Nurture' and 'Challenge'. Not an assessment of attachment but may give indications. Extensive clinical experience necessary. Recording usually made for discussion with carer. Associated with Theraplay.

Picture Response Tasks

Method	Reference	Age	Accessibility for Clinical Assessment
Separation Anxiety Test (SAT) and variants	Hansburg (1972) Jacobsen *et al.* (1994) Slough and Greenberg (1990)	11–17 years 7–15 years 4–7 years	Uses pen and ink drawings or photographs of separation-related themes from mild to stressful. Child is asked how the child in the picture feels and what they will do. Most recent version eradicates emotional expression from pictures. Variable in terms of reliability and validity about which limited information is available.
	Wright *et al.* (1995)		This variant uses nine photographs designed to assess children's narrative responses to representations of separation from parents.
School-age Assessment of Attachment (SAA)	Crittenden *et al.* (2010)	5–12 years	Seven picture cards are used to elicit fantasy stories and recalled episodes. A preliminary validity and reliability study has been conducted. Yields one of 13 classifications within the Dynamic-Maturational Model of attachment and adaptation (DMM).

(Continued)

Method	Reference	Age	Accessibility for Clinical Assessment
Bené–Anthony Family Relations Test	Bené and Anthony (1957) Revised 1978 and 1985	Less than 6–8 years Over 6–8 years Adult version Couples version	Uses posting boxes on the front of which are drawn line figures which the child selects to represent family members. The respondent posts a series of cards on which are written positive and negative outgoing and incoming feelings. The test provides an indication of degree of emotional involvement, rather than attachment style, based on total cards posted into each character, and of the direction and degree of feelings expressed towards each character. Can be purchased from: www. gl-assessment.co.uk. Restricted access.

Narrative Story Stem Approaches

Method	Reference	Age	Accessibility for Clinical Assessment
MacArthur Story Stem Battery (MSSB)	Bretherton and Oppenheim (2003)	3–8 years	Variation in coding dependent on purpose. There is a rigorous manual but the measure has not been standardised.
Attachment Story Completion Test (ASCT)	Bretherton *et al.* (1990)	3 years	Story stems include themes of spilled juice, hurt knee, monster in the bedroom, departure and reunion. Bretherton *et al.* reported good validity
Story Stem Assessment Profile (SSAP)	Hodges *et al.* (2004, 2009)	4–8 years	Unpublished coding guidelines. Story stems can be accessed in Hodges *et al.* (2003).

(Continued)

Method	Reference	Age	Accessibility for Clinical Assessment
Manchester Child Attachment Story Task (MCAST)	Green *et al.* (2000)	4½–8½ years	Coding and analysis of response requires specialised training.
Electronic version available (CMAST)	Minnis *et al.* (2008)	4½–8½ years	Aim of its development was to create a measure with enhanced reliability for large-scale use. Requires minimal training and can be used on any PC. Classifies as Insecure-avoidant, Secure, Insecure-resistant/ ambivalent and Insecure-disorganised. Training workshops are available contact: jonathan.green@ manchester.ac.uk
Additional story stem approaches	Bettmann and Lundahl (2007)	3–10 years	The authors review 13 story stem approaches and summarise key characteristics and sources.

Interview Methods

Method	Reference	Age	Accessibility for Clinical Assessment
Adult Attachment Interview (AAI)	George *et al.* (1996)	Adults	Unpublished coding manual. Specialist training required for administration and interpretation. AAI interview questions can be accessed at: http://www. psychology.sunysb.edu/ attachment/measures/content/ aai_interview.pdf
Current Relationship Interview (CRI)	Crowell and Owens (1998)	Adults	Parallels the AAI but the questions reflect the reciprocal nature of adult relationships. Logic and procedures for scoring the CRI closely parallel those for the AAI. Scoring can be accessed at: http://www. psychology.sunysb.edu/ attachment/measures/content/ cri_manual_4.pdf
Child Attachment Interview	Target *et al.* (2003)	7–12 years	Protocol available as appendix in Shmueli-Goetz *et al.* (2008).

(Continued)

Method	Reference	Age	Accessibility for Clinical Assessment
Friends and Family Interview	Steele and Steele (2003, 2005)	11 years and above	Unpublished manual. Training is required for administration and coding. The full FFI protocol and scoring system are available from the authors: steeleh@newschool.edu
Attachment Interview for Childhood and Adolescence (AICA)	Ammaniti *et al.* (1990)	10–14 years	Unpublished protocol. Specialist training required for administration and coding.
Disturbances of Attachment Interview (DAI)	Smyke and Zeanah (1999)	Childhood disorders of attachment	Assesses for reactive attachment disorder. Training advised before utilisation. Unpublished but questionnaire and scoring can be downloaded from: http://download.lww.com/wolterskluwer_vitalstream_com/PermaLink/CHI/A/00004583-920020800-00014.doc
Attachment Style Interview	Bifulco *et al.* (1998, 2002)	Adults	Assesses quality of close relationships, social support and attachment style on a three-point scale in the five categories: Secure, Enmeshed, Fearful, Angry-dismissive and Withdrawn.
Versions for Adoption and Fostering (ASI-AF) and Child Care (ASI-CC)	Bifulco *et al.* (2008)		Developed with a view to assessing prospective adopters and foster carers. Attendance at four-day training workshop required to ensure reliability and obtain ASI pack. Information can be obtained from: http://www.rhul.ac.uk/Health-and-SocialCare/Research/LRG.html

Questionnaire Methods

Method	Reference	Age	Accessibility for Clinical Assessment
Relationship Questionnaire	Bartholomew and Horowitz (1991)	Adults	Explores adult attachments to partners, resulting in classification into Secure, Preoccupied, Dismissive and Fearful.

(Continued)

Method	Reference	Age	Accessibility for Clinical Assessment
Experiences in Close Relationships – Revised (ECR-R)	Fraley *et al.* (2000)	Adults	Questionnaire assessing adult experiences in romantic relationships. Downloadable from: http://www.psych.illinois.edu/~rcfraley/measures/ecrritems.htmOnline version available from: http://www.web-research-design.net/cgi-bin/crq/crq.pl
Attachment Questionnaire	Hazan and Shaver (1987)	Adults	A single-item measure of three attachment styles was designed by translating Ainsworth's descriptions of infants into terms appropriate to adult love.
Attachment Style Classification Questionnaire	Finzi *et al.* (1996) Published in Hebrew	Children in middle childhood	An adaptation of the Attachment Questionnaire with 15 items. Attachment classification in three categories: Secure, Anxious/Ambivalent and Avoidant. Can be obtained from author at: http://www.biu.ac.il/faculty/rikifnz
Vulnerable Attachment Style Questionnaire (VASQ)	Bifulco *et al.* (2003)	Adults	Brief self-report measure based on Attachment Style Interview. Designed to assess attachment style in relation to depression and poor social support. Two factors of 'insecurity' and 'proximity-seeking' were devised.
Attachment Style Questionnaire	Van Oudenhoven *et al.* (2003)	Adults	Assesses the attachment categories, Secure, Dismissing, Preoccupied and Fulfilling.
Parent Attachment Diary	Dozier and Stovall (1997)	Child attachment behaviours	Formal training recommended. Authors will send examples of coded diaries to try to establish reliability of new coders. Can be accessed at: http://icp.psych.udel.edu/Publications.html

Appendix 2   Questionnaires for assessment of adults

In this appendix, I list questionnaire measures that I have found useful in supplementing interview data, the results of which can contribute to the process of triangulation. The results need to be viewed with caution, given the motivation of respondents in family proceedings to second guess 'right' answers. The majority of these measures do not require particular professional qualifications for administration but results may indicate referral to a specialist. Companies that sell assessment materials often provide information about the nature of the qualifications needed. Pearson UK, for example, use the category system 'UNAS' (unassigned and available to all), 'CL3' for which advanced training is not needed, 'CL2R' for which the practitioner needs to be certified by a professional organisation. This includes speech therapists, psychologists, health professionals and social workers. 'CL2' requires a qualification that indicates competence in test administration. This includes social workers who hold a postgraduate diploma, postgraduate degree or certificate of quality in social work. Questionnaires that require greater specificity of qualification are generally not included in my selection.

The *Mental Measurements Yearbook* is a source of independent reviews of such assessment measures. The reviews contain descriptive information and an evaluation of each measure's technical properties including studies of validity and reliability. Reviewers do not mince their words: 'There is continued doubt ... that the test "conveys any useful information additional to simply asking the client if they have an alcohol-drug problem, if they are violent, and how they cope with stress"' (Toneatto, 1995: 891). The Yearbook is published by the Buros Institute of Mental Measurements. Reviews can also be accessed online at: http://www.unl.edu/buros.

Self-esteem

The Internalised Shame Scale (ISS) (Cook, 1994, 2001) is a self-report questionnaire from which a 'Shame Score' is derived. It includes self-esteem items that can be scored separately and used as an indication of positive self-esteem. Cook argues that feelings of shame can be translated into feelings of inferiority, worthlessness, inadequacy and emptiness. The scale is marketed by MHS (https://ecom.mhs.com). It incorporates some items from the Rosenberg Self Esteem Scale.

The **Rosenberg Self Esteem Scale** (Rosenberg, 1989) is widely used in social science research. It can be downloaded from several websites including http://www.bsos.umd.edu/socy/research/rosenberg.htm.

The **Self-Image Profile for Adults** (Butler and Gasson, 2006) has been validated on a large British population and is published by Hogrefe.

The **Test of Self-Conscious Affect-3** (**TOSCA-3**) presents 11 negative and five positive scenarios and yields scores on the dimensions of Shame-proneness, Guilt-proneness, Externalization, Detachment/Unconcern, and Pride. It is published together with scoring guidelines in Tangney and Dearing (2002: 207). There are adapted versions for adolescents and children. The relevance of the TOSCA scales is limited by the nature of the scenarios presented. They were designed for use with college students. Many of the scenarios address work situations which are unlikely to be encountered by the adults being assessed in family proceedings. They were found to be similarly unsuited to the assessment of people admitted to an acute psychiatric hospital in the USA (Averill *et al.*, 2002).

The **Harder Personal Feelings Questionnaire-2** (**PFQ2**) (Harder and Zalma, 1990) has been shown to distinguish feelings of shame from guilt.

Excellent descriptive summaries of multiple scales designed to assess shame and related constructs can be found in Robins *et al.* (2007) and Robinson *et al.* (1991).

Sociability

Personality Test Subscales. The interpersonal characteristics of warmth and sociability are factors that are measured by some personality assessment instruments such as the California Psychological Inventory, of which one 'folk scale' is 'sociability'. One of the interpersonal scales of the Personality Assessment Inventory (PAI) assesses 'warmth'. The MMPI-2 has a scale entitled 'social discomfort' which in lay terms might be thought of as 'shyness' or unsociability. Users require specific qualifications.

The **Inventory of Interpersonal Problems–Circumplex** (**IIP–C**) (Alden *et al.*, 1990) is a self-report instrument that assesses a person's most salient interpersonal difficulties. There is a short version, the IIP–SC (Hopwood *et al.*, 2008) which has been validated both with college students and used with clinical samples. It yields scores on the dimensions: Domineering/Controlling (a high score indicates that the person finds it difficult to relax control over other people), Vindictive/Self-Centred (the person readily experiences and expresses anger and irritability, is preoccupied with revenge, and tends to fight with others), Cold/Distant (a high score indicates minimal feelings of affection for and little connection with other people),

Socially Inhibited (a high score indicates feelings of anxiety, timidity, or embarrassment in the presence of other people), Non-assertive (a high score indicates a significant lack of self-confidence, low self-esteem, and reluctance to show assertiveness), Overly Accommodating (a high score indicates excessive readiness to yield in a friendly way to the influence of others), Self-Sacrificing (a high score indicates a tendency to empathise with others in need and nurture them, even when so doing requires sacrifice of own needs), Intrusive/Needy (a high score indicates a need to be both friendly and controlling, sociable to the extent that others experience as excessively intrusive into their affairs). It can be obtained from Mind Garden at: http://www.mindgarden.com/products/iip.htm

The Revised Cheek and Buss Shyness Scale (RCBS) (Cheek, 1983) is designed to assess the 'unsociable' or shyness aspect of temperament. It is a development from the original nine-item scale devised by Cheek and Buss (1981). It can be downloaded free from: http://www.wellesley.edu/Psychology/Cheek/research.html.

Anger

The State-Trait Anger Expression Inventory (STAXI-II) (Spielberger *et al.*, 1985), available from Psychological Assessment Resources, attempts to measure to what extent people's angry feelings constitute a stable trait and to what extent they are responsive to current stressors. The questionnaire results also give an indication of the manner in which people handle their angry feelings; the degree to which these are suppressed and the extent to which they are expressed. 'State anger' is defined as an emotional state marked by subjective feelings that vary in intensity from mild irritation to intense fury and rage. 'Trait anger' is defined in terms of individual differences in the disposition to perceive a wide range of situations as annoying or frustrating and by the tendency to respond to such situations with elevations in state anger.

The Novaco Anger Scale and Provocation Inventory (NAS-PI) (Novaco, 1994) can be obtained from Western Psychological Services and Hogrefe UK. It is a self-report measure comprising the Novaco Anger Scale of 60 items which focus on how an individual experiences anger and the Provocation Inventory of 25 items which focus on the kinds of situations that can generate anger. It is regarded as having predictive capability for violent behaviour for people with mental health difficulties who are being considered for discharge from hospital into the community.

Resilience

The Resilience Scale (Wagnild and Young, 1993) can be obtained from: http://www.resiliencescale.com/. The scale is free to download and the user guide can be purchased from this site.

The Connor-Davidson Resilience Scale (CD-RISC) (Connor and Davidson, 2003), a more recently constructed measure, was designed to assess the capability to cope with stress. Twenty-five items are rated on a five-point scale. On this measure, clinical populations of clients showed lower resilience than the standardisation sample, especially those who had received a diagnosis of Post-Traumatic Stress Syndrome.

Anxiety, depression and mental health screening questionnaires

The General Health Questionnaire (GHQ-28) (Goldberg and Hillier, 1979) is a 28-item self-administered screening questionnaire designed for use in community settings to detect those with a diagnosable psychiatric disorder. The scale gives a useful measure of relative psychological difficulty. It is obtainable from GL Assessment (http://shop.gl-assessment.co.uk/home. php?cat=416), and also as one of the measures in a pack designed to aid clinicians in working with people experiencing symptoms of post-traumatic stress disorder (Measures in Post Traumatic Stress Disorders: A Practitioner's Guide, edited by Stuart Turner and Deborah Lee). This pack allows the purchaser to make multiple copies of the assessment questionnaires that are included. It is out-of-print at the time of writing. The GHQ measures symptoms within four categories: somatic symptoms; anxiety and insomnia; social dysfunction; and severe depression. The overall total can be used as an indicator of 'caseness'. A total score above the cut-off of seven is regarded as positive for mental health difficulties (Goldberg *et al.*, 1997) and a score over 13 has been used to indicate the presence of a psychiatric condition (Easton and Turner, 1991).

The World Health Organization WHO-Five Well-being Index (WHO-Five) and the Major (ICD-10) Depression Inventory (MDI) (World Health Organization, n.d.) may both be downloaded from: http://www.gp-training.net/protocol/psychiatry/who/whodep.htm#Scoring. The WHO-Five Well-being Index is a brief self-report questionnaire of five items. The five items address positive well-being related to quality of life. The measurement of positive well-being encourages a constructive focus. Lack of positive well-being is an indicator for depression. It is suggested that the questionnaire is completed and the results interpreted during an interview. If a low score is obtained on the WHO-Five, The Major Depression Inventory (MDI) can be completed. It contains 10 items reflecting the presence or absence of depressive symptoms described in the International Classification of Diseases (ICD-10) and is a useful screening measure which gives an indication of the severity of depressive symptomatology.

The Adult Well being Scale assesses anxiety, depression and irritability. It is one of the measures in a pack produced as part of the UK Framework for the Assessment of Children in Need and Their Families which was jointly issued by the Department of Health, the Department for Education and Employment and the Home Office in 2000. It can be downloaded free from: http://www.dh.gov.uk/en/Publicationsandstatistics/Publications/PublicationsPolicyAndGuidance/DH_4008144.

The **GAD7** is designed to screen for generalised anxiety disorder (Spitzer *et al.*, 2006), and the **PHQ9** for depression. These two measures can be photocopied under licence and are free to download from: http://www.phqscreeners.com/pdfs/02_PHQ-9/English.pdf and http://www.phqscreeners.com/pdfs/03_GAD-7/English.pdf. Terms of use are at: http://www.phqscreeners.com/terms.aspx.

The **Hospital Anxiety and Depression Scale (HADS)** (Zigmond and Snaith, 1983) is marketed by GL Assessment (http://shop.gl-assessment.co.uk/home.php?cat=417). It can be used to screen for anxiety and depression, yielding scores in the ranges 'normal' (0–7), 'mild' (8–10), 'moderate' (11–14) and 'severe' (15–21).

Other widely-used measures include the **Beck Inventories for Anxiety** (Beck and Steer, 1993) and **Depression** (Beck *et al.*, 1996), the **Beck Hopelessness Scale**, and the **Symptom Checklist 90 Revised (SCL-90-R)** (Derogatis, 1994). **The Brief Symptom Inventory (BSI)** (Derogatis, 1993) consists of 53 items covering nine symptom dimensions: Somatization, Obsession-Compulsion, Interpersonal Sensitivity, Depression, Anxiety, Hostility, Phobic anxiety, Paranoid ideation and Psychoticism; and three global indices of distress: Global Severity Index, Positive Symptom Distress Index and Positive Symptom Total. The global indices measure current or past level of symptomatology, intensity of symptoms and number of reported symptoms, respectively. The BSI is the short version of the SCL-R-90. These measures are all marketed by PsychCorp (http://psychcorp.pearsonassessments.com).

The **Hamilton Depression Scale** (Hamilton, 1980) and the **Edinburgh Postnatal Depression Scale** (Cox *et al.*, 1987) can be downloaded free from: http://www.real-depression-help.

The **Quick Inventory of Depressive Symptomatology-Self-Rated (QUIDS-SR)** (Rush *et al.*, 2003) is a 16-item self-report measure based on the DSM-IV criteria for a major depressive disorder. It is a shorter version of the **Inventory of Depressive Symptomatology (IDS-SR)** which gives an indication of levels of anxiety in addition to depression. The standardisation process undertaken for these measures is deemed to have been excellent by Jacqueline Persons (2008). They may be downloaded free from: http://www.ids-qids.org/.

The **State-Trait Anxiety Inventory for Adults** (a children's version is also available) aims to discriminate between anxiety as a temporary or more long-standing state (Spielberger *et al.*, 1970). It is available from: http://www.mindgarden.com.

The **Burns Anxiety Inventory (Burns AI)** (Burns, 1997) is a 33-item scale of anxiety symptoms which explores anxiety feelings, thoughts and physical symptoms. Limited validation data is available. It is restricted to use by licensed mental health professionals and is one of the measures in a pack designed to screen for all the mental health disorders described in DSM-IV. Full information and a license to photocopy can be purchased at www.feelinggood.com.

Drug and alcohol use

The FAST alcohol screen can be downloaded free from: www.nice.org.uk/ niceMedia/documents/manual_fastalcohol.pdf. One of the strengths of the FAST questionnaire is said to be that that just one question successfully identifies hazardous and non-hazardous alcohol use for over 50 per cent of most sample populations. This is the question, 'How often do you have eight (for men) six (for women) or more drinks on one occasion?' The FAST is an abbreviated version of the World Health Organization screening device AUDIT (Babor et al., 2001).

The Drug Abuse Screening Test (DAST) (Gavin *et al.*, 1989) is one of the most widely used screening tests for drug abuse and addiction. It can be downloaded free from: http://counsellingresource.com/quizzes/drug-abuse/ index.html.

The Personal Experience Screening Questionnaire for Adults (PESQ-A) (Winters, 1991, 1992) provides self-reported preliminary information about an individual's drug use. It also identifies psychosocial problems that often accompany substance misuse, incorporates 10 items related to social and emotional adjustment and five items that assess respondents' tendency to 'fake good'. It can be obtained from Western Psychological Services.

The Adult Substance Abuse Subtle Screening Inventory – 3 (SASSI-3) (Lazowski *et al.*, 1998) marketed by the SASSI Institute (http://www.sassi. com/products/SASSI3/shopS3-pp.shtml) and Pearson Assessment (http:// www.pearsonassessments.com/HAIWEB/Cultures/en-us/Productdetail. htm?Pid=015-8136-934&Mode=summary) addresses not only substance use but also gives an indication of defensive responding, clients' level of insight and awareness of the effects of their substance misuse, evidence of emotional pain and relative risk of involvement with the legal/judicial system. Accuracy is reportedly very high with the sensitivity (i.e. the percentage of respondents diagnosed as having a substance use disorder who screened test positive on the SASSI-3) reported as being 95 per cent for the development sample and 93 per cent for the validation sample, giving an overall sensitivity of 94 per cent. The specificity (i.e., the percentage of respondents diagnosed as not having this type of disorder who screened test negative on the questionnaire) was 93 per cent for the development sample and 95 per cent for the validation sample, giving an overall specificity of 94 per cent.

T-ACE and TWEAK (Russell, 1994) are questionnaires devised for the assessment of drinking in pregnancy. They can be obtained free from Marcia

Russell at: russell@prev.org. They are described at: http://pubs.niaaa.nih.gov/publications/assesing%20alcohol/InstrumentPDFs/74_TWEAK.pdf.

Learning difficulties

The Activities of Daily Living (Katz *et al.*, 1963) is based on an evaluation of the functional independence or dependence of people in bathing, dressing, toileting,transferring, continence, and feeding. It may be downloaded from: http://www.healthcare.uiowa.edu/igec/tools/function/katzADLs.pdf.

The Instrumental Activities of Daily Living (Lawton and Brody, 1969) may be downloaded from: www.positiveaging.org/provider/pdfs/functioning_iadl.pdf.

The Adaptive Behavior Assessment System (ABAS II) (Harrison and Oakland, 2003) is a norm-referenced assessment that uses a behaviour rating format to assess adaptive behaviour and related skills for individuals across the lifespan. Information used to complete the assessment can be provided by significant others, care providers, supervisors, and/or the client independently. It provides composite norms for three general areas of adaptive behaviour (conceptual, social and practical) and assesses functioning in the skill areas: communication, community use, functional academics, school/home living, health and safety, leisure, self-care, self-direction, social and work (for older adolescents and adults). The assessment encompasses practical, everyday skills required to function and meet environmental demands, including those needed for independence and social interaction. It can be purchased from Multi-Health Systems (MHS) at: http://www.mhs.com/ or Pearson Assessments at: http://www.psychcorp.co.uk.

The Vineland Adaptive Behavior Scales (Sparrow *et al.*, 2005) are norm-referenced and assess self-sufficiency and the personal and social skills needed for everyday living. The scales address communication, skills of daily living, socialisation, motor skills and an optional maladaptive behaviour index is provided. The scales include both a rating system and a semi-structured interview format. They can be purchased from: http://psychcorp.pearsonassessments.com.

A set of non-standardised checklists has been published by Alexander Tymchuk (1990, 1991). They are designed to assess knowledge and skills in dealing with common household emergencies such as fires, cuts or they address dangers within the home environment and the vulnerability of children to them.

Social support

The Multidimensional Scale of Perceived Social Support (Zimet *et al.*, 1988) explores relationships with friends, family and significant others. Its psychometric properties are discussed in a paper by Canty-Mitchell and Zimet (2000). It can be downloaded from: http://www.yorku.ca/rokada/psyctest/socsupp.pdf.

Benjamin Gottleib and Anne Bergen (2010) reviewed a range of questionnaires designed to measure social integration and support. On the basis of their psychometric properties they selected three measures as of particular use:

The Inventory of Socially Supportive Behaviors (ISSB) (Barrera *et al.*, 1981) which can be downloaded from: http://chipts.cch.ucla.edu/assessment/IB/List_Scales/ISSB.pdf. It measures the frequency of receipt of a wide variety of verbal and behavioural expressions of social support from people in the individual's social circle.

The Social Provisions Scale (SPS) (Russell and Cutrona, 1984) can be downloaded from: chipts.cch.ucla.edu/images/Social%20Provisions%20Scale.pdf. It comprises 24 items concerning sources of social support. In addition to an overall score there are subscales addressing Attachment, Social Integration, Reassurance of Worth, Reliable Alliance, Guidance and Opportunities for Nurturance.

The ENRICHD Social Support Inventory (ESSI) is a short seven-item measure designed specifically for patients recovering from myocardial infarction. The protocol and questionnaire can be downloaded from: http://www.cscc.unc.edu/enrichd/protocol/ENRICHDProtocol072103.pdf.

These three measures were designed for the purpose of assessing and comparing populations and need to be used with caution when making interpretations about the experience of social support by individuals. Although there are no norms, the Social Provisions Scale can be a useful adjunct to an assessment of perceived social support and, as with many questionnaires, can provide a useful focus for discussion and elaboration.

Couple relationships

The Marriage and Relationship Questionnaire (Russell and Wells, 1993) can encourage couples to think about their relationships with each other. This measure yields scores on twelve dimensions: 'Roles' (relating to the division of labour within the relationship), 'Values' (concerning attitudes towards marriage and care of the children), 'Family Ties' (addresses the history and current status of relationships with the extended family), 'Partnership' (the extent to which they experience understanding from and feel valued by their partner), 'Love' (emotional bond with partner), 'Attractiveness' (explores each individual's perception of how physically attractive they are to their partner) 'Sexual Jealousy' (gives an indication of how secure they feel in the relationship), 'Conciliation' (partners give a perspective on which person is more likely to begin a process of reconciliation after a disagreement, which is the more or less assertive or submissive), 'Problems: Personal' (gives an indication of the extent to which couples have problems with communication and feelings of isolation in the relationship), 'Problems: Partner' (gives insight into the degree of satisfaction that each partner has with their partner's personal characteristics), 'Problems: Relationship' (addresses commitment to the relationship), 'Problems: Circumstances' (gives an indication of how each partner feels about the negative impacts such as money and housing on their relationship). It is designed to give a comprehensive picture of the respondents' feelings about themselves and about their relationship with their partner. The measure is out of print but the headings can provide a useful structure for assessing the quality of the partnership.

The Golombok Rust Inventory of Marital State (GRIMS) is a companion questionnaire to the Golombok Rust Inventory of Sexual Satisfaction (GRISS), and concentrates on aspects other than the sexual in a dyadic relationship between two adults living together. The 28 items explore interests shared, degree of dependence, communication, warmth, trust, roles and expectations, decision-making and coping strategies. It is marketed by PsychCorp and can be obtained from: http://www.psychcorp.co.uk.

The Dyadic Adjustment Scale (Spanier, 1976) was originally standardised on a sample of 218 married and 94 newly-divorced individuals. There is a more recent revised version (Revised Dyadic Adjustment Scale, RDAS) (Busby *et al.*, 1995). The scale gives an overall satisfaction score, and also includes the sub-scales Consensus (agreement on decision making, values and affection), Satisfaction (conflict and the likelihood of breakup) and Cohesion (the extent to which the couple do things together and discuss matters). It can be downloaded from: http://www.gurufortwo.com/userfiles/21203/file/Dyadic_Adjustment_Scale.pdf. The test is considered to have reasonable reliability and validity and yields a general cut-off score of 97 to distinguish between adjusted and distressed couples (Frances and Guzzo, 2009; Graham *et al.*, 2006). The revised version is available as an appendix from: http://russcrane.byu.edu/Assets/MarriageResearch/1995_Revision_of_the_DAS.pdf.

The Family Environment Scale (FES) (Moos, 1990; Moos and Moos, 1994) provides a method for exploring each family member's perceptions of the way they view the family as functioning, their ideal, and how they anticipate that it will function in new situations. It focuses on three dimensions: family relationship, personal growth and system maintenance and change. The information can be used to contrast the perceptions of different family members, including children, and to assess family strengths and problems. It can be obtained from Mind Garden at: http://www.mindgarden.com/products/fescs.htm.

Intimate partner violence

The Conflict Tactics Scale (Straus, 2007) is one of the most widely used questionnaires for the assessment of domestic violence. The CTS assesses conflict tactics; the behaviours adopted by respondents to progress their case within a conflict, and the behavioural responses of their partners. Ideally, the questionnaire is completed both by respondents and their partners in order to examine the extent of concordance in their responses. The results yield scores for Physical Assault, Injury, Psychological Aggression, Sexual Coercion and Negotiation. There are variants for partners and addressed to parent-child relationships. The Scales are not copyrighted but permission to reproduce them needs to be obtained from: http://pubpages.unh.edu/~mas2/ctsb.htm. Copies of the questionnaires can also be purchased from Western Psychological Services (WPS) at: http://portal.wpspublish.com/portal/page?_pageid=53,70488&_dad=portal&_schema=PORTAL.

The Intimate Justice Scale is a questionnaire designed by Brian Jory (2004) to measure ethical dynamics of couple relationships which are evident in patterns of action and attitude expressed over the course of their relationship. It does not attempt to measure specific acts of abuse. Intimate justice is based on the idea that relationship satisfaction derives from how partners embrace equality, fairness and responsible caring in their actions and attitudes. Failure to embrace and enact these qualities is associated with physical or mental abuse (Jory and Anderson, 2000). The total overall score is regarded as a predictor of violence and preliminary reliability and validity was established in the study reported by Jory (2004). The author recommends caution in drawing inferences from the result without taking account of data from additional sources. The scale can be downloaded free from: http://www.creativeconflictresolution.org/bhr/IJS%20-%20The%20Intimate%20Justice%20Scale.pdf.

The Spousal Assault Risk Assessment (SARA) (Kropp *et al.*, 1995) adopts a structured professional judgement approach to assessing the risk of future domestic violence. It consists of 20 items that have been identified as correlated with domestic violence. The items reflect the four areas of criminal history, psychosocial adjustment, spousal assault history and the details of the current index offence. The **Brief Spousal Assault Form for the Evaluation of Risk (B-SAFER)**, also designed by Randall Kropp and colleagues, is a screening measure designed for use in situations where limited time is available for risk assessment. They are available from Pearson Assessment (www.psychcorp.co.uk).

Appendix 3   Questionnaires for the assessment of care-giving

Parenting Stress Index (PSI) (3rd edition)

The PSI is a parent self-report, 101-item questionnaire, devised by Richard Abidin (1990, 1995), designed to identify potentially dysfunctional parent-child systems. There is a short form (PSI-SF) consisting of 36 items which comprise three scales: Parental Distress, Difficult Child Characteristics and Dysfunctional Parent-Child Interaction. The Index is based on the idea that the total stress a parent experiences is a function of salient child characteristics, parent characteristics and situations that derive from the role of parent. The questions are largely relevant to parents of preschool children and refer to just one child in the family. It is advised that the parent be requested to think about the child they have found most difficult when completing the measure.

The child domain of the measure assesses characteristics displayed by children that make them difficult to parent. Subscales address 'distractibility and hyperactivity', 'adaptability', the extent to which it is reinforcing for a parent to be with the child, 'demandingness', 'negative mood' and 'acceptability', the extent to which the child fulfils the parent's expectations. The adult domain comprises 'competence', which is associated with a parent feeling criticised for the way he or she parents the child, 'isolation', 'attachment' and 'health'. Parents with chronic physical ill health often score highly on this subscale. The measure also provides scores for 'role restriction' (the degree to which parents feel their freedom has been restricted as a result of the parenting role), 'depression' and 'spouse' which provides an indication of the emotional and practical support that the parent perceives from the child's additional carers. There is a 'defensiveness' scale which gives an indication of those parents who are seeking to minimise expressions of their distress.

The PSI has been subject to empirical validation in terms of its capability to predict observed parenting behaviour and children's current and future behavioural and emotional adjustment. Research data is available from its application in a wide range of different cultures. It is obtainable from Hogrefe at: http://www.hogrefe.co.uk/?/test/show/177/, Western Psychological

Services at #http://portal.wpspublish.com/portal/page?_pageid=5369223&_
dad=portal&_schema=PORTAL and from Psychological Assessment
Resources at: http://www4.parinc.com/ProductSearch.aspx?q=parenting%20
stress%20index.

A practitioner's tool for child protection and the assessment of parents

This is the title of a book published by Jeff Fowler in 2003. Within the
text are a variety of non-standardised checklists on topics such as 'perception
of parenting', 'parental stress', 'parenting knowledge and style', 'living
arrangements', 'finances', 'child protection concerns' and 'parenting skills
and abilities'. These may be useful for stimulating ideas about what to ask
parents in interview. In my view, some of the questions would need to be
asked with caution for they risk generating defensiveness (Do you think
you are someone who suffers from stress? How often do you think parents
should play with children?), are leading (Do you think children like to be
cuddled? Do you think children should know that parents are 'in charge'?
Should parents encourage imaginary play with small children, for example,
having a tea party?), or may be beyond the parent's verbal and intellectual
skills (How do you think children learn?).

Parental Acceptance-Rejection Questionnaire (PARQ)

This is a set of self-report questionnaires designed for children, parents
and teachers (Rohner, 2005). The questionnaires are designed to measure
individuals' perceptions of parental acceptance-rejection (i.e. the warmth
dimension of parenting). Parental rejection may be expressed in coldness/lack
of affection, hostility/aggression, indifference/neglect, and in 'undifferenti-
ated rejection', which refers to conditions as a result of which individuals
perceive their parent to be rejecting, but where the expression of rejection
is not clearly unaffectionate, aggressive or neglectful. Questions addressed
to young people include, 'Says nice things about me,' 'Wants me to bring
my friends home, and tries to make things pleasant for them,' 'Talks to me
about our plans and listens to what I have to say,' and 'Pays no attention
to me as long as I do nothing to bother her.' Details of the instruments and
their validity and reliability can be found in Rohner and Khaleque (2005)
and they may be purchased from: http://home.earthlink.net/~rohner_research/
index.htm.

Parent–Child Relationship Inventory (PCRI)

The PCRI, compiled by Anthony Gerard (1994), is a self-report inventory
exploring how parents view the tasks and role of parenting including their

feelings towards their child. It is designed for use with parents of 3–15-year-old children and provides scores for 'parental support', 'satisfaction with parenting', 'involvement', 'communication', 'limit setting', 'autonomy' and 'role orientation'. There are two validity scales which aim to assess inconsistency or parents who are trying to portray their relationship with the child in an unrealistically positive light. The test has been standardised and reasonable reliability reported (Coffman *et al.*, 2006). It can be obtained from Western Psychological Services at: http://portal.wpspublish.com/portal/page?_pageid=53,70187&_dad=portal&_schema=PORTAL.

Parent–child communication scales

These comprise individual questionnaires for parents and children which assess care-givers' perceptions of their own openness to communication and awareness of their children's communication skills. The scales include questions such as, 'Does X admit mistakes without trying to hide anything?' and 'Are there certain topics which you do not allow X to discuss with you?' The child's version includes, 'Does your carer try to understand what you think?' and 'Can you let your carer know what is bothering you?' The materials can be downloaded from: http://www.fasttrackproject.org/techrept/p/pcp/

Parenting Relationship Questionnaire

This questionnaire is designed to explore parents' perspectives on their relationship with their child. It comprises a number of subscales: 'attachment', 'communication', 'discipline practices', 'involvement', 'parenting confidence', 'parental satisfaction with school' and 'relational frustration'. It allows comparison with the results of a normally distributed sample and can be purchased from Pearson Assessments.

Further questionnaire measures

Schmidt *et al.* (2007) reviewed additional instruments including the Crowell Procedure and Atypical Maternal Behavior Instrument for Assessment and Classification (AMBIANCE). The Ackerman-Schoendorf Scales for Parent Evaluation of Custody (ASPECT) give rise to an overall score (Parental Custody Index (PCI), which is said to give an indication of the effectiveness of a parent (Ackerman, 2005). The scales comprise a self-report measure for individual carers and a series of questions for the practitioner who is carrying out the assessment. Consideration of multiple data sources is required. The Perception-of-Relationships Test and Bricklin Perceptual Scales (Bricklin and Halbert, 2004) have also been used to assess parenting. Structured methods for observation of parent-child relationships are extensive and reviewed by Daniel Hynan (2006). The Fast Track Project website lists many additional relevant measures which can be accessed at: http://www.fasttrack-project.org/data-instruments.php.

Many of these measures have good face validity; their item content makes sense and appears to assess factors relevant to decisions about care-giving but, 'significant questions remain regarding their utility, and their appropriateness for use in custody evaluations at the present time' (Otto *et al.*, 2000: 317). Referring to forensic assessment instruments, such as those described in the preceding paragraph, Emery *et al.* (2005: 8) go further and argue that, 'all measures that purport to assess constructs directly relevant to child custody determinations suffer from significant limitations ... no study examining the properties of these measures has ever been published in a peer-reviewed journal and ... the absence of scientific support should preclude the use of any of these forensic assessment instruments for any purpose other than research.' These authors argue for restriction of assessment in disputes between separating parents to matters of direct relevance such as whether a child has special needs, whether a parent is depressed, or when substance misuse results in risk to the child.

In my view, questionnaire results can never be taken alone as reliable indicators of parenting knowledge and skills. But they can usefully serve to open up areas for discussion with carers and constitute a piece amongst the many in the overall jigsaw.

Appendix 4   Examples of actuarial and consensual family risk assessment instruments

Actuarial instruments

Structured Decision Making (SDM) Tools

Structured Decision Making models aim to bring a greater degree of consistency, objectivity and validity to child welfare case decisions and to enable agencies to focus their limited resources on families presenting with the highest levels of risk. Such models prescribe a course of action arising from decision choice points in a hierarchical tree formation. Structured measures are completed at specific points in the case decision-making process (e.g. initial response to allegations, child removal, case opening/closing, reunification). One of the key measures is a research-based risk assessment that estimates the probability of future abuse or neglect. A number of different versions of a risk assessment instrument have been developed in the USA for various jurisdictions by the Children's Research Center (CRC). The following two scales are examples:

California Family Risk Assessment Scale (CFRAS)

This comprises am 11-item Neglect Scale and a 12-item Abuse Scale. It produces four categories of risk; low, moderate, high and very high. Research about the predictive capability of this measure has shown that the Californian families that were assessed as presenting low risk had a resubstantiation rate of less than 8 per cent. For families classed as high risk the resubstantiation rate was 44 per cent. The researchers argue that the differences between family characteristics associated with abuse and with neglect warrant the use of two separate scales. Information about the scales is available at: www.ncjrs.gov/pdffiles1/ojjdp/187759.pdf.

Minnesota SDM Family Risk Assessment (FRA)/ Family Risk of Abuse and Neglect (FRAAN)

The SDM Family Risk Assessment (FRA) aims to determine the probability that a family will continue to abuse or neglect their children. The instrument has been validated in South Australia (Johnson et al., 2000), California

(Johnson, 2004) and in other States in the USA. It comprises an 11-item Abuse Scale and an 11-item Neglect Scale.

The FRA categorizes families as low, moderate, high or intensive risk of future child abuse and neglect. An evaluation study (Loman and Siegel, 2005) reported a specificity of 77.2 per cent and a sensitivity rate of 89.7 per cent for families with no child protection services. The evaluation concluded that the FRA could accurately classify risk in only two out of three cases and should therefore not be used in isolation.

Child Abuse Potential Inventory (CAPI) (2nd edition)

This is a 160-item self-administered questionnaire which is a screening instrument for physical child abuse compiled by Joel Milner and published in 1986. It comprises a 77-item Abuse Scale and has three Validity Scales designed to identify respondents who are attempting to give a false impression. There is a comprehensive technical manual and the instrument has been standardised. Norms are provided for different client groups. The inventory was designed to screen parents reported for physical child abuse. Abuse rates in reported cases range from 35–50 per cent, a high base rate in this population which increases the utility of the instrument. The many research studies based on the administration of the questionnaire have produced correct classifications of between 80–90 per cent (reported in Milner, 1995). Although this is impressive data, false positives and negatives cannot be eliminated and parental responses to the validity scales may invalidate the results. Copies can be obtained from Psychological Assessment Resources at: http://www4. parinc.com/Products/Product.aspx?ProductID=CAP.

Consensual instruments

California Family Assessment and Factor Analysis (CFAFA, or the 'Fresno Model')

This measure has 23 items from within five domains: (1) precipitating incident, (2) child assessment, (3) caregiver assessment, (4) family assessment and (5) family-agency interaction. All types of maltreatment are considered together. The measure is reported as performing poorly in terms of predictive validity and for inter-rater reliability (Baird and Wagner, 2000).

Child Emergency Response Assessment Protocol (CERAP)

The CERAP is a single list of 14 items focused on child safety. All types of maltreatment are considered together. The assessor notes the presence or absence of each item; if any of the items are present, the worker decides whether the child is 'safe' or 'unsafe'. Findings regarding its predictive validity are mixed (Fuller *et al.*, 2001).

Child At Risk Field System (CARF)

The CARF focuses on safety as distinct from risk. It has 14 items within the five domains: child, parent, family, maltreatment and intervention. Four 'qualifiers' are applied: duration of a negative influence, pervasiveness of a negative influence, acknowledgement by parents of a negative influence and control of the negative influence. All types of maltreatment are considered together. Tests of its predictive validity have given mixed results. Families assigned to the high risk group were found to be more likely to be re-referred than those assigned to the low risk group although statistical significance was not reached (Doueck *et al.*, 1993).

Risk Estimation System (RES)

The RES was developed in New Zealand in the 1990s as a nationally-adopted, computer-based, consensual model identifying areas of severity of abuse, vulnerability of children and likelihood of further abuse. It comprises a 22-item scale used to assess the characteristics of care-givers, focusing on the actions, intentions, beliefs, attitudes and behaviours of the carers. It produces estimates on three scales of vulnerability, re-occurrence and future severity. The manual can be retrieved from: http://www.practice-centre.cyf.govt.nz/documents/policy/practice-tools/p-pt-resource-risk-estimation-system.pdf.

Washington Risk Assessment Matrix (WRAM)

This is a consensus based instrument with 37 items within the domains Child Characteristics, Severity of Abuse/Neglect, Chronicity of Abuse and Neglect, Caretaker Characteristics, Caretaker/Child Relationship, Socio-economic Factors and Perpetrator Access. The predictive validity has been reported as relatively poor. Rates of substantiated maltreatment for families in low, moderate and high risk groups identified by the measure were not significantly different (Baird and Wagner, 2000; Camasso and Jagannathan, 2000).

A major review of risk assessment measures relating to child maltreatment is, at the time of writing, being undertaken by Aron Shlonsky, Michael Saini and Meng-Jia Wu. The protocol can be accessed at: http://www.campbellcollaboration.org/lib/index.php?go=browse&sort=title&view=all&.

Appendix 5   The process of application for a care order

In England and Wales, all applications for care orders made on or after 6 April 2011 must follow the Rules and Practice Direction which can be accessed at: http://www.justice.gov.uk/guidance/docs/preparing-care-supervision-proceedings.pdf.

A care order is an order of the court made under Section 31 of the Children Act 1989. It allows the local authority to share parental responsibility and decide issues such as where the child should live and with whom. In order to remove a child from a carer with parental responsibility the local authority needs an interim (temporary) care order, full care order or an emergency protection order.

Parents in care proceedings are publicly funded as a matter of course and can instruct their own solicitor who may appoint a barrister.

The court will decide whether a child has suffered or is at risk of suffering significant harm and if the threshold criteria are met that suggest this to be the case, an interim care order will be made in order for the child to be kept safe whilst the matter is investigated. A core assessment will be carried out by the local authority. If there are areas which require specialist assessment, reports will be commissioned from appropriate expert witnesses. These will generally be jointly instructed by all of the parties. The duty of experts is to assist the court in making best interest decisions with regard to the welfare of the child.

The birth mother automatically holds parental responsibility and is known in the proceedings as a 'respondent'. Birth fathers, whether or not they hold parental responsibility, must be served notice of the case and have the option to bring an application to the court to be directly involved. Other members of the extended family are not automatically notified and if they wish to be involved they must request permission from the court. When this is granted it is called 'party status'.

Anyone who is provided with information about the proceedings has no right to share it with anyone else and if it is shared this may be adjudged as contempt of court.

For the first hearing, which must take place within 6 weeks of the local authority making an application, a children's guardian from CAFCASS

(Children and Family Court Advice and Support Service) and a solicitor will be appointed to represent the child. This solicitor is normally known as the 'lead solicitor'. The local authority will prepare an 'interim care plan' outlining how the child will be looked after whilst the matter is investigated.

The judge decides on the level of complexity of the case and whether it should be transferred to another court. If the threshold criteria are reached, an *Interim Care Order* will be made. The children will usually be removed from the care of the parents. They can be placed with a relative following a 'viability assessment' and should be so placed if a suitable carer is available in the wider family. Otherwise they will usually be placed with a foster family. The judge may also make the following orders:

Interim supervision order

An interim supervision order does not give the local authority parental responsibility but it requires them to monitor how the child is being cared for.

Interim residence order

The child is placed with someone in the wider family until the final hearing. That person shares parental responsibility. The local authority does not have parental responsibility.

Interim contact order

This sets out details of what contact the birth parents and other members of the family will have with the child.

The local authority arranges regular meetings to review the arrangements. The meetings are chaired by an independent reviewing officer. Parents and involved professionals are invited, including health visitors, teachers, general practitioners, foster carers and social workers. Specified time periods are set at which reviews must take place. Minutes are kept and distributed to all participants and anyone else whom the local authority considers should have access.

Before the final hearing the court will hold a Case Management Conference at which a decision will be made as to what information will be needed in order to make a judgement at the final hearing. The court will decide if the case needs to be transferred to a higher court.

It is the final hearing at which the long-term plans for the child are determined. Parents make statements and respond to statements from professionals.

If parents agree to the plans of the local authority, they are asked to sign a consent order. If the parent disagrees, the hearing is contested and each of the parties gives evidence in chief and then is cross examined by the representatives of the other parties. The local authority puts its case first. The guardian gives evidence last after hearing that of all the other witnesses.

The court can only make a care order or supervision order if the judge decides that the threshold criteria have been met: the child has been seriously harmed or is at risk of serious harm in the future, the harm has resulted from the quality of care provided by the parent or because the child is deemed out of control, and the harm may include seeing or hearing the ill treatment of another person. The judge decides what is in the child's best interests according to the 'welfare checklist'.

Unless otherwise changed or discharged, a care order remains in force until a child reaches the age of 18 years. Local authorities can only place a child for adoption if they have a care order and the parent consents. If the parent does not consent the local authority can seek a 'placement order' which dispenses with the need for parental consent.

Appendix 6 Supplementary information relevant to expert witnesses in England and Wales

In this section I have drawn attention to some of the issues that are specific to expert witnesses in England and Wales. The glossary also provides the definition of many of the terms that an expert will encounter in the family court. For experts who are new to the role it will be important to study these issues in much greater depth than is summarised here.

Definition of expert witness

An expert witness is a person having special training or experience in a particular specialist field who is asked to provide an opinion concerning those specialist matters. Non-expert witnesses are only permitted to testify about facts they observed and not their opinions about these facts. In family law proceedings, expert witnesses include paediatricians, other medical specialists, psychiatrists and psychologists who give opinions about risk of harm to children, child and adult functioning, and the capability of parents to provide adequate care.

Guidance for experts

This is provided in the Practice Direction for Experts in Family Proceedings Relating to Children which can be obtained from: http://www.justice.gov.uk/downloads/guidance/protecting-the-vulnerable/care-proceeding-reform/experts-pd-flagB-14-01-08.pdf. It is essential to have read, understood and remembered the contents of the Practice Direction since experts affirm this at the end of their report and may be cross-examined on this knowledge.

Competence and supervision

An expert is responsible for ensuring that he or she has the relevant knowledge and skills to offer an opinion on the matter at hand. Criteria by which to judge this include formal qualifications, nature and extent of post-qualification experience in the claimed area of expertise and relevant publications. Experts summarise this in their reports and may be asked to give an outline in the witness box before giving evidence. Experts are expected to be knowledgeable about the court processes in addition to their domain of expertise. Experts are not expected to need supervision regarding their opinion *per se,* and supervisors cannot be provided with court documents without the permission of the court. Supervision is helpful regarding approaches to conducting an assessment for this purpose, how opinion can be stated, and how the court process works.

Daubert and Kumho principles for admissibility of expert testimony

The Daubert[1] standard is a rule established in the USA regarding the admissibility of expert witness testimony on the basis of whether it is the product of reliable principles and methods. The Kumho[2] case established that the Daubert principles applied not only to scientific evidence but to all expert testimony. Daubert required that expert evidence met the requirements of being based on a theory which could be tested and falsified, had been established through peer review and achieved general acceptance in the relevant scientific community. Techniques and tests based on the theory should have been rigorously applied and should have clearly stated acceptable rates of error. Ironically, the aim of the Daubert judgement was to encourage more liberal admissibility of expert witness evidence but it actually created a more stringent test (Graham, 1999–2000).

In a thorough review of the principles enshrined in Daubert and Kumho, Graham (1999–2000: 356) concludes that the trial judge has simply to ask, 'Has the explanative theory as actually applied to facts, data or opinions sufficiently established to exist been shown to possess sufficient assurances of correctness to warrant jury acceptance?' The judge's role is not to decide whether an explanative theory actually works but to determine if there are sufficient assurances of correctness when applied to the specific case. This is largely determined by a test of 'widespread acceptance' within a specific professional community. In my view this means that it is wise for experts to consider alternative explanations for their findings and make a case for acceptance or rejection of a particular account. It is wise to be aware of relevant data concerning validity, reliability and error rates of test materials. Standardised tests need to be administered and interpreted by a professional with the relevant qualifications and experience. Theories, techniques and methods should be broadly accepted within the specific community of experts.

1 Daubert v. Merrell Dow Pharmaceuticals, Inc., 509 U.S. 579, 588 (1993).
2 Kumho Tire Co. V. Carmichael, 119 S.Ct. 1167, 1171 (1999).

Communication with others

The expert's report belongs to the court and is usually submitted via the lead solicitor. All correspondence and any queries should be directed to this advocate. Letters of instruction may, as a matter of course, require the expert to speak to the lead solicitor prior to discussing the family with a specific professional. It is appropriate to err on the side of caution. Any discussions that are held with any parties must be recorded and there is no confidentiality. This is with the aim of protecting the expert's impartiality.

Time-scales

The court specifies a time-scale for the lodging of the report. It is critical to adhere to the filing date because it is one date in a series leading up to the final hearing. The Practice Direction for Expert Witnesses makes it clear that experts should not agree to take on the case unless they are able to guarantee that they can meet the deadline for the report.

Structure of report

The Practice Direction clearly lays out the content and structure of an expert's report. The front sheet should specify the type of report, the names and dates of birth of the parties being assessed. If these are adults, the child's name/s and dates of birth should also be included. The case number and date of the report are also items on the cover sheet. The report ends with a statement of compliance, a statement regarding conflicts of interest and a statement of truth. It must be signed and dated.

Fees

A fees estimate will be requested by the lead solicitor. This enables prior authority for the costs to be agreed by the Legal Services Commission (LSC). I allow up to 6 hours of contact time for assessments of each adult, 1–4 hours for children depending on their ages, a number of hours for observation of contact dependent on the number of adults and children and the arrangements for contact, an hour an inch (thickness) for reading files and background information, 2 hours for conversations with other involved professionals or family members, and 1–2 hours to analyse test results. The total number of hours is doubled to cost for the time spent writing the report. Travelling time and costs need to be estimated. At the time of writing these are capped by the LSC at £40 an hour and 45 pence a mile. In 2011 the LSC proposed a cap to hourly fees which came into force on 3rd October 2011. Rates can be found at: http://www.jspubs.com/experts/ewire/itemtext. cfm?ewid=221&ewdid=3992. Higher rates may be justified in complex cases and in those where there are very few experts in highly specialist areas.

An invoice is submitted with the report, laying out actual time spent and costs. This may be submitted to the lead solicitor with the report with a request for it to be circulated to the other parties along with the report. Practices vary between solicitors. Some collect all shares of the fees on behalf of the expert; in other instances individual invoices need to be constructed and distributed to each party. Payment can be slow and it is as well to have a good system for following up unpaid and inaccurate amounts.

Retention of documents

All documents copied to the expert should be retained by the original party. At the conclusion of the case the expert may return these documents to the firm by whom they were originally supplied or arrange for shredding as confidential waste. Documents that are particular to the expert, such as the expert's report and raw data from test and questionnaire completion need to be retained for a minimum of 6 years, and in the case of proceedings relating to children, for much longer. More detailed advice is available from the UK Register of Expert Witnesses at: http://www.jspubs.com/Experts/fs/58.pdf and from: http://www.cambridgeshire.gov.uk/NR/rdonlyres/CB13BCCD-E3A0-42F2-B1D3-2FC46340912D/0/general54.pdf. The latter indicates that for children looked after by the local authority, 'all case records must be retained until the person's 75th birthday, or if the child has died before reaching 18 years old, a period of 15 years beginning with the date of his/her death.'

Support and advice

For 'new' experts, it may be worth working for a company in the first instance. There is also advice and information available from a number of organisations:

The Academy of Expert Witnesses (AEW) provides a directory of experts and runs training events. These can be accessed at: http://www.academy-experts.org/

The American Psychological Association provides links to useful articles and publications on its website at: http://search.apa.org/search?query=expert+witnesses

Bond Solon offer accredited courses in writing reports and giving evidence. Information can be accessed at: http://www.bondsolon.com/expert-witnesses/. They also offer a directory of expert witnesses at: http://www.expertfamily-law.co.uk/

The British Psychological Society provides a directory of experts and offers guidance to psychologists undertaking the role. It can be accessed at www.bps.org.uk. It has also published useful advice in: British Psychological

Society Expert Witness Advisory Group (2010). *Psychologists as expert witness: guidelines and procedure for England, Wales and Northern Ireland* (3rd edition), Leicester: British Psychological Society.

Expertpages lists experts based in the USA and Canada. The website hosts a number of relevant articles at: http://expertpages.com/

The Expert Witness Institute (EWI) has a directory of experts and runs training events. It can be accessed at: http://www.ewi.org.uk/main/index.asp

An excellent source for expert witnesses is the annually updated Expert Witness Year Book published by Chris Pamplin, an extract of which can be accessed at: http://www.jspubs.com/YearBook/Samples/YB.pdf. The UK Register of Expert Witnesses is also published at this site.

The *Family Law* journal is a good resource containing up-to-date information and judgements that bear on expert witnesses' practice.

The General Medical Council provides online advice to medical professionals which is more widely relevant at: http://www.gmc-uk.org/guidance/ethical_guidance/expert_witness_guidance.asp

The Law Society of Scotland Directory of Expert Witnesses website provides useful information about codes of conduct for expert witnesses at: http://www.expertwitnessscotland.info/

Legal Hub provides a directory of expert witnesses and has a bank of articles which may be searched at: http://www.legalhub.co.uk/legalhub/app/main?rs=BOL1.0&vr=1.0&sttype=stdtemplate

The Online Directory of UK Expert Witnesses is available at: http://www.expertsearch.co.uk/. In addition to the directory, relevant articles are published at this site.

The Society of Expert Witnesses (SEW) provides a directory of experts and runs conferences. Information can be accessed at: http://www.sew.org.uk

In the UK, Local Family Justice Councils offer mini-pupillages for medical practitioners and psychologists involved in child protection. They offer up to a week shadowing barristers undertaking cases involving the welfare of children. The objective is to provide experience both in and outside the court. There is a network of 39 Local Family Justice Councils across England and Wales and it is the local councils which provide the mini-pupillage schemes. Contact details for local councils can be accessed at: http://www.judiciary.gov.uk/about-the-judiciary/advisory-bodies/fjc/local-fjcs

Author index

Subject index